# REVISITING AMERICA

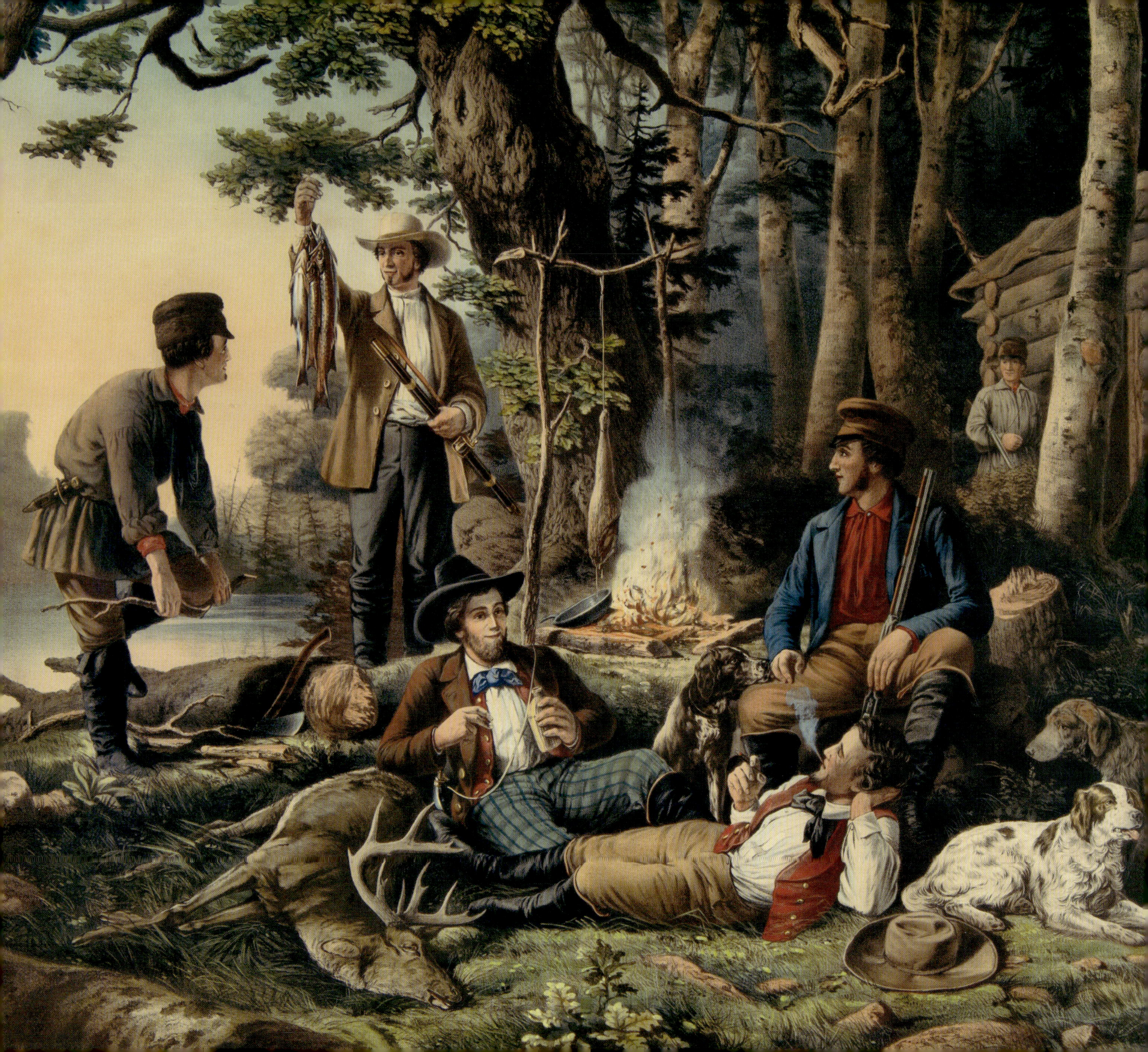

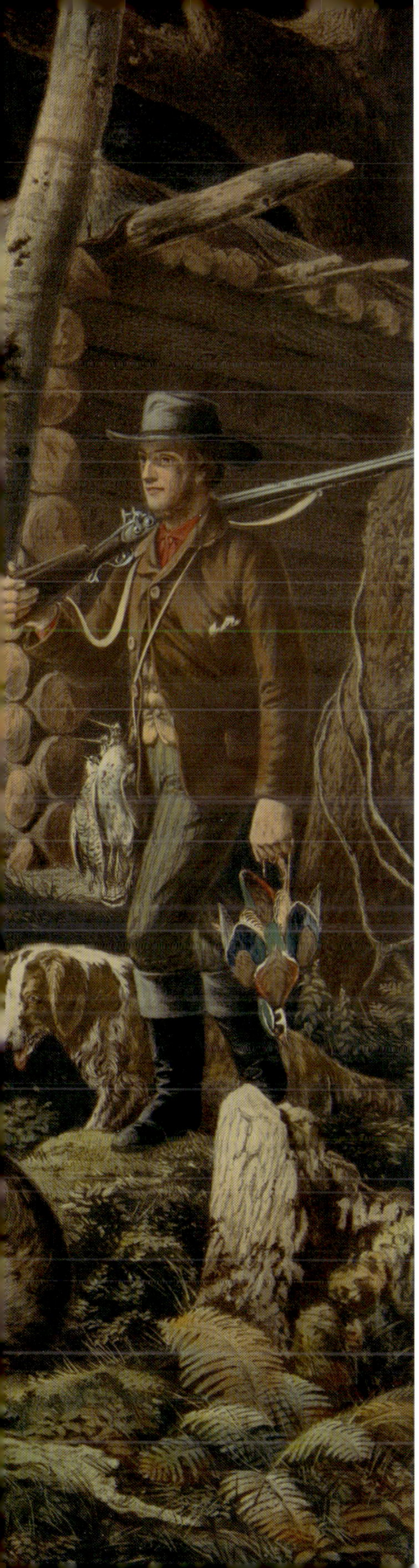

# REVISITING AMERICA

## *The Prints of Currier & Ives*

Joslyn Art Museum
Omaha, Nebraska

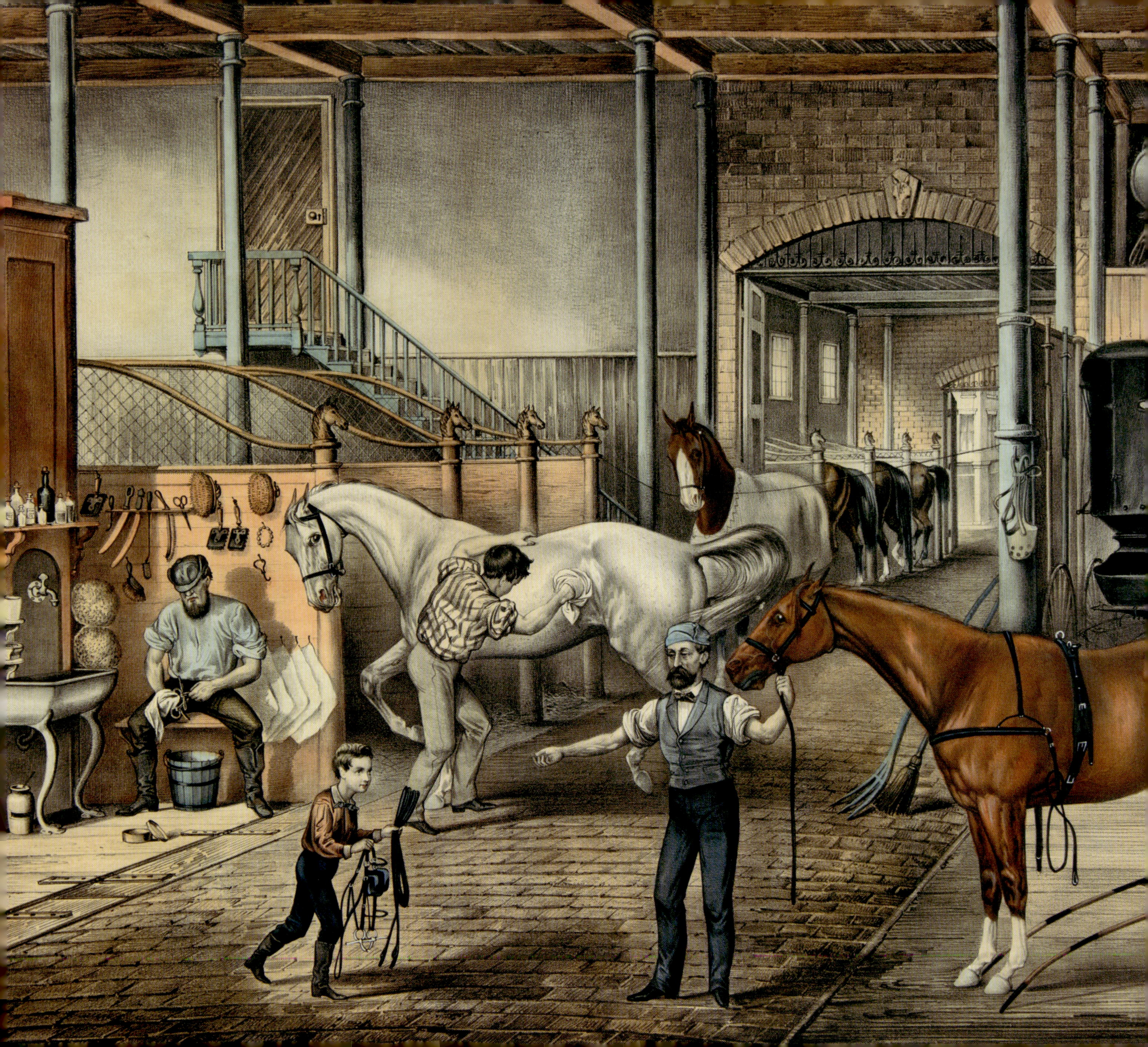

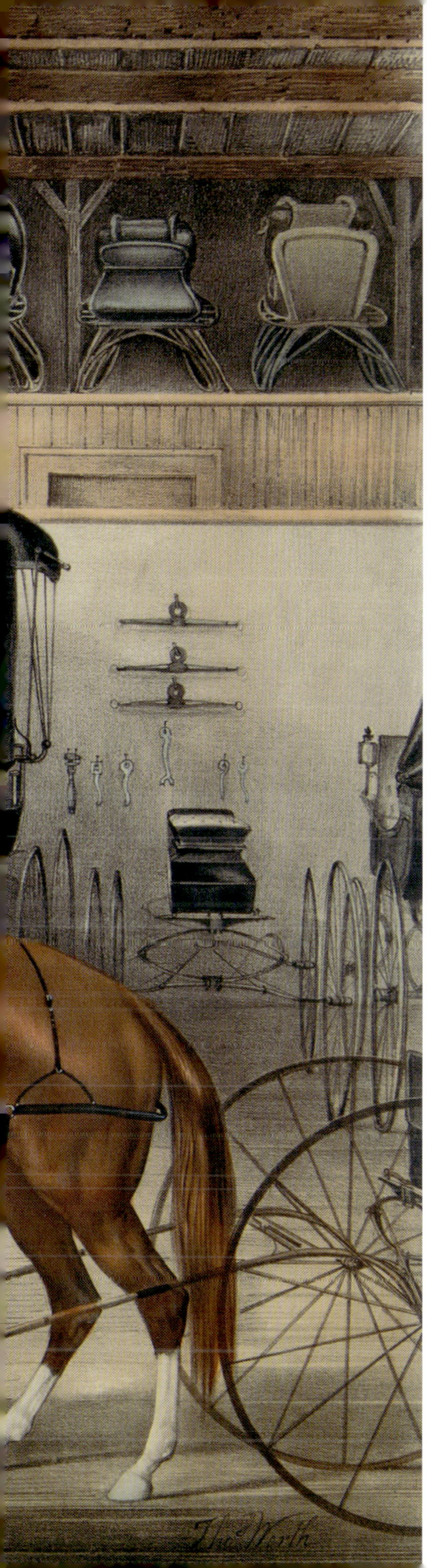

# CONTENTS


**DIRECTOR'S FOREWORD**
JACK F. BECKER
**07**

**ENGRAVINGS FOR THE PEOPLE**
*A Collection History, from Private Treasure to Public Trust*
EMMA WESTBROOK
**09**

**BETWEEN ART AND INDUSTRY**
*Making Currier & Ives Lithographs*
MARIE-STÉPHANIE DELAMAIRE
**15**

**EXCITING REASSURANCES**
*Popular Art and Contemporary Life in Currier & Ives Prints*
MICHAEL CLAPPER
**31**

**THE POLITICAL BROADSIDES OF CURRIER & IVES**
*A Reconsideration*
BAIRD JARMAN
**45**

**PLATES**
**59**

**CATALOGUE CHECKLIST**
**177**

**CONTRIBUTORS**
**184**

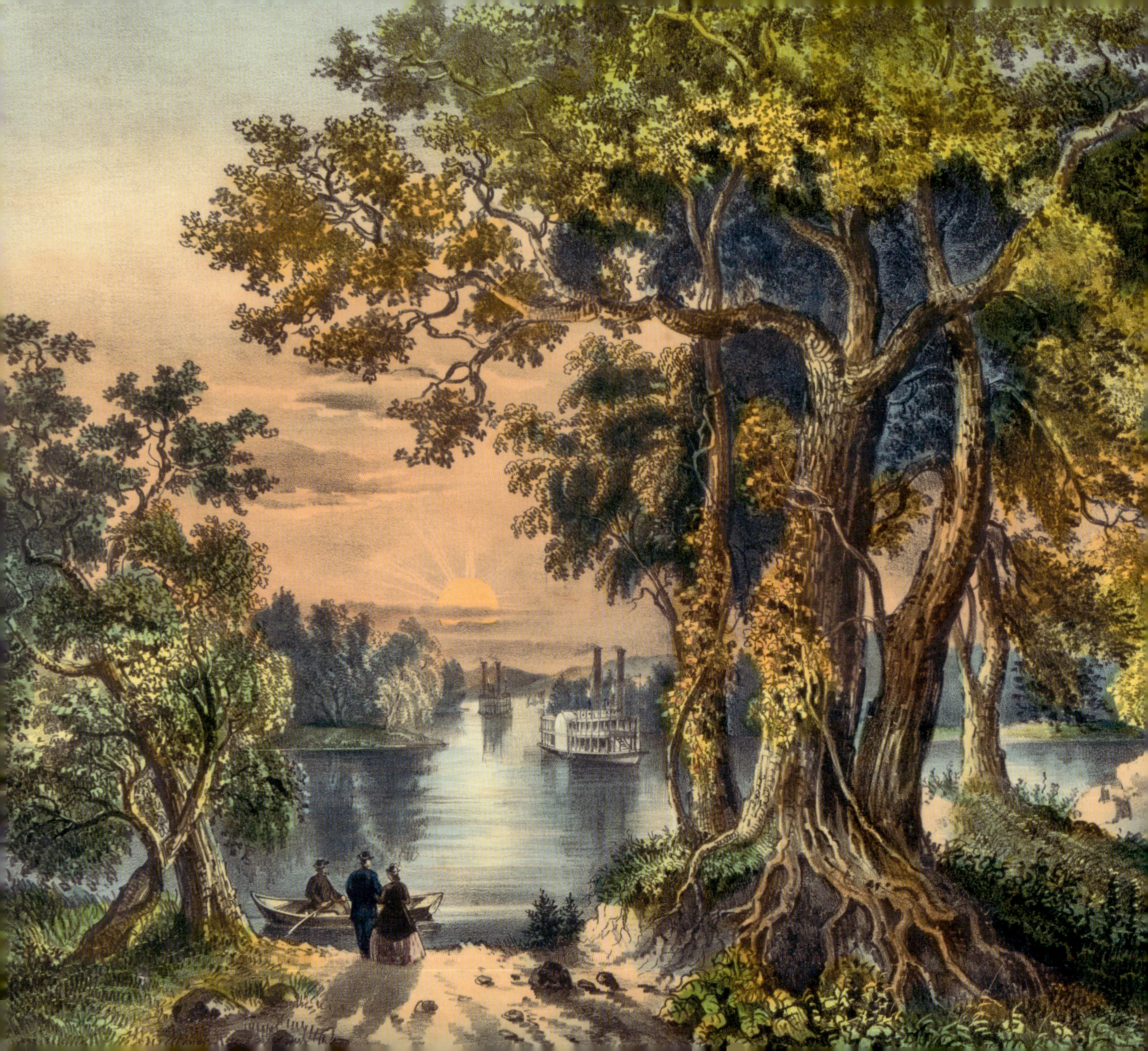

# DIRECTOR'S FOREWORD

*Jack F. Becker*

For three decades, Conagra Brands had a major presence in downtown Omaha. In 1990, the company opened a new campus in the Old Market neighborhood that included an expansive corporate headquarters and Heartland of America Park, which attracted visitors from across the city. Inside the corridors of the Conagra Brands complex was an installation featuring over four hundred prints from the company's Currier & Ives collection, obtained in the late 1980s with the acquisition of Beatrice Foods, the collection's former owner. When Conagra Brands moved its headquarters to Chicago in 2015, the company wanted to recognize its long-standing relationship to the Omaha community. In June 2016, Conagra Brands announced the donation of its entire corporate collection of nearly six hundred original Currier & Ives prints to Joslyn Art Museum. This remarkable gift immediately established the Museum as one of the largest public collections of these popular and historically important illustrations and ensured that the collection is permanently available to share with the Omaha community, as well as Joslyn's many visitors from across the United States and beyond.

Joslyn Art Museum would like to thank Sean Connolly, President and Chief Executive Officer, Conagra Brands. We would also like to acknowledge Chris Kircher, a member of Joslyn Art Museum's Board of Governors from 2014 to 2017 and former Vice President, Corporate Affairs at Conagra Brands, for his enthusiastic support of this significant gift.

Our guest authors have done much to make this a lively and insightful catalogue. Michael Clapper, Marie-Stéphanie Delamaire, and Baird Jarman bring new light to this important addition to the Museum's collection in their three original essays. Emma Westbrook, who came to the Museum in 2018 as a Weitz Fellow and extended her stay as a curatorial assistant, contributed the collection history and has been of invaluable assistance with the publication. Spencer Wigmore, the inaugural Weitz Fellow in 2011–2012 and current Assistant Curator at the Amon Carter Museum of American Art, offered critical assistance in the early stages of this project.

Finally, this publication would not have been possible without the assistance of the Henry Luce Foundation, whose ongoing encouragement of American art scholarship, exhibitions, and publications has been instrumental to institutions across the nation. We are grateful for their support.

*Revisiting America: The Prints of Currier & Ives* celebrates a major new addition to Joslyn Art Museum's permanent collection. We hope you will share our enthusiasm for these enjoyable and enlightening prints that reveal the complex and challenging story of our American past.

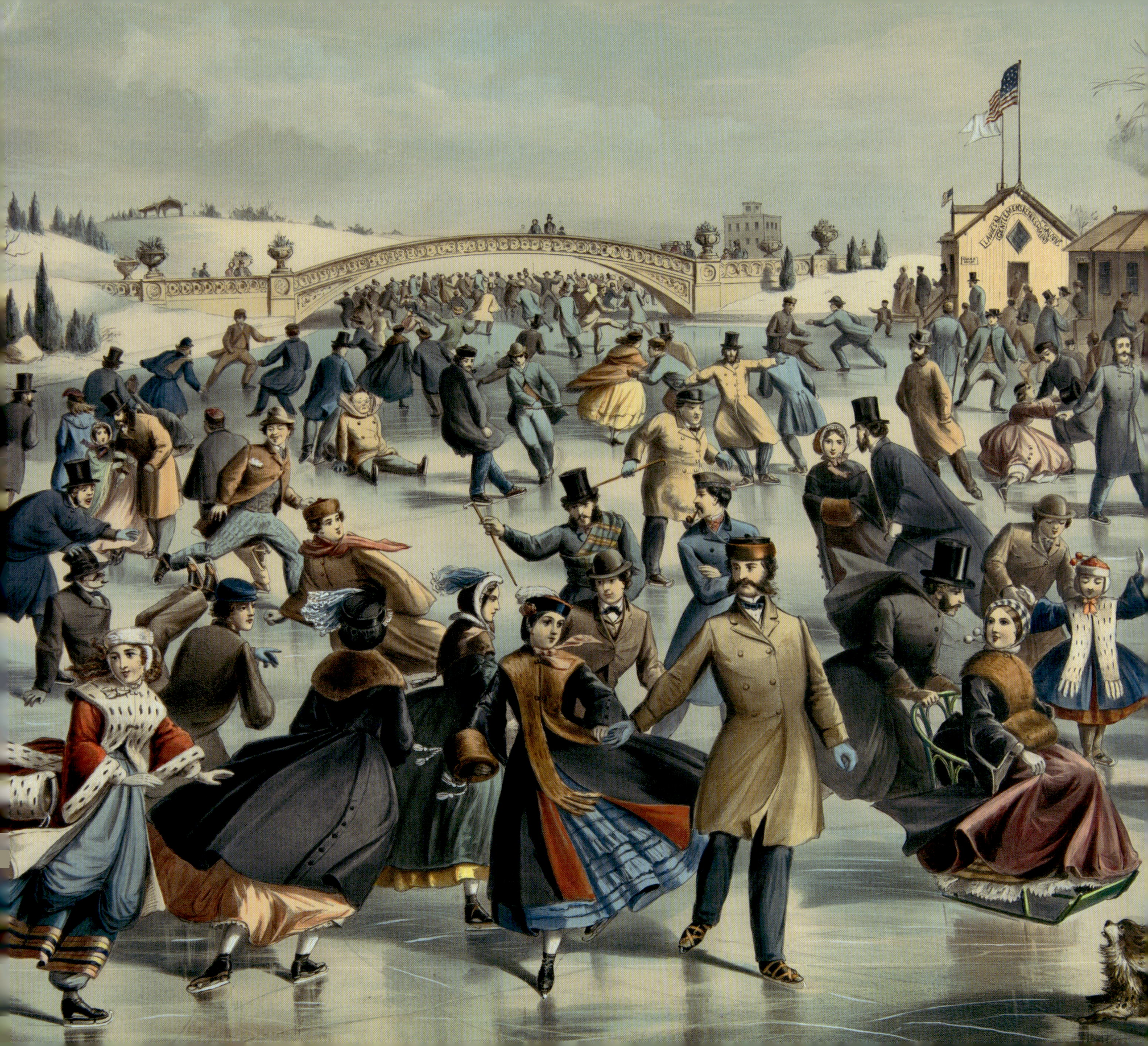

# ENGRAVINGS FOR THE PEOPLE

*A Collection History, from Private Treasure to Public Trust*

*Emma Westbrook*

The timeless appeal and accessibility of Currier & Ives prints have buoyed their popularity across three centuries. Having started the most famous commercial lithography firm of their era, Nathaniel Currier and James Merritt Ives were at the center of a quintessentially American image culture that remains familiar to this day. Mass-produced and affordable, the company's prints were marketed as "engravings for the people" and were readily available to collectors, enthusiasts, and common households. The Currier & Ives workshop produced images of quotidian scenes of daily life, allegorical narratives, national history, and sporting events, as well as newsworthy events and political broadsides, which hung on the walls of American homes across the economic spectrum. Although these images now seem far removed from our contemporary lives, the enduring fascination with Currier & Ives prints demonstrates how these pictures touch on themes that remain deeply integrated into the American visual vernacular and notions of our national past.

Joslyn Art Museum's collection of Currier & Ives lithographs is one of the largest in the United States, and the most extensive in the Midwest and Plains states. Assembled in the 1960s and 1970s by Roy King, a private collector, it comprises over six hundred prints, along with a variety of ephemera from the firm. Over the collection's history, it has shifted from a private enthusiasm to a corporate resource to a public trust, after it was donated by Conagra Brands to Joslyn Art Museum in 2016. During the time it was held by corporate entities, the collection served as a facet of their public relations campaigns, and was seen by tens of thousands of people across the world. Not only were these lithographs exhibited in institutional settings, such as museums and college galleries, but they were also seen in stores and corporate headquarters. Shoppers and employees would encounter Currier & Ives prints on their daily rounds, adding an unexpected brush with beloved and familiar American images to an otherwise mundane experience. By the time Conagra Brands acquired this collection in 1990, these lithographs had visited 23 other countries and more than 116 museums, college galleries, and department stores. Conagra Brands and the other companies that have held this collection emphasized their accessibility and appeal to a wide variety of audiences, allowing these images to act as visual ambassadors for their corporate profiles.

## Roy King

Over a period of three decades beginning in the 1950s, New York collector Roy M. King assembled one of the finest collections of

Currier & Ives prints in the country, numbering over 672 lithographs, as well as other documents and ephemera from the company's workshop. His extensive collection represented years of travel and study. An overwhelming majority of the prints were purchased individually, with only a few transactions involving multiple prints. Over two hundred of the prints in his collection came from the Old Print Shop, a dealer of works on paper in Midtown Manhattan specializing in Currier & Ives prints. King developed a close relationship at the gallery with Kenneth Newman, who shared his love and connoisseurship of the workshop's prints. Kenneth was the son of Harry Shaw Newman, who bought the Old Print Shop in 1928. Harry had first fallen in love with print works on paper after finding two folios of Currier & Ives lithographs in his grandmother's attic. He helped popularize the practice of collecting prints from the workshop and established the Old Print Shop as one of the premiere dealers of Currier & Ives prints in the country. In the 1930s, Harry elected juries to determine the fifty "best" Currier & Ives lithographs, both in large- and small-sized folios. These lists helped to shape the tradition of collecting lithographs from the workshop for decades to come. Both Harry and his son Kenneth were instrumental in helping King expand and develop his collection, and Kenneth was known to brag that King bought his first Currier & Ives impression at the Old Print Shop.

In 1968, King collaborated with author Burke Davis to publish *The World of Currier and Ives*, which used prints from his collection as its illustrations. Davis contributed text placing the prints in historical context, as well as an essay on the nuances of collecting Currier & Ives lithographs. In his essay, he remarked that Currier & Ives prints had fallen out of fashion in the early twentieth century, and it was not until the 1930s that they again became widely popular. King's interest in print connoisseurship was also communicated in another essay Davis wrote for the book, in which he identified desirable characteristics in the prints and guided collectors toward those that would be most valuable. Among other qualities, a sharp, crisp image is important, indicating it was one of the early impressions off a stone, as the images deteriorated quickly as the stone was reprinted. At the time of their production, the frame was usually more costly than the print, and therefore the prints' wide margins would often be cut down to fit an available frame. The wider the print's margins, the more valuable it is to a collector—especially considering some margins were truncated to such an extent that the publishing line and title were lost. Finally, since the prints were hand colored (although with very precise and largely uniform techniques), images with more vivid coloring are prized over those that may be irregular or faded. The passion both King and Davis demonstrated in this publication is apparent, and its wider release delighted King, who was very invested in bringing his collection to the public. This book marked the beginning of King's desire to share his collection with a broader audience.

As King aged, he began to worry about the future of his collection, fearing that it would be broken up at auction or otherwise dispersed. As he sought the collection's next owner, he emphasized his desire to keep the 672 prints together—even if it meant eschewing profit and donating the collection to an institution. In 1975, King found a buyer in a New York corporation, the holding company Esmark. A division of Swift and Company, Esmark wished to use the collection as part of a public relations effort and as an opportunity to reach out to the community. This sale began a long period of travel for the collection, fulfilling King's wish to have his Currier & Ives lithographs shared with the public.

## Esmark

Esmark acquired King's collection of Currier & Ives prints as a part of their celebration of the American Revolution Bicentennial

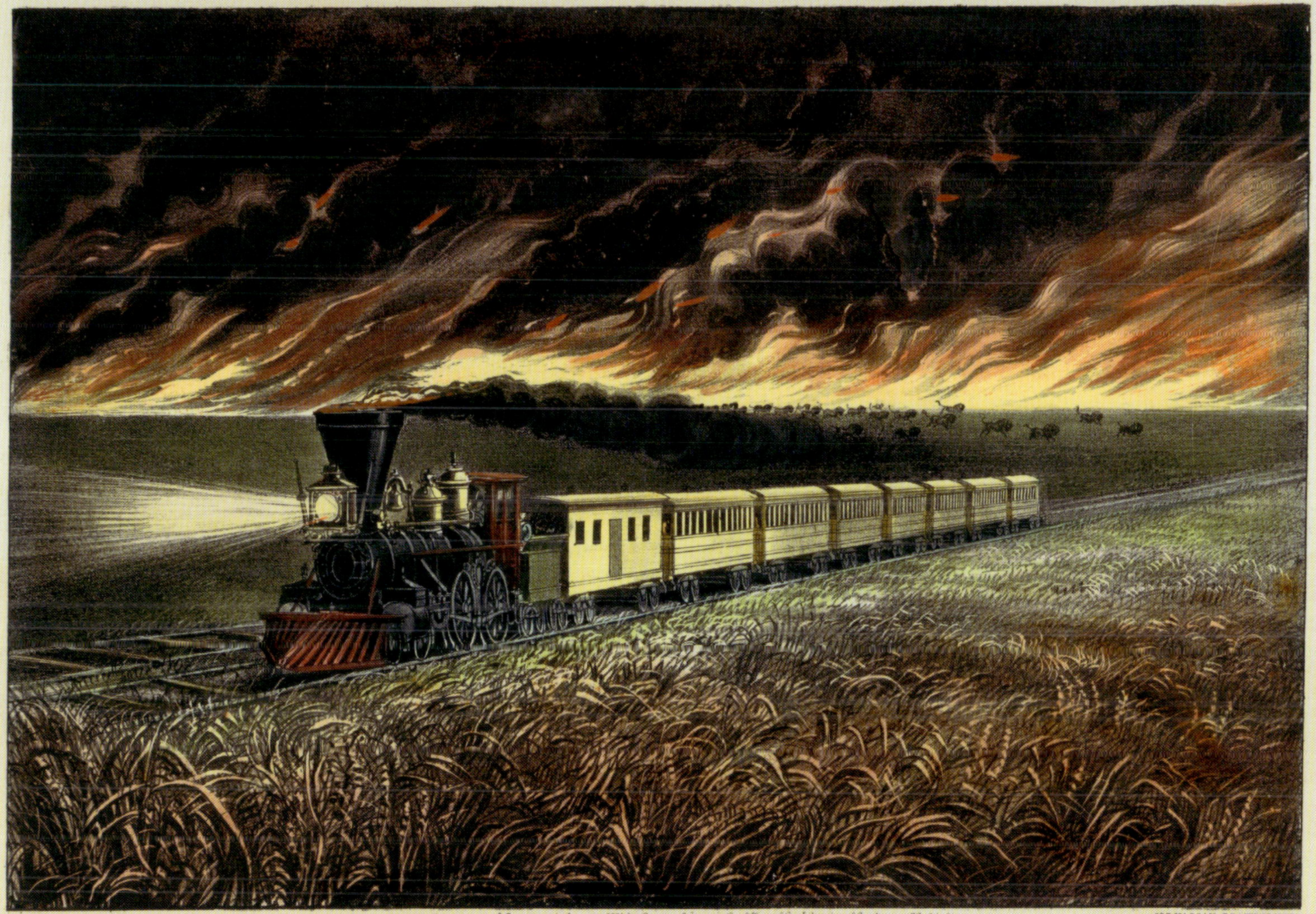

PUBLISHED BY CURRIER & IVES

Entered according to act of Congress in the year 1871, by Currier & Ives, in the Office of the Librarian of Congress at Washington.

125 NASSAU St NEW YORK

PRAIRIE FIRES OF THE GREAT WEST.

in 1976. The company purchased the collection for much less than it would have fetched if it had been broken up and sold individually, but King was delighted his impressions would remain together. The prints were shown at universities and museums across the country, beginning a long pattern of Esmark bringing its collection of Currier & Ives prints to the public. For each exhibition's opening reception, Esmark invited local public officials, such as politicians and dignitaries, to enjoy the artwork on view. This program gave these prints a wide reach, and King and Esmark developed a close correspondence regarding the plans for the collection.

In 1982, King arranged for conservation of the prints and frames, which was financed by Esmark. That same year, Kenneth Newman of the Old Print Shop appraised 660 prints in the collection and remarked that the collection had already more than doubled in value. Esmark continued to lend its collection to other corporate holdings of Swift throughout the 1980s, sending packaged exhibitions to headquarters and department stores across the country and the world. Venues included department stores such as J. W. Robinson's, Dayton's, and Marshall Field's, and corporations like International Playtex and Danskin. The collection was organized into six thematic touring exhibitions, although installations frequently included more than one of these categories if space allowed. "Commerce and Industry and the Challenges Therein" recorded the rapid industrial and commercial growth that America experienced in the second half of the nineteenth century with images of clipper ships, steamboats, railroads, and advertising images. "Life on the Mississippi/ U.S. at War" communicated the central role of the Mississippi River in the United States' economic expansion, and included depictions of the most important events of the Civil War. "The American Sporting Life" provided a window into the sports played and watched by mid-nineteenth-century Americans, such as horse racing, baseball, and sailing. "The American Expansion, Politics, and Satirical Humor" included prints concerning subjects as wide-ranging as westward expansion, presidential portraits, satirical comics, and political cartoons. "The Four Seasons of Rural Life" featured many of the firm's most popular images, often depicting a balanced relationship between man and nature, and the ways in which American life revolved around the seasonal cycle. Finally, "American Middle Class Values, Recreation, and Education" contained images of social gatherings, entertainment, and societal issues of the period, such as skating scenes, images of the temperance movement, and depictions of P. T. Barnum's "Gallery of Wonders."

Each exhibition was accompanied by labels provided by Esmark, as well as an educational film about the history of the printmaking firm. By 1984, the Esmark collection of Currier & Ives had been exhibited in over one hundred museums, college galleries, and department stores in the United States and nearly two dozen other countries where Swift had commercial interests. Esmark also licensed the images to a host of other commercial ventures to use on dishware, cards, album covers, and needlepoint designs. Roy King's collection of Currier & Ives had a wider audience than ever before, and brought these quintessentially American images to audiences and consumers all over the world. In internal correspondence, Esmark highlighted the positive impact this extensive touring schedule had on its brand image, noting that it brought, free of charge, historical images of everyday life to the kinds of people they wanted to buy their products. Esmark was able to further the American fascination with Currier & Ives prints, as well as familiarize their patrons with traditional images of American history. However, new company leadership would change the way these prints were circulated and displayed. In June of 1984, Beatrice Companies, Inc. acquired Esmark and soon ended the collection's extensive touring schedule.

## Beatrice and Conagra Brands

By 1986, the prints had almost all been placed in storage, except for a handful installed in Beatrice's Chicago headquarters, ending their days of traveling around the globe. In 1990, Conagra Brands purchased Beatrice Companies, Inc., at which point the collection was transferred from Chicago to the new Conagra Brands campus in downtown Omaha. The company installed over four hundred prints across its headquarters in spaces that were open to the public, allowing visitors and residents of Omaha easy access to the collection. The installation, entitled "Recapturing the American Spirit," wound down the corridors that connected the four buildings of the campus. Joslyn Art Museum curator David Hunt was engaged to arrange and install the lithographs in forty-nine thematic groupings, each preceded by commentary on the subject or theme of the group, as well as additional information about the firm itself. This unusually large number of groupings was dictated by architectural partitions within the campus, but they could also be categorized into larger thematic sets such as city life, life in the country, American history, the Civil War, the American West, and sporting events. Scattered among the groupings were prints Currier & Ives sold as "comics," which could be lightly humorous or bitingly satirical. The installation provided an admirable overview of the workshop's oeuvre, and was beloved by many employees of the company. Brochures and maps of the Conagra Brands campus highlighted this collection as a source of pride, and the company encouraged employees and other guests to visit. Although the collection did not travel to off-site venues during this period, it still served as public relations ambassador for Conagra Brands, which encouraged the citizens of Omaha to visit and enjoy the collection.

## Joslyn Art Museum

In June of 2016, Conagra Brands announced its plans to donate the entire corporate collection of nearly six hundred Currier & Ives prints to Joslyn Art Museum. Following the move of its corporate headquarters to Chicago the previous year, the company wanted to provide a permanent home for the collection, ensure greater public access, and cement the collection's ongoing presence as a cherished part of the Omaha community. The gift immediately gave Joslyn one of the premiere collections of the workshop's prints in the country. The Museum just as quickly recognized the opportunity not only to celebrate this notable gift with a major traveling exhibition, but to encourage the scholarly reevaluation of these seemingly comprehensively studied American prints. Indeed, as the three essays that follow ably demonstrate, the avenues for understanding and interpreting Currier & Ives are as broad as their subjects, and these familiar accounts continue to challenge our understanding of our national history. The demise of Currier & Ives came in conjunction with the advent of inexpensive and easily reproducible photography, but the legacy of the firm is apparent in the continued popularity of their images. The story of Currier & Ives is one of everyday people, in subject and in audience, and their continued fascination with how we describe and define America, past and present.

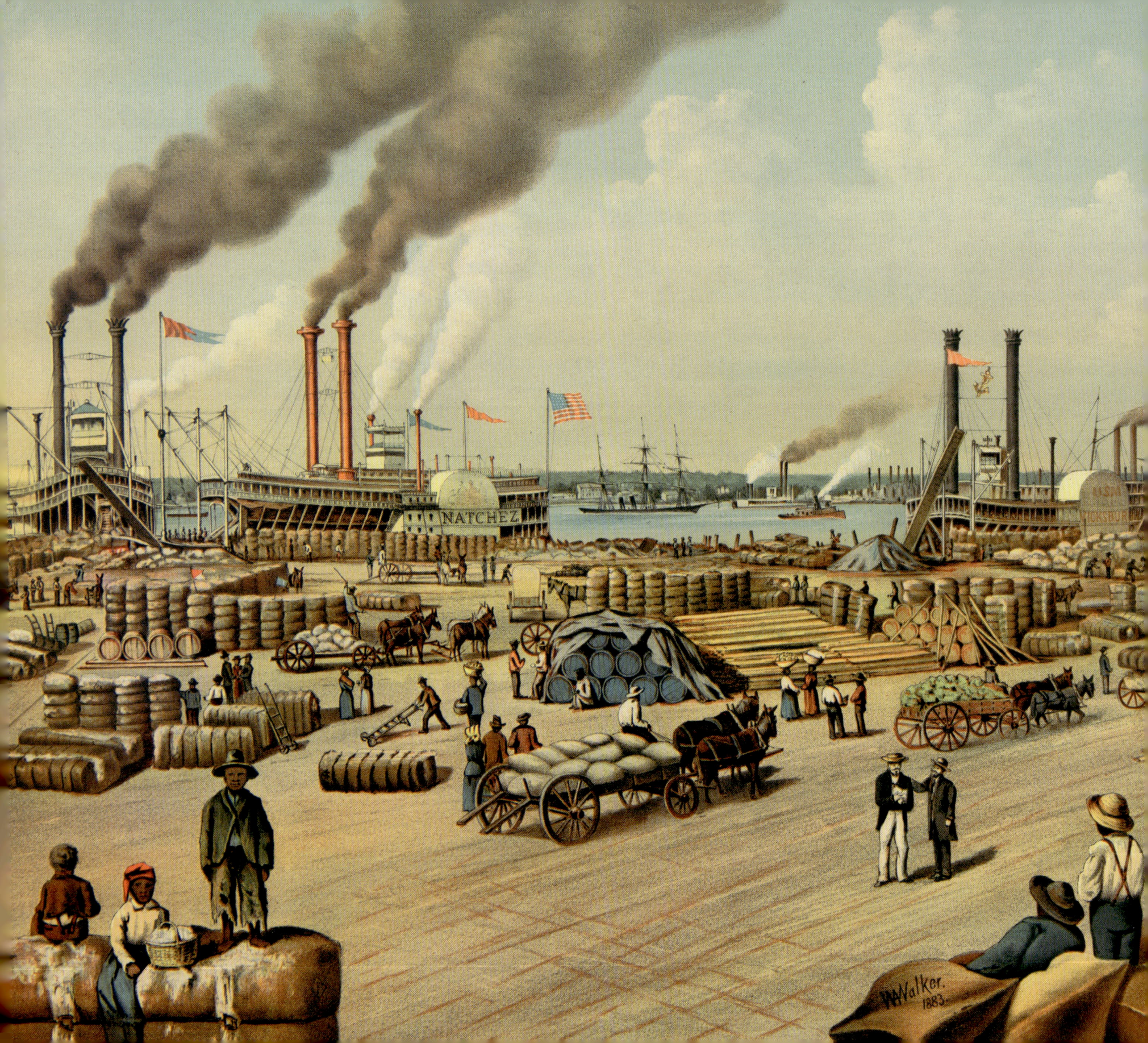
NATCHEZ
WAWalker.
1883.

# BETWEEN ART AND INDUSTRY

## *Making Currier & Ives Lithographs*

*Marie-Stéphanie Delamaire*

The self-proclaimed "Grand Central Depot for Cheap and Popular Prints," Currier & Ives was a firm of printmakers and publishers founded in New York in 1834 by Nathaniel Currier (1813–1888) and, after 1857, headed by Currier and his partner, James Merritt Ives (1824–1895). Based in New York, the firm produced and distributed a vast range of images, from expensive, large-folio lithographs and imported engravings to cheap prints and trade cards.[1] Whether large or small, coarse or delicate, Currier & Ives's pictures represented a broad assortment of subjects. Rural landscapes, genre scenes, portraits of presidents, and sporting pictures have endured in the form of Christmas cards, stamps, and calendars. Portraits of celebrities, generic "female heads," and devotional pictures have more often survived in many nineteenth-century albums and scrapbooks. Whether belittled for their cheap production process and debasement of high art, or hailed as the successful transmitter of the "romance of America," Currier & Ives and their lithographs have long come to define the democratic culture of Victorian America.[2]

In spite of scant archival evidence from the firm, more has been written on Currier & Ives and their prints than on any other nineteenth-century American publisher, giving the firm a disproportionate weight in the history of American lithography, sometimes aggrandizing the firm's contributions while obscuring its real innovations.[3] Yet connecting comparative archival evidence with the careful examination of Currier & Ives's prints and ephemera has the potential to shed light on many aspects of the firm's business and place within the history of American printmaking. This essay looks at Currier & Ives from this perspective. I consider the historic transformations that helped Nathaniel Currier's lithographic workshop rise from a typical small operation to a large publishing firm of national prominence. I look at how Currier & Ives produced its pictures and highlight the differences between the prints manufactured on a mass scale in the firm's factory and the large, hand-colored lithographs created on demand by independent workshops headed by a single artist. Considering the differences in production, techniques, and craftsmanship, this essay not only shows Currier & Ives's dependence on outside talent, but also how the firm's network of collaborators made possible the production of a vast catalogue of images that came to be seen as representative of Victorian America.

### Currier & Ives, Lithography, and American Mass Visual Culture

Lithography, derived from Greek for "writing on a stone," is a planographic printing process developed in Germany by the playwright Alois Senefelder (1771–1834) at the end of the eighteenth century. One of the most important innovations of the modern printing industry, it is based on the principle that water and oil do not mix. Rather than creating a design on a copper plate, the new printing method required the use of limestone slabs with uniform surfaces. An artist would draw a design on the surface of the stone using a greasy medium such as lithographic crayon or liquid tusche (ink). To prepare the stone for printing, a solution of gum arabic and acid affixed the image on the stone. Then, moistened with water, the stone would receive an application of oil-based ink from a roller, which would only adhere to the oil-based medium of the artist's design. The printer finally laid a sheet of paper on the stone and passed it through the press, transferring the inked drawing to the paper as a mirror image of the original (fig. 1).

Simple in principle, lithography is a rather demanding technique that requires training as well as specific materials, presses, and drafting methods.[4] Limestone is a very sensitive surface and any greasy mark on the stone will alter the design during printing. Nineteenth-century artists used a wooden bridge to avoid touching the stone's surface while drawing. They had a wide variety of tools and materials to draw their pictures and create various effects. For instance, a hammer and mallet helped artists chisel out broken edges and imperfections on the stone. They also used scrapers, pen-knife rockers with fold-out burnishers, steel-tip lithographic pens, and crayons, held in a portcrayon, to compose their designs (fig. 2).[5] Despite the difficulties entailed in this drawing technique, lithography held enormous advantages vis-à-vis former methods of image making. In contrast to copper and steel engraving or etching, the design process was faster, and it allowed the direct transfer of a design from stone to sheet of paper. It was therefore conceptualized as allowing the creation of a multiple originals

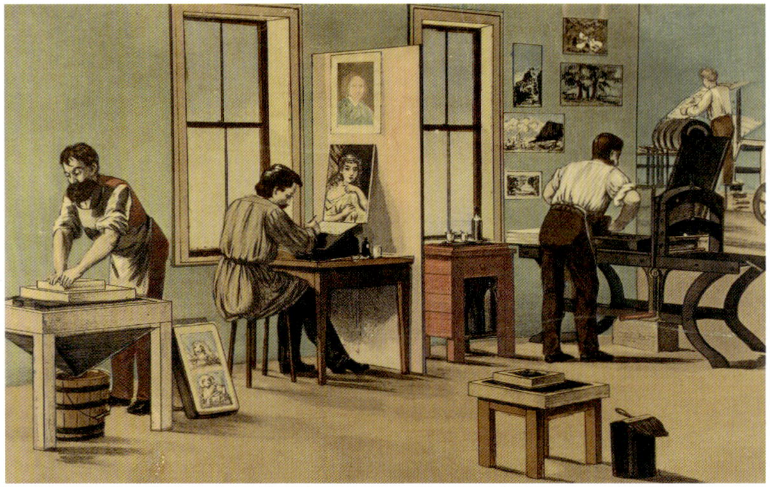

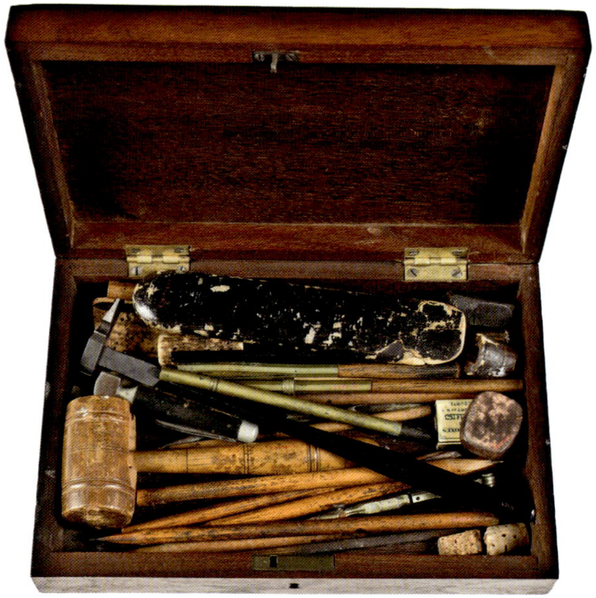

FIG 1 *Prang's Aids for Object Teaching: Lithography*, L. Prang and Co., lithographers, Boston, Massachusetts, 1874. Hand-colored collotype. Courtesy of Winterthur Museum, Museum purchase with funds drawn from the Centenary Fund, 2016.0022.002. Photo funded by NEA

FIG 2 Louis Maurer's wooden toolbox. Louis Maurer Collection, Courtesy, American Antiquarian Society rather than an adaptation of one medium into another. Secondly, this original could be multiplied faster, more cheaply, and with a virtually infinite print run as long as the stone itself was properly maintained. This latter quality positioned the medium at the forefront of the transformations taking place in the printing industry of the United States starting in the 1830s, which led to the rise of mass visual culture.

In the United States, the practice of lithography emerged within the context of Franco-American exchanges and became widespread after the 1820s.[6] Originally invented as a cheap alternative to publishing text, lithography's first widespread application began in France with the printing of sheet music. An active lithographic trade soon emerged when printers Godefroy Engelmann (1788–1839) and Charles Philibert de Lasteyrie (1759–1849) were able to recruit fine artists to invest in this new drawing technique. According to Peter S. Duval, a French lithographer who emigrated to Philadelphia in 1831, the biggest obstacle the new medium encountered in the United States was to find skillful artists ready to explore this challenging drawing and printing technique.[7] Nathaniel Currier happened to be one such artist.

Born in Roxbury, Massachusetts, in 1813, Currier first learned the craft in Boston from John and William Pendleton, who had imported pressmen and materials from France and operated one of the earliest lithographic workshops in the country. As an apprentice and journeyman in the Pendleton workshop, Currier learned how to prepare, draw on, and print lithographic stones, together with the manufacture of transfer paper, lithographic crayons, and varnish.[8] In 1834, Currier bought the Pendleton New York workshop and established a new lithographic firm at 137 Broadway with a man named Stodart. The partnership lasted less than a year, however, and in 1835 the business was all in the hands of Currier.[9]

Currier established his business in the right place and at the right time. The printing industry was booming in New York during the second quarter of the nineteenth century. Thanks to several newly founded institutions supporting the visual arts, lithographic workshops were able to rely on talented artists to sustain this development. New York's art institutions were fast expanding in the early 1830s. The National Academy of Design, the American Art-Union, the American Institute for the City of New York, and the Mechanics' Institute of the City of New York all promoted artistic education and careers. Equally important, they held annual exhibitions or fairs that included significant displays of printed pictures and promoted the utility of the visual arts for various industries and society at large.[10] New York thus became an attractive location for many artist lithographers who emigrated mainly from France, Germany, and England. The city's lithographic industry, including Nathaniel Currier's establishment, benefitted tremendously from this growing pool of talent. Three of the artists most often associated with the firm, Frances Flora Bond Palmer (Fanny Palmer) (1812–1876), Louis Maurer (1832–1932), and Otto Knirsch (active 1853–67), were foreign-born individuals who immigrated to the city during this period.[11]

In the early years of the business, the Currier workshop subsisted largely through job printing. Like other lithographers in the city, Nathaniel Currier started by producing thousands of prints on commission: sheet music, charts, advertisements, certificates, trade cards, etc. It was during the late 1830s and the early 1840s that he moved toward publishing, not only operating as an on-demand printmaker, but also producing, copyrighting, and selling the press's own work. What drove this new line of business was the representation of the news and the firm's association with newspapers.[12]

Even though the earliest known collaboration between Currier and a newspaper dates back to 1837, it was not until the reporting of a steamship fire in 1840 that the firm's stature in the New York's lithographic industry was transformed and expanded into publishing.[13] On January 13, 1840, the *Lexington*, a luxury passenger steamboat sailing from New York and bound for Stonington, Connecticut, caught fire off Eatons Neck in Long Island Sound. Soon the fire spread to the flammable cotton bales on deck and the entire ship burned, with only four people surviving. New York newspapers broke the disaster to the public two days later, and the *Sun* advertised its lithographic representation in the morning paper of January 16th. Several versions of that image—an anonymous monochrome lithograph representing the fire as a day scene—and its accompanying text were published as a news extra within a week. It was Nathaniel Currier's version, however, that would become an iconic representation of the disaster (fig. 3). Published first by the *Sun* as an extra on January 23, Currier's lithograph depicted a night scene, accompanied by a map of Long Island and the Sound showing the exact location of the disaster. The *Sun* announced that the lithograph would be colored and "executed with much more accuracy and finish than any others."[14] Five days later, the newspaper announced its plans to stop publishing the image, adding that already more than 12,000 copies had been distributed. At that time, Currier took over the lithograph's publication, issuing his own combination of colored lithograph and letterpress text in a mock-up news extra that went at least through at least three different states before he decided to publish the picture as a stand-alone small folio.

Despite the success of the *Lexington* lithograph, such images would not come to be the primary medium for illustrating the news in America. (Instead, wood engraving illustrations would take the lead as they could be printed together with text on a letterpress.) Nevertheless, the impact of the *Lexington* on the New York lithographic industry and Nathaniel Currier's firm

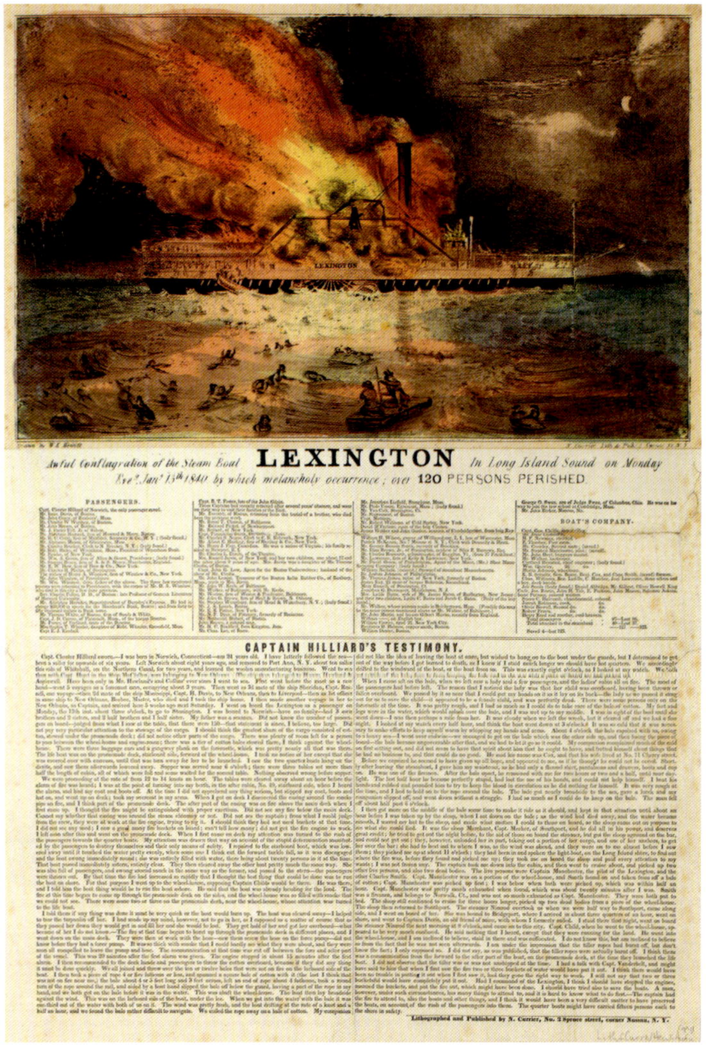


FIG 3 *Awful Conflagration of the Steam Boat Lexington*, 1840. Courtesy, American Antiquarian Society

is difficult to overstate. Considering that a good lithographic printer on a handpress could produce about three hundred prints in a day, the publication and distribution of one image as popular as the *Lexington* would have kept busy at least three pressmen and three lithographic presses per day, a considerable workforce and equipment for the size of the industry at that time. Although we do not know exactly how many lithographic presses were available in Nathaniel's workshop or in the entire city of New York in 1840, we have a sense of the industry's size through information about a competitor, Endicott's New York establishment. Endicott employed about twelve people at that time, including apprentices, draftsmen, pressmen, and a bookkeeper. Less than ten years earlier, according to Peter S. Duval, there were only eight presses in the entire country. Three presses were therefore likely to occupy an entire workshop production in the early 1840s.[15]

The success of the *Lexington* image marks a turning point in the history of the American lithography industry. Its popularity demonstrated the public's desire for sensational and dramatic colored lithographs, ushering in a decade of significant expansion for the industry. Both the demand for equipment and labor pushed the industry's investments, creating a labor market attractive to talented lithographic printers and artists, supported in part by the city's art institutions. In Hartford, Connecticut, for instance, Daniel W. Kellogg had started his lithographic business with just one press in 1830. In 1849, he had moved to a large building at 130 Main Street with about ten lithographic presses.[16] Currier, like Kellogg, was one of the key figures of that expansion. By 1845, he had entirely transformed his business model. From a small workshop primarily offering all kinds of job printing services, and only occasionally investing in the publication of a picture, Currier had become a large publisher of prints ranging from common domestic scenes to patriotic and historic images, portraits of presidents, and (of course) disaster prints. Currier had expanded its operations so as to be able to publish close to a hundred titles a year, about seven times the number of lithographs he published in 1840. A catalogue of prints from 1851 demonstrates the firm's continued expansion, proudly listing more than four hundred titles available, monochrome or hand colored, framed or unframed, in the shop at 152 Nassau Street or by mail order. Currier's business had expanded so much that the firm now operated from two locations, a shop on Nassau, and its original workshop on Spruce Street, which had been transformed into a factory.

## Factory, Workshops, and Artists' Homes: The Making of Currier & Ives Prints

Currier & Ives produced and sold a wide range of printed images, including trade cards and foreign prints. Its focus, however, was the lithograph for display, from the large folios that are considered the crown jewel of many Currier & Ives collections today, to numerous small decorative images of landscapes, fruits, female heads, and devotional subjects, as well as caricatures that would play a particularly important role in the final twenty years of the firm's history. In the almost total absence of archival records, our knowledge of Currier & Ives's modes of production relies primarily on comparative archival material, on the physical and visual examination of print collections, and on the firm's oral history, gathered in large part by Harriett Endicott Waite and Harry T. Peters.[17] Much of what we know about the firm's relationships with its artists, in particular, was limited to Peters's and Waite's interviews with people who had been involved with the firm or with their relatives. Since then, the discovery of a handful of documents has shed light on some of the stories Peters told in his book. Going back to the archives and examining prints has thus become essential to constructing a more accurate account of the firm's production methods and the roles of its artist lithographers.

One of the first important features of Currier & Ives's business model was how the firm separated the production of its cheap prints from their more prestigious counterparts. Their pictures greatly varied in price. The cheapest images were small, plain lithographs printed in black ink and sold either uncolored or coarsely painted for six to ten cents each. The costlier examples were large lithographs printed on the best papers and delicately hand colored by professional artists. These sold between $1 and $3.75 apiece, prices on par with foreign imports such as the lithographs sold by Goupil & Co, a Parisian art dealer established in New York in 1848.[18]

The small and inexpensive lithographs were not manufactured in the same manner or by the same people who created the large folios. They were designed, printed, and colored by anonymous artists who worked in the factory on Spruce Street. The factory operations were very similar to those of the Kellogg firm in Hartford.[19] The spaces were divided and separated by task. In the artists' rooms, apprentices ground the stones and helped the draftsmen with their drawings. The stones were then sent to the pressroom where they were printed on handpresses. From there, the prints went to the sizing room, where the sheets of paper were coated for watercoloring. Currier & Ives's New York operations were distributed across three upper floors of a five-story building. According to Peters, coloring took place on the fifth floor and was mostly done by "young women and girls, all trained colorists and mostly of German descent."[20] Since none of the artists and printers are identified on the prints, and there is no surviving staff list, it is impossible to verify the accuracy of this statement. From the very few pieces of evidence from prints and other firms, we know that coloring was carried out in various ways. An invoice between Nathaniel Currier and James Baillie, a New York print colorist and lithographer, dated December 1840, indicates that he had painted 2,378 impressions for $23.78 (these included 125 impressions of *The Awful Conflagration of the Steam Boat Lexington*).[21] In this particular case, coloring likely took place on the premises, since the invoice withheld money for rent. In contrast, Virginia Penny's survey *The Employments of Women* reported that many women colorists worked from home in order to protect their middle-class status. Penny also recounted an interview with Nathaniel Currier who explained that small girls were employed in the Spruce Street factory, earning between $3 and $7 dollars per week, coloring prints under the direction of a forewoman.[22] Currier's statement is confirmed by the examination of extant examples of some of the cheap prints likely produced at the factory: looking at them reveals that sometimes only one or two colors were applied, often by a combination of stencil and hand coloring, suggesting a low level of craftsmanship and an assembly-line method.

In contrast to the firm's cheap prints at the lower end of the catalogue, Currier & Ives's largest series of prints were colored by professional artists in their studios and were works of art in and of themselves. Technical analysis of several examples conducted in Winterthur Museum's conservation laboratories has led to a new appreciation of their status and role in Currier & Ives's catalogue. All of them were printed on the highest grade of lithographic paper available in New York at the time. Additionally, the watercolor palette used by some of the colorists included new and expensive colors such as viridian, a transparent green pigment synthesized in 1838 in Paris and only available on the market after 1850.[23]

What is more, Currier & Ives's large folios were not anonymous. They were designed by a handful of artists who are identified in the prints' margins: Louis Maurer, Thomas B. Worth (ca. 1834–1917), Arthur Fitzwilliam Tait (1819–1905), James E. Butterworth (1817–1894),[24] George Henry Durrie (1820–1863), Otto Knirsch, Charles Parsons (1821–1910), John Cameron (ca. 1828, active 1848–62), and Fanny Palmer. Other artists less frequently associated with the firm included Eastman Johnson (1824–1906), Napoleon Sarony (1821–1896), and George Inness

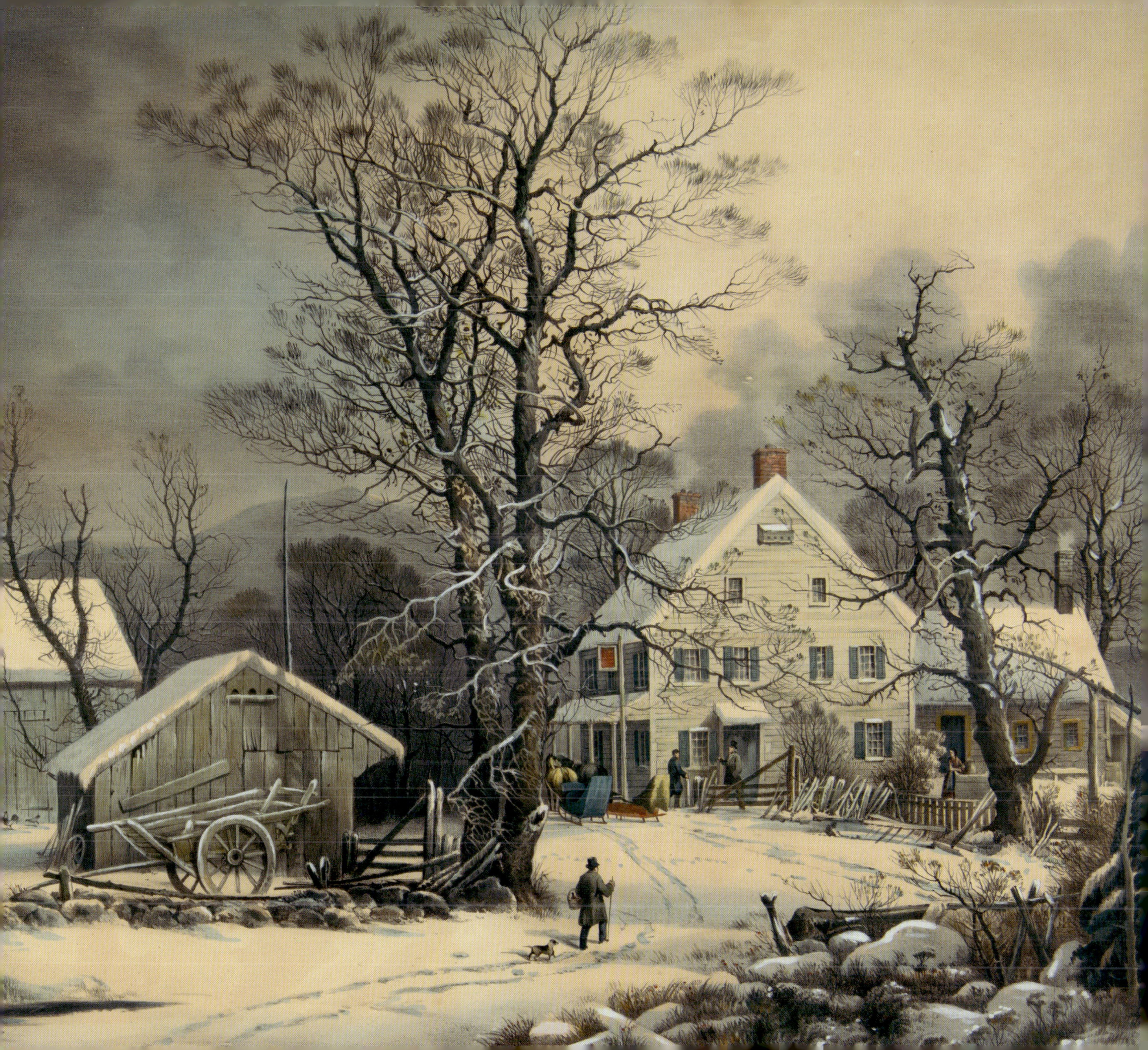

(1825–1894). Knirsch, Maurer, Palmer, and Parsons were all artist lithographers who contributed many of the pictures that are considered to be the best of Currier & Ives's production today. None of these artists trained with Currier. Parsons had apprenticed in the Endicott firm, while Maurer, Palmer, and Knirsch were trained in Europe and thus contributed to the dissemination of lithographic technical knowledge from Europe to the United States. Maurer had started as a staff artist in the firm but left and established his own workshop. Parsons worked for Endicott on contract for Currier & Ives. The others, including Palmer, worked at the head of their own workshops, contracted by Currier & Ives for the production of specific stones.[25]

As lithographers, Knirsch, Maurer, Palmer, and Parsons either drew their own compositions or adapted another artist's drawing or painting for the lithographic stone. In contrast, the large folios bearing the names of Tait, Butterworth, Johnson, Durrie, or Inness can all be considered reproductive prints, since they are all adaptations of the artists' paintings on stone. Out of these, Durrie, a painter of landscapes from New Haven, Connecticut, became particularly popular for his idealized visions of the New England countryside and winter scenes. By the late 1850s, his reputation had grown and he was exhibiting at New York City's major art institutions such as the National Academy of Design. Butterworth and Tait were both born in England. They immigrated to the United States as adults, and exhibited at the American Art-Union and the National Academy of Design. Butterworth specialized in marine paintings, while Tait was better known as a painter of sporting pictures.[26]

Tait's collaboration with the firm was the longest and most productive one, although not without its difficulties. The artist was first trained as a lithographer. Once in the United States, however, he abandoned lithography for painting, and attracted critical attention for his western scenes (though he painted without firsthand knowledge of the West). Nathaniel Currier and James Ives took notice of the artist because of his pictures' narrative and dramatic potential. The publishers wanted to capitalize on the appetite for images representing the lands recently acquired by the United States in the aftermath of the Mexican-American War. The firm became an important patron of Arthur Tait, commissioning forty-two paintings for publication between 1852 and 1865, and hiring artist lithographers to translate them on the stone. Among these, two large folio series—American Hunting Scenes and American Field Sports (pp. 113 and 117)—depicted groups of men hunting and fishing in Upstate New York, a region Tait visited every summer. The large lithographs were handsomely colored by hand and heavily advertised by the publishers, defining Tait's reputation as a successful painter of sporting images for years to come.

At first, the collaboration between painter and publishers worked to everyone's advantage: the success of the prints increased the value of Tait's paintings on the art market and built his artistic reputation on a national scale. As for the publishers, since they owned the copyright to the artist's prints, they could reproduce popular compositions in a variety of formats and prices, reaching a broader range of customers. This practice, which Currier & Ives used with many of their artists, became a source of conflict between Tait and the firm in 1865, a time when painters were becoming increasingly preoccupied with controlling the reproduction of their pictures. *The Cares of a Family* (p. 116), a picture depicting a family of quails with a brood of eleven chicks, led to a falling-out between the painter and Currier & Ives. The large folio print published in 1855 had been very popular, and Currier & Ives, following their usual practice, decided to reissue the picture in a smaller and cheaper version. The print, distributed with the same title, was intended for less-discerning audiences; it was not as carefully drawn and lacked the refined coloring of the earlier print. Tait, who had not been consulted, was outraged by what he perceived to be a debased representation of his talent in the print. What especially upset him was not that Currier & Ives reused an earlier composition—there was no copyright for paintings in America until 1865, and Currier & Ives legally owned the legal right to copy the earlier image—but rather that his signature had been prominently inserted into the new lithograph. The dispute led to Tait's decision to no longer work with Currier & Ives and turn to their Boston competitor Louis Prang, who was then developing a method to adapt chromolithography, the latest technique in color lithography, to the exact reproduction of fine paintings.

Collaborations between artists and lithographers were woven in the very fabric of the printing industry and the American art world. From its very beginnings, lithography depended on the combined abilities of talented artist lithographers and skilled lithographic printers.[27] Collaborative practices were thus instrumental in the emergence of lithography as a viable form of printing in the 1820s and 1830s, and they had a profound impact on American art and visual culture as the industry expanded in the middle decades of the century. In a typical workshop, several artist lithographers often worked with one another on the production of a stone, such as when Louis Maurer and John Cameron joined forces to create the *Life of the Fireman* series (pp. 86 and 87). Even when only one artist lithographer's name appears on a print, such as Charles Parsons's lithograph after Tait's *Brook Trout Fishing: An Anxious Moment* (fig. 4; see also p. 112), the image was likely created by several artists working under Parsons's direction. Collaborative art making was not even restricted to the lithographic workshop. Tait, who was a member of the National Academy of Design, worked on at least twenty-four paintings with a Düsseldorf-trained landscape painter named James McDougal Hart. Since Tait had

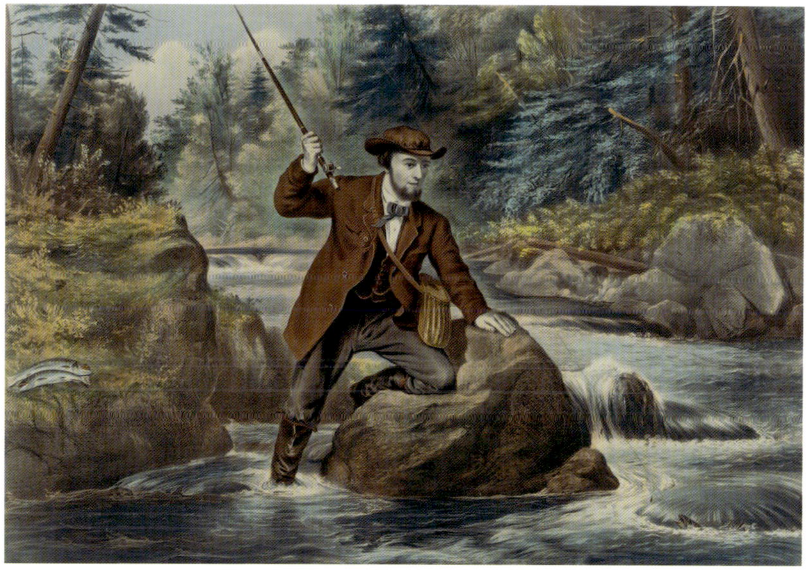

FIG 4 *Brook Trout Fishing: An Anxious Moment*, 1862. Joslyn Art Museum, Gift of Conagra Brands, 2016.20.484

first trained in England as a lithographer, one ponders whether his collaborative attitude toward artistic creation in painting was not a direct extension of practices learned in the printing workshop. Indeed, many a draftsman like Tait, Fitz Henry Lane (1804–1865), or Winslow Homer (1836–1910) first learned lithography before dedicating themselves and their careers to painting and the fine arts.

## Fanny Palmer: An Artist's Impact on a National Firm

The relationship between lithographic printer and artist lithographer remained an important feature of both small and large firms throughout the nineteenth century. Nathaniel Currier's workshop was in fact unusual in its abandon of this system when Currier dissolved the partnership with Stodart in 1835 without taking on a new partner. What Nathaniel Currier lacked in the absence of a partner, however, he replaced with an abundance of contracts with outside artists. Throughout his leadership, the firm worked with many independent lithographers, including his own brother Charles. Currier's fruitful collaborations with such artist lithographers as Palmer, Maurer, Cameron, and others, who worked on contract had significant repercussions on Currier & Ives's business. Examining the life and work of Fanny Palmer sheds light on the impact that Currier & Ives's collaborations with artists had on the firm's production and on the field of American lithography at large.

Born in Leicester, England, in 1812, Frances Flora Bond Palmer was among the most talented and prolific female artists of the nineteenth century. Known as Fanny from her childhood, she received her first artistic education at an academy for girls run by Mary Linwood (1755–1845), located not far from her home.[28] At the school, Fanny received solid instruction in drawing, perspective, and watercolor—three areas that were key to the training of lithographers in the early Victorian era. As her family weathered economic hardship in the wake of her father's death in 1839, Fanny and her husband, Seymour, decided to establish themselves in the lithographic business. She went to London to train with Louis Haghe (1806–1885), one of the founders of Day & Haghe, the leading art lithography firm of early Victorian London. Likely training in the same workshop was her husband, who became a professional printer. In 1842 the Palmers established their own lithographic workshop in Leicester, and Fanny taught students in her "Drawing Academy." By January 1844, the couple had immigrated to New York, where they established themselves as "F. & S. Palmer, Lithographers." The Palmers collaborated with Nathaniel Currier as early as 1849 with a series of panoramic views of New York City. By the end of 1851, however, F. & S. Palmer, Lithographers had ceased to exist. Seymour was now a tavern keeper, and Fanny was on her way to becoming one of Currier & Ives's most prolific artists, designing at least two hundred of the firm's most famous prints between 1851 and 1868.

The only interview published during Palmer's lifetime indicates that she ran a lithographic workshop in her home during this period, rather than working as a staff artist in Currier & Ives's factory, as she is commonly described in the literature.[29] In her studio, she designed pictures, drew them on lithographic stones, and supervised apprentices and emerging lithographers. Conscious of the gender imbalance in her field, she acknowledged giving "instruction to several youths, but never to one of her own sex." "To an apprentice," Palmer said, "after two or three years' practice, a small premium is paid," adding that "she had one youth to learn of her, who, after four years' time, received $7 a week from her for his work."[30] Like other lithography studios in New York at the time, hers functioned as a form of art school and followed a hierarchical system of education from apprentice to master lithographer.[31] Palmer thus worked for Currier & Ives, but independently. Her work was so popular with the firm that she did not have to search for commissions elsewhere: between 1852 and 1868, we only know of one composition she created for a competitor.

Leading an independent workshop, Palmer recruited and instructed several apprentices. Some of them would make significant contributions to their field. One was Joseph Knapp (1832–1891), who became a partner in Sarony & Major in 1855.[32] An important competitor of Currier & Ives, Sarony & Co. would become the well-known American Lithographic Company at the end of the nineteenth century. Another one was likely James M. Ives, who became Currier's partner in 1857. According to the early histories of the firm, James started working for Currier as a bookkeeper in 1852, although he had artistic leanings. His input is credited with a major role in the firm's success in the 1860s.[33] A recently discovered receipt of payment dated August 27, 1845, and signed by him, indicates that Ives was already working with Nathaniel Currier by the mid-1840s, likely as a printseller in the shop.[34] Ives, however, aspired to become a lithographer in the early 1850s. He lived in Brooklyn at several addresses that are all a few blocks from Fanny Palmer's home.[35] In the early 1850s, Palmer's career was in transition as she and her husband liquidated their business, and she began work as an independent lithographer in Brooklyn. Meanwhile, Ives moved from being a printseller (according to the census of 1850) to a lithographer (1855), and finally to his role as partner in Currier & Ives (1857). The signature "J. M. I. del." on the stone of the 1868 print *Low Water in the Mississippi* is evidence that Ives's early experience as a lithographer continued to play an important role in the firm. While Ives's children claimed that he was self-taught in the medium, it is very unlikely. Lithography was a difficult art to learn, requiring, in Palmer's words, "a regular course of advancement in order to follow it advantageously."[36] It seems reasonable to believe that Ives must have learned lithography from a master, and there is no more likely teacher than Palmer, whose studio was close to his home, and who was working for his employer.[37]

Visual examination of lithographs from both Palmer and Currier & Ives also suggests that Palmer's knowledge and talent had a direct impact on the technical skills of Currier & Ives's printers and lithographers working on Spruce Street. Nathaniel collaborated with many artists at that time, including his own brother Charles, who worked on printing the finest lithographs. Charles is also well known for developing new lithographic crayons with the help of Fanny Palmer. What is less known is how he learned from her and her husband the fine printing technique of tint lithography, which became critical to the production of the firm's high-end series. According to Harriet Endicott Waite's interview with Louis Maurer, such lithographs were not printed by the thousands at the factory, but were printed on a handpress by Charles Currier and purely on demand.[38] When the Palmers arrived in New York, Nathaniel had been in business for a decade. Almost all the Currier's prints until then were one-stone crayon lithographs. None show the refined drawing and the multiple-stone tint lithography found in the Palmer's production, as seen in *Church of the Holy Trinity* (fig. 5). This large three-stone lithograph was designed by Fanny and printed by Seymour soon after their arrival in the United States. Particularly adapted to landscape, the tint lithography technique employed transparent color inks (often only beige and blue) printed from separate stones on which areas might be stumped, rubbed, abraded, or stopped to create reserves of white. The effect evoked watercolor washes, and was particularly popular for high-end lithographic publications such as David Roberts's *Sketches in the Holy Land and Syria, 1842–1849*, illustrated with lithographs designed and printed in the Day & Haghe workshop. Currier & Ives's large prints only started showing evidence of the proper use tint lithography after Currier started working with Palmer. Some of Palmer's most successful lithographs published by Currier—for instance, *Wooding Up on the Mississippi* (p. 68)—were printed with two or three stones. Charles may have learned printing with tint stones from the artist herself, or from Seymour between his retirement from the lithography business in 1851 and his death in 1859.

Currier & Ives's collaboration with Fanny Palmer and other artists sheds light on the real impact the firm had on American lithography and Victorian culture at large. Their innovation did not lie in the partners' drive for technological change or improvement. Currier & Ives's mastering of tint lithography certainly allowed the firm to take full advantage of Palmer's lithographic style. However, when chromolithography rose to prominence in the second half of the nineteenth century,

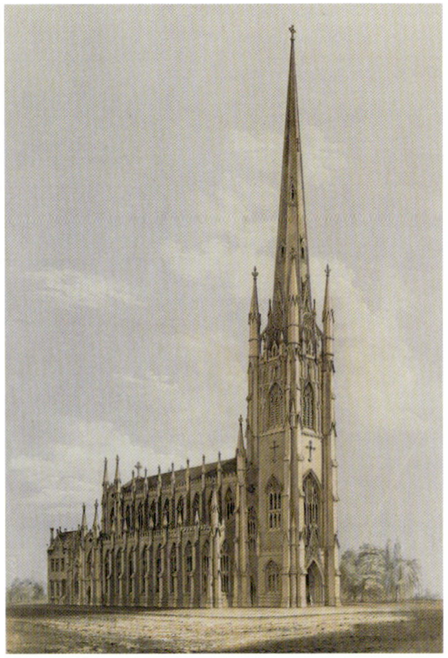

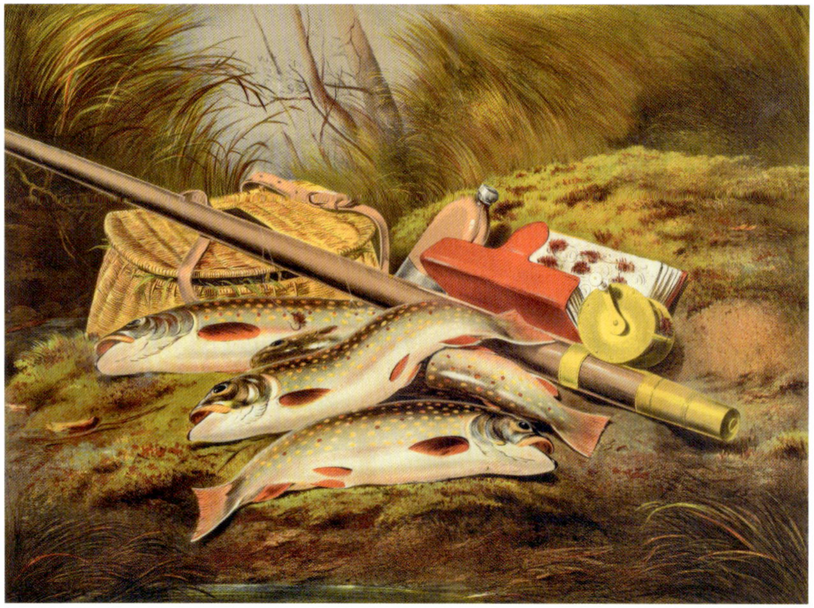

FIG 5 *Church of the Holy Trinity. Brooklyn Heights*, Frances B. Palmer, artist, F. and S. Palmer, lithographers, New York, New York, 1845. Three-stone lithograph printed in black, tan, and blue. Courtesy of Winterthur Museum, Library purchase, 1973.0567. Photo funded by NEA

FIG 6 *American Speckled Brook Trout*, Currier & Ives, publisher, Charles Parsons, lithographer, Arthur Fitzwilliam Tait, painter, New York, New York, 1864–72. Chromolithograph. Courtesy of Winterthur Museum, Bequest of C. Porter Schutt, 2000.0019.019 A. Photo funded by NEA

Currier & Ives only explored it on a small scale—for instance, producing a five-stone large lithograph after Tait's *American Speckled Brook Trout* (fig. 6). They did not invest in the mass production of pictures entirely printed in color like Duval, who produced full chromolithographs as early as 1848, or Prang in postwar Boston. Instead, Currier & Ives's innovation lay in their relationships with artists and independent workshops, and in their strategy of print reproduction.[39]

Often considered the prize of contemporary collections, Currier & Ives's largest lithographs were not the "cheap and popular" prints sold by the thousands that the brand name brings to mind.[40] Produced in collaboration with independent artists, these prints were exploratory endeavors in many ways. Aimed at a discerning public, they were not expected to generate a lot of income directly through their sale. The firm's major income stream derived from the cheap lithographs discussed earlier in this essay. Currier & Ives commissioned the large and ambitious pictures directly from an artist or a workshop, and they acquired its copyright at the same time. The assumption was that the picture would generate profits by being reissued in smaller, simplified, or partial reproductions, which would be printed and colored cheaply on an industrial scale. Currier & Ives were thus able to produce an impressive catalogue of more than 7,500 titles in their seven decades of operation, and they sold hundreds of thousands of images to individuals, communities, and printsellers throughout the country.

On the one hand, Currier & Ives's relationships with New York's independent workshops demonstrate the critical role that singular artists such as Fanny Palmer, a remarkably talented and prolific woman lithographer of Victorian era, played in the history of one of the largest publishing firms in America. On the other hand, looking at the firm's wide range of activities also points to Currier & Ives's strategy to capture market shares spanning areas from the art of fine prints to ephemeral political cartoons. Working with independent artists not only allowed the firm to test the potential of a picture to become an item of popular culture, it helped Currier & Ives produce quickly a vast number of prints that were largely variations of one another, and reflected the partners' vision of what was desirable in American visual culture. Between the steamboats and trains, western and sporting scenes, pictures of domestic harmony and wealth, portraits of celebrities, and social and political caricatures, Currier & Ives's prints presented both the possibility of customization as well as some uniformity through series that embodied a consensus of white and middle-class Victorian values and belief systems, widely spread across the country, and reflecting those of the founding figures of the business itself.

## NOTES

1 Nathaniel Currier, and later Currier & Ives, sold various types of images, including steel engravings and imported foreign prints. The lithographs were the firm's major line of production and will be the subject of this chapter. For other images published or sold by Currier & Ives, see James Bruce and Wendy Shadwell, "Unconventional Currier & Ives," *Imprint* 24, no. 1 (Spring 1999): 2–26.

2 Harry T. Peters, *Currier and Ives: Printmakers to the People* (Garden City, NY: Doubleday, Doran, 1929), 7.

3 Harry T. Peters's account of the history of the firm and its artists, *Currier and Ives: Printmakers to the People,* is largely responsible for the identification of Currier & Ives with nineteenth-century America. Peters saw in the form and content of the firm's prints an embodiment of the epic story of American democratic culture and its expansion. Bryan Le Beau's recent *Currier & Ives: America Imagined* (Washington, DC: Smithsonian Institution Press, 2001) revisits this narrative to engage with the way that Currier & Ives's pictures embodied Victorian values and beliefs. Michael Clapper's essay in this volume expands on Le Beau to consider the success of particular Currier & Ives's themes, such as disaster prints, cheap black-and-white representations of domestic animals, and still lifes.

4 Michael Twyman, "The Process of Lithography and the Technique of Drawing on Stone," in *Lithography, 1800–1850, The Techniques of Drawing on Stone in England and France and their Application in Works of Topography* (London, New York, and Toronto: Oxford University Press, 1970), 61–163.

5 For a full explanation of Currier & Ives's tools, materials, and techniques, with close-ups of examples from the Winterthur collection, see http://lastingimpressions.winterthur.org/creating-currier-ives-prints/.

6 Georgia B. Barnhill, ed., *With a French Accent: American Lithography to 1860* (Worcester, MA: American Antiquarian Society, 2012).

7 Peter S. Duval, "Lithography," in *American Encyclopaedia of Printing,* ed. J. Luther Ringwalt (Philadelphia, PA: Menamin & Ringwalt, J. B. Lippincott & Co., 1871), 278.

8 Georgia B. Barnhill, "Business Practices of Commercial Nineteenth-Century American Lithographers," *Winterthur Portfolio* 48, no. 2/3 (Summer/Autumn 2014): 213–232.

9 Nathaniel still regarded 1834 as the date of his start in business since Currier & Ives's various letterheads and advertisements would later bear the inscription "Founded in 1834."

10 For the cross-pollination between art institutions and the printing industry, see Ethan Robey, "The Utility of Art: Mechanics' Institute Fairs in New York City, 1828–1876," (PhD diss., Columbia University, 2000), and Elliot Bostwick Davis, "The Currency of Culture: Prints in New York City,"

in *Art and the Empire City,* ed. Catherine Hoover Voorsanger and John K. Howat (New York: Metropolitan Museum of Art, 2000), 188–225.

11 According to Georgia B. Barnhill, the largest proportion of lithographs produced in the United States at that time were drawn by foreign-born artists, especially men and women born in France and Germany. See Barnhill, "French Technology and Skills in the United States," in Barnhill, ed., *With a French Accent,* 25.

12 The first copyrighted image for N. Currier dates 1838. For Currier & Ives's early production and move toward publishing, see G. R. A. Goyle, "An Addition to Currier Incunabula," *Antiques* 20 (September 1931): 100–101; Bella C. Landauer, "Some Trade Cards with a Particular Emphasis on the Currier & Ives Contributions," *The New-York Historical Society Quarterly* 17 (October 1933): 5–8; and Brust and Shadwell, "Unconventional Currier & Ives." For Currier & Ives's role in the representation of the news, see Michael Leja, "News Pictures in the Early Years of Mass Visual Culture in New York: Lithographs and the Penny Press," in *Getting the Picture: the Visual Culture of the News,* ed. Jason Hill and Vanessa R. Schwartz (London and New York: Bloomsbury Academic, 2015), 146–153.

13 In 1837, Currier collaborated with the *Sun* on a lithographic representation of another disaster, the *Dreadful Wreck of the Mexico.* See James Brust and Wendy Shadwell, "The Many Versions and States of the Awful Conflagration of the Steam Boat Lexington," *Imprint* 15, no. 2 (Autumn 1990): 8.

14 Brust and Shadwell, "The Many Versions," 6.

15 Duval compared the only three American lithographic firms of 1831—occupying only eight presses—with the 55 large establishments employing 450 handpresses and about 35 steam presses of 1870. (Duval, "Lithography," 278.)

16 Barnhill, "Business Practices," 217.

17 Peters, *Currier and Ives: Printmakers to the People*. Peters's research files are at the Museum of the City of New York. Harriet Endicott Waite gathered testimonies and materials for Peters. Her extensive research notes are available at the Archives of American Art.

18 See *First Supplement to Catalogue of Goupil & Co. New York, January 1855* at the American Antiquarian Society. The catalogue lists lithographs at various prices depending on the printing technique (crayon, tinted, or with dark background) and the presence or absence of hand coloring.

19 Barnhill, "Business Practices," 213–232; Nancy Finlay, ed., *Picturing Victorian America: Prints by The Kellogg Brothers of Hartford, Connecticut, 1830–1880* (Hartford, CT: Connecticut Historical Society, 2009).

20 Peters, *Currier and Ives: Printmakers to the People*, 33.

21 A photograph of this invoice is reproduced in Peters's *Currier and Ives: Printmakers to the People,* 33.

22 Virginia Penny, *The Employments of Women, A Cyclopaedia of Woman's Work* (Boston, MA: Walker, Wise, 1863), 8–69.

23 Marie-Stéphanie Delamaire and Joan Irving, "Fine or Commercial Lithograph? A Reappraisal of Fanny Palmer's Prints Published by Currier & Ives," in *Laid Down on Paper: Printmaking in America During the Life of Fitz Henry Lane,* ed. Caroline Sloat (Gloucester, MA: Cape Ann Museum, forthcoming); see also http://lastingimpressions.winterthur.org/creating-currier-ives-prints/materials/.

24 James E. Butterworth was born James E. Buttersworth but changed his name after he arrived in the United States. The Currier & Ives prints usually are inscribed with the name Butterworth.

25 Out of all the artists named above, Fanny Palmer is the only one whom Harry Peters considered a staff artist of Currier & Ives. Peters did not believe she could be a lithographer. For the most recent and complete monograph on the artist, see Charlotte S. Rubinstein, *Fanny Palmer: The Life and Works of a Currier & Ives Artist* (Syracuse, NY: Syracuse University Press, 2018). Recent research shows that Palmer worked independently in her own workshop in Brooklyn. See Delamaire and Irving, "Was Fanny Palmer the Powerhouse behind Currier & Ives?" *Art in Print* 8, no. 2 (July/August 2018): 25–31.

26 More information on the lives of these artists can be found in M. B. Cowdrey, *George Henry Durrie, 1820–1863* (Hartford, CT: Wadsworth Atheneum, 1947); Richard B. Grassby, *Ship, Sea & Sky: The Marine Art of James Edward Buttersworth* (New York: South Street Seaport Museum with Rizzoli, 1994); and Warder H. Cadbury, *Arthur Fitzwilliam Taint: Artist in the Adirondacks* (Newark, DE: University of Delaware Press; London and Toronto:

Associated University Presses, 1986).

27 See Twyman, *Lithography, 1800–1850*. For American lithography, see Delamaire and Irving, *Laid Down on Paper*, 34–37.

28 Mary Linwood was a needlework artist who had gained international fame for her full-scale needlework representations of old master paintings made with irregular stitches that evoked brushstrokes. As Linwood's student, Fanny not only had the opportunity to observe a professional artist at work and the successful career of a woman artist, she also had access to the paintings brought to the studio for their adaptation into needlework.

29 For a full discussion of Palmer's status vis-à-vis Currier & Ives, see Delamaire and Irving, "Was Fanny Palmer the Powerhouse behind Currier & Ives?" 25–31.

30 Penny, *Employments of Women*, 69.

31 David Tatham, "The Lithographic Workshop, 1825–1850," in Georgia B. Barnhill, Diana Korzenik, and Caroline F. Sloat, eds., *The Cultivation of Artists in Nineteenth-Century America* (Worcester, MA: American Antiquarian Society, 1977), 46.

32 Charles Hart, *Lithography, Its Theory and Practice, Including a Series of Short Sketches of the Earliest Lithographic Artists, Engravers, and Printers of New York,* Manuscript Division, New York Public Library, 196. I am grateful to Diann Benti for pointing out this important source.

33 Harry T. Peters's book is the source of this story.

34 James Brust, "Notes on the Life of James Merritt Ives, with a Reappraisal of When he Joined Nathaniel Currier," *Imprint* (Autumn 2008): 36–45.

35 Delamaire and Irving, "Was Fanny Palmer the Powerhouse behind Currier & Ives?" 30–31.

36 Penny, *Employments of Women*, 69.

37 In 1851, James Ives married Nathaniel Currier's sister-in-law.

38 See Harriet Endicott Waite's research material concerning Currier & Ives, 1923–1956, Archives of American Art, Smithsonian Institution.

39 Duval is known to have introduced steam presses to his establishment in the late 1840s. See Erika Piola, ed., *Philadelphia on Stone: Commercial Lithography in Philadelphia, 1828–1878* (Harrisburg, PA: Pennsylvania State University Press, 2012). According to the Harriet E. Waite's papers, Currier & Ives did not use steam presses in his business.

40 Calculating the equivalent value of a large folio print in today's market is a difficult task. However, we have comparative values. The cheapest prints were sold between 6 and 10 cents each, while the most expensive ones were priced at 10 to 40 times more than the cheapest price. As a comparison, the average salary for a male laborer in the state of New York in 1850 was 67 cents per day with board, 90 cents without board. See J. D. B. De Bow, *Statistical view of the United States, embracing its territory, population, white, free colored, and slave—moral and social condition, industry, property, and revenue* (Washington, DC: B. Tucker, State Printer, 1854), 164.

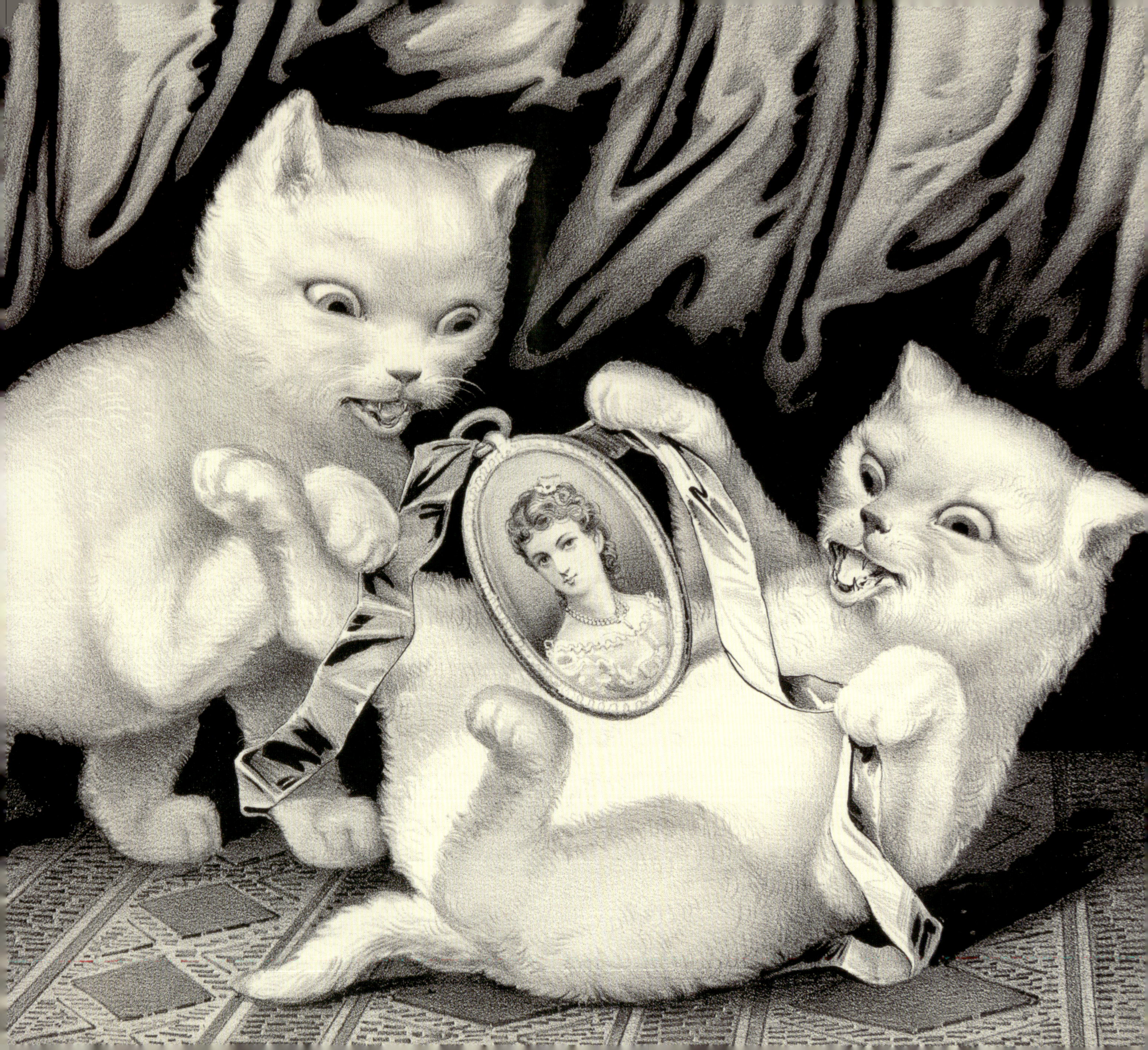

# EXCITING REASSURANCES

## *Popular Art and Contemporary Life in Currier & Ives Prints*

*Michael Clapper*

Currier & Ives seem to portray an American past that we can return to through their striking and often impressive prints. Their images, which are both productions of and documents of an era, take us back to a time of booming cities, idyllic farmsteads, open frontiers, vigorous leisure, and warm sentiment. In this sense, as the title of this exhibition suggests, we are "Revisiting America," returning to a shared national yesteryear. Yet this project also offers the opportunity to critically "revisit" our understanding of America and of these prints, to acknowledge the kind of art they are, the reasons why they were made, and the market conditions which both enabled and constrained their creation, and the cultural purposes that they served for their original audience. As popular art, Currier & Ives prints paradoxically both offered nineteenth-century viewers exciting visions of their dynamic present moment, reassurance that idealized traditional values and ways of life remained intact, and that social change and conflict were manageable. Popular art, of which Currier & Ives prints are the best-known nineteenth-century example, is distinctive in that it necessarily aims at, responds to, and shapes popular taste. From the outset, the makers and marketers of popular art have in mind broad appeal, machine reproduction, and commercial success. The target group of potential customers is more amorphous and uncertain than a known client, yet nonetheless has definite concerns and preferences, conveyed to manufacturers through critical responses and even more powerfully through sales. There is a close relationship between mass appeal, mass reproduction, and mass market. Machine reproduction is the key to a dramatic decrease in the price per copy to the point where many people can afford to buy art. Previous production efficiencies, such as mechanical aids, artistic conventions within genres, and relief and intaglio printmaking techniques, had made it possible to produce art for a market, as for instance seventeenth-century Dutch artists had done, but not yet a mass market. The machinery and assembly-line production methods used by Currier & Ives and other manufacturers of popular art from the mid-nineteenth century onwards made art not just affordable, but cheap, provided that many copies could be sold. The incremental cost of creating another copy, or another ten thousand copies, became relatively small. Yet the initial investment in equipment and skilled labor was large, and so popular art could only be profitable, and thus could only remain viable, by deliberately trying from the outset to create art that many people would like.

The way that Currier & Ives knew what people wanted was through a mass market, and indeed addressing a mass market rather than producing work on commission was one of the main ways in which the firm differed from earlier lithography businesses. Nathaniel Currier had come up in the business in the usual way, as an apprentice, in the pioneering and influential Boston lithography shop of the Pendleton brothers. Though they employed some artists who later went on to notable fine arts careers, such lithography firms were not art publishing houses, but rather commercial printing businesses serving the needs of particular customers by executing "job work," dictated printing done on commission. Currier's business in New York began in a similar way starting in 1834, but in the 1840s, he and a few other New York lithography firms moved into print publishing, making and marketing their own works rather than working as printers for hire. From the time James Ives joined as bookkeeper in 1852 (he became partner in 1857) through the 1870s, Currier & Ives did almost no job printing, focusing instead on prints made on speculation for a sizable but uncertain and heterogeneous market. Identifying and satisfying the tastes of that market was the chief success of their enterprise.[1] The market exerted a powerful influence on Currier & Ives prints and whatever sold well, whether rural homesteads or presidential portraits or burning buildings, would be repeated with variations or expanded into a series. As producers of popular prints, Currier & Ives were more interested in satisfying their customers than with shaping taste or pursuing their own cultural agenda. This does not negate the aesthetic and cultural achievements of the company, but it does help explain the repetition of types within its body of work. Market forces encouraged clusters of similar images, but also the production of different kinds of images, so thinking of a "Currier & Ives print" as a coherent entity flattens the marvelous breadth and diversity of the firm's output. The most complete and authoritative catalogue of Currier & Ives prints lists 7,500 different images, though some of these are minor variations on what is basically the same design. Within this great array, there are certain types of images, such as idealized scenes of country life, that seem to exemplify the sort of prints commonly associated with the company name, but there are many other kinds of images that are rather generic (for instance, the bust-length portraits of notable presidents), unusual (the disasters), or wacky (*My Little White Kitties*, p. 104). There were prints suitable for many different settings, including parlors, dining rooms, bedrooms, offices, hotels, bars, and barbershops. Billing itself as "The Grand Central Depot for Cheap and Popular Pictures," Currier & Ives was more concerned with the variety of offerings than with their coherence.[2]

Size, fineness, and amount of handwork generally corresponded with the price. The prints vary considerably in size, from images approximately eight by twelve inches to those over thirty inches wide. Currier & Ives's "lowest wholesale price" to dealers was six cents per print, plus postage, and this was at some time after 1877. A "New Catalogue of Cheap and Popular Pictures" from the mid-1870s offered 903 subjects on 13½ × 17¾-inch sheets for twenty cents each, colored. In the company's heyday in the late 1850s, their catalogue offered, in the "Cheap Colored Prints" section toward the back, hundreds of small colored prints retail priced at eight cents, postage included. Medium-sized prints cost about twenty-five cents. Large prints went for about a dollar to as high as three seventy-five. Even the most expensive Currier & Ives prints were affordable to the middle class, and the cheapest ones were within the reach of just about anyone with any disposable income. Slightly later makers of popular art in the 1860s and 70s would find that even higher prices were bearable. Louis Prang of Boston sold many of his chromolithographs for five to ten dollars, and John Rogers priced most of his cast plaster sculptures between ten and fifteen dollars.[3]

Lithography helped take the mass production of prints to a new level. In earlier printmaking techniques such as woodcut and engraving, the block or plate's design wore down during the printing process so that at most a few thousand high-quality impressions could be printed. Lithography, invented in 1819 and commercially developed in the next several decades, could produce tens of thousands of copies without significant degradation of the printing matrix. The process entailed starting with a sketch, drawing, or finished painting, drawing that image on the stone, chemically processing the exposed areas, and then printing from the dampened stone, relying on the physical property of oil and water to repel one another. Producing a Currier & Ives print involved several distinct functions, often performed by separate people: artist, lithographer, printing shop, colorist, and publisher. The company's lithographs were printed in oily black ink, with the resulting black-and-white prints pulled from the presses and then on to the colorists, who hand colored with watercolor, and sometimes highlighted with gouache (opaque water-based paint). The dramatic difference in their print prices was due not only to size, but also to the fineness and complexity of the drawing and coloring, which in turn related to means of executing the handwork. The smaller, simpler prints were often rather roughly rendered by anonymous artists, while the larger, more finely wrought pieces were executed by skilled artists and specialist draftspersons. Coloring methods also varied considerably. The large landscapes, farms, and hunting and camping scenes which sold for over two dollars at the front of the catalogue could be had uncolored for a dollar to a dollar fifty at the back of the catalogue, indicating that the coloring accounted for about forty percent of the price. Large, elaborately colored examples, such as *The Four Seasons of Life: Middle Age* (p. 102), include subtle shading of colors to convey the effect of natural light, a refinement not attempted in the coloring of cheaper prints. At the high end, batches of the large prints were sent out with a color model to aspiring artists who worked on their own premises. The less expensive prints were colored in-house by a staff of young women who sat around a table, again with a color model, and each person painted a single color before passing the print to the next colorist. For the cheapest prints, or in times of extremely high demand, additional temporary colorists could be brought in to use stencils to wash in flat areas of color quickly.[4]

The coloring, executed by various hands, was always anonymous, but notations at the bottom margins or in the lower corners of the image field gave credit to the various people involved in making a given print. "Published by Currier & Ives" is clear enough, but "Lith. by Currier & Ives" or a similar phrase meant that this was a production of their lithography firm, not that the proprietors drew the image on the stone, though Currier was trained as a lithographer. Even initials or a name *within* the image field, most commonly in the lower right corner, likely credited the artist who drew the design, not the artisan who copied it onto the stone. In the rare instances in which a Currier & Ives print reproduced a signed painting, the signature might be copied into the print by the lithographer as part of the image. Much more often, the prints were made from drawings, and the draftsperson was frequently credited in the margin with their name and "del." for "delineavit," Latin for "drew it."

The firm distributed their finished prints from their showroom and through local commission vendors, but mail order from their catalogues was crucial for increasing their sales volume. Through most of their existence, Currier & Ives had two main locations, a factory on Spruce Street and a showroom on Nassau Street. At the factory on the upper floors, lithographers, printers, and colorists ground the lithographic stones, drew the designs on them, produced the prints on hand-operated presses, and, on the top floor, colored them. The showroom, on the ground floor, with a wide frontage and large display windows, was geared to attract and serve customers. Clerks also packed and shipped prints from the showroom. Local peddlers stocked their pushcarts in the morning and left a deposit for the prints they selected, returning in the evening to settle their daily accounts. Currier & Ives recognized, however, that "many persons living at a distance from the city have no opportunity of examining our large collection of Pictures," so they compiled a descriptive catalogue (fig. 1). They promised to fill and send orders on the same day they received them, provided the customer sent payment along with the order. The United States Postal Service became more reliable and less expensive in the second half of the nineteenth century, allowing Currier & Ives to ship prints to any post office in the country, whether direct to customers or to local agents. An office in London later served as a hub for European distribution. Thus, though based in New York City, Currier & Ives developed extensive national and international markets for their prints.[5]

Currier & Ives prints are similar to genre painting in that they seem to portray an encyclopedic range of aspects of American life, but in fact they treat a limited array of subjects over and over again. In its portrayal of typical characters (rather than nameable individuals) and situations, genre art avoids deep unhappiness, emotional conflict, and grueling labor. The emotional register tends toward the lighter side—joy, wonder, relish, playfulness, humor, or reverent contemplation; hardly ever mournfulness or despair. The emotions elicited are usually straightforward: the trains and ships are exhilarating, the home life is warm, and the furry animals are cute. Labor does sometimes occur, but it is always portrayed as gratifying and never as arduous. The selectivity and tenor of these scenes of apparently everyday life clues us in that they are idealizations. Rather than

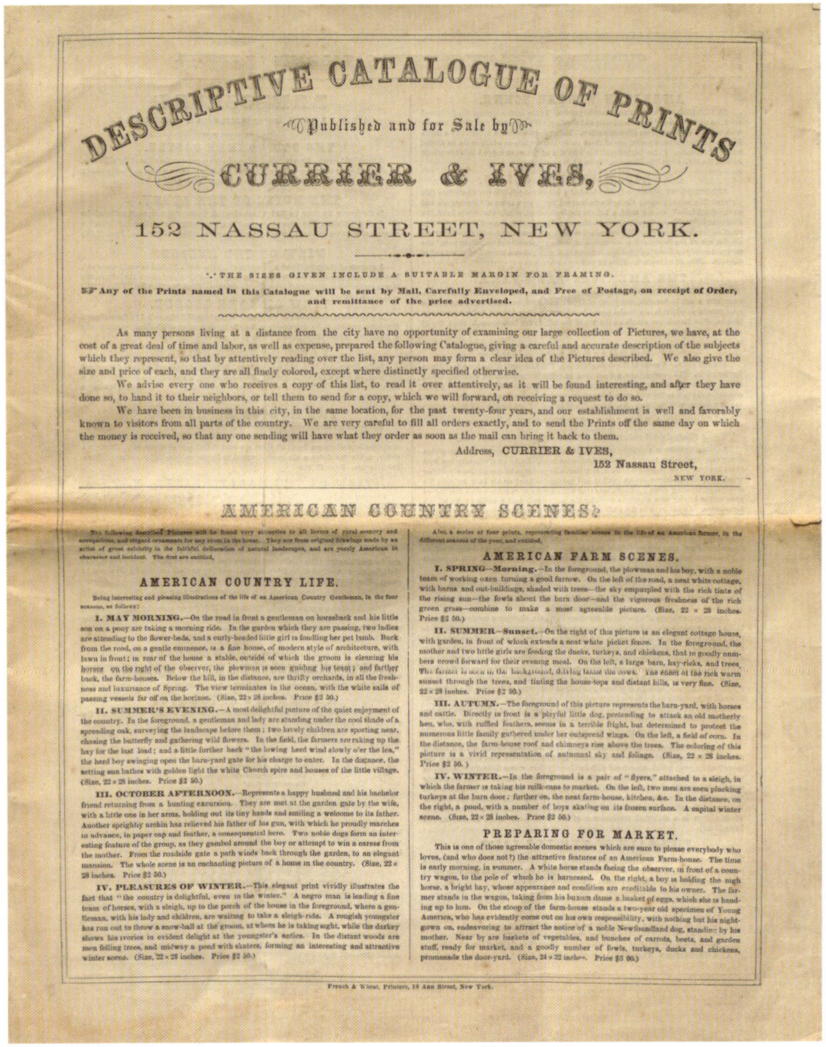

DESCRIPTIVE CATALOGUE OF PRINTS

Published and for Sale by

CURRIER & IVES,

152 NASSAU STREET, NEW YORK.

∴ THE SIZES GIVEN INCLUDE A SUITABLE MARGIN FOR FRAMING.

☞ Any of the Prints named in this Catalogue will be sent by Mail, Carefully Enveloped, and Free of Postage, on receipt of Order, and remittance of the price advertised.

As many persons living at a distance from the city have no opportunity of examining our large collection of Pictures, we have, at the cost of a great deal of time and labor, as well as expense, prepared the following Catalogue, giving a careful and accurate description of the subjects which they represent, so that by attentively reading over the list, any person may form a clear idea of the Pictures described. We also give the size and price of each, and they are all finely colored, except where distinctly specified otherwise.

We advise every one who receives a copy of this list, to read it over attentively, as it will be found interesting, and after they have done so, to hand it to their neighbors, or tell them to send for a copy, which we will forward, on receiving a request to do so.

We have been in business in this city, in the same location, for the past twenty-four years, and our establishment is well and favorably known to visitors from all parts of the country. We are very careful to fill all orders exactly, and to send the Prints off the same day on which the money is received, so that any one sending will have what they order as soon as the mail can bring it back to them.

Address, CURRIER & IVES,
152 Nassau Street,
NEW YORK.

AMERICAN COUNTRY SCENES.

The following described Pictures will be found very attractive to all lovers of rural scenery and occupations, and elegant ornaments for any room in the house. They are from original drawings made by an artist of great celebrity in the faithful delineation of natural landscapes, and are purely American in character and incident. The first are entitled,

AMERICAN COUNTRY LIFE.

Being interesting and pleasing illustrations of the life of an American Country Gentleman, in the four seasons, as follows:

**I. MAY MORNING.**—On the road in front a gentleman on horseback and his little son on a pony are taking a morning ride. In the garden which they are passing, two ladies are attending to the flower-beds, and a curly-headed little girl is fondling her pet lamb. Back from the road, on a gentle eminence, is a fine house, of modern style of architecture, with lawn in front; in rear of the house a stable, outside of which the groom is cleaning his horses on the right of the observer, the plowman is seen guiding his team; and farther back, the farm-houses. Below the hill, in the distance, are thrifty orchards, in all the freshness and luxuriance of Spring. The view terminates in the ocean, with the white sails of passing vessels far off on the horizon. (Size, 22 × 28 inches. Price $2 50.)

**II. SUMMER'S EVENING.**—A most delightful picture of the quiet enjoyment of the country. In the foreground, a gentleman and lady are standing under the cool shade of a spreading oak, surveying the landscape before them; two lovely children are sporting near, chasing the butterfly and gathering wild flowers. In the field, the farmers are raking up the hay for the last load; and a little further back "the lowing herd wind slowly o'er the lea," the herd boy swinging open the barn-yard gate for his charge to enter. In the distance, the setting sun bathes with golden light the white Church spire and houses of the little village. (Size, 22 × 28 inches. Price $2 50.)

**III. OCTOBER AFTERNOON.**—Represents a happy husband and his bachelor friend returning from a hunting excursion. They are met at the garden gate by the wife, with a little one in her arms, holding out its tiny hands and smiling a welcome to its father. Another sprightly urchin has relieved his father of his gun, with which he proudly marches in advance, in paper cap and feather, a consequential hero. Two noble dogs form an interesting feature of the group, as they gambol around the boy or attempt to win a caress from the mother. From the roadside gate a path winds back through the garden, to an elegant mansion. The whole scene is an enchanting picture of a home in the country. (Size, 22 × 28 inches. Price $2 50.)

**IV. PLEASURES OF WINTER.**—This elegant print vividly illustrates the fact that "the country is delightful, even in the winter." A negro man is leading a fine team of horses, with a sleigh, up to the porch of the house in the foreground, where a gentleman, with his lady and children, are waiting to take a sleigh-ride. A roguish youngster has run out to throw a snow-ball at the groom, at whom he is taking sight, while the darkey shows his ivories in evident delight at the youngster's antics. In the distant woods are men felling trees, and midway a pond with skaters, forming an interesting and attractive winter scene. (Size, 22 × 28 inches. Price $2 50.)

Also, a series of four prints, representing familiar scenes in the life of an American farmer, in the different seasons of the year, and entitled,

AMERICAN FARM SCENES.

**I. SPRING—Morning.**—In the foreground, the plowman and his boy, with a noble team of working oxen turning a good furrow. On the left of the road, a neat white cottage, with barns and out-buildings, shaded with trees—the sky empurpled with the rich tints of the rising sun—the fowls about the barn door—and the vigorous freshness of the rich green grass—combine to make a most agreeable picture. (Size, 22 × 28 inches. Price $2 50.)

**II. SUMMER—Sunset.**—On the right of this picture is an elegant cottage house, with garden, in front of which extends a neat white picket fence. In the foreground, the mother and two little girls are feeding the ducks, turkeys, and chickens, that in goodly numbers crowd forward for their evening meal. On the left, a large barn, hay-ricks, and trees. The farmer is seen in the background, driving home the cows. The effect of the rich warm sunset through the trees, and tinting the house-tops and distant hills, is very fine. (Size, 22 × 28 inches. Price $2 50.)

**III. AUTUMN.**—The foreground of this picture represents the barn-yard, with horses and cattle. Directly in front is a playful little dog, pretending to attack an old motherly hen, who, with ruffled feathers, seems in a terrible fright, but determined to protect the numerous little family gathered under her outspread wings. On the left, a field of corn. In the distance, the farm-house roof and chimneys rise above the trees. The coloring of this picture is a vivid representation of autumnal sky and foliage. (Size, 22 × 28 inches. Price $2 50.)

**IV. WINTER.**—In the foreground is a pair of "flyers," attached to a sleigh, in which the farmer is taking his milk-cans to market. On the left, two men are seen plucking turkeys at the barn door; further on, the neat farm-house, kitchen, &c. In the distance, on the right, a pond, with a number of boys skating on its frozen surface. A capital winter scene. (Size, 22 × 28 inches. Price $2 50.)

PREPARING FOR MARKET.

This is one of those agreeable domestic scenes which are sure to please everybody who loves, (and who does not?) the attractive features of an American Farm-house. The time is early morning, in summer. A white horse stands facing the observer, in front of a country wagon, to the pole of which he is harnessed. On the right, a boy is holding the nigh horse, a bright bay, whose appearance and condition are creditable to his owner. The farmer stands in the wagon, taking from his buxom dame a basket of eggs, which she is handing up to him. On the stoop of the farm-house stands a two-year old specimen of Young America, who has evidently come out on his own responsibility, with nothing but his night-gown on, endeavoring to attract the notice of a noble Newfoundland dog, standing by his mother. Near by are baskets of vegetables, and bunches of carrots, beets, and garden stuff, ready for market, and a goodly number of fowls, turkeys, ducks and chickens, promenade the door-yard. (Size, 24 × 32 inches. Price $3 00.)

French & Wheat, Printers, 18 Ann Street, New York.

FIG 1 *Descriptive Catalogue of Prints Published and For Sale By Currier & Ives, 152 Nassau Street, New York.* Museum of the City of New York, Anonymous gift in memory of Harry T. Peters, 1956

thinking of Currier & Ives prints as representing life as it was, we might instead consider the images as representations of what viewers desired but did not have, a kind of antidote, balance, or supplement to their own experiences. The prints were mostly displayed indoors, in urban areas, and seen in the course of everyday life by ordinary people. They depict the opposite: the outdoors, the country, extraordinary events, paradigmatic types, and remarkable individuals. After all, if the prints represented life as it was, what social function would they serve? It is in the gap between actual life and imagined life that artistic representation does important cultural work. Merging the actual and imaginary, it makes them both seem possible to some extent, despite the contradictions between them. One cannot, for instance, live at once in the woods and in the city, nor work hard while also enjoying recreation. How about, then, choosing to do one while hanging a picture of the other? The prints were not so much an encouragement or spur to change one's daily life as they were a way to rationalize not doing so.

In this manner, Currier & Ives prints were meant to be both exciting and reassuring. The prints allowed viewers to embark on fictional adventures, large and small: train or boat voyages, retreats to country homesteads, camping or hunting trips, encounters with famous leaders, delectation in fashionable dress, an afternoon at the racetrack or other sporting venue, or being a vicarious witness to a fiery disaster. While these fantasies speak to aspects of experience that were desired but missing in everyday life, the alternative or supplementary existence imagined through the prints reinforces rather than challenges their audiences' values. The prints envision the people of the United States as daring, undaunted, sentimental, patriotic, competitive, fun loving, and responsible. Entrenched race and gender roles define acceptable behaviors. Embracing new technologies coexists harmoniously with nostalgia for older ways of life, as the prints help to assimilate the innovations of the present with enduring standards. Even a massive conflagration is more of an invitation to mourn and rebuild than a call to systemic change.

It is difficult to neatly survey or summarize the subjects of the vast range of Currier & Ives prints. The types considered below are trains, disasters, and hunting and camping scenes. Other authors might well group the prints differently or choose different types on which to focus (see, for instance, Baird Jarman's essay later in this catalogue for a thorough consideration of Currier & Ives's political prints). What we can do is get started looking carefully at this fascinating body of work and trying to make sense of it in terms of the pictorial conventions of certain types of images, some of the implied preoccupations and world views of Currier & Ives's nineteenth-century audience, and critical consideration of the cultural purposes that these prints served in their time and for more recent viewers.[6]

Currier & Ives train prints tell a story of modern technological marvels powering through the landscape and opening new frontiers. After the Civil War, trains and steamboats predominated over the images of sailing ships and whaling that the firm had published in the antebellum period. Like analogous images of steamboats, the train images show an interest not just in the latest technology, but in the travel and trade that these conveyances made possible. Never merely mechanical drawings, these works portrayed the ventures and adventures enabled by these new modes of transportation. These are mostly celebratory images, in which innovation and determination span vast distances, open new frontiers, and exemplify human prowess. They never show trains as static objects in isolation, but rather always on the move. Variations in pictorial structure deliberately connote particular understandings of the character and achievement of each train and its journey.

One basic type is shown in *American Express Train* (fig. 2; see also p. 73), in which the train slices across from left to right and bends out toward the viewer's space, trailing a nearly horizontal

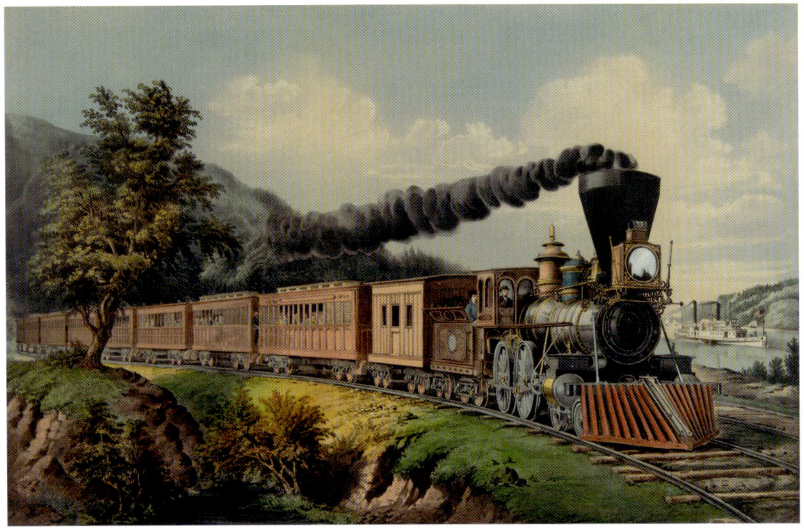

FIG 2 *American Express Train*, 1864. Joslyn Art Museum, Gift of Conagra Brands, 2016.20.416

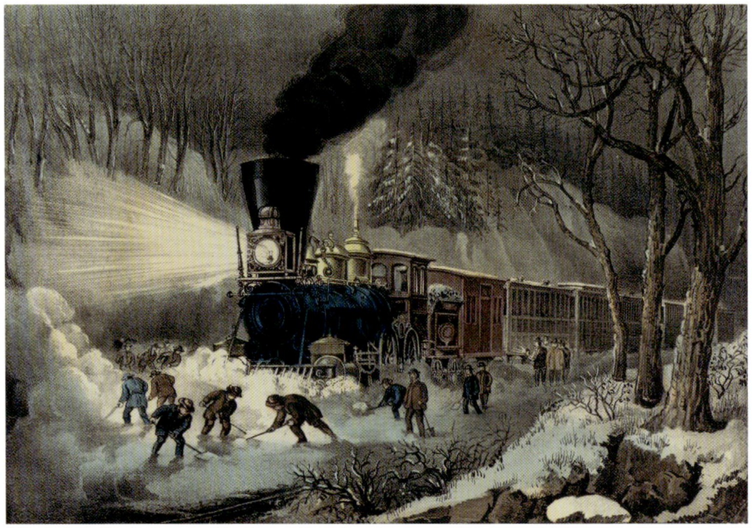

FIG 3 *American Railroad Scene: Snow Bound*, 1871. Joslyn Art Museum, Gift of Conagra Brands, 2016.20.80

plume of smoke, emphasizing the train's speed and momentum. This train has the customary arrangement of cars also seen in most other train prints: a locomotive, a tender, a baggage car, and passenger cars. It traverses the land, as the paddle-wheel riverboat in the middle distance navigates the water. Highlighting with white gouache makes the glassy headlight at the front of the train stand out brightly, even against the white clouds behind it. These clouds are a languid counterpoint to the purposeful puffs of black pouring out from the smokestack. That the direction of the train's movement corresponds to our conventional direction of reading emphasizes its smooth trajectory. It also glides forcefully out from the distance on the clean lines of the rails, the regular diminution of the cars toward the rear giving a powerful sense of deep space, yet the angle of its approach not so direct as to alarm viewers. The broad, alternating sections of green and yellow in the vegetation along the track are not naturalistic renderings of lighting or color, but they too emphasize dramatic spatial recession, as well as forming an engaging pattern of bold hues. The lone tree on a rise at the left serves as a *repoussoir*—its large scale and overlapping branches push the rear of the train and the hill behind it further back into space. Although the engineer gazes ahead along the track and many passengers are visible in the windows of the cars in the middle of the train, the train itself is the main character in this drama, forging effortlessly through the landscape. Currier & Ives repeated this composition in several images, for instance the smaller *Express Train* (p. 76), in which a rocky cliff at the right presses the train out toward the viewer and a bridge in the middle ground articulates the space through which the train passes.

When the point is to stress the difficulties that trains were able to overcome, the train is usually shown moving from right to left. This is the case, for instance, in *American Railroad Scene: Snow Bound* (fig. 3; see also p. 75). Here, heavy snow has slowed the train's progress, despite its pilot (the pointed, slatted prow attached to the front of the engine) acting as a plow, churning and deflecting the snow before it. Men with shovels work

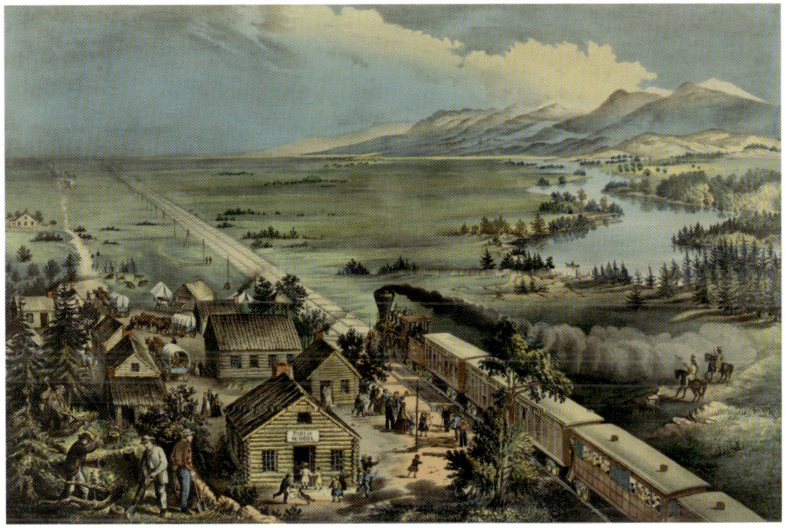

FIG 4 *Across the Continent: Westward the Course of Empire Takes Its Way*, 1868. Joslyn Art Museum, Gift of Conagra Brands, 2016.20.474

strenuously to clear its path. The headlight pierces the night's gloom ahead, but the almost vertical wafting of the smoke from the chimney shows that the train is moving forward only very slowly as it comes slightly uphill. Though beset by snow and darkness and moving against our conventional direction of reading, the train, with people's help, presses on. In *The Route to California* (p. 74), the horizontal stream of smoke indicates that the train is moving at speed, while the boulders in the river show the impracticality of water travel here, and the mountains in the background and the rocky hillside at the right show that this train too faces formidable challenges, once again subtly emphasized by its right-to-left path. Even the distant train in *Pensylvania* [sic] *Rail Road Scenery* (p. 77) moves toward the left, a counterpoint to the horse carriage directly below it moving in the opposite direction, as a way to highlight its impressive achievement in swiftly traversing this rugged terrain.

More unusual are images in which the train moves from the foreground out to the distant horizon, an arrangement that stresses the function of trains in opening new frontiers, as in *Across the Continent: Westward the Course of Empire Takes Its Way* (fig. 4; see also p. 128). In this case, the frontier is the real subject, and the train the vehicle and emblem. The train separates the burgeoning new settlement on the left from the isolated pair of Native Americans on horseback on the right, stymied by the train and its trail of smoke. The train moves toward the left and off into the distance, along a dead straight track. Left and right in this instance represent conventions of mapping at least as much as conventions of reading. The rolling hills, meandering water, and trees of an eastern landscape on the right peter out and give way to the flat, open grasslands of the central plains on the left. Conestoga wagons move out from the new town along a slightly irregular dirt road parallel to the westward track of the train. The white swath of clouds at the top mimics the shape of the black train smoke below it, suggesting that the train is an analogue of natural forces, and that it is indeed the Manifest Destiny of European-American pioneers to move westward, eventually settling the continent from coast to coast. The straight, unimpeded course of the train out to the distant horizon is a visual symbol of the inevitability of this process.[7]

Oddly enough, some of Nathaniel Currier's earliest and most influential successes were images of disasters, notably *Ruins of the Merchant's Exchange N.Y.* (p. 90) and *Awful Conflagration of the Steam Boat Lexington* (see p. 18, fig. 3), which spawned related images for decades. That Currier himself was a volunteer fireman may account for his firm's ongoing fascination with images of fires (and that Ives kept trotting horses might help explain a similar imbalance of horse racing images), but the prints must have connected with an audience as well.[8] Why would people favor images of fires and explosions? Part of the answer is that such subjects make for terrific pictures. The images are dramatic, engaging, and beautiful even if tragic. Flames and blasts afford pictorial opportunities to juxtapose darkened environments with brilliant light and bold red and orange. Flowing flames and billowing smoke contrast with the orderly structure of vessels and buildings. Linear perspective and differences in scale between figures and the built environment create a sense of vast spaces teeming with people. There is also a satisfying combination of thrill and safety and exhortation. People are always present in the scene, as responders and as observers. Viewers, just outside the frame, are close enough to gawk and marvel, but distant enough to be out of danger. Looking on, there is no need to offer help, knowing that the tragedy portrayed has already occurred, the response galvanized, the wreckage cleared, the cost counted. As witnesses we were spared, and now gaze on the image as a stirring entertainment and perhaps a moment of reflection. It is not so much a matter of taking pleasure in the misfortunes of others, but rather marveling at the destructive power of fire from a comfortable remove. And yet, might we too be subject to the vicissitudes of fortune and the always present dangers of catastrophe? We are safe for now, but there is a moralizing message, urging us to be grateful, circumspect, and not smug.

The most typical elements of the disaster prints are city buildings in flames surrounded by spectators and firefighters, as seen in *Burning of the City Hall New York* (fig. 5; see also p. 89), where the onlookers serve as stand-ins and models for the viewer, and give some sense of how the prints were viewed. Massive fires were a spectacle, which citizens came out to witness from a safe distance, and this print abounds with hundreds of such figures. The firefighters can be distinguished by their crested helmets, as distinct from the top hats and less formal broad-brimmed hats worn by most of the men in the foreground. The colorist of this copy has picked out the firemen with orangey shirts (the red shirts shown in the two *The American Fireman* (pp. 86 and 87) prints are probably more accurate), though apparently confusing one top-hatted figure in the center right foreground for a fireman because he, like the helmeted fireman to his right, is running forward. In contrast with the fire crew pulling a hose carriage in the center, the well-dressed figures in the very foreground stand calmly and steadily, their clothing and demeanor evincing remarkable composure given the turbulent events unfolding before them. Most face the burning city hall and the crowd surrounding it, though a few, their eyes indicated only as dots, look out toward the viewer. Even the many figures at the balustraded outermost corners of the roof appear to be spectators rather than responders, and presumably out of any immediate danger. The viewer's eye level is at about twice the height of a standing figure, thus allowing us to survey the scene more comprehensively, but also to meld in with the less densely packed crowd at the periphery. This degree of proximity and slightly elevated point of view are typical of the disaster prints. Looking at the prints was an extension of the common practice of flocking to the scene of an urban disaster, though we have a more expansive view being higher up.

Such disaster prints were well able to dramatize the event, but had less potential than written accounts for narrating the progression of circumstances or adjudicating the social failures which resulted in the fires. In the case of the Lexington print, several versions appeared as an extra of the *New York Sun* newspaper, and included extensive columns of text below the image, although this was unusual. Most Currier & Ives prints limited textual explanations to fairly terse captions. In *Burning of the City Hall*, we learn that the supposed cause of the disaster was fireworks set off in celebration of the laying of the Atlantic telegraph cable. Newspaper accounts in the next several days detailed the timeline: the initial discovery of an

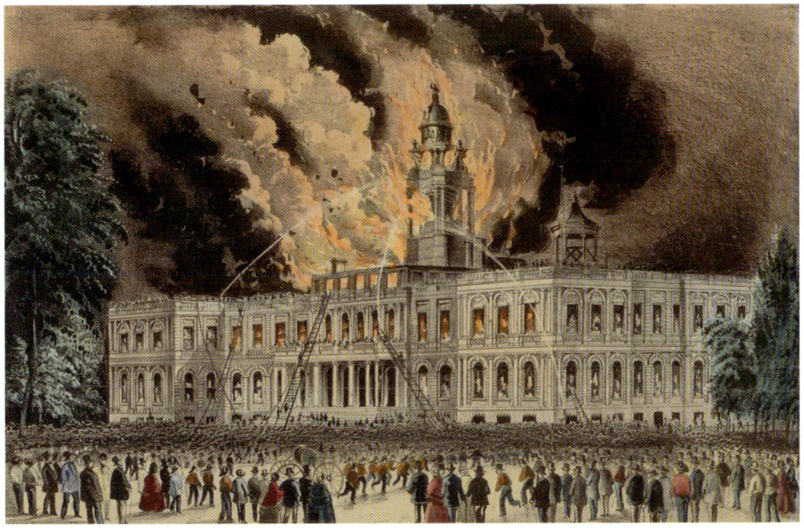

FIG 5 *Burning of the City Hall New York*, 1858. Joslyn Art Museum, Gift of Conagra Brands, 2016.20.196

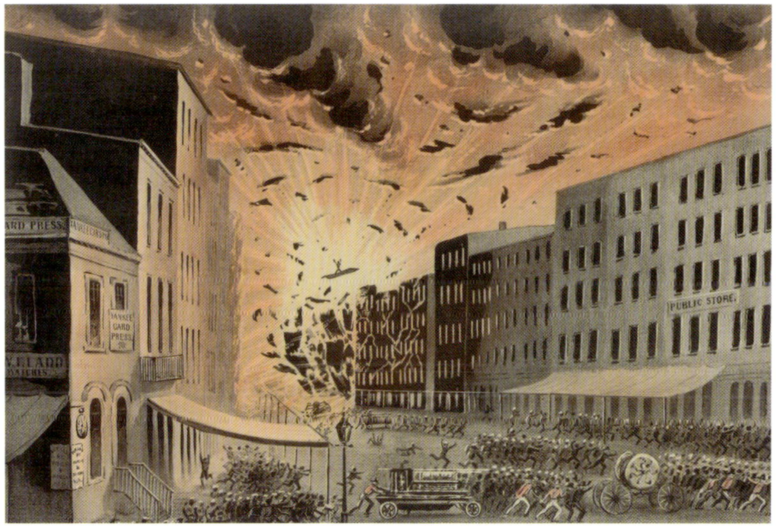


FIG 6 *View of the Terrific Explosion at the Great Fire in New York*, 1845. Joslyn Art Museum, Gift of Conagra Brands, 2016.20.112

outbreak of fire from boxes containing fireworks at the base of the cupola, the fire being extinguished several times and then breaking out again after midnight, and then, finally, flames consuming the entire cupola and ravaging the top floor of the building, but leaving the city records stored on the lower floors mostly unscathed. The print depicts the moment of maximum drama, with the cupola engulfed and the allegorical figure of Justice atop it silhouetted, the floor below also ablaze, which actually happened later, after the tower had already fallen. The large crowds were a fiction, given that the events shown happened in the early hours of the morning, and the heat was so intense as to drive the bell ringer from his post at the bell tower at the foremost corner of the roof. Newspaper accounts included depositions from those on the scene, and the wrangling of aldermen about who was to blame and how to investigate. For viewers of the print, the unfolding story and details of personal interactions were replaced by a lasting moment of memorable spectacle.[9]

In some ways, the character and the moralizing implications of the disaster prints can be understood most clearly in the simplest examples, for instance *View of the Terrific Explosion at the Great Fire in New York* (fig. 6; see also p. 88), in which we observe the moment of devastation from a safe distance, yet sense its force and empathize with the headlong response of the crowd. The explosion in the middle distance rips apart the streetscape of commercial buildings, shattering the orderly facade into jaggedly cracked rubble. The caption gives a tally of the damage: "Engine No. 22 destroyed, and several lives lost. 17 stores blown up." The wrecked engine is swept up and tipped by the force of the blast at the far end of the street. Nearer to the viewer, fire crews wheel several more pieces of equipment toward the blaze, but most of the throng flees in panic. In the middle of the street, one figure has been thrown onto their back, while another crawls away on hands and knees. The generic "public store" at the right and the printing shop and watch store at the left are mercifully beyond the sphere of destruction, but the pocket watch sign on the corner of the building suggests the possibility that disaster can strike in a moment. Silhouetted at the center of the radiating beams of the fireball, drawing our eye, a lone figure casts up its hands and rides a slab of debris like a surfboard more than five stories above the street. Less an individual victim than an emblem of the danger, this person is at once transfigured and destroyed. The viewer, bathed like the buildings on the left in a hellish orange-red light, can only be glad to have escaped by luck and distance and the tenuous protective cordon of the brave firemen. The warning is not so much about urban centers and business districts as it is, more broadly, about the hazards to materialism and the vagaries of fate. The disaster prints give evidence not just of a gawking enjoyment of the misfortunes of others, but of a concern that rapid growth might bring with it spectacular reversals, as economic boom and bust cycles increasingly did.

The disaster prints offer a dramatic contrast to the idyllic rural scenes more commonly associated with Currier & Ives. City buildings are shown ablaze or burned down, but a country homestead is never threatened. The burning of a single home would be a less newsworthy event, but there is more to it than that. Currier & Ives prints helped to construct ways of thinking about urban and rural environments. Cities were conceived as places of heady but dangerous aspiration, while rural areas were thought of as places of traditional values and established ways of life. Paradigmatic images such as *Winter Moonlight* and *Winter in the Country: A Cold Morning* (pp. 96 and 97) portray a rustic, humanized world of taverns, barns, and cottages. Anonymous figures move calmly but purposefully. Each has their own untrammeled psychological domain, yet also companionship, whether a faithful dog following behind, a farm animal waiting to be tended, or an acquaintance or family member with whom to chat before moving on. Sometimes the homesteads were more decisively contemporary, as in *American Country Life: May Morning* (p. 101), which features a new house in the Italianate style that had recently become popular in the United States and figures in fashionable attire. Nonetheless, there is a consistent fantasy of being able to live in touch with nature and the seasons while still maintaining social connections. In addition to human and/or animal companions close by, pathways or roads in the foreground and middle ground, and often ships in the distance, link the people depicted to larger networks. In cities, Currier & Ives prints imply, such connections could be taken for granted; the question was whether the frenetic density of human activity and separation from nature would result in a thrilling but terribly destructive cataclysm. Prints of country homesteads could inoculate viewers, psychologically if not physically, against such dangers.

Hunting and camping prints were a way to inject a dose of vigorous masculinity into viewers' lives. This may have been in deliberate contrast to the generally feminized environment of a middle-class home, or to fortify an already masculine environment such as a professional office. The sense that urbanization, white-collar work, and comfortable domesticity threatened to render men effete was a widespread concern in the late nineteenth century. Prints of manly exertion and leisure acted as a counterbalance. The basic fantasy of the hunting prints combined nature, sport, and companionship, as in *Snipe Shooting* (fig. 7; see also p. 110). The hunter is rarely shown alone, but usually with another hunter and several hunting dogs. By the time these prints were made, hunting was no longer a necessity for obtaining food. What was instead in short supply for urban gentlemen was strenuous physical activity, practice of masculine skills and know-how, and opportunities to commune with nature. The series of hunting scenes that

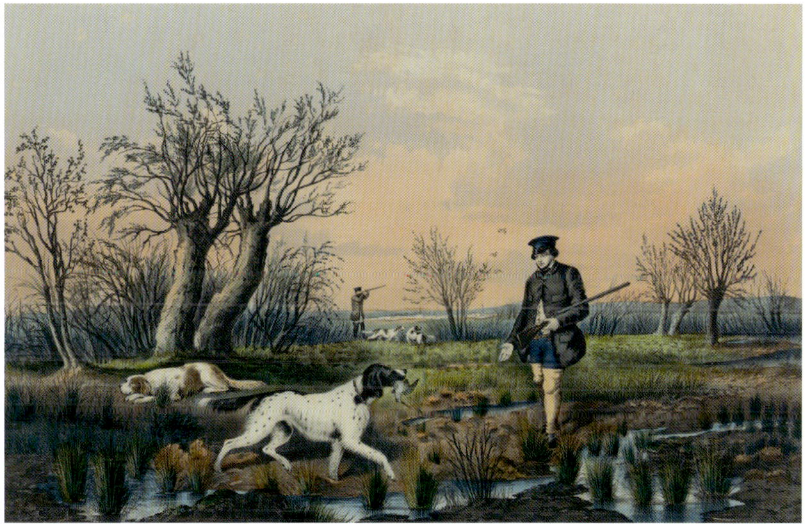

FIG 7 *Snipe Shooting*, 1852. Joslyn Art Museum, Gift of Conagra Brands, 2016.20.338

in-house Currier & Ives artist Frances Palmer made in 1852, including *Snipe Shooting*, are particularly convincing and engaging because she both drew the scenes on site and did the final drawings on the lithographic stones—"from nature and on stone by F. F. Palmer," as noted at the bottom left of the image. Unlike Arthur Tait, the other main artist who created hunting scenes for Currier & Ives, Palmer herself was not a hunter, but her husband was, and she featured him and his dogs in these prints. The combination of personal knowledge of the activity portrayed and carefully observed landscape details, such as the idiosyncratic forms of the trees or the waves softly crashing on the beach in the middle distance, gave these prints a special sense of authenticity. Viewers also could appreciate the quiet drama of the two main phases of shooting, the hunter in the distance taking aim at the birds in flight as his dogs prepare to retrieve, and the open palm of the hunter in the foreground awaiting the downed bird in his dog's mouth. Palmer also often executed the color models for large prints like this one, which likely accounts for the evocative soft pink light in *Snipe Shooting*.[10]

Camping scenes are a variant of the hunting and fishing scenes, with dogs, guns, and game still prominently featured, but with a greater sense of camaraderie and relaxation. The men cook over a campfire some of what they have brought, caught, or killed, and sit and smoke and drink. The image of the camp, while out in nature, as the home base for rustic shelter and sustenance, is a daydream of a simpler, less stressful, more basic lifestyle. The presence of like-minded companions is crucial. In *Camping Out: Some of the Right Sort* (p. 114), being with peers in the same contented mindset ("the right sort") is as important as being "out" in nature and beyond the concerns and constraints of civilization. The communing that occurs here is at least as much between people as it is between one person and the natural world. The men sit or stand close to one another, and those on the periphery move toward the center. Each individual attends to his own activity, but all are clearly aware of those around them, linked by nearness, direction of posture or movement, and gaze. As viewers, we join the outermost figures and make our way visually toward the central group of three men.

As befits their generally urban, relatively well off, and cultured audience, camping in Currier & Ives prints is the recreation of gentlemen. The central standing figure in *Camping in the Woods: A Good Time Coming* (p. 115) wears a bow tie, patterned vest, and a jacket of studied refined rusticity, and sports a carefully trimmed beard and moustache and artfully tousled hair. The campers have brought along pots, pans, cups, knives, plates, and boxes, baskets, and jugs of provisions, including bread, coffee, and even a case of imported port (in the lower left) from the storied Osborne company, of which the standing figure pours himself a cup. This is an enjoyable diversion ("a good time"), a long anticipated and too slow to arrive respite ("a good time coming"). The pictorial structure of these two camping images is remarkably similar, and helps to create a sense of communal retreat. Dense, dark woods in the middle ground close off most of each scene. The only view into the distance is at the far left, where the surface of a placid body of water leads smoothly to faraway hills and trees. The water is a point of entry to this enclosed space, not an exit, as is made explicit in *Camping in the Woods* by the presence of two canoes in which the campers have arrived. Imagine, given our convention of reading from left to right, the much different effect if these open vistas were on the right side, where our attention would drift past the edge. Instead, the right-hand boundaries are barricaded by trees, a lean-to or cabin, and figures facing left. Diagonals bracing the lower right and left corners help to define a circular area in the foreground occupied by a central group of figures. Viewers, positioned at the edge of these open yet isolated spaces, easily move a short distance over minimal obstacles to take part. Like the men depicted, a male-identified viewer need not engage intensely with any one fellow camper to enjoy the pleasant combination of refuge in nature and casual sociability.

If the appeal of Currier & Ives prints is grounded in technological and social developments particular to the middle of the nineteenth century, why do they still interest us today? One answer is that the prints may seem like a uniquely American form of art, not too beholden to European precedents and embodying, through the wide range of subjects on offer, deeply held values of democratic participation and a trust in markets and the collective perspicacity of the citizenry. There is also surely an element of nostalgia, of yearning for a simpler time in the past, but we should recognize that nineteenth-century viewers felt similar psychological needs. The middle of the nineteenth century was, like our own present moment, complex and conflicted. Yet in the images, there is mostly pure adventure, innovation, and emotion. This dramatization and simplification of actual social conditions and experiences appealed to the original audiences for these prints, and appeals to us too, now with an added layer of wistfulness. Perhaps because of our distance in time we more readily interpret as transparent depictions of reality images that were—in their own day—idealizations. We do not have nineteenth-century life histories and everyday experience against which to measure what we see in this art.

## NOTES

1 Harry T. Peters, *Currier & Ives: Printmakers to the American People* (Garden City, NY: Doubleday, Doran & Co., 1942), 5–7; Bernard F. Reilly, Jr., *Currier & Ives: A Catalogue Raisonné* (Detroit, MI: Gale Research, 1984), xxi–xxiii. Peters, a wealthy New York City-based executive of and heir to his father's coal company, Williams and Peters, and a notable collector of Currier & Ives prints, was largely responsible for establishing the scholarly and cultural standing of Currier & Ives prints and a wistful, romantic interpretation of them as reflecting nineteenth-century life. His nostalgia for an idealized earlier, supposedly simpler, United States is typical of his historical moment, in which many, from industrial magnates to ordinary homeowners, directed considerable cultural energy toward colonial revivals. His work, especially his first book, cited above and initially published in 1929, remains a foundational source upon which subsequent scholars have relied. His papers at the Museum of the City of New York (MCNY) include drafts

and research notes for his scholarly projects.

2 Reilly's two-volume *Catalogue Raisonné* is the definitive reference work. The company's tag line is from one of their letterheads, quoted in Peters, *Currier & Ives: Printmakers to the American People*, 16. Reilly, *A Catalogue Raisonné*, xl, reproduces a letter on this letterhead. Another, substantively quite similar letter on the same letterhead in the same hand is in the Harry T. Peters papers, MCNY.

3 The six cents wholesale price is that stated by Currier & Ives in business letters replying to inquiries, basically a handwritten form letter, including the two examples cited above. The "New Catalogue" is reproduced in Reilly, xli. The date for it is based on the street addresses given. The rest of the pricing information cited here is drawn from a *Descriptive Catalogue of Prints Published and for Sale by Currier & Ives, 152 Nassau Street, New York* in the Harry T. Peters papers, MCNY. Internal evidence, including the dates of the prints offered for sale and the statement in the introduction that the firm has been in business for twenty-four years, dates the "Catalogue" to c. 1858. Small prints were on 13½ × 18-inch sheets, medium prints on 16 × 20-inch sheets, large prints about 22 × 28 inches, and the very largest prints about 24 × 32 inches. These sizes included a broad margin for framing, about two inches on each side. Good introductions to chromolithographs and Rogers Groups are Peter Marzio, *The Democratic Art: Pictures for a 19th-Century America* (Boston, MA: David R. Godine, 1979), and David H. Wallace, *John Rogers: The People's Sculptor* (Middletown, CT: Wesleyan University Press, 1967).

4 See *Descriptive Catalogue* (c. 1858), 1–2, 15, to compare colored and uncolored offerings. On the various work arrangements for colorists, see Peters, *Printmakers to the American People*, 14–15.

5 Reilly, xvi, lists Currier & Ives business addresses at various times. On Currier & Ives production and distribution channels, see Peters, *Printmakers to the American People*, 10–12, 14. The quote is from the *Descriptive Catalogue*, 1.

6 My approach, though necessarily more selective, is similar to that of a number of books on Currier & Ives, which, following the model of the final chapter on "The Prints" in *Printmakers to the American People*, attempt to organize and survey the firm's output by type of subject matter. For example, Russel Crouse, *Mr. Currier and Mr. Ives: A Note on Their Lives and Times* (Garden City, NY: Garden City Publishing, 1936), offers witty, historical anecdotes and glosses on various industries, inventions, and cultural practices in eighteen chapters, the first biographical and the rest each about a subject matter category. John Lowell Pratt, ed., *Currier & Ives: Chronicles of America* (Maplewood, NJ: Hammond Inc., 1968), breaks down fifteen kinds of subjects and divides several of those into subtypes. The most lavish and enormous compendium is Walton Rawls, *The Great Book of Currier & Ives' America* (New York: Abbeville Press, 1979), which does well in combining historical developments and cultural concerns with thematic groupings of the firm's output. None of these books (and this is typical) discuss the particulars of specific images much, nor do they include source citations. More recently, Bryan F. Le Beau's *Currier & Ives: America Imagined* (Washington, DC: Smithsonian Institution Press, 2001) offers a more in-depth, scholarly, critical interpretation, with extensive footnotes, while still organizing his consideration by categories of subject.

7 See Le Beau, 121–122, for his take on *Across the Continent*.

8 For a thoughtful analysis of Currier's early disaster prints and their cultural context, see Conoa Shepley, "By Which Melancholy Occurrence: The Disaster Prints of Nathaniel Currier, 1835–1840," *Panorama* 1.2 (Fall 2015).

9 The *New York Times* published three articles on the city hall fire, August 18, 1858, 5, and August 19, 1858, 4, 8.

10 On Palmer's involvement with Currier & Ives hunting scenes, see Rawls, 330. A recent, comprehensive consideration of Palmer is Charlotte Rubinstein, *Fanny Palmer: The Life and Works of a Currier & Ives Artist*, ed. Diann Benti (Syracuse, NY: Syracuse University Press, 2018).

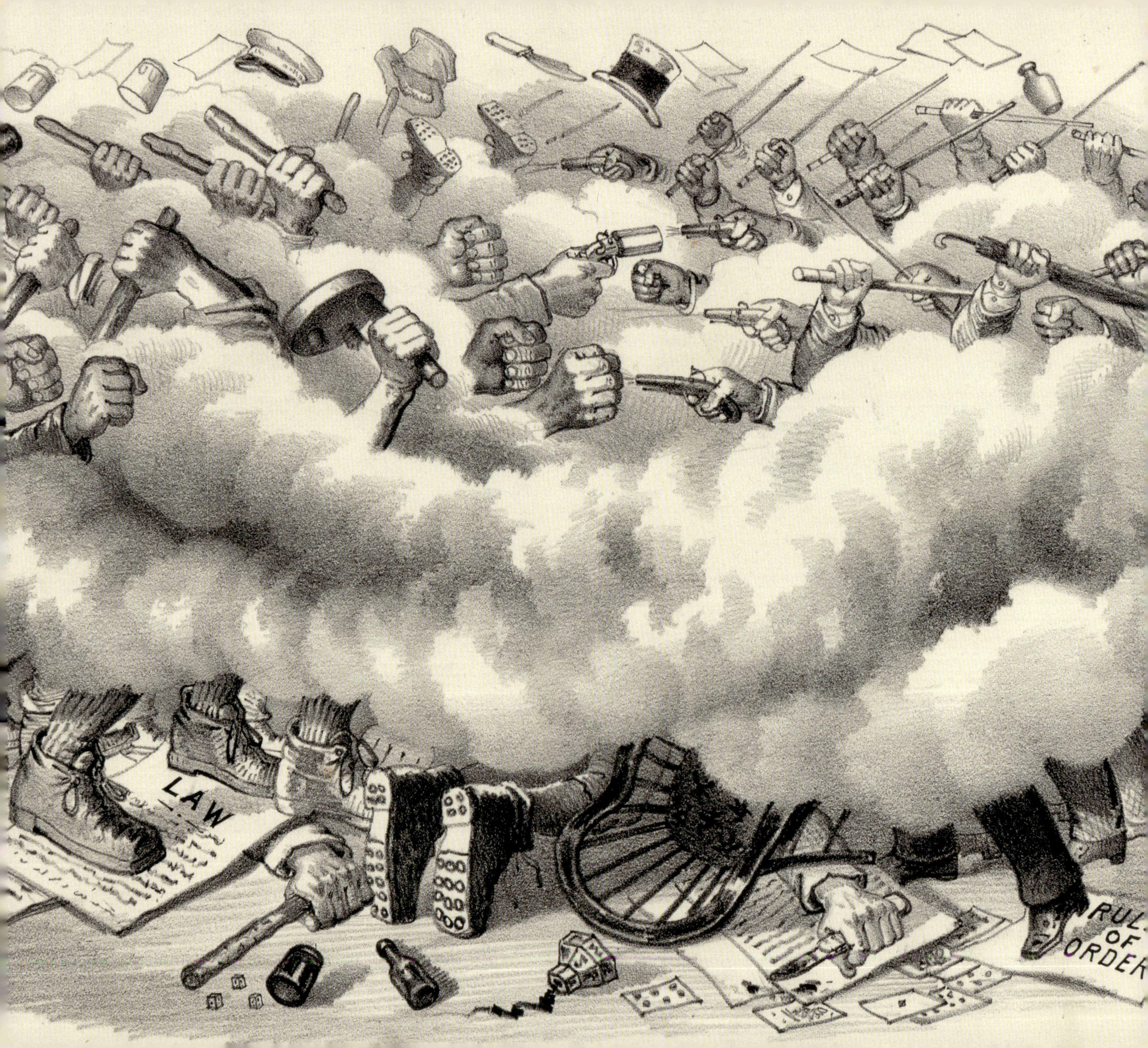
LAW
RUL
OF
ORDER

# THE POLITICAL BROADSIDES OF CURRIER & IVES

## *A Reconsideration*

*Baird Jarman*

From the end of the Mexican War through the early Reconstruction Era, Nathaniel Currier's lithography firm published substantially more political caricature than any other printer in North America.[1] Yet Currier's partisan satire has generally been neglected by chroniclers of his company, and denigrated by historians of political caricature. Despite appearing amid the vital political circumstances of the Civil War, and its onset and aftermath, the firm's political broadsides are often dismissed as leaden and lackluster. They are routinely judged inferior to contemporaneous European caricature and the subsequent "golden age" of editorial cartooning that emerged in mass-circulation periodicals in the United States during the 1870s. Such critical accounts conventionally assume that a wide gulf separates the tradition of political broadsides—loose, individual prints released occasionally by publishers—from the journalistic practice of regularly published editorial cartoons. But a richer history of political caricature emerges from setting aside such compartmentalization by manner of distribution. Viewed in a broader context, the political caricatures of Currier & Ives appear as a crucial early phase of mass-market satirical imagery rather than solely the closing chapter of an outmoded broadside tradition.

### Caricatures for Campaign Seasons

Despite dominating the market for political caricature between the presidential elections of 1848 and 1868, political broadsides never rested comfortably within Currier's larger strategy of supplying idealized imagery for mass audiences. The vitriol common to political satire diverged markedly from the sentimentality permeating much of his firm's iconic imagery. Of course, it is a mistake to oversimplify the company's offerings solely to its most famous nostalgia-laden scenes. It published a vast array of different print types: disaster scenes of contemporary calamities, fashion plates, still lifes, social satires, and likenesses of famous racehorses, locomotives, and clipper ships. Yet, more than any other genre, political caricature presented a risky category of imagery for Currier's firm, threatening to embroil it within rancorous partisan disputes and personal animosities.

Likely concerned about angering potential customers, or even about libel lawsuits, Currier kept both his name and primary business address off his political caricatures for a decade. He initially employed the pseudonym Peter Smith to register copyrights for his caricatures.[2] Several years later he began omitting all names, providing only the simple inscription: "For sale at

No. 2 Spruce St., N.Y." This diverged from his standard credit line at the time: "N. Currier, 152 Nassau St." By using an outdated address for his large corner lot, and by simply listing the prints for sale rather than claiming credit for their creation, Currier continued to obscure his identity as publisher. He only began routinely crediting his firm on political broadsides after forming his business partnership with James Merritt Ives in 1857.[3]

Political satire constituted only a fraction of Currier & Ives's output during its seven decades in business. Their prevalence in the market reflects an unrivaled scale of operations and robust distribution network rather than commitment to frequent partisan commentary. The firm released over eight thousand different print designs, but perhaps only about eighty of these—around 1 percent of the total—offered satirical partisan imagery.[4] Yet some of these broadsides were probably among the most widely distributed prints produced by the firm.

Reliable circulation figures for midcentury political caricatures remain stubbornly elusive. Only with the rise of political cartooning for illustrated newspapers and magazines in the 1870s, and the concomitant emergence of periodical directories with estimated circulation figures for the benefit of advertisers, does quantified data appear.[5] Prior to this, during the broadside era, only anecdotal information is available. But according to Joseph B. Bishop, who interviewed James Merritt Ives, at least two of the firm's satires from 1860, *The Impending Crisis* and *The Irrepressible Conflict* (p. 175), both mocking William Seward for failing to secure the Republican Party nomination, "had a very large sale, exceeding 50,000 copies each."[6] Such vast circulation figures probably extended immensely beyond that of even their most prolific forerunners in the field of political caricature.

Whereas most earlier caricature publishers consistently endorsed one political party, and typically the Whigs over the Democrats, Currier routinely produced multiple caricatures to appeal to rival constituencies simultaneously.[7] Further, though many of his predecessors produced political commentaries year after year, Currier rarely released political broadsides except during the height of presidential campaigns. In these narrow windows of a few months every fourth year, from 1848 through 1872, his firm often circulated ten or more political caricatures.[8] During the fateful election of 1860, for instance, when the company released about one-fifth of its known political broadsides, caricature temporarily became a major priority, surely constituting a large percentage of its sales.

Caricature was not the only genre Currier marketed cyclically during presidential election seasons. He also routinely produced campaign posters, termed "Grand National Banners." These popular banners generally presented oval portraits of presidential and vice-presidential running mates amid allegorical scenes of national prosperity, with party slogans emblazoned below. Currier entered this market during the presidential election of 1844, four years before he began publishing political broadsides. From that year until 1880, the firm produced campaign posters for every party with a sufficient following to hold a national nominating convention, including such third parties as the Free-Soilers, the Know Nothings, the Constitutional Unionists, and the Liberal Republicans. Similarly, Currier produced comical broadsides both extolling and mocking the candidates for these minor parties as well.

The firm also published individual portraits of presidential candidates during these campaign seasons, often in multiple versions. For instance, in 1860 Currier & Ives published at least eight different portrait variants of Abraham Lincoln (pp. 158 and 159).[9] The firm also prepared, or reissued, portraits of the winning candidate after each election. Currier typically arranged permission to copy commercial portrait photographs for such works.[10] Prior to the Civil War, one popular series of the firm's politician portraits used a recurring pictorial convention of half-length seated figures, often beside a table, in front of a large curtain tied back to a classical column with a tasseled cord. By printing similar portrayals of every earlier president, stretching back to George Washington (p. 157), Currier established a consistent pictorial formula for antebellum presidential portraits. But after the Civil War, the firm abandoned this tradition, generally preferring more detailed, bust-length vignettes without the curtained *mise en scène*. This style of presidential portrait appeared at least as early as 1856, with Currier's print of James Buchanan based on a photograph by Mathew Brady (fig. 1).

Just as Currier treated his political broadsides as a sideline endeavor, scholarship about the firm long downplayed the subject. Not until the 2001 study by Bryan F. Le Beau, *Currier & Ives: America Imagined*, did a monograph about the firm dedicate a robust section to political caricature. This tendency to ignore political broadsides presumably stemmed from a lack of enthusiasm about the genre on the part of print collectors, whose interests dominated the study of the firm and its prints throughout most of the twentieth century.[11] Whereas most collectors sought large, colorful prints, political broadsides—by Currier & Ives and other firms—generally appeared only as "plain," meaning untinted, prints in small formats. According to the established measurement system, the company's broadsides fall into the "small" and "medium" size classifications, rather than the "large" category.[12] In addition, unlike the alluring nostalgia of romanticized scenery appearing in many popular prints, the ephemeral topicality of political caricature often struck later generations as arcane.

But if writing about the firm has tended to ignore its political broadsides, historians of political cartooning have discussed these works. However, such attention has been predominantly

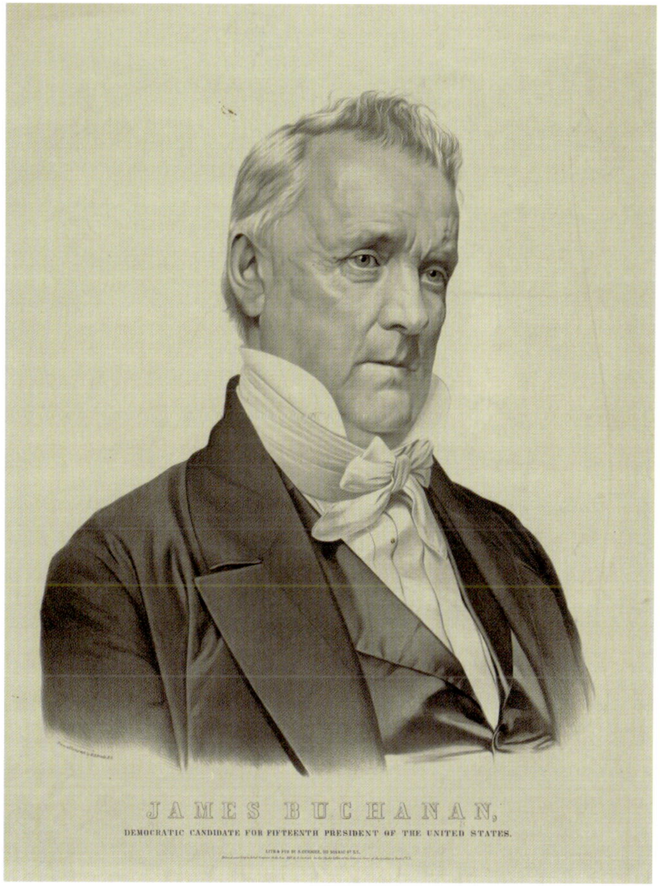


FIG 1 *James Buchanan, Democratic Candidate for Fifteenth President of the United States*, 1856. Courtesy of the Library of Congress, LC-DIG-pga-00797

unfavorable. Negative critiques often fault Currier & Ives for two distinct but compatible reasons. First, their caricatures have been viewed as inexcusably feeble and halfhearted at a time when the nation, amid the cataclysmic upheaval of the Civil War, desperately needed clarion calls to duty and moral uplift through propagandistic imagery. Second, their caricatures have been seen as awkwardly antiquated in their artistic conventions. But, in many respects, these unsympathetic critiques largely present the flipside of certain positive and even innovative aspects of the firm's broadsides that were readily appreciated by many nineteenth-century observers.

In order to analyze the contributions of Currier & Ives to a caricature tradition, it is useful to outline standard accounts of the genre. Histories of print culture commonly divide nineteenth-century political caricature from the United States into four phases defined by broad shifts in print media and dissemination methods. According to this taxonomy, an early period of scarce and sporadic intaglio prints, mostly copperplate engravings and etchings, persisted from colonial times through the first three decades of the nineteenth century. A second period dawned as the cheaper printing process of lithography, becoming increasingly common during the 1820s, provided unprecedented levels of graphic satire during the presidency of Andrew Jackson. In 1832, as various scholars have noted, lithographic firms waged the first pictorial "large-scale American war of political satires" over the issue of the national bank.[13] Currier & Ives became the dominant publisher of lithographic broadsides during the latter half of this long second phase, which lasted around four decades until shortly after the Civil War.

Though political broadsides continued to circulate into the final quarter of the century, weekly editorial cartoons in the periodical press began overshadowing them by the presidential election of 1872, marking the onset of a third phase. During this period, illustrated newspapers featuring black-and-white wood engravings, most notably *Harper's* and *Leslie's*, began supplanting the tradition of single-sheet broadsides. And, within a decade, humor magazines with eye-catching chromolithographs, such as *Puck* and *Judge*, continued this process. Finally, in a fourth period commencing around 1890, photographic transfer techniques and process engraving ushered in an era of daily newspaper cartooning that attained faster and cheaper results by accepting decreased image size and quality. Thus, the cartoonist Frank Beard noted in 1895 that the "poor processes of printing" recently adopted by the daily newspapers made even "the sketches of the best artists look scarcely better than those of the amateurs who scratch out pictures on the chalk plates in the country newspaper offices."[14]

Within this taxonomy, the third phase, often termed the "golden age" of editorial cartooning, has received by far the greatest amount of attention and acclaim. Although Thomas Nast is perhaps the only figure from this era who still retains much name recognition, this third phase saw an entire class of celebrity caricaturists rise abruptly to national prominence. Though little remembered today, several became household names, such as Bernhard Gillam, Joseph Keppler, Matt Morgan, William Allen Rogers, and James Albert Wales.

The fame of these prominent editorial cartoonists seems a world apart from the largely anonymous artists of the preceding broadside era. Like many midcentury publishers, Currier & Ives seldom credited the creators of their political prints. The firm retained a corporate identity while evenhandedly mocking prominent politicians across the political spectrum. Though many of their broadsides are thought to have been drawn by Louis Maurer, such attributions rest largely upon stylistic arguments rather than signed prints.[15] Maurer never emerged as a political commentator in the public eye. The only artist to sign broadsides for the firm regularly was John Cameron, who also commonly worked as a copyist, thereby complicating questions of authorship.[16] Rare are broadsides, such as *The Radical Party on a Heavy Grade* from 1868 (fig. 2), that credit both the artist, in this instance Ives himself, as well as the copyist, here Cameron.

Dominating the final stretch of the lithographic broadside era, Currier & Ives's political caricatures often appear as an unsympathetic foil against which to measure the success of

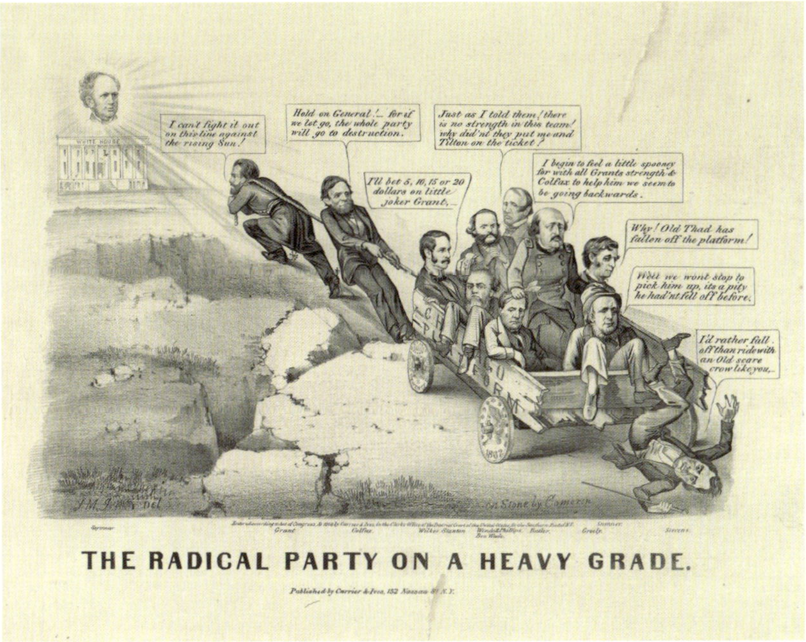


FIG 2 *The Radical Party on a Heavy Grade,* 1868. Courtesy of the Library of Congress, LC-DIG-pga-04990

the ensuing generation of periodical caricaturists. It is tempting both to overstate the innovations of this wave of celebrity caricaturists as well as to portray the broadsides of the 1850s and 1860s, by Maurer and Cameron and others, as a creative wasteland from which the imaginative editorial cartoons of the "golden age" successfully emerged. The situation, however, is not so cut-and-dried. Though Currier & Ives followed many of the established visual conventions for lithographic broadsides, their approach to political caricature differed distinctly from their forerunners. In several crucial ways the firm significantly altered conventional approaches to political caricature. Rather than simply a hidebound vestige of antiquated practices mired in an outmoded technology, Currier & Ives's political broadsides helped prepare the way for the new school of editorial cartooning.

## Caricatures Across the Continent: From a Regional to National Market

The celebrity caricaturists who rocketed to popularity in the 1870s, Thomas Nast above all, are typically described as the founders of a national caricature tradition. But Currier & Ives offer a logical earlier starting point for such discussions. Their broadsides helped develop the market for such graphic satire from regional centers, often concerned with local matters, to a continental scale, thereby contributing to a greater centralization of popular visual culture. And, crucially, they demonstrated that such caricature could prove profitable, despite a long and doleful history of satirical caricature as a financially bleak business venture. As many chroniclers have noted, most political humor magazines published in the United States prior to *Puck* failed very quickly.[17] While monetary rewards would seem to be the underlying consideration for any publisher, some of Currier's forerunners in the production of political broadsides might have been just as interested in political messaging as financial gain. In the early nineteenth century, both newspaper and lithograph publishers were often expected to contribute to party efforts, as a long-standing custom involved with larger networks of political patronage. But with Currier, this pattern of overtly partisan printers shifted to an entirely business-minded model.

Beginning with his early forays into political satire, Currier circulated imagery calculated to appeal to each substantial voting bloc. In 1848, he released caricatures variously supporting and ridiculing each of the three major presidential candidates: Zachary Taylor, Lewis Cass, and Martin Van Buren. Rather than a consistently moderate political voice, the business adopted multiple voices tailored for different audiences. Even during the Civil War, the firm seems always to have prioritized sales over partisanship. Thus, during the crucial referendum on the continuation of the war posed by the 1864 election, Currier & Ives supplied nearly as much anti-Lincoln and pro-McClellan imagery as they provided in support of the Republican cause.[18]

Currier was not the first publisher to adopt this tactic of releasing a spectrum of prints calculated to appeal to rival partisan groups at the same time, though he seems to have been uniquely successful in profiting from such a mass-market strategy. For example, the printmaker James S. Baillie, located for a time just a few doors down Spruce Street from Currier, issued dozens of broadsides during the 1844 presidential campaign, alternately favoring the Whigs and the Democrats. In doing so, Baillie offered a clear template for Currier to emulate four years later. With his immense distribution network and production capacity, Currier could reach far greater audiences—both in terms of geographical extent and overall market saturation—than Baillie or any other publishers of caricature from that era. Tellingly, Baillie shifted away from producing caricatures soon after Currier entered the market.

These nationally circulated broadsides of Currier & Ives exemplify a period often judged harshly by historians. Stephen Hess and Milton Kaplan, authors of *The Ungentlemanly Art: A History of American Political Cartoons*, first published in 1968, particularly scorned the firm's broadsides, finding that their "figures were stiff and spiritless." Especially vexing were the ubiquitous speech balloons, "a method of story-telling by then abandoned in Europe," that marked such works as embarrassingly hackneyed and outdated. Further, the humorous content of the company's lithographs "continued to rely heavily on the pun" though many, "unfortunately, were no more inspired than plays on people's names." Also, these prints were seen as often hopelessly banal. "About as predictable as the cartoonists' puns were the sports motifs that they dusted off every fourth year." Thus, in this influential account, the political broadsides of Currier & Ives were branded as insipid, trite, and monotonous—especially compared to contemporaneous European caricature. With a final, dismissive summation of the firm's broadsides, Hess and Kaplan griped that while "cartoonists on the west side of the Atlantic were experiencing a spiritual and artistic near bankruptcy, their counterparts in France were toppling a throne."[19] Later writers frequently followed in this vein of criticism. "The static figures are frozen," noted a 1973 exhibition commenting on the firm's campaign prints from 1860. "In a year filled with drama, action and decision, Currier & Ives were doing business at the same wooden stand."[20]

But these very aspects so disliked by some writers probably contributed to the successful mass marketing of Currier & Ives's broadsides. Needing to make timely images comprehensible to wide audiences, it is not surprising that the firm relied on familiar or universal themes and settings, leaning heavily upon conventional scenarios—such as barnyard genre scenes and sporting metaphors—and sometimes preferring obvious puns to quips that might make sense only to select audiences. But it is wrong to assume that more complex allusions and topical references are absent from these prints, though they might be harder for later audiences to comprehend. As Bishop notes, "caricaturists of the period were quick to seize upon whatever happened to be uppermost in the public mind at the moment, with which to add point to their pictures."[21]

An example is provided by the 1860 print *Taking the Stump or Stephen in Search of His Mother* (p. 173), which derides presidential candidate Stephen Douglas for his much-discussed campaigning tactics. The central pun here hinges upon the phrase "taking the stump," meaning both to speak on the campaign trail and to rely upon a prosthetic leg (eerie imagery given the many amputations soon to occur on Civil War battlefields). Though most current historians would point to the split of the

Democratic Party and its nomination of two competing candidates as the most significant aspect of this election, many period accounts found the "most remarkable" feature of the campaign to be the precedent-shattering speechifying of Douglas. "He is going to 'stump' the Union for himself as President—a course never pursued before," noted one Iowa paper.[22] The *Chicago Tribune*, squarely in the Republican camp, noted that "while Mr. Douglas has become the itinerant candidate, showing himself at the various railroad depots and college commencements, and making stump speeches in his own behalf," Lincoln, in stark contrast, "is staying quietly at home and preserving that modest reticence that proper decorum in a candidate has always demanded, until this shameless era of Presidential demagogues and self-puffery."[23] Thus, though the "stump" pun might perhaps be strained, it was far from commonplace. On the contrary, it directly commented upon the most distinctively novel aspect of the campaign.

As for the dreaded "loops," the period term for speech balloons, they may have been old fashioned, but they also seem to have remained familiar and popular with consumers. Informed by personal interviews with Ives, Bishop reported that "the public demanded" these traditional textual devices, and that "a picture without the loops would not sell." In Bishop's opinion, however, rather than relying upon such outmoded devices, the firm's broadsides clearly did not need the "loops" at all, since "the pictures told their story perfectly without these aids." Singling out various Currier & Ives prints, Bishop described "how plainly their meaning appears at a glance" without recourse to the dialogue balloons.

Bishop also provides an alternative assessment of the aesthetic quality of the firm's political imagery. Though many later critics found the company's broadsides on the eve of the Civil War banal and pedestrian, Bishop, writing in 1892, considered the firm's prints referencing the election of 1860 to be "the most successful of the kind ever issued in this country."[24] Rather than the allegedly stiff poses noted by many twentieth-century critics, the lithographs impressed him favorably. "In all of them the faces are carefully drawn portraits, and the figures are presented in natural attitudes." More than this, many of these works presented "vigorous" caricatures that compared "favorably with the caricatures of the present day," meaning the heyday of the magazines *Puck* and *Judge*.

The emphasis on easily recognizable faces, as many observers have noted, spurred the firm's broadsides to depart from the traditional core notion of caricature—namely the exaggeration or distortion of distinguishing personal features. The common description of "stiffness" in figures probably results in large part from the care taken to imitate specific likenesses from circulating commercial portraits, helping ensure that mass audiences would successfully identify the public figures. And this emphasis on clearly recognizable countenances continued in the work of many "golden age" artists, such as Nast and Gillam, who each amassed extensive collections of photographs of politicians in order to copy their faces as needed in their caricatures.

## Caricature and Propriety: From the Pool-Hall Wall to the Parlor Table

Several late nineteenth century authors pinpointed Currier's entry into the caricature market as the turning point away from the crudeness common to early nineteenth-century broadsides toward the refinement appreciated later in the century. Even some authors who faulted Currier & Ives for producing meek broadsides during the Civil War still acknowledged the firm's prints as the first "campaign caricatures of sufficient merit to have been a serious factor in influencing public opinion" rather than merely scurrilous political attacks.[25] Unlike the lewdness

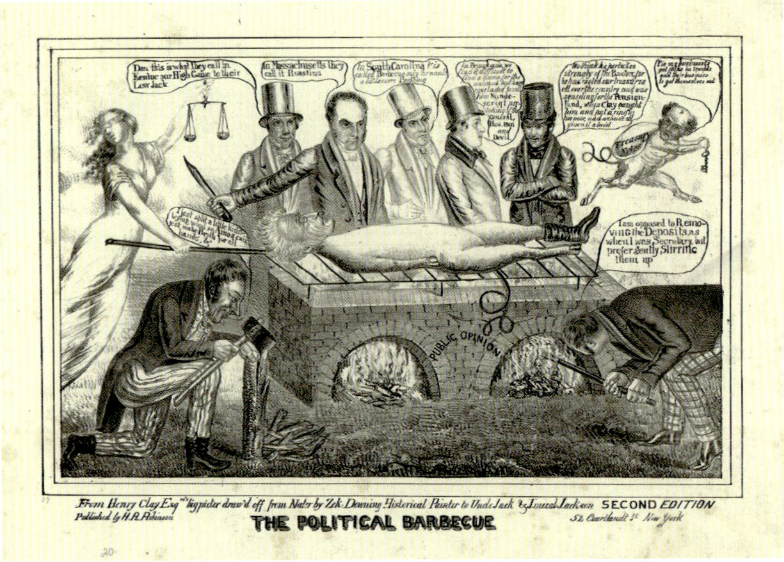


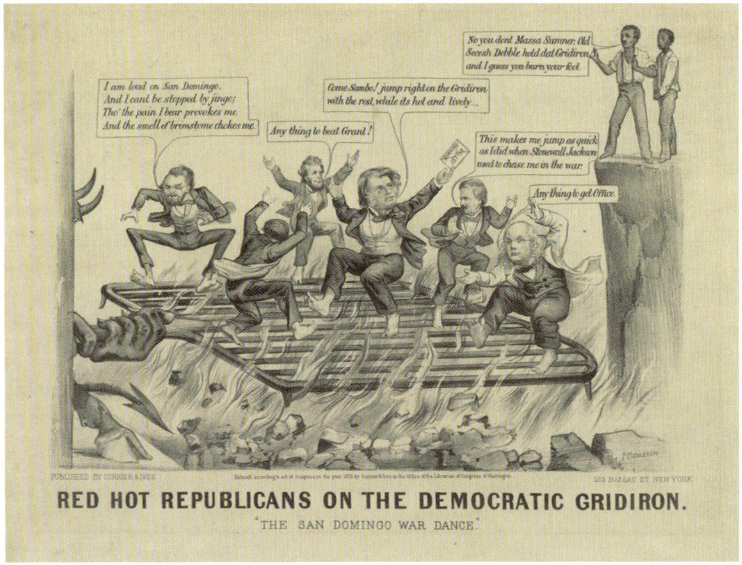


FIG 3 *The Political Barbecue,* published by H. R. Robinson, 1834. Courtesy of Tennessee State Library and Archives

FIG 4 *Red Hot Republicans on the Democratic Gridiron: The San Domingo War Dance,* 1872. Courtesy of the Library of Congress, LC-DIG-pga-04993

of some early British caricature, in the United States violations of propriety in caricatures from the second quarter of the nineteenth century tended more toward graphic violence than bawdy licentiousness. This type of imagery, from which Currier notably retreated, is exemplified by the most prolific New York caricaturist of the 1830s, Henry R. Robinson.

Two images sharing the conceit of grilling politicians help elucidate the differing approaches to visual proprieties of Robinson and Currier. Print historians have pointed to *The Political Barbecue* (fig. 3) from 1834 as an image that "has seldom been outdone for sheer wishful violence."[26] Perhaps first published by Ezra Bisbee, but then copied and circulated by Robinson, the grisly image portrays President Andrew Jackson with cloven hooves and a spiked curly tail—a monstrous amalgamation of "Hog, Man and Devil"—being roasted atop a gridiron held by the allegorical figure of Justice, who, even blindfolded, recoils from the abomination. Standing beside a roaring fire labeled "public opinion" and holding a large knife to carve the carcass, Senator Daniel Webster chats cheerily with other prominent Whigs about different methods for cooking the creature.

By comparison, even the unusually graphic Currier & Ives broadside *Red Hot Republicans on the Democratic Gridiron* (fig. 4), drawn by Cameron in 1872, appears far less vicious. Unlike Bisbee's disturbingly literal barbecue of a partisan foe, Cameron's gridiron metaphorically presents the discomfort of an awkward political stance, namely Liberal Republican opposition to President Grant's Caribbean foreign policy. The menacingly large horns and cloven hoof visible at the left margin belong not to the devil but rather to "Old Secesh," the demonized spirit of southern secession, as two clear-eyed, African-American freemen point out to the overheated politicians. Merely uncomfortable rather than in mortal peril, these northern Liberal Republicans—including Carl Schurz, Charles Sumner, Nathaniel Banks, and Horace Greeley—jump barefoot

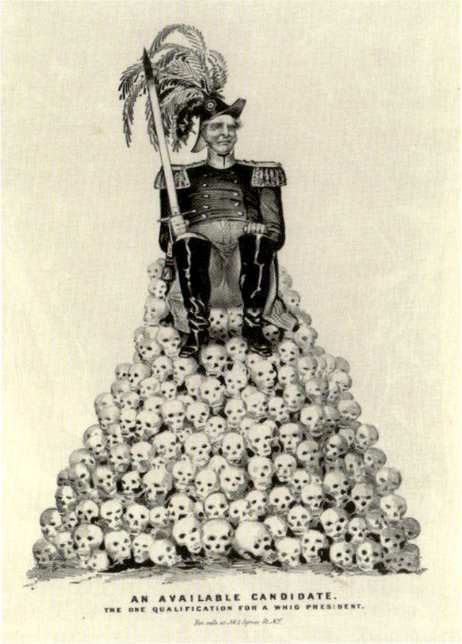


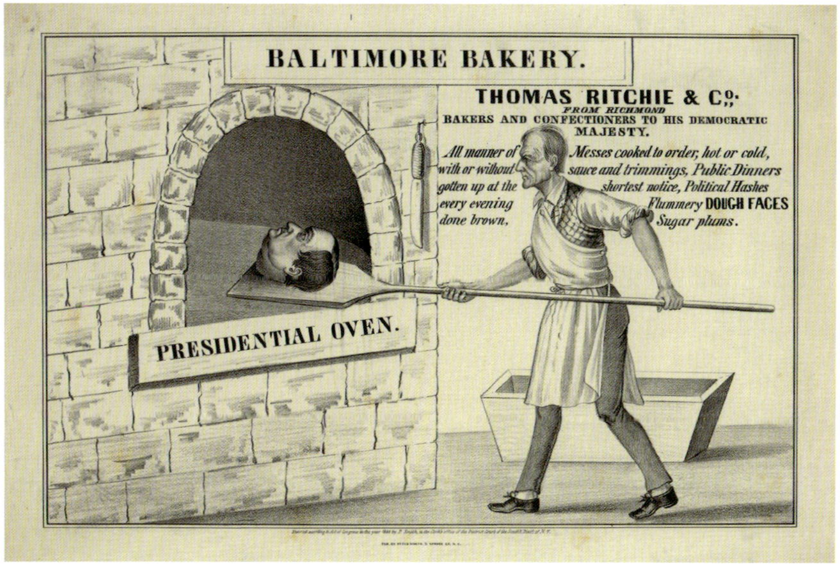


FIG 5 *An Available Candidate: the One Qualification for a Whig President*, 1848. Courtesy of the Library of Congress, LC-DIG-pga-04723

FIG 6 *Baltimore Bakery*, 1848. Courtesy of the Library of Congress, LC-DIG-ppmsca-15778

on their comically mammoth grill, performing a "San Domingo War Dance" in allegedly foolish sympathy with an unreconstructed Confederate worldview, while clamoring for others to join their fiery torment.

Currier's most morbid political images, *An Available Candidate* and *Baltimore Bakery* (figs. 5 and 6), are among his very earliest broadsides. *An Available Candidate* depicts Whig candidate Zachary Taylor seated atop a mound of skulls, a grisly reference to his military career in Mexico.[27] *Baltimore Bakery*, showing the Democratic publisher Thomas Ritchie using a baker's peel to place the head of candidate Lewis Cass into an oven, also makes for an interesting comparison with *The Political Barbecue*. But here a seeming decapitation is driven by a punning reference to the period term "doughface," applied to northern Democrats such as Cass, a Michigander, who staunchly supported southern slaveholding interests (the derogatory phrase implied dough-like manipulability). *Baltimore Bakery* downplays any corporeal reality in its depicted doughface; the disembodied head appears uncanny rather than abhorrent. And the cooking metaphor of a "presidential oven" implies the preparation of Cass as a candidate, not as a meal. Far more gruesome is *Political Guillotine* (fig. 7), a decapitation scene published that same year by Robinson, emphasizing the violent action of beheading. Here Cass leads shackled turncoat Democrats toward President Polk, shown as an executioner wielding an enormous axe. A bound victim lies atop a chopping block, his head tumbling into a sewer piled with lifeless remains of other disloyal politicos.

After releasing mildly macabre political commentaries in 1848, Currier quickly eschewed any gruesomeness in his satire. In his ensuing election images, physical violence generally tended more toward prankish slapstick: Franklin Pierce falls to the floor as Winfield Scott unexpectedly pulls the 'presidential chair' out from under him; Horace Greeley dunks William Seward in a harbor by shoving him off a pier; Thaddeus Stevens

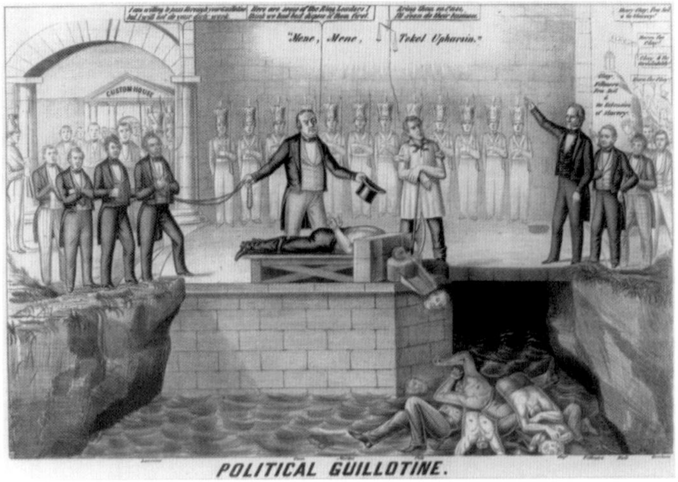


FIG 7 *Political Guillotine*, 1848. Courtesy of the Library of Congress, LC-USZ62-69613

tumbles off the back of a wagon (see fig. 2). By 1876, the convention of not showing violence could contribute itself to satirical messaging. In *Democratic Reformers in Search of a Head* (p. 174) a cloud of dust kicked up from an awful brawl cloaks the fighting. Only hands grasping weapons—revolvers, shillelaghs, bottles, umbrellas, knives, canes, and a broken stool—appear around a haze of combat. The ruthlessness of Democratic infighting is thus denounced as inexpressibly uncivilized.

Currier probably worried about alienating viewers by wading too far into the aggressive realm of male sporting culture, where the hard-nosed realities of political contests traditionally resided. With his business resting squarely upon the sanctified parlor culture of the home, the very antithesis of the down-and-dirty culture of the streets, Currier must have remained concerned about debasing his firm, whose reputation and earnings derived from its large colored prints intended for framed display in polite domestic environments.[28] The raw political broadsides of Robinson and his ilk obviously jarred with the genteel aspirations of parlor culture, which prioritized wholesome, edifying, and respectable imagery. Traditionally, broadsides circulated within male-dominated environments of the semipublic sphere, such as political headquarters, newspaper offices, saloons, fire stations, and other masculine preserves. Striving to bring political broadsides more in line with his larger business venture, Currier began transforming the practice of caricature into a genre more suitable for the domestic sphere. This shift parallels the firm's humorous prints about sporting society, such as *The Beauties of Billiards* from 1869 (p. 170), which sanitize the roguish associations of such masculine resorts into harmlessly comical, mild-mannered, and genteel venues.

Unlike many of his predecessors, Currier not only refrained from pushing the limits of acceptable graphic representation in political broadsides but also reversed their violent pictorial excesses, and in this way helped usher in a new phase in which caricature became increasingly acceptable within polite society. Despite issuing his political prints during the hostilities of the sectional crisis, Civil War, and Reconstruction period—arguably the most violently divisive period in the nation's history—his broadsides refrain from the excessively acrimonious and gory imagery common in earlier lithographs. This move toward respectability for political caricature was readily appreciated by many observers in the late nineteenth century. In 1880, the *New York Times* noted that the artistic refinement of caricature had been continually improving. "In caricatures there are many new hands at work, in which the higher canons of art influence the pictures."[29] The paper particularly praised Bernhard Gillam, who had worked for both *Leslie's* and *Harper's* before joining the staff of *Puck*. That same year, another paper declared approvingly that "the pertinent caricatures of the day" appearing in *Leslie's* and *Harper's* "bring laughter and instruction always" rather than presenting any unseemly content.[30] In other words, suitably presented in illustrated weekly magazines that positioned themselves as genteel purveyors of current events and cultured civility, caricature had attained the respectability needed for inclusion within the middle-class parlor.

Thus, rather than viewing the broadsides of Currier & Ives as pale imitations of their venomous precursors, dithering meekly amid the sectional crisis, they might instead be seen as successfully pioneering attempts to tame the unsavory excesses of earlier visual repertoires into formats acceptable for domestic consumption. In this way, the firm planted the seeds for a greatly expanded audience for caricature, thereby laying the necessary groundwork for the ensuing "golden age" of editorial cartooning, wherein illustrated journals greatly concerned with respectability—like *Harper's*, which billed itself as "A Journal of Civilization"—adopted caricature as an acceptable format for political commentary.

After the election of 1896, the *Philadelphia Times* surveyed the history of caricature during the nineteenth century. "While the political cartoon is to-day one of the great features of a daily newspaper, two-score years ago it was unheard of, and a professional caricaturist would have looked in vain for a position where he could earn his daily bread and butter." Further, the paper noted, generations earlier political broadsides had been "crude affairs," unfit for polite audiences. "They were often cruel, brutal and positively indecent. This is all in great contrast to the best cartoons of to-day, which are in most cases finished and perfect as any picture."[31] Though working within the broadside tradition rather than the emergent popular medium of the periodical, Currier & Ives arguably influenced this shift more than any other publisher.

In sum, the political satire of Currier & Ives might be viewed as the start of a mass-market caricature tradition in the United States, while at the same time participating in the final phase of the political broadside tradition. At least two departures from the practice of earlier lithographers position the firm's works as significant forerunners to the editorial cartooning of the ensuing "golden age." Currier cultivated a vastly larger market for political prints than his predecessors, successfully operating on a national scale rather than relying chiefly upon local or regional audiences. And the firm led the shift from the mean-spirited, bruising, and often crude format of graphic politicking to a more restrained mode of satire. Both of these developments, unrelated to common taxonomical concerns with shifting technical processes, bolstered crucial preconditions for the mass-market circulation of political caricature in the pages of illustrated newspapers and magazines.

## NOTES

1 Precise circulation statistics do not exist. By 1846, Currier already boasted in advertisements that his collection of prints for sale was "the most extensive in the United States, and consists almost exclusively of original drawings executed by the best artists in the country." See, for instance, "Lithographic Prints, &c.," *Washington Union*, September 10, 1846, 4. None of his prolific predecessors in the market for political broadsides, such as Henry R. Robinson and James S. Baillie, had the capacity to print and circulate so many lithographs as Currier. And *Harper's Weekly*, the first of the mass-market periodicals to feature political caricature, did not do so with regularity until around 1870.

2 Writers in the late nineteenth and early twentieth century routinely acknowledged Currier's activity in the political caricature market beginning in 1848. See, for instance, Joseph B. Bishop, "Early Political Caricature in America," *Century Magazine* 44, no. 2 (June 1892): 222 or Frank Weitenkampf, *American Graphic Art* (New York: H. Holt and Company, 1912), 255. But Harry T. Peters seems to have been the first to note the use of Currier's old business address and also the presence of many prints by "Smith" in the final remainder sale of the firm. See, for instance, Anne Marie Serio, *Political Cartoons in the 1848 Presidential Campaign*, Smithsonian Studies in History and Technology, no. 14 (Washington, DC: Smithsonian Institution Press, 1972), 18.

3 The political broadside *Capability and Availability* from 1852 bears a standard credit line, "N. Currier, 152 Nassau St," but this anomalous case likely stemmed from a clerical error. In general, the name Peter Smith appears routinely from 1848 until 1852, when the phrase "For sale at No. 2 Spruce St., N.Y." becomes the default text.

4 It is hard to define political caricature with precision. For example, differences are often drawn between caricatures involving political satire and social satire, but such distinctions easily enter gray areas. The estimate of eighty political prints appears in Stephen Hess and Milton Kaplan, *The Ungentlemanly Art: A History of American Political Cartoons* (New York: Macmillan, 1968), 73.

5 Even these guides are not terribly reliable during their early years since they often depended upon publisher-supplied data. Only later did processes emerge for verified data.

6 Bishop, "Early Political Caricature in America," 226–227.

7 On the predominance of Whig caricature, see, for instance, Nancy R. Davidson, "E. W. Clay and the American Political Caricature Business," in David Tatham, ed., *Prints and Printmakers of New York State, 1825–1940* (Syracuse, NY: Syracuse University Press, 1986), 104.

8 Most presidential campaign broadsides arrived during the summer months, following shortly after the presidential nominating conventions typically held between late May and early July. Some election years offered quite abbreviated intervals for publishing broadsides. For instance, in 1864, during the Civil War, the unusually late Democratic convention that nominated the McClellan and Pendleton ticket only wrapped up on the last day of August, just over two months before election day.

9 See Frederic A. Conningham, *Currier & Ives: An Illustrated Check List*, updated by Colin Simkin (New York: Crown Publishers, 1970), 3–4, 135, 161–162. See also the discussion in Harold Holzer, *Lincoln at Cooper Union: The Speech That Made Abraham Lincoln President* (New York: Simon & Schuster, 2004), examining four different Currier & Ives variations upon Mathew Brady's celebrated "Cooper Union" portrait of Lincoln.

10 Thus, Currier's 1852 portrait of Franklin Pierce notes its source is "a daguerreotype by T. Dunlap," while many later portraits, such as James Buchanan in 1856 and Abraham Lincoln in 1860, credit Mathew Brady.

11 The work of Harry T. Peters stands out in this regard, but many other publications also targeted collectors, often providing specific suggestions for readers interested in acquiring Currier & Ives prints.

12 Though Bernard F. Reilly's two-volume *Currier & Ives: A Catalogue Raisonné*, first published by Gale Research in 1983, later became the standard reference source, Frederic A. Conningham's *Currier & Ives: An Illustrated Check List*, first published in 1949, established the standard measurement classifications: very small (prints whose images, without captions,

measure no larger than 7 × 9 inches), small (no larger than 9 × 14 inches), medium (up to 14 × 20 inches), and large (more than 14 × 20 inches). Though overall most Currier & Ives prints fall into either the small or the large categories, many of the partisan prints fall into the medium category.

**13** Bernard F. Reilly, Jr., *American Political Prints, 1766–1876: A Catalog of the Collections in the Library of Congress* (Boston, MA: G. K. Hall & Co., 1991), xv.

**14** Frank G. Carpenter, "Chalk Talk," *St. Joseph* (Missouri) *Weekly Herald*, September 19, 1895, 12.

**15** Late in life, Maurer was also interviewed about some of the firm's political broadsides by the collector and scholar Harry T. Peters.

**16** Cameron sometimes used the phrase "on stone" alongside his signature on prints, presumably to indicate designs he had copied onto the lithographic stone from drawings or sketches made by others.

**17** For example, Frank Luther Mott, *A History of American Magazines 1850–1865* (Cambridge, MA: Harvard University Press, 1938), 179.

**18** See, for example, anti-Lincoln prints such as *Running the "Machine"* and *Abraham's Dream!*, and pro-McClellan imagery like *The True Issue or "That's What's the Matter."*

**19** Hess and Kaplan, *The Ungentlemanly Art*, 73–81.

**20** *Made in America: Printmaking, 1760–1860* (Philadelphia, PA: Library Company of Philadelphia, 1973), 59.

**21** Bishop, "Early Political Caricature in America," 226.

**22** "Douglas Pitches into Breckinridge," *Muscatine* (Iowa) *Weekly Journal*, September 7, 1860, 1.

**23** "The Presidential Stumpers," *Chicago Tribune*, July 31, 1860, 2.

**24** Bishop, "Early Political Caricature in America," 225.

**25** Arthur Bartlett Maurice and Frederic Taber Cooper, *The History of the Nineteenth Century in Caricature* (New York: Dodd, Mead & Co., 1904), 143.

**26** Reilly, *American Political Prints, 1766–1876*, xiv.

**27** This print is often identified as depicting General Winfield Scott, who was also in the running for the Whig nomination in 1848. The connection to Scott is often made through his nickname "Old Fuss and Feathers," which would seem to accord with the impressive plumage atop the bicorn hat. But an earlier Currier portrait of Taylor, *General Z. Taylor*, from 1847, shows him in profile wearing a similar hat. The Whig candidacy and the pyramid of skulls applies equally well to both men. But the facial features would seem closer to those of Taylor, judging from the half-plate daguerreotype of Taylor taken by James Maguire belonging to the National Portrait Gallery. Since this would seem to be an early, and possibly even the first, political caricature published by Currier, it is perhaps inappropriate to reason from the firm's later standard approach to releasing election-year imagery; however, if the work depicts Scott, meaning that it would date from before the nomination, then it constitutes an exception to the firm's typical practice of releasing broadsides after conventions. It is also conceivable that the work is deliberately meant to blur the identity of the two men, though this would seem unlikely as a rather complicated conceit. See entry in Reilly, *American Political Prints 1766–1876*.

**28** See, for example, Bryan F. Le Beau, "Art in the Parlor: Consumer Culture and Currier and Ives," *Journal of American Culture* 30, no. 1 (March 2007).

**29** "Our Best Illustrators," *New York Times*, November 7, 1880, 5.

**30** "The Illustrated Weeklies," *St. Joseph* (Missouri) *Weekly Gazette*, December 2, 1880, 6.

**31** "Cartoons and the Cartoonists," *Times* (Philadelphia), April 25, 1897, 27.

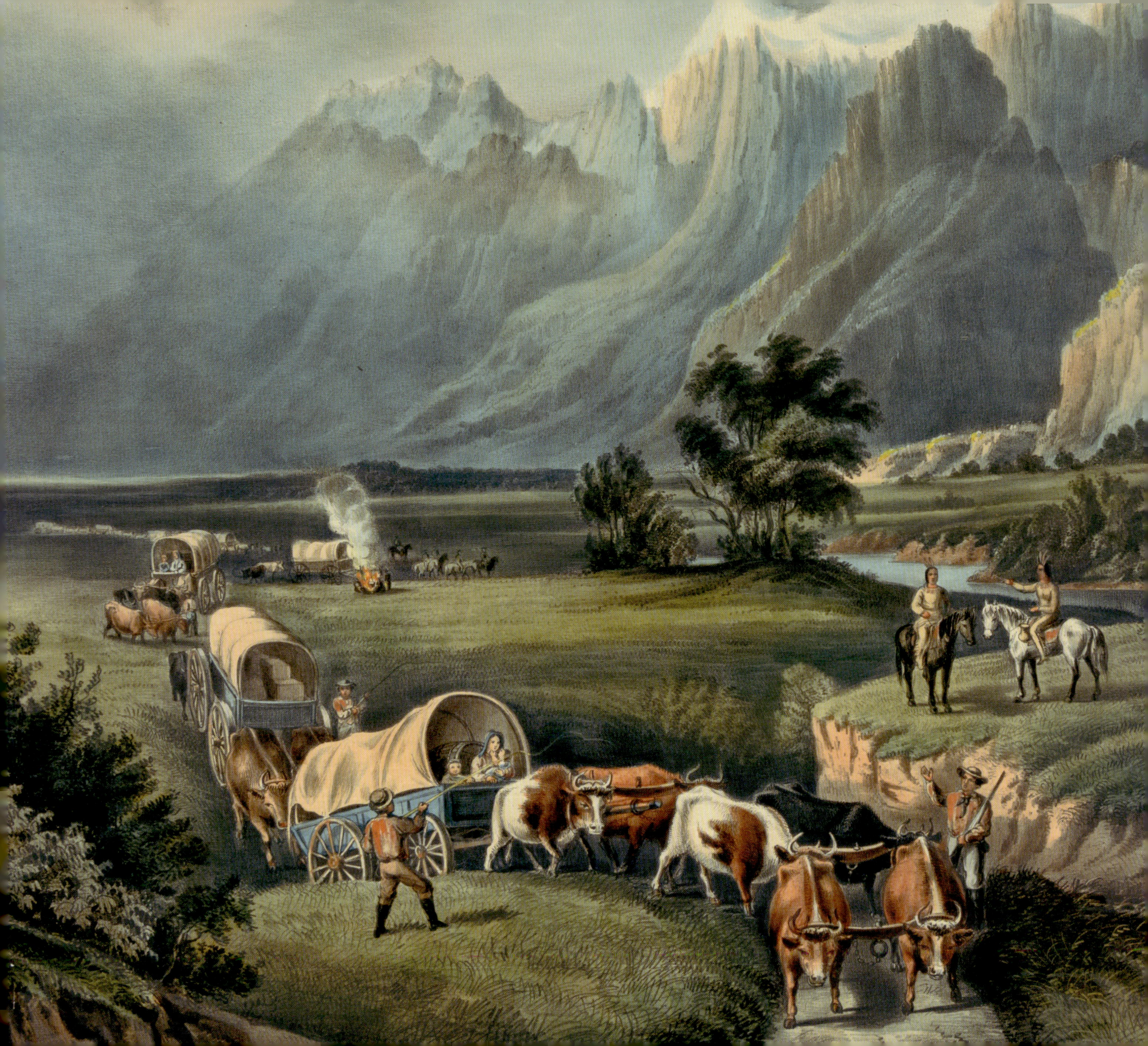

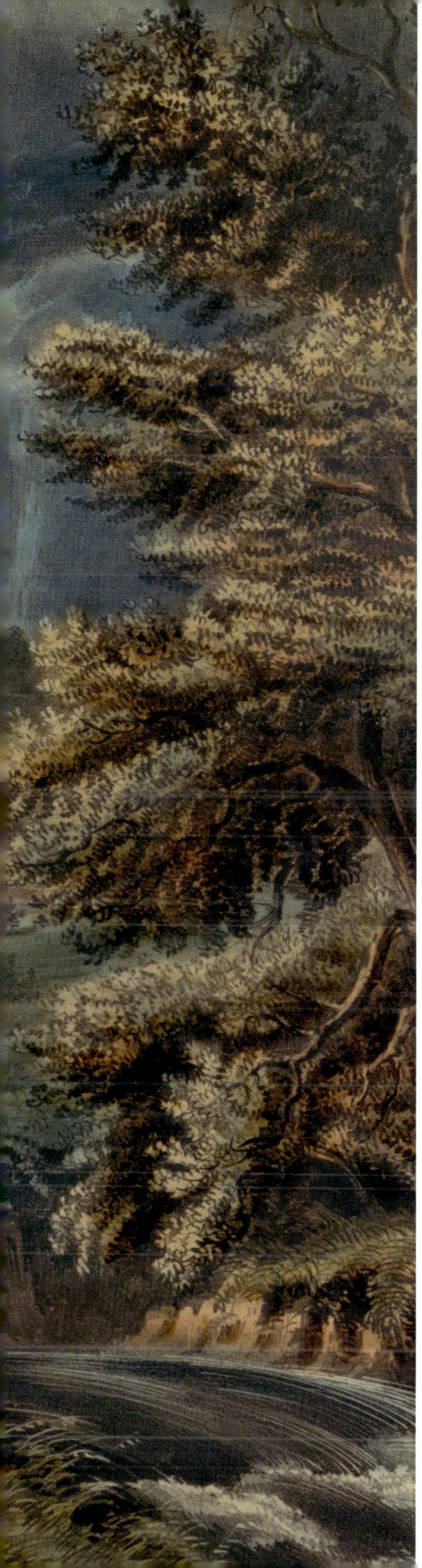

# REVISITING AMERICA

*Plates*

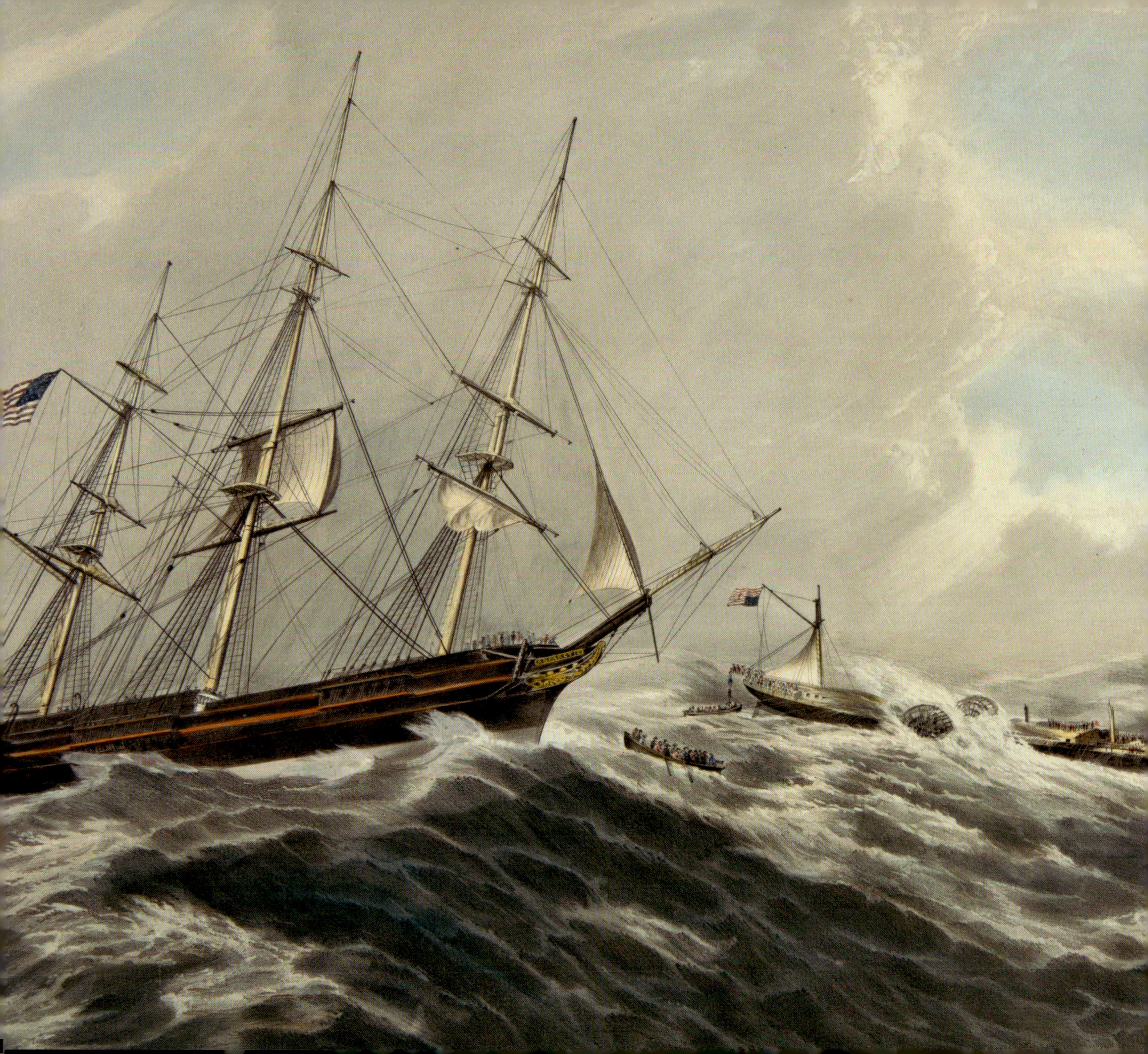

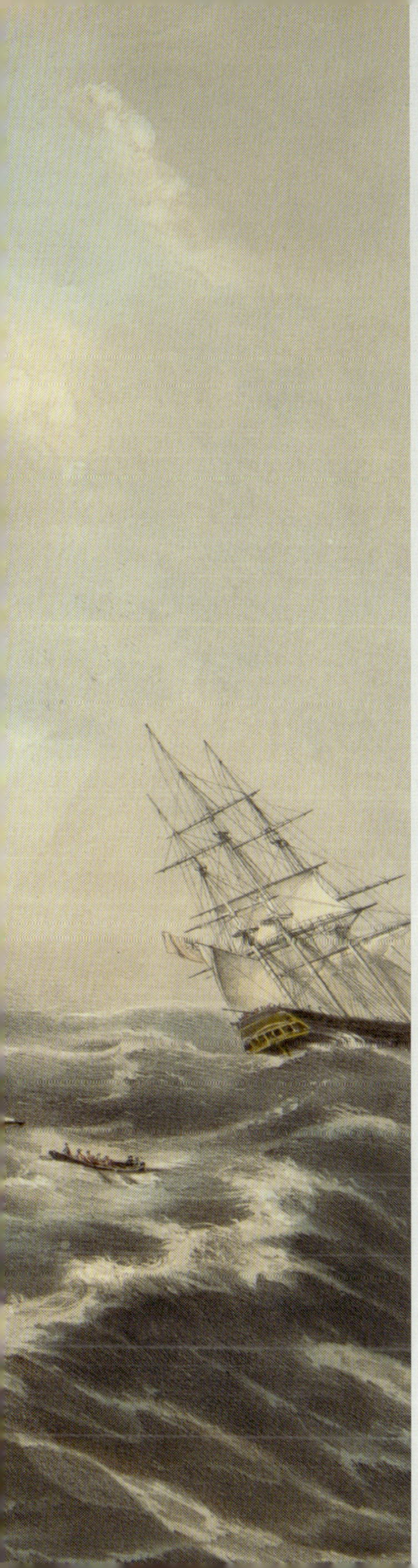

# SAILS, STEAM, AND SPEED

Nineteenth-century Americans took pride in the technological advancements being made across their nation. A rapid and wide-reaching revolution in transportation led the country from majestic clipper ships to powerful steam-driven boats and locomotives in a matter of decades. At their height in the middle of the century, clipper ships—three-masted merchant ships designed for speed—ruled the seas and allowed for the faster-than-ever transportation of goods and people across the Atlantic and along the coasts. The might of steamboats followed shortly thereafter, which turned America's waterways into high-traffic thoroughfares bringing culture and commerce to riverside towns like St. Louis, Memphis, and New Orleans. Reconstruction efforts following the Civil War standardized and expanded railroads throughout the nation, allowing Americans to travel westward more quickly and comfortably than ever before. Not limited to riverways, the railroads encouraged economic growth from coast to coast. Currier & Ives's large-format prints of clipper ships, steamboats, and trains emphasized a seamless continuity between these new technologies and the American landscape. Often composed on a diagonal racing toward the horizon, their prints showed locomotives and steamboats speeding across the country throughout the day and night to keep pace with American progress and ambition.

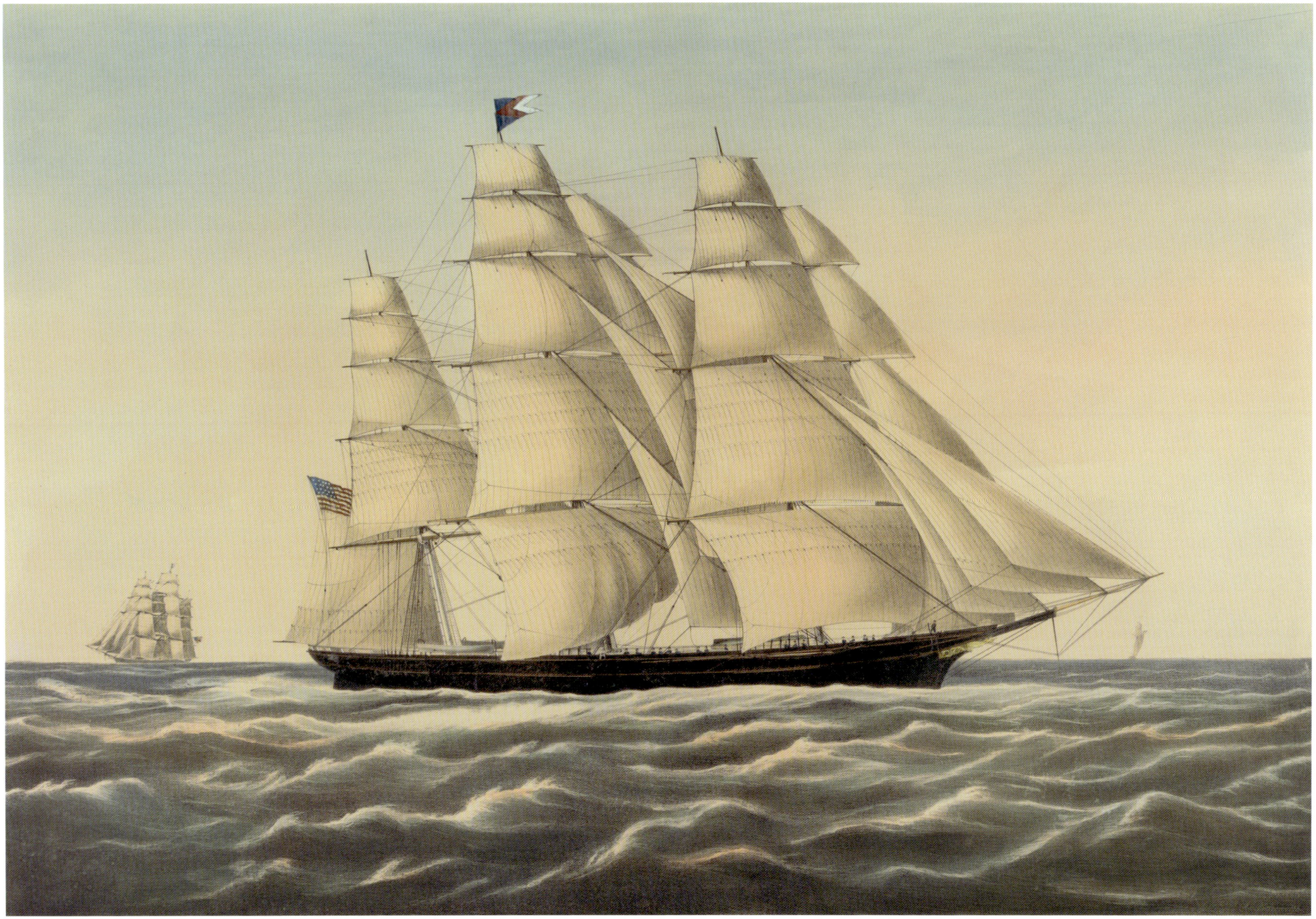

*Clipper Ship "Flying Cloud"*

1852

James E. Butterworth, AMERICAN (BORN ENGLAND), 1817–1894

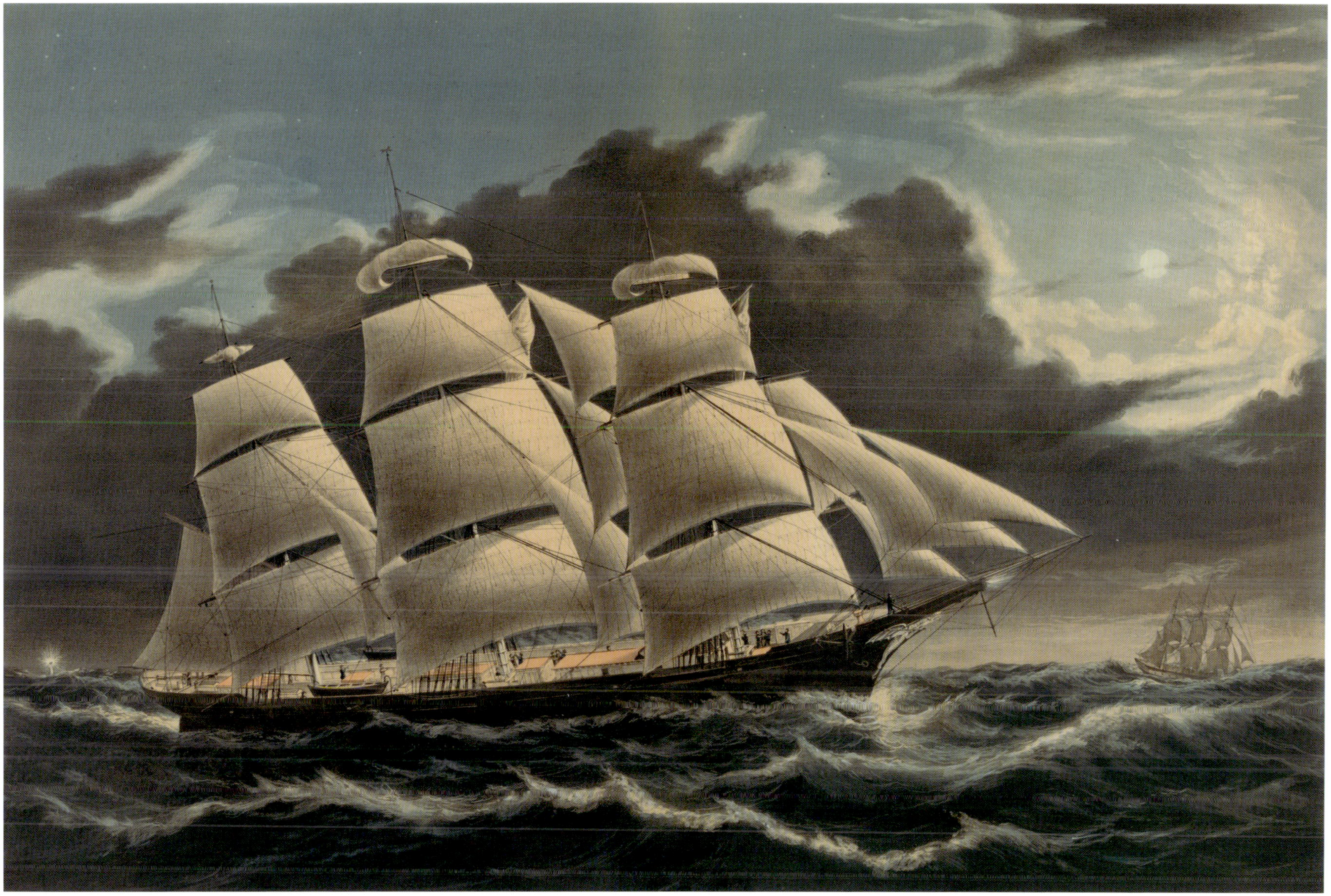

*Clipper Ship "Dreadnought" off Tuskar Light*

1856

Charles Parsons, AMERICAN (BORN ENGLAND), 1821–1910

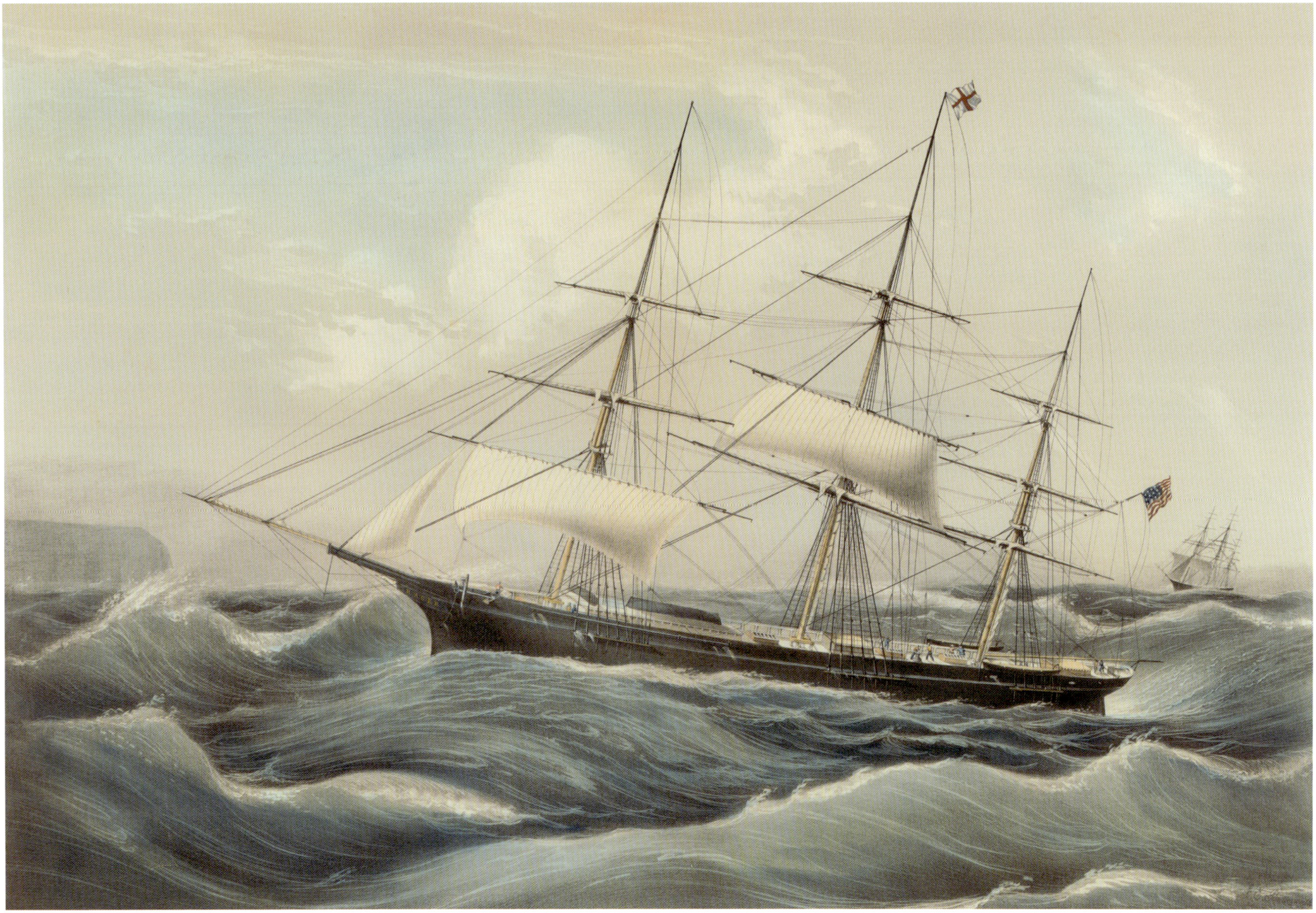

*Clipper Ship "Racer"*

1854

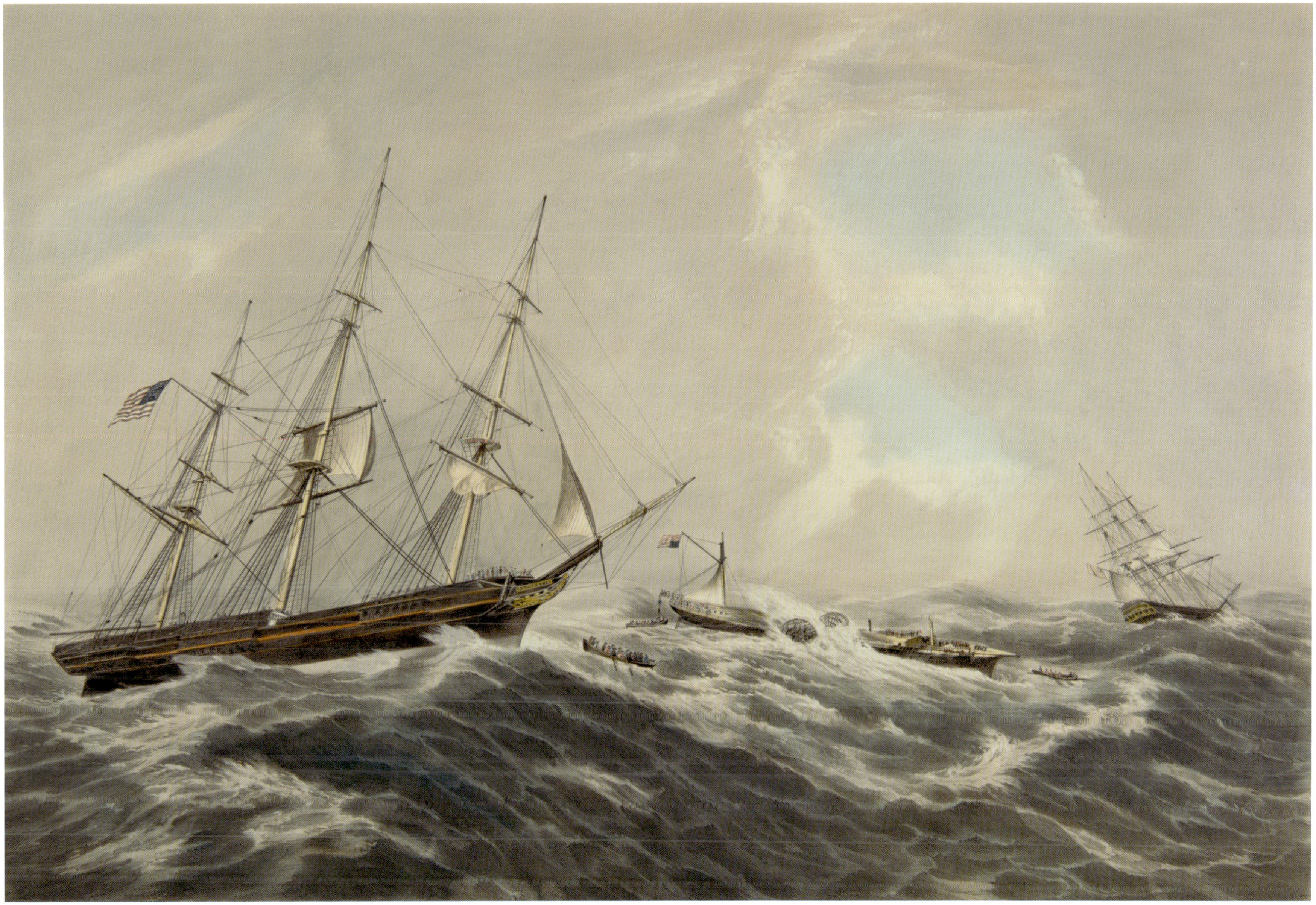

*The Wreck of the Steam Ship "San Francisco"*

1854

James E. Butterworth, AMERICAN (BORN ENGLAND), 1817–1894

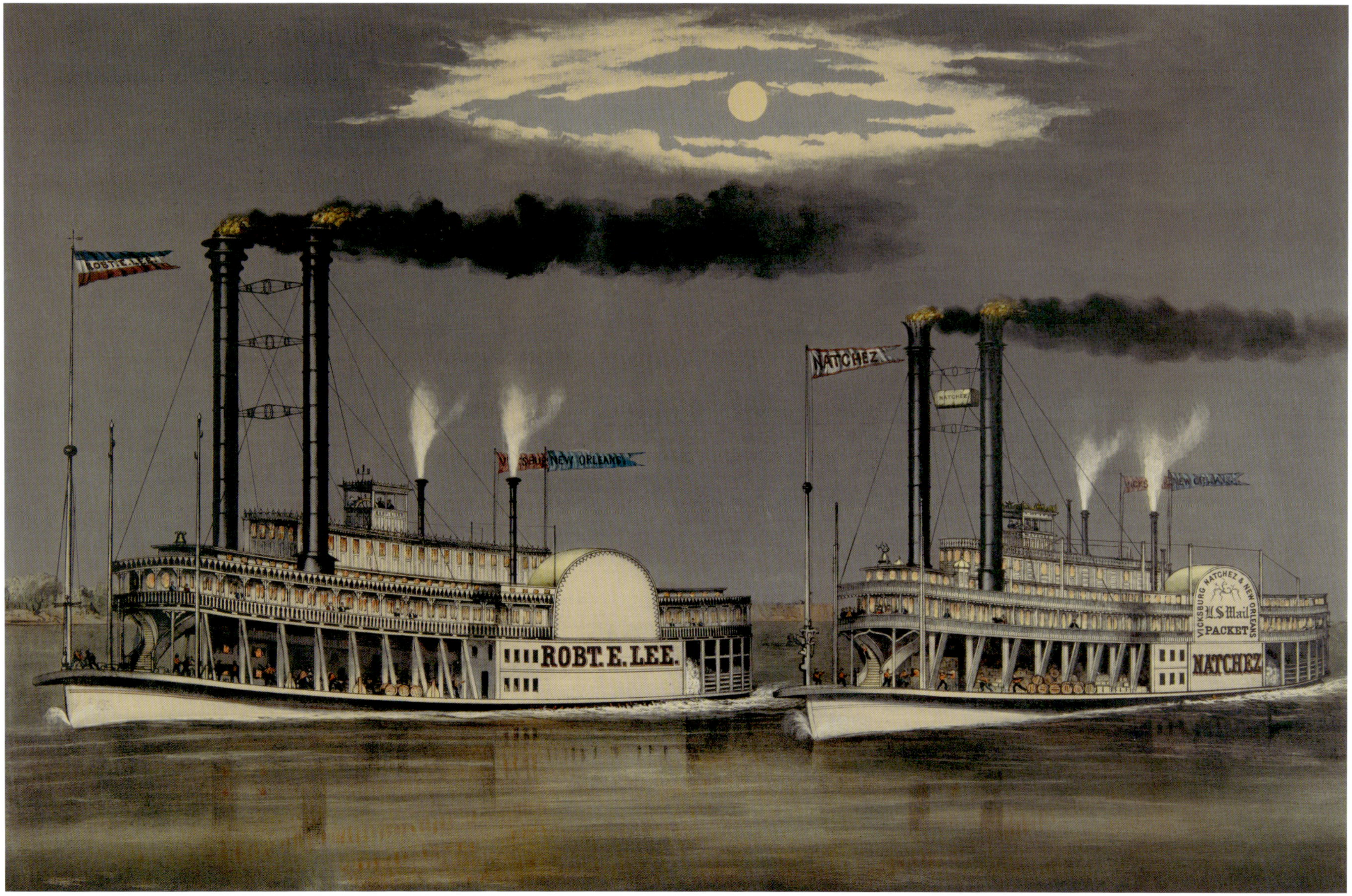


*The Great Race on the Mississippi*
*From New Orleans to St. Louis 1210 Miles*
1870

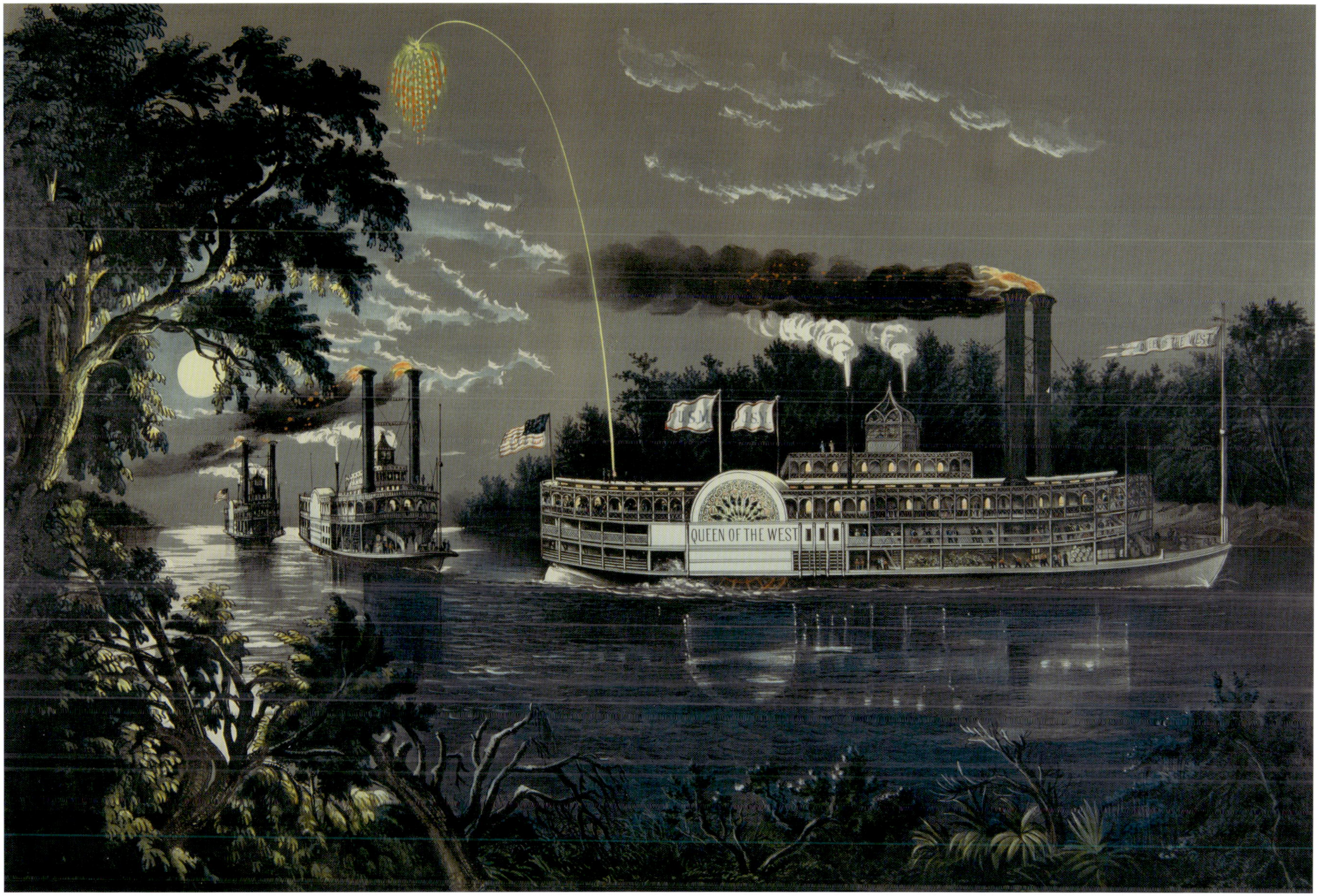


*Rounding a Bend on the Mississippi*

*The Parting Salute*

1866

Frances Palmer, AMERICAN (BORN ENGLAND), 1812–1876

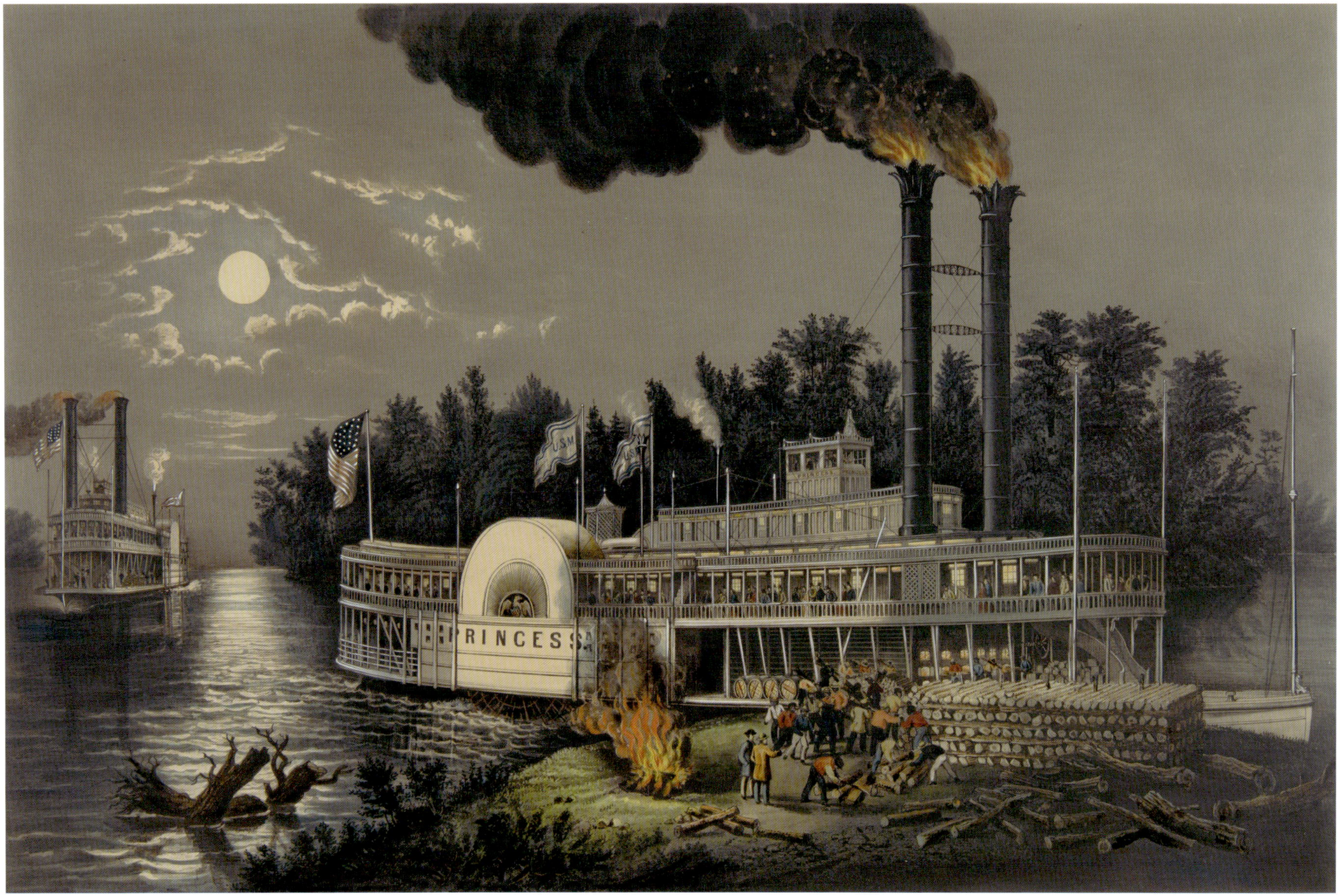


*Wooding Up on the Mississippi*

1863

Frances Palmer, AMERICAN (BORN ENGLAND), 1812–1876

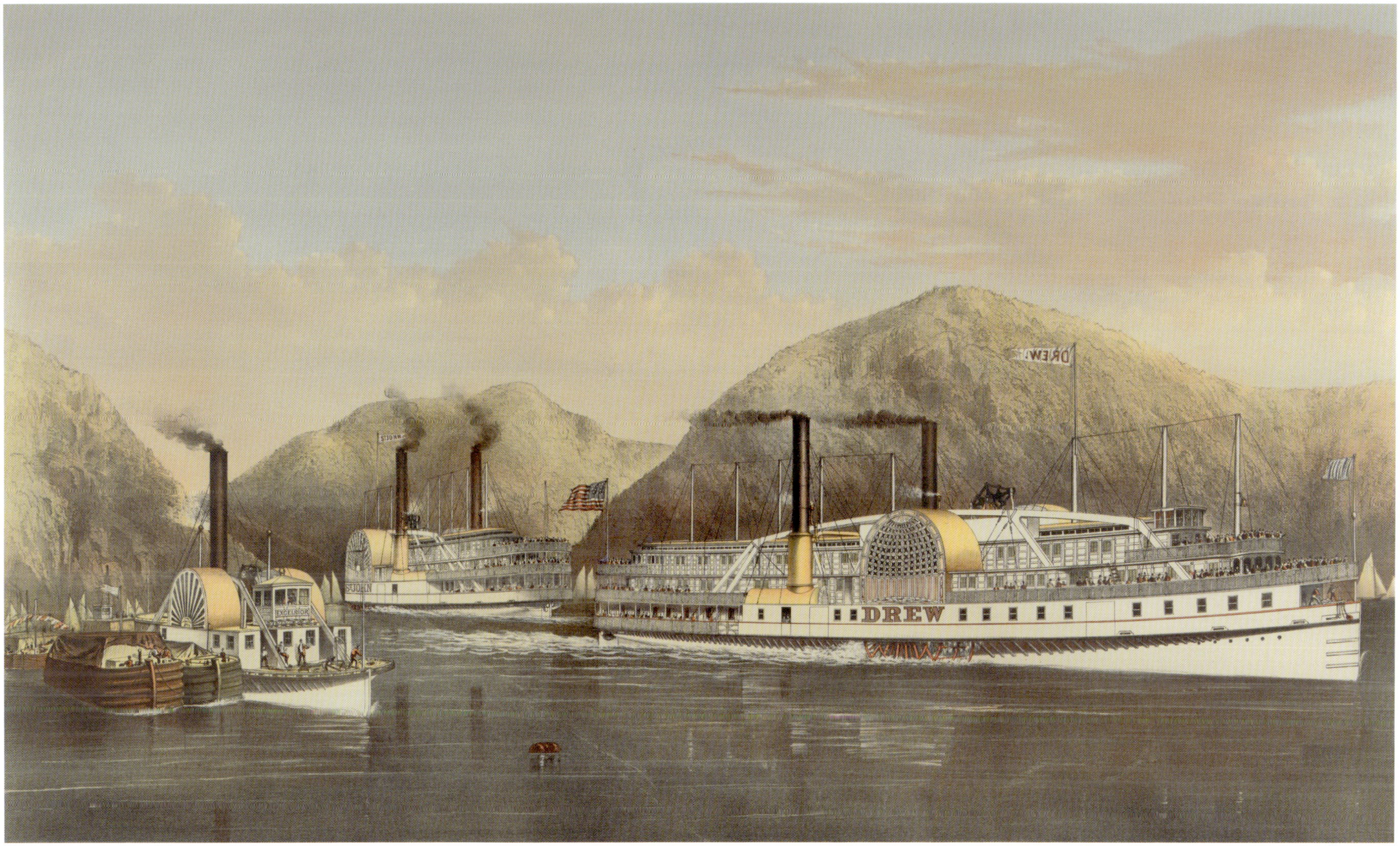


*American Steamboats on the Hudson*

*Passing the Highlands*

1874

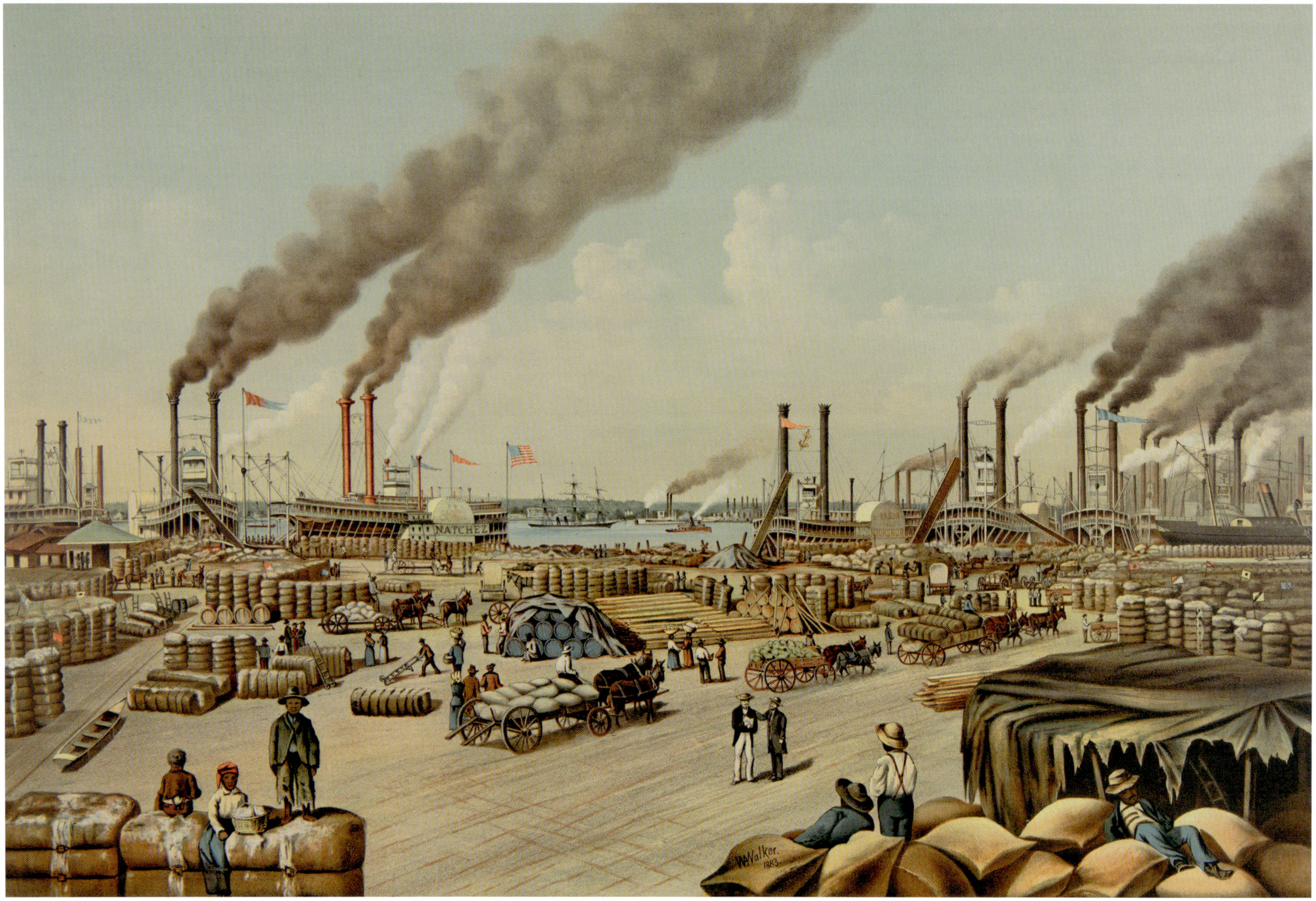


*The Levee—New Orleans*

1884

William A. Walker, AMERICAN, 1838–1921

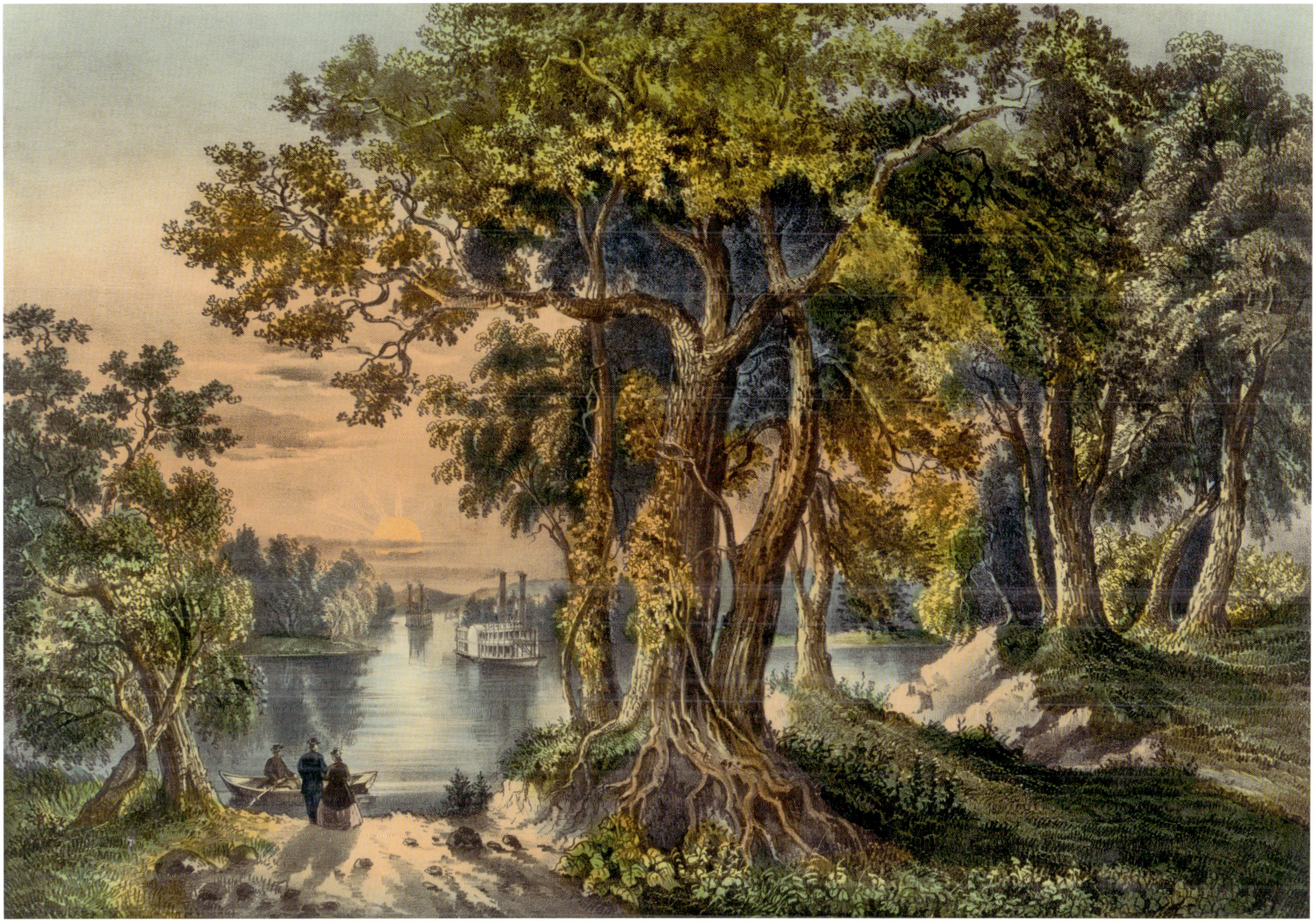

*Western River Scenery*

1866

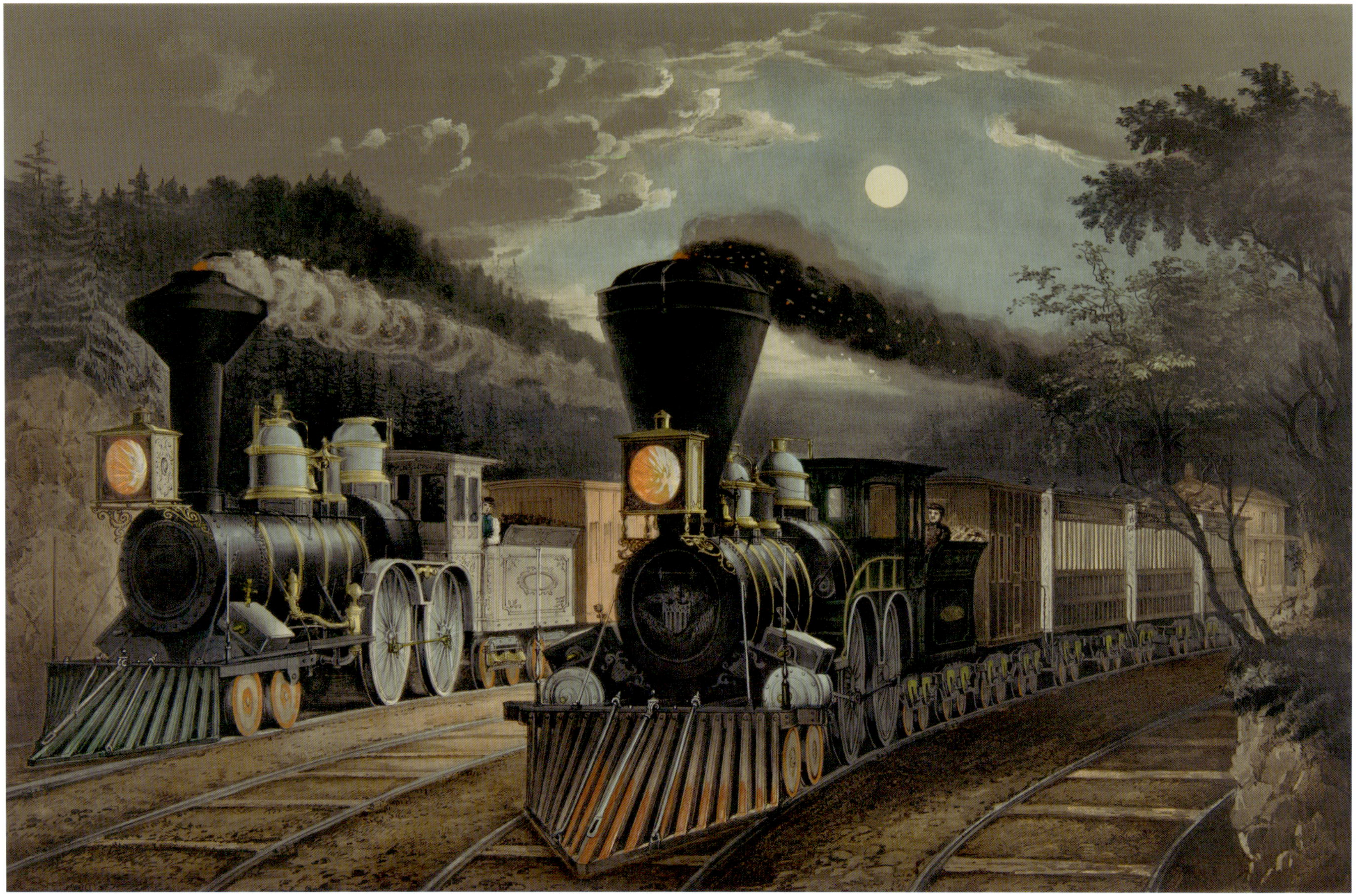

*The Lightning Express Trains*
***Leaving the Junction***
1863
Frances Palmer, AMERICAN (BORN ENGLAND), 1812–1876

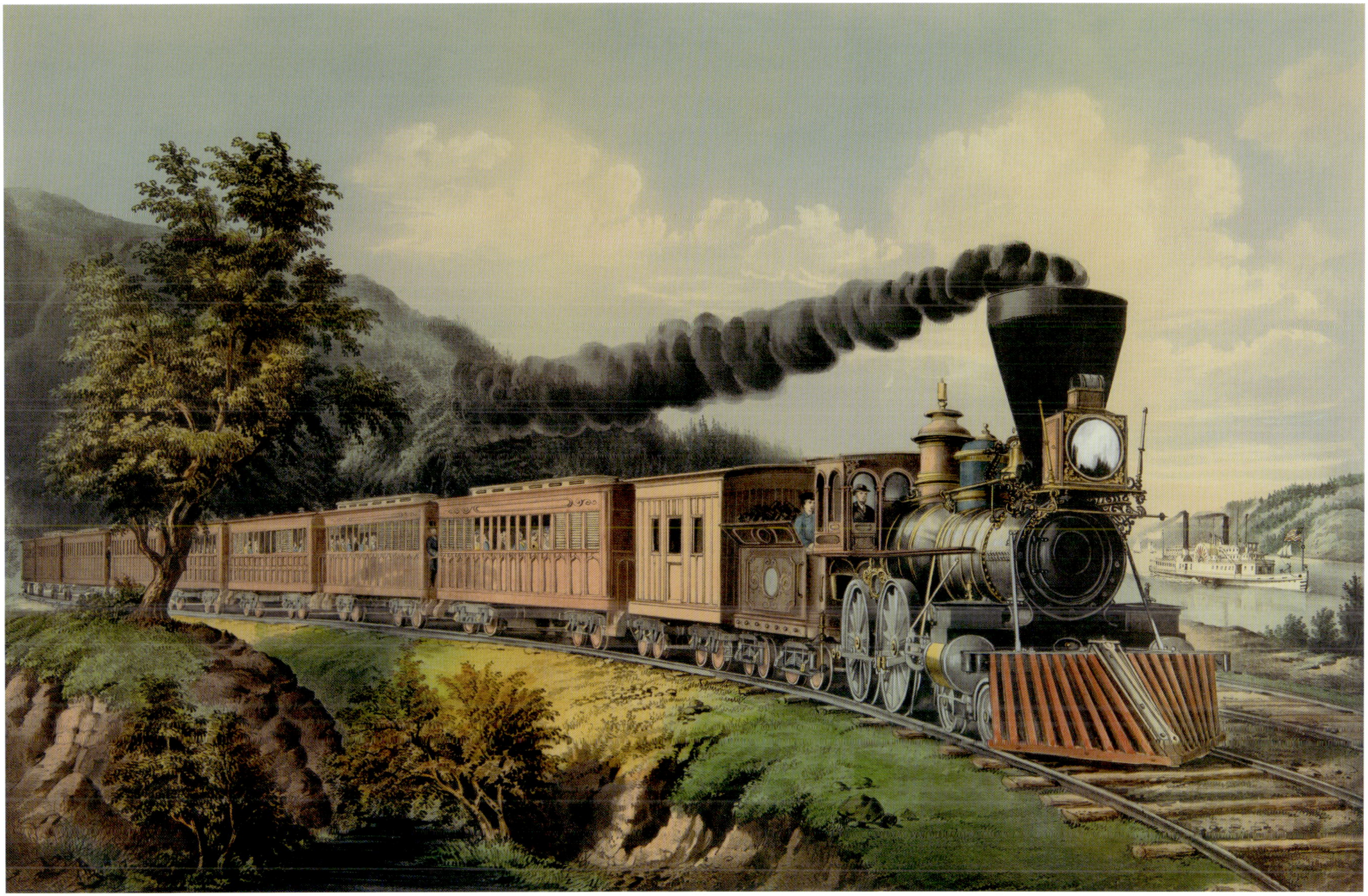

*American Express Train*

1864

Frances Palmer, AMERICAN (BORN ENGLAND), 1812–1876

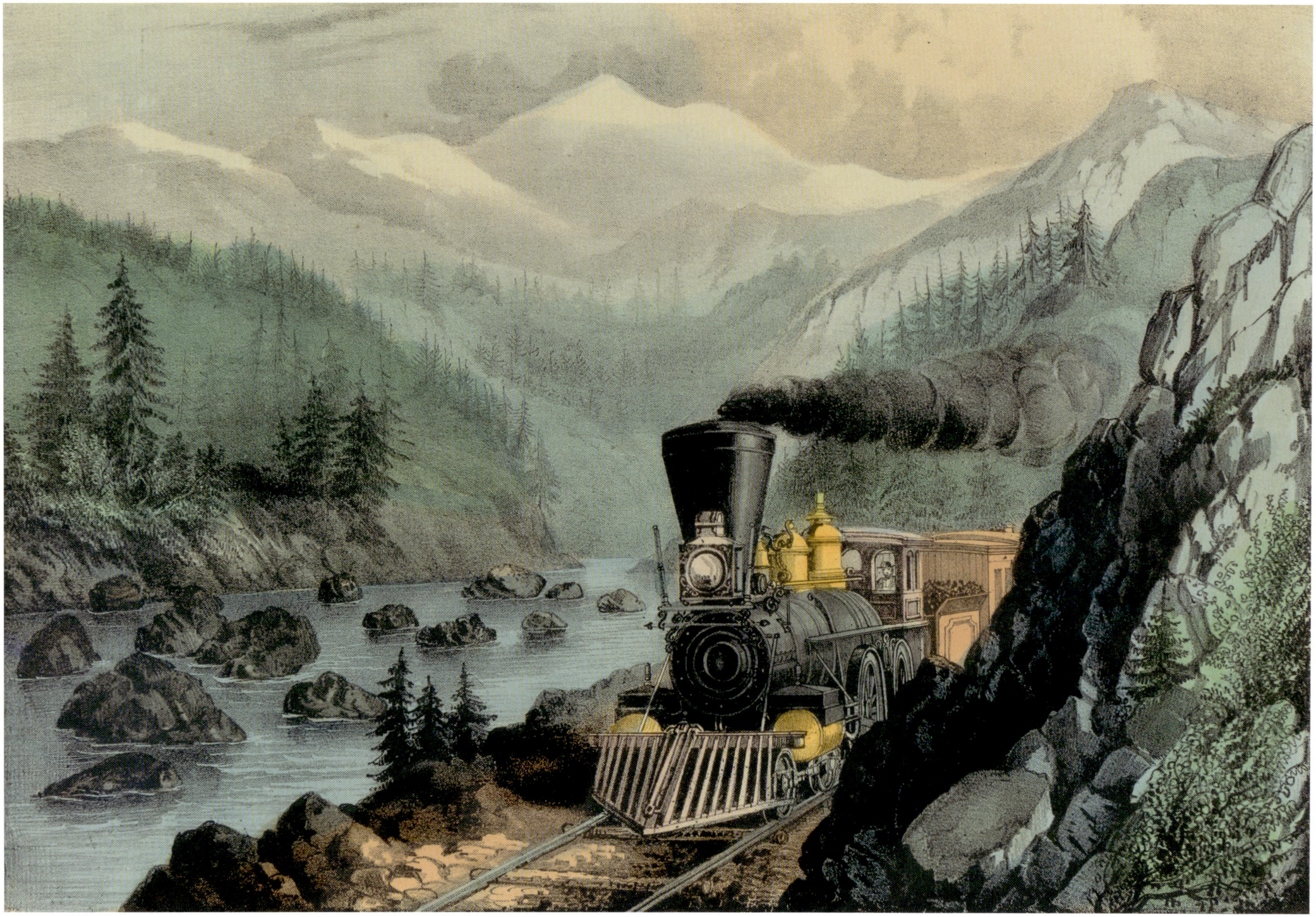

*The Route to California*
*Truckee River Sierra-Nevada*
1871

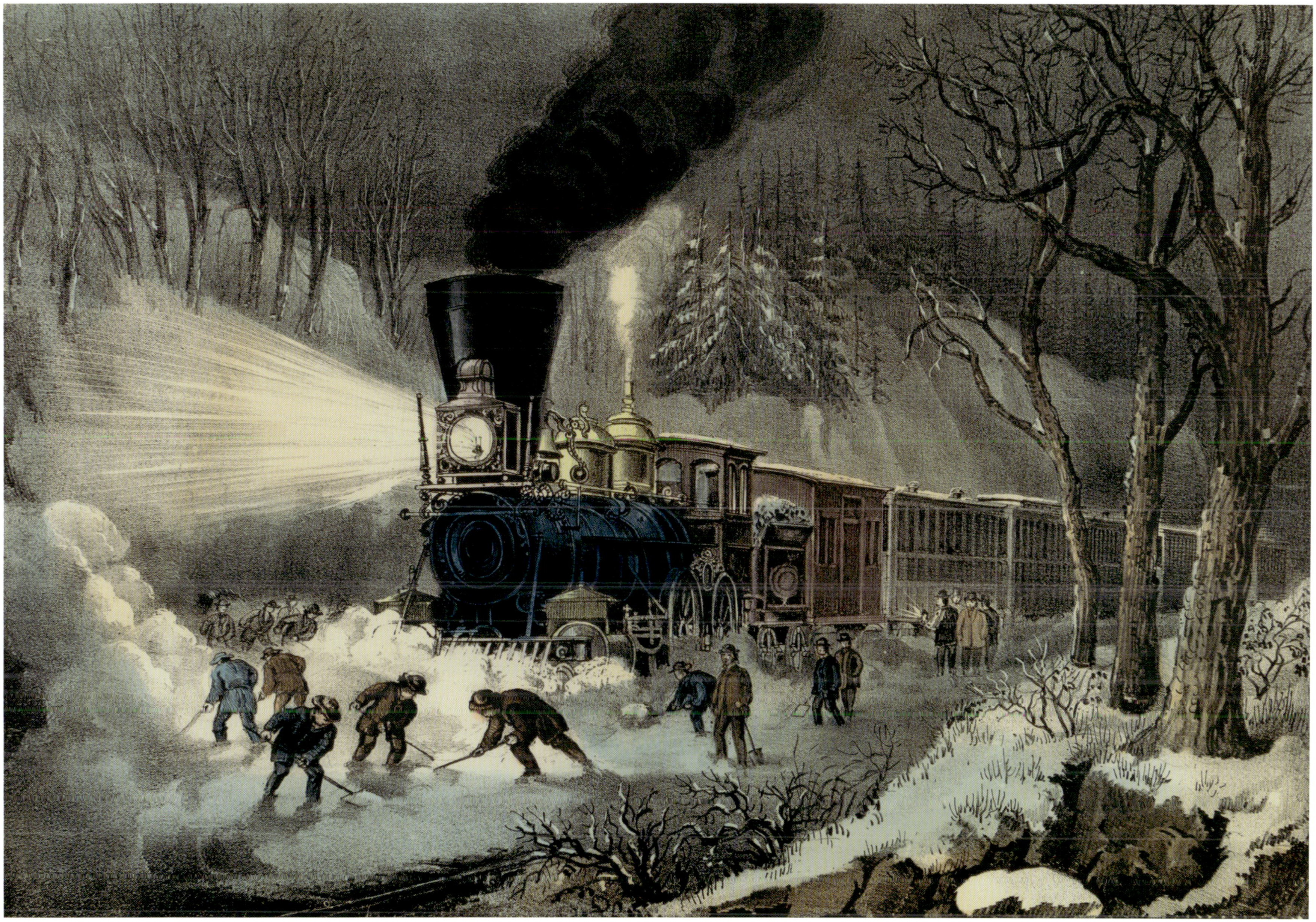

*American Railroad Scene*
***Snow Bound***
1871

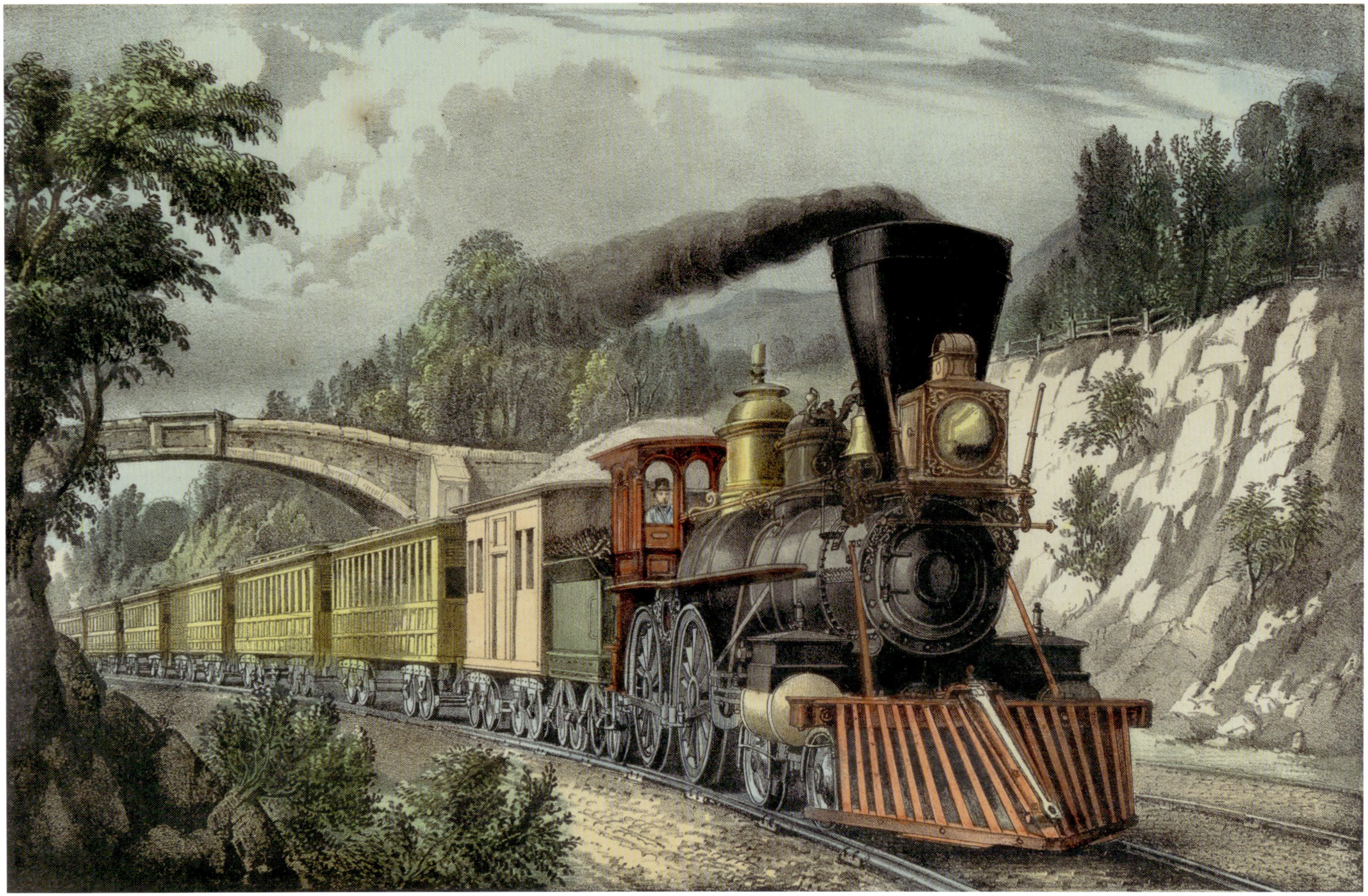

*The Express Train*

1870

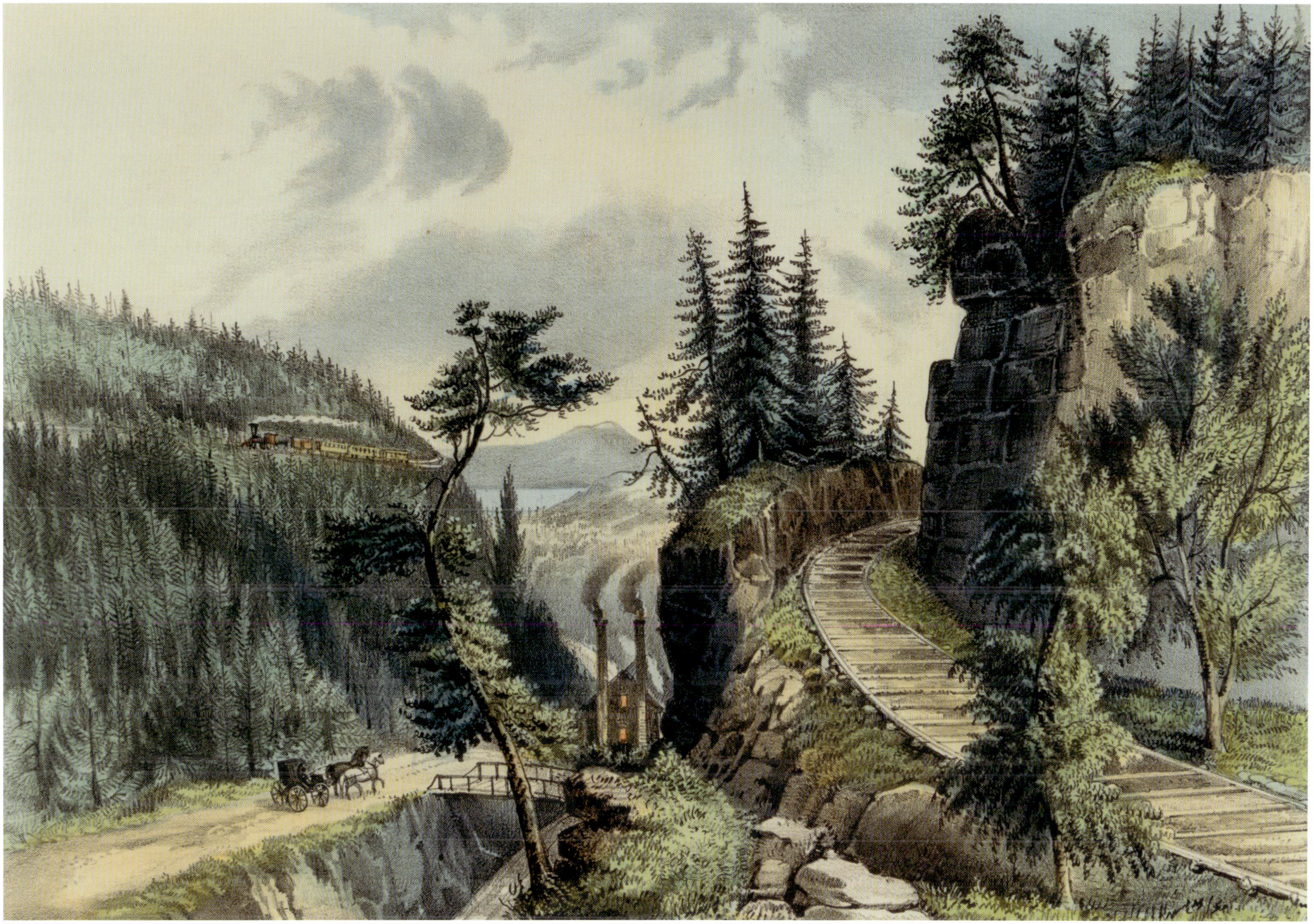

*Pensylvania* [sic] *Rail Road Scenery*

n.d.

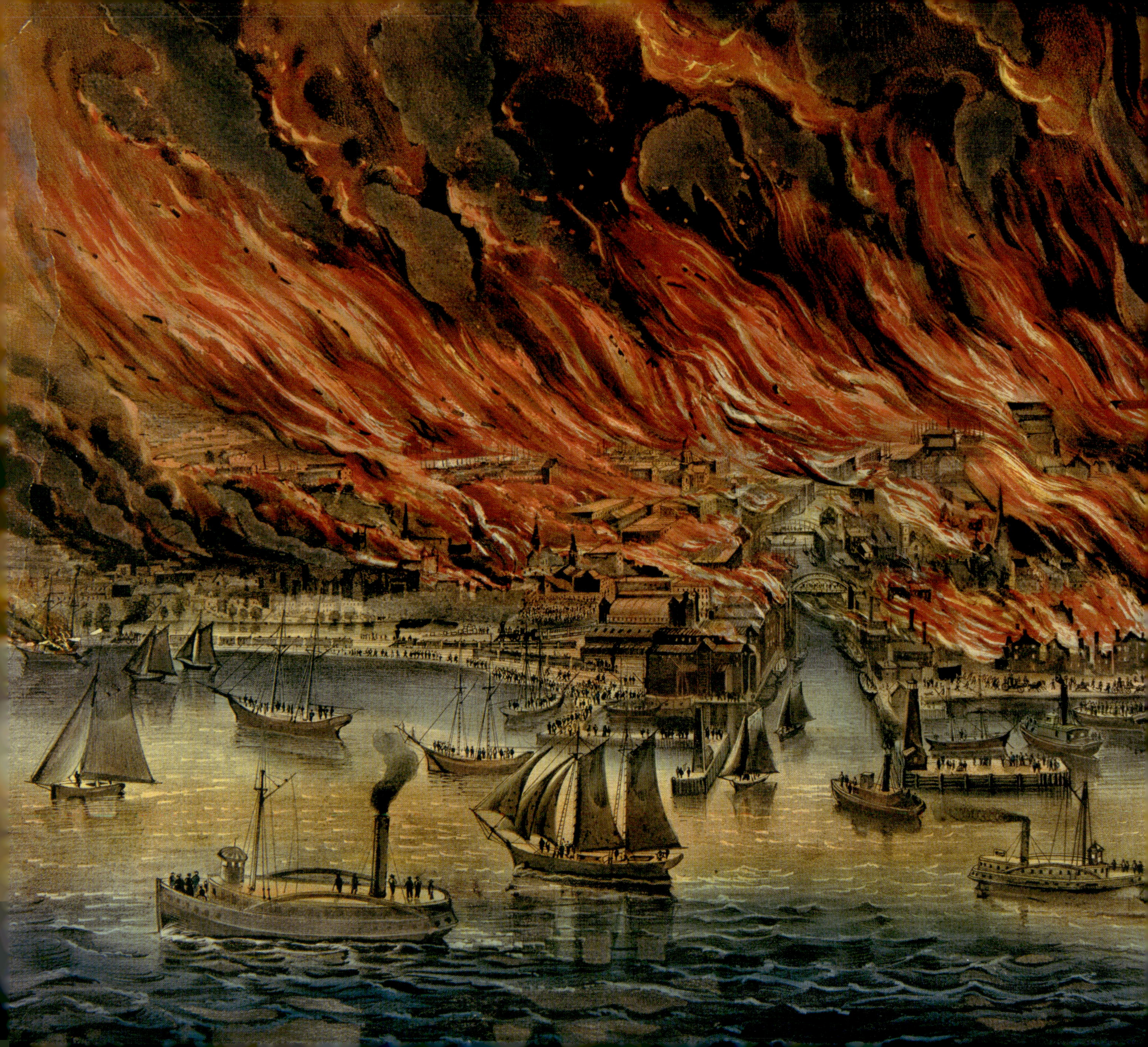

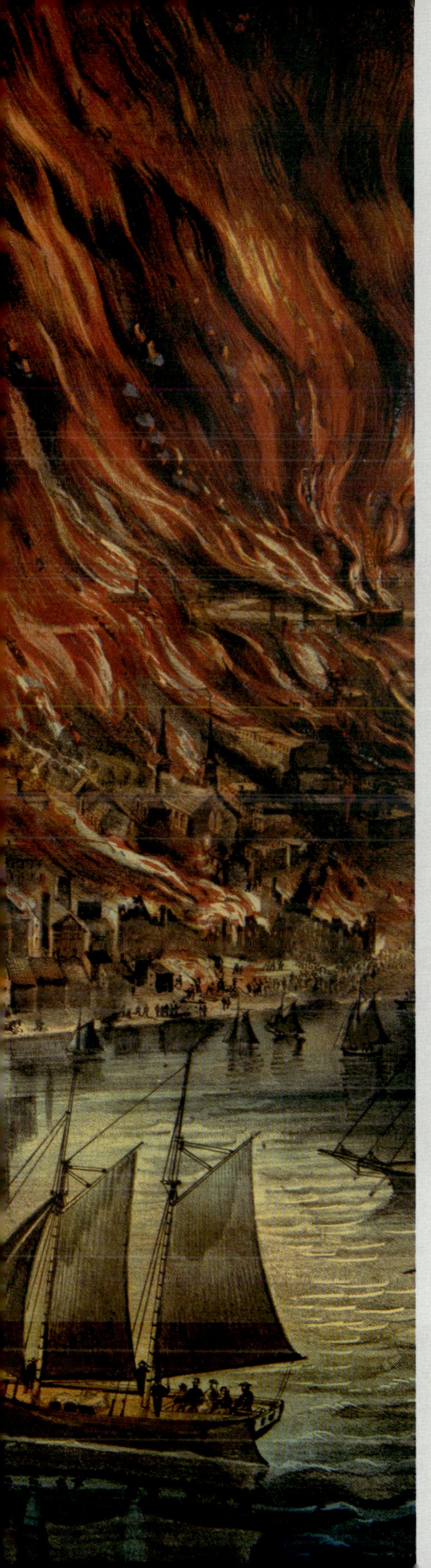

# URBAN EXPERIENCES

Along with changes in transportation technology came innovations in manufacturing. Cities filled with factory jobs and economic opportunities that attracted people from all over the country and around the world. Urban development elicited pride in economic growth and national expansion, but the workforce that sustained the American industrial revolution also brought with it social upheaval. Young men seeking economic opportunity flocked from rural areas to cities, leaving their families and communities behind, while millions of migrants to the United States settled in urban areas, bringing with them new languages, customs, and cultures. Americans had uncertain feelings about these transformations—while technological and engineering innovations gave a sense of pride and bolstered the economy, the single young men and poor immigrants who facilitated these modernizations were seen as a threat to the social fabric of the country. In their lithographs, Currier & Ives carefully avoided this social turmoil and depicted cities as clean places full of marvelous architecture and fashionable citizens, able to live lives of leisure. But many of their most popular prints of urban centers illustrated disasters, such as fires and explosions, speaking to Americans' interest in both the fantasy of city life and its dangerous reality.

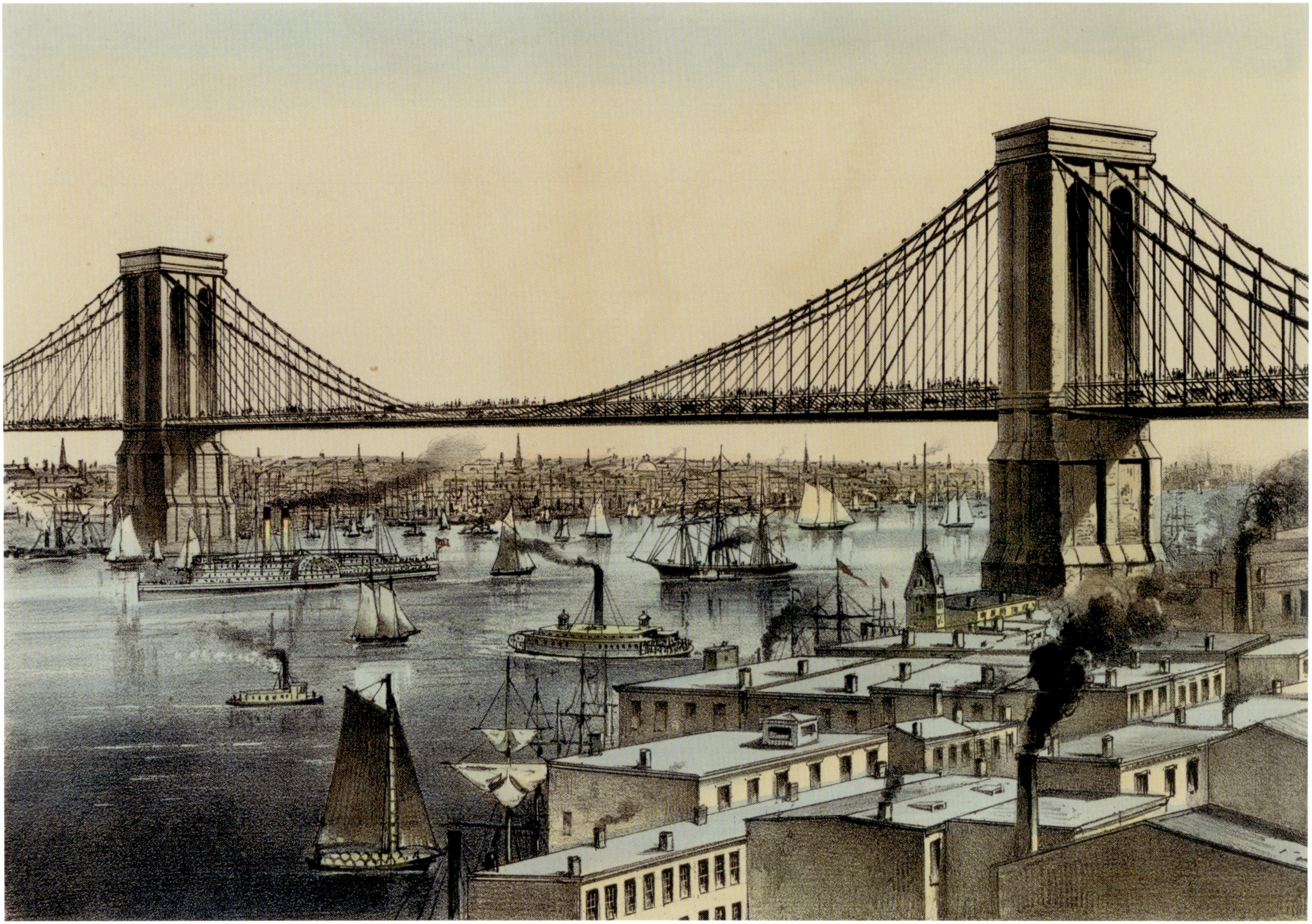

*The Great East River Bridge*
*To Connect the Cities of New York & Brooklyn*



1872

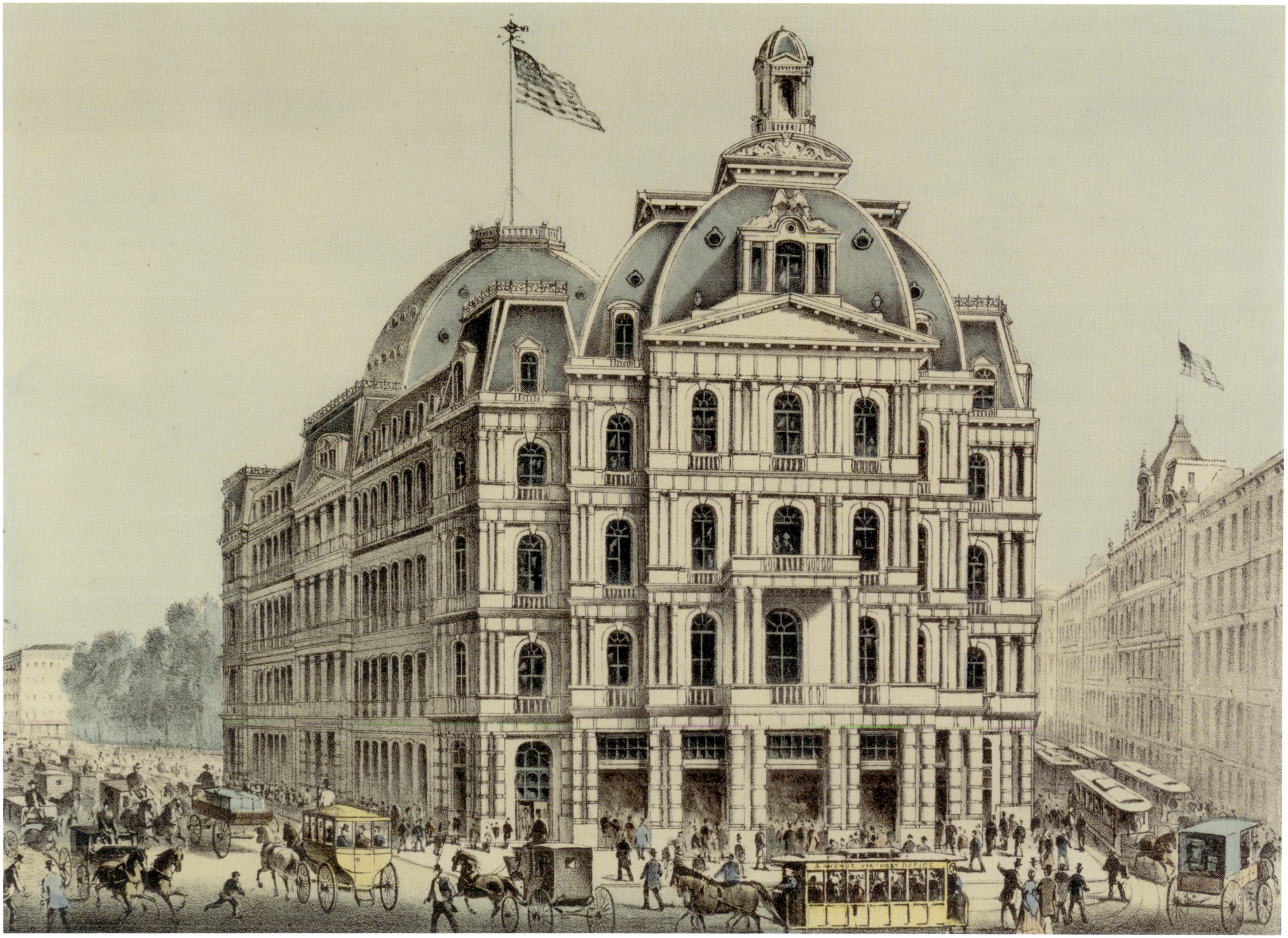

*U.S. Post Office, New York*

n.d.

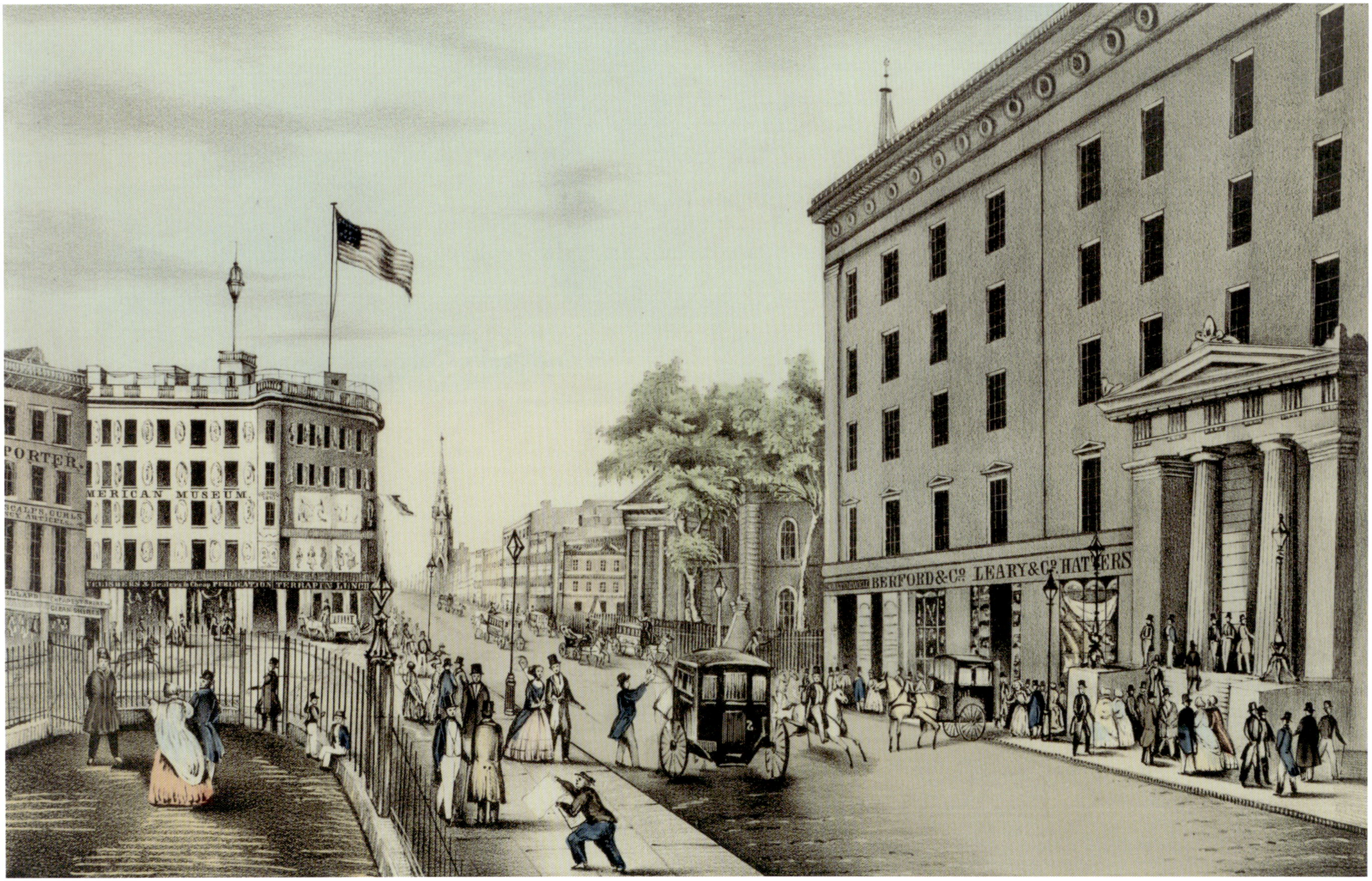


*Broadway New York*

n.d.

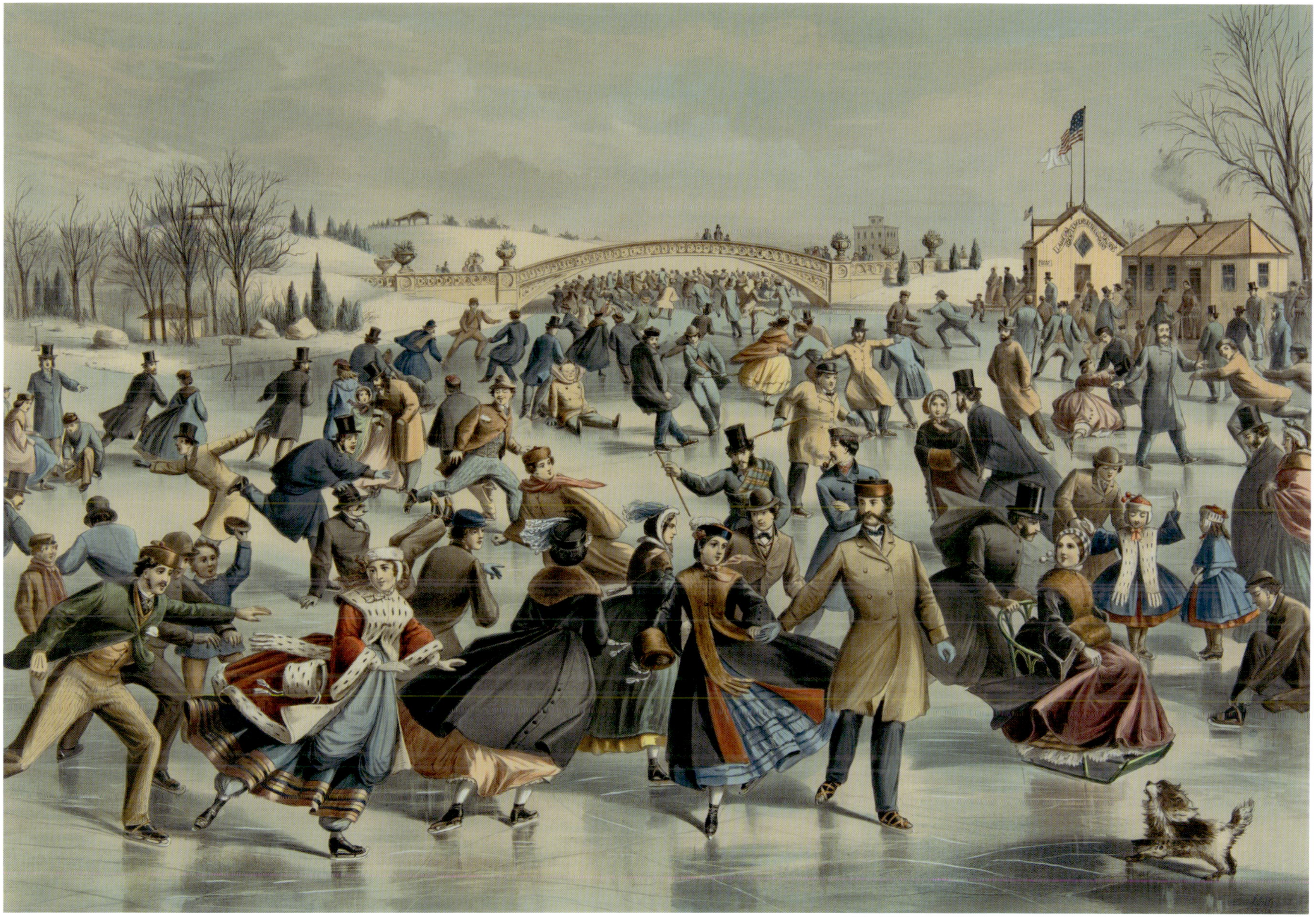

*Central-Park, Winter*

***The Skating Pond***

1862

Charles Parsons, AMERICAN (BORN ENGLAND), 1821–1910

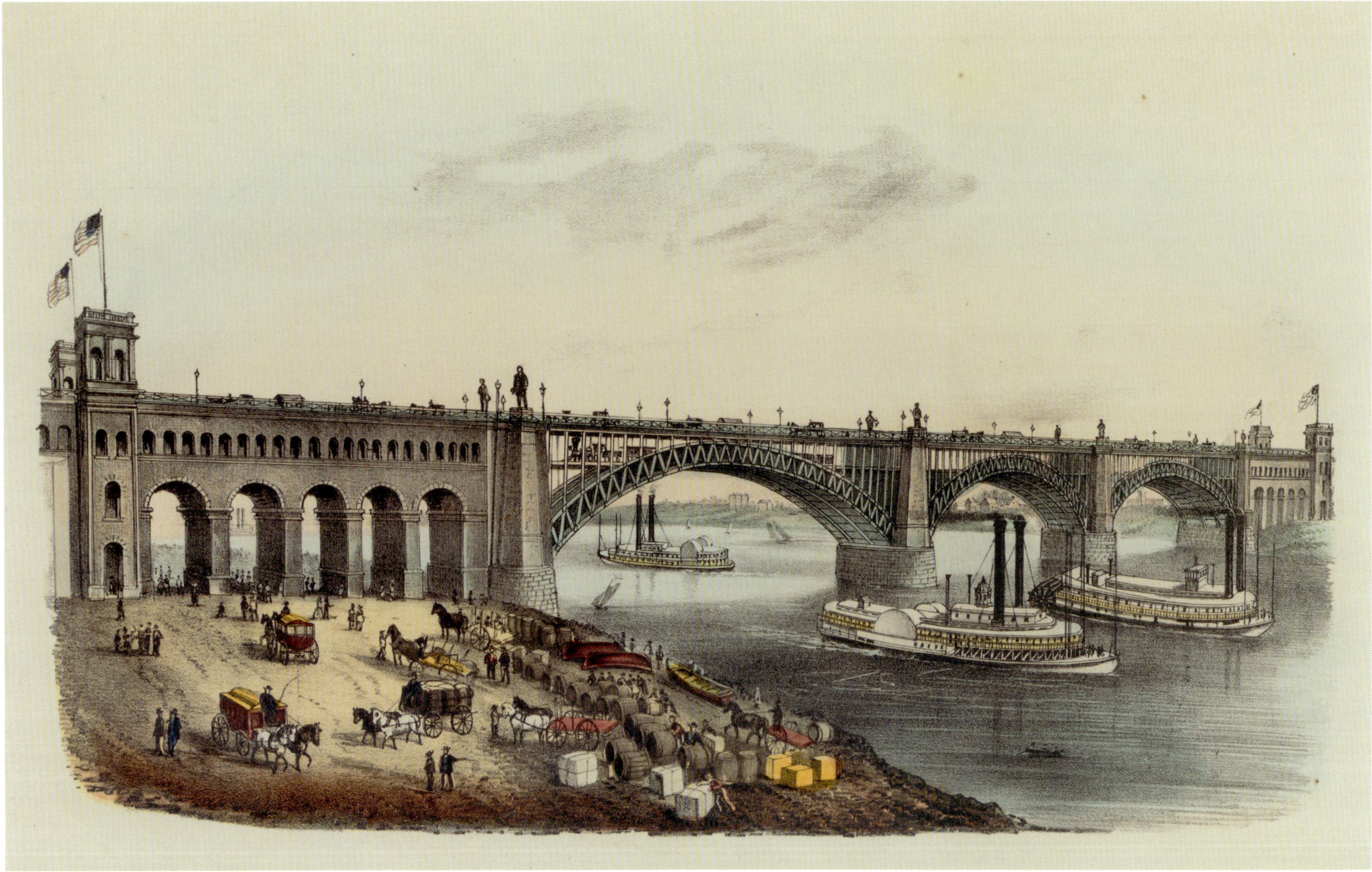

*The Great St. Louis Bridge*

*Across the Mississippi River*

ca. 1874

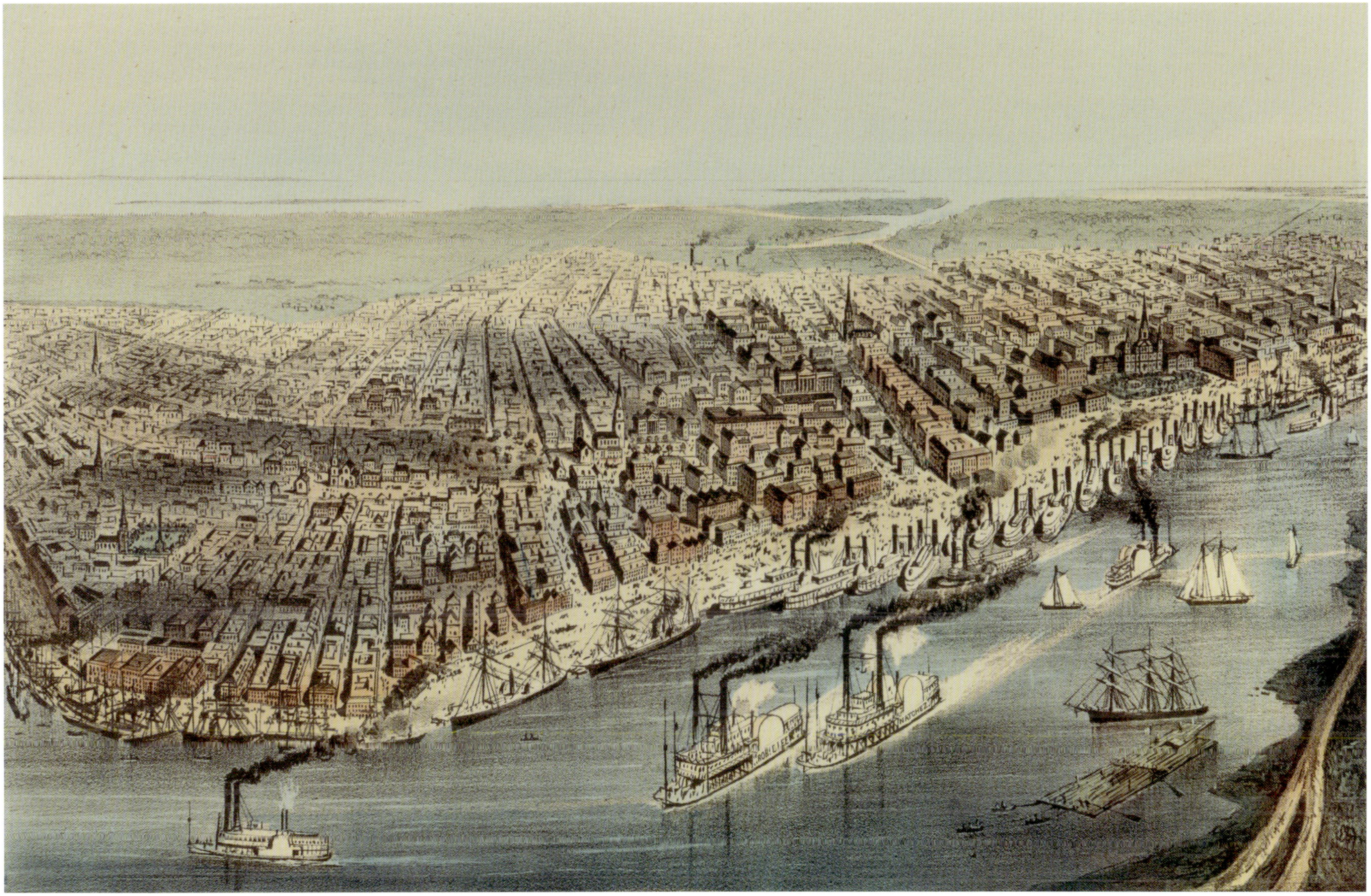

*City of New Orleans*

n.d.

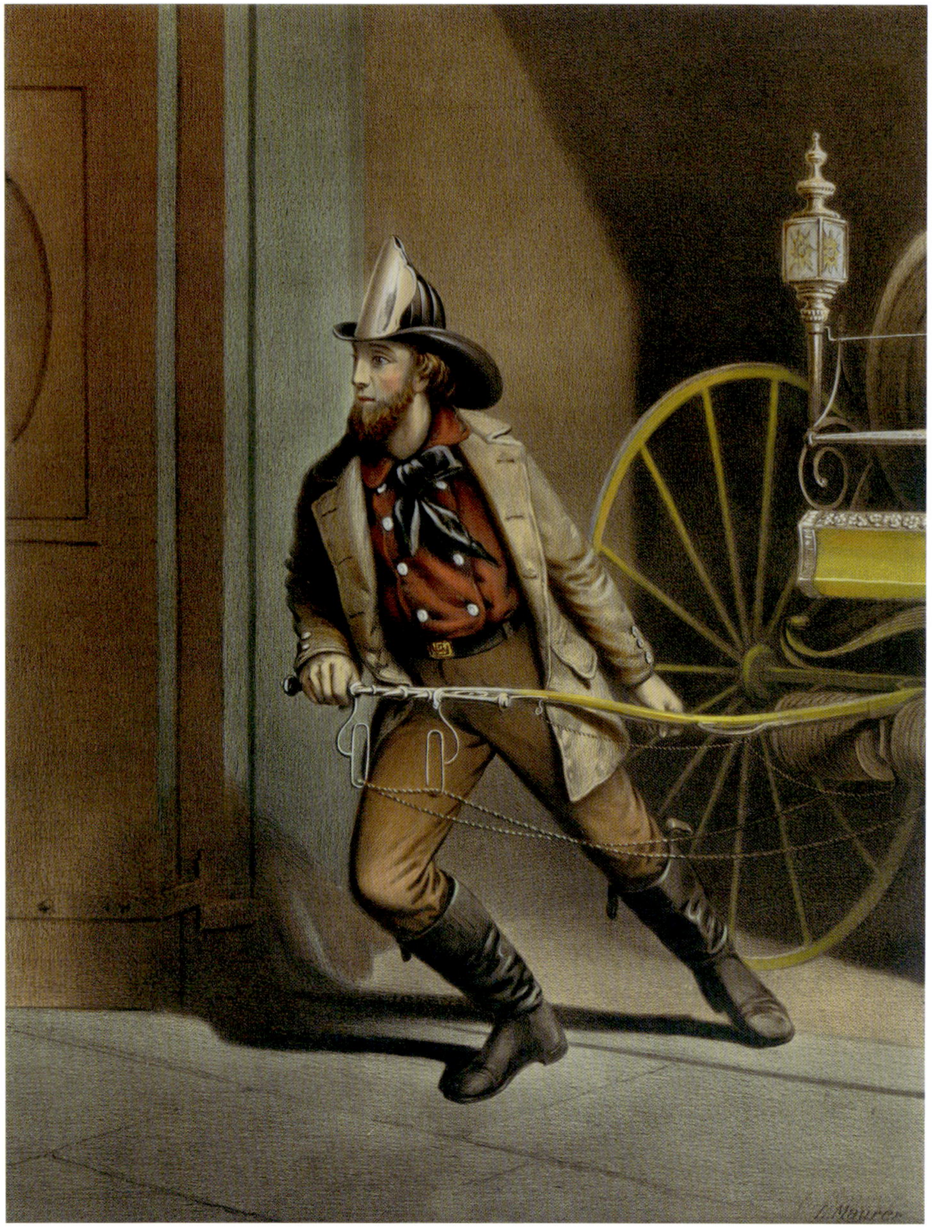


*The American Fireman*

***Always Ready***

1858

Louis Maurer, AMERICAN (BORN GERMANY), 1832–1932

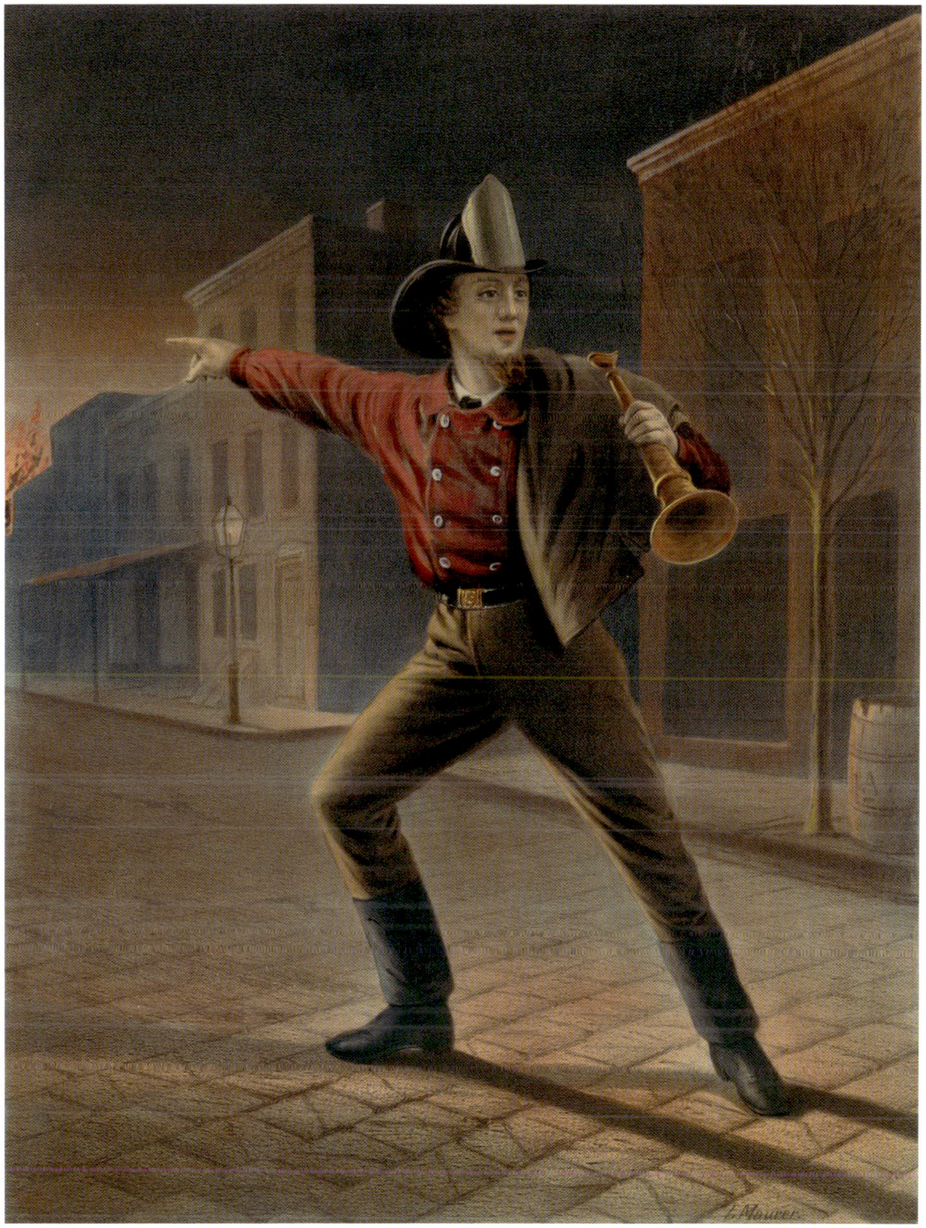

*The American Fireman*

***Rushing to the Conflict***

1858

Louis Maurer, AMERICAN (BORN GERMANY), 1832–1932

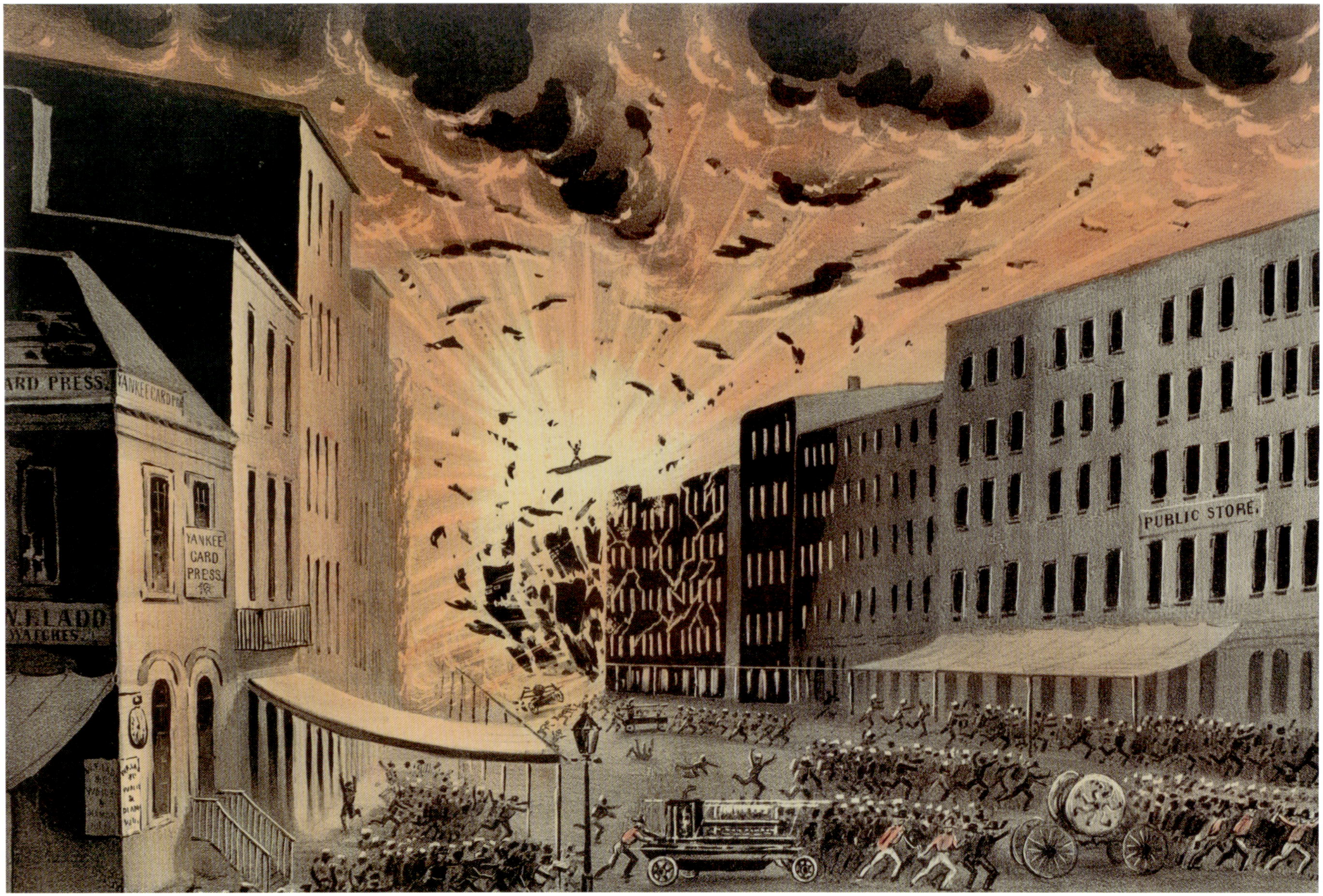


*View of the Terrific Explosion at the Great Fire in New York*
*From Broad St. July 19th 1845*

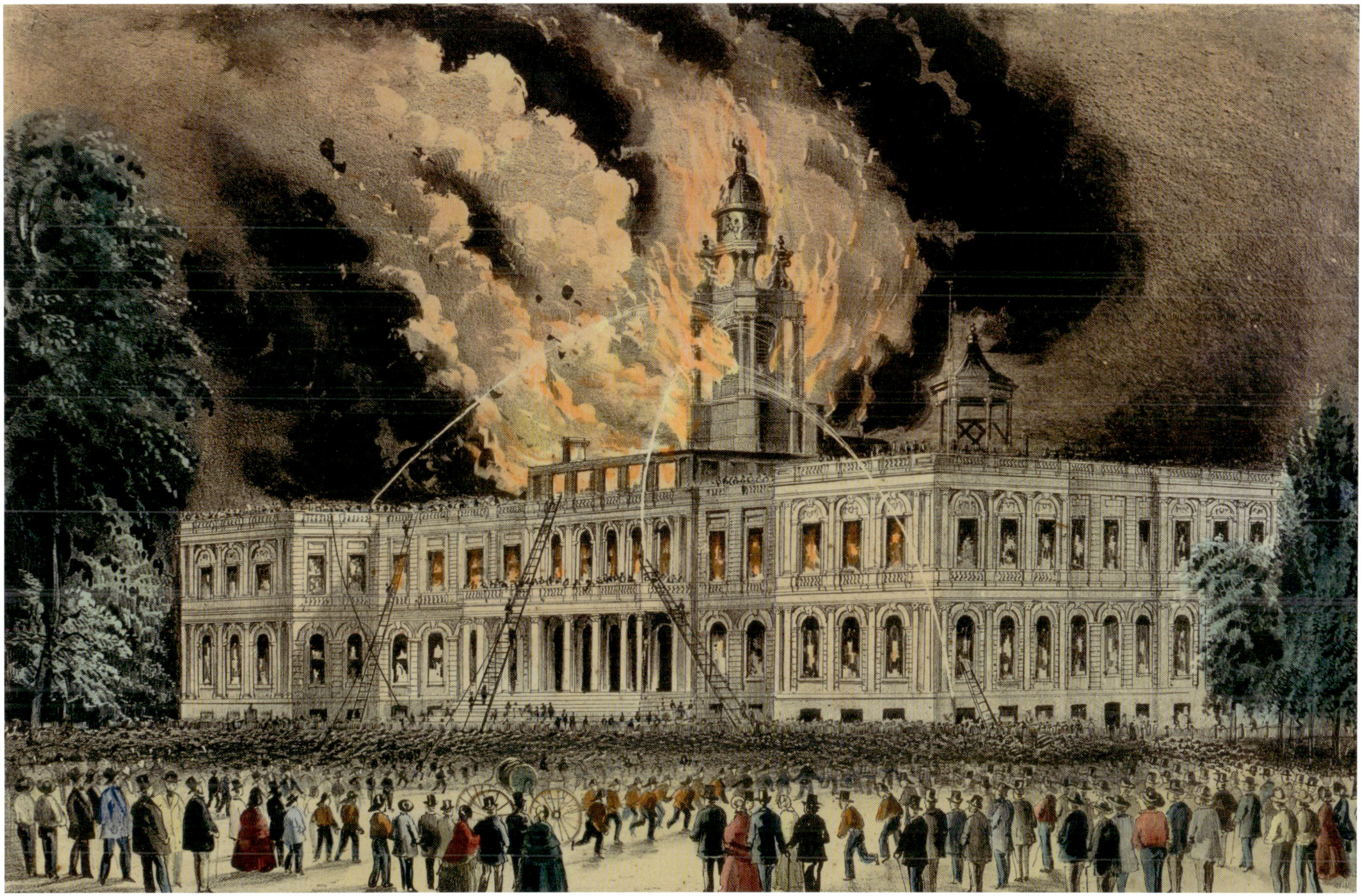

*Burning of the City Hall New York*

1858

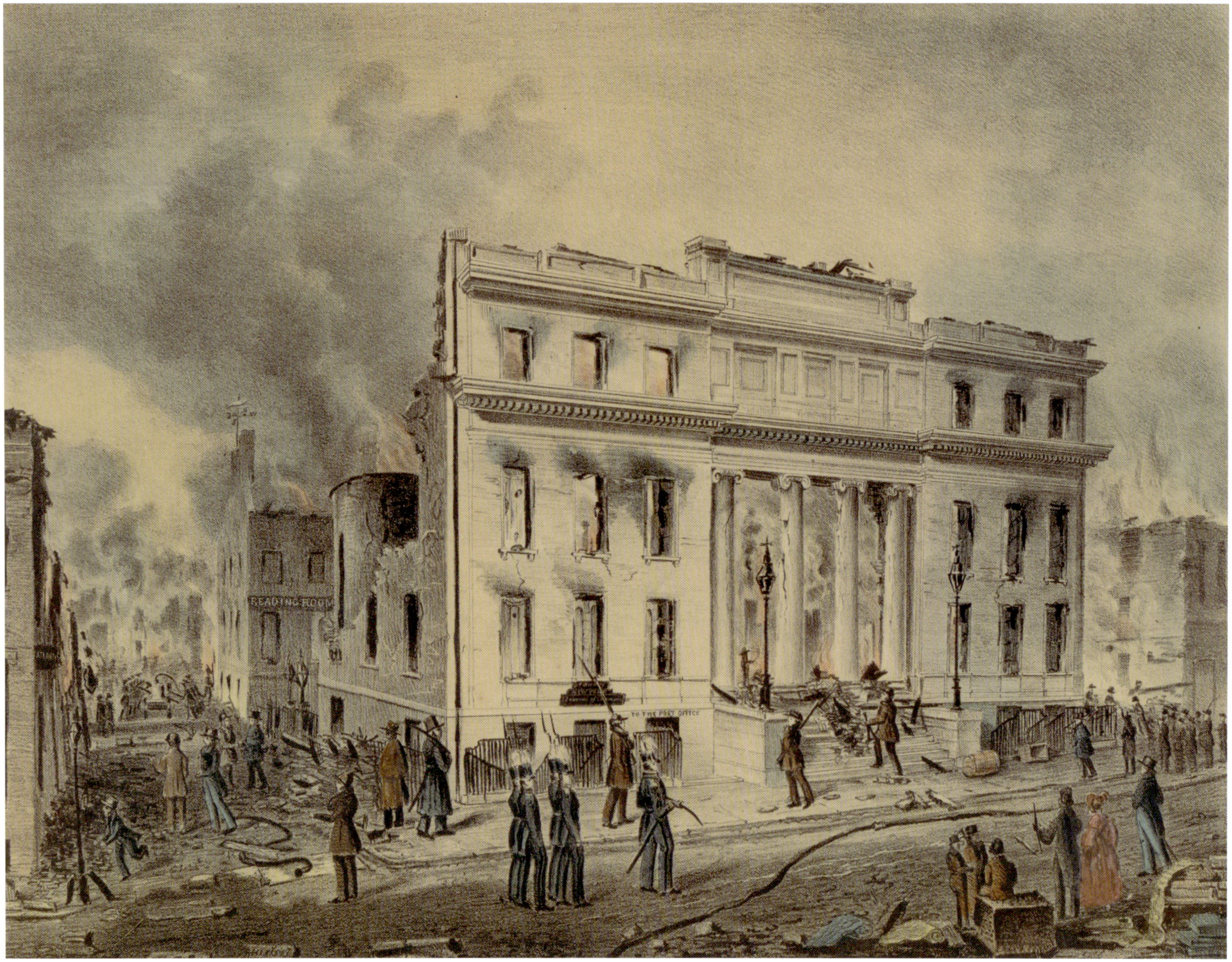


*Ruins of the Merchant's Exchange N.Y.*
*After the Destructive Conflagration of Decbr. 16 & 17 1835*

1835

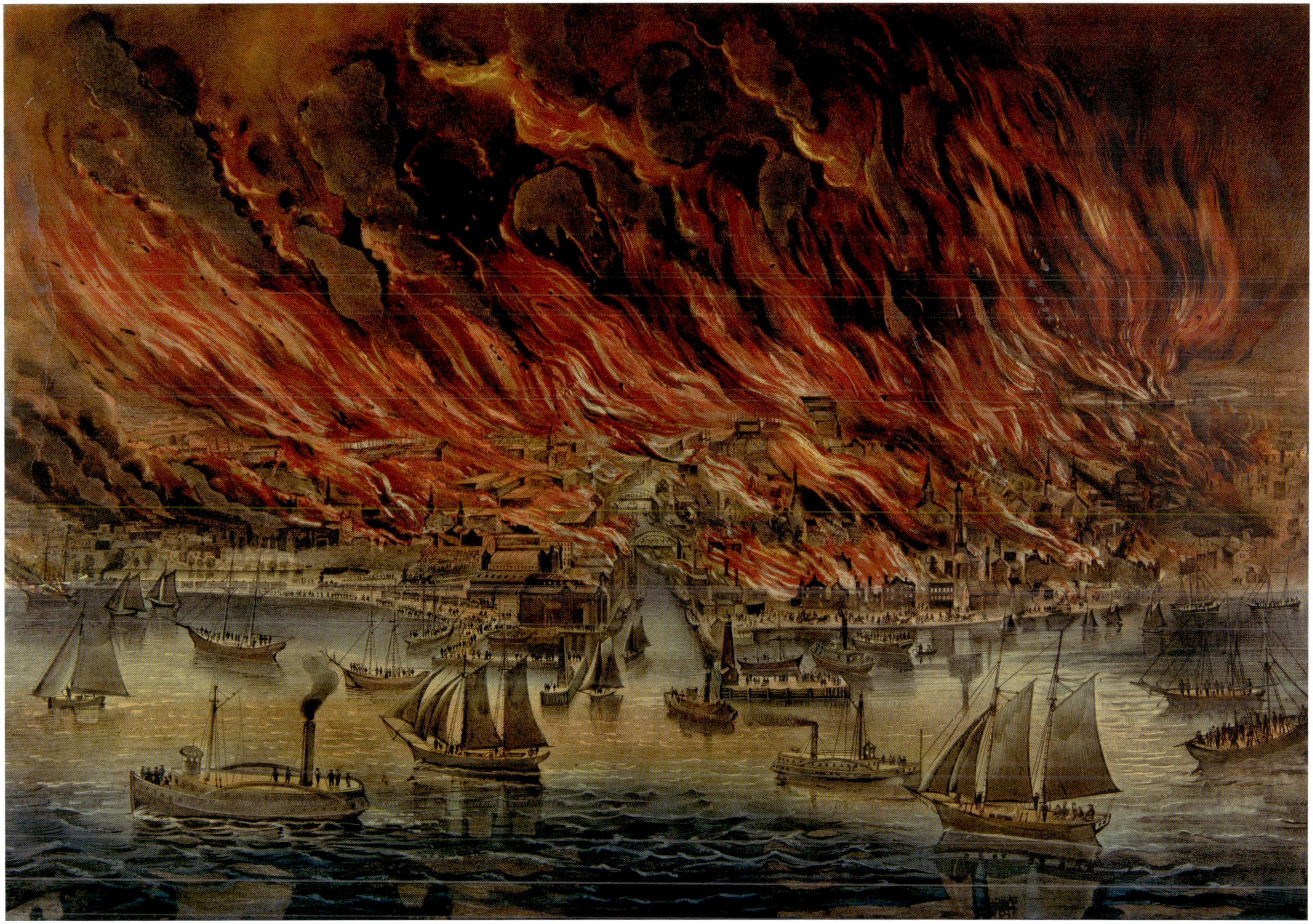

*The Great Fire at Chicago, Octr. 8th. 1871*

1871

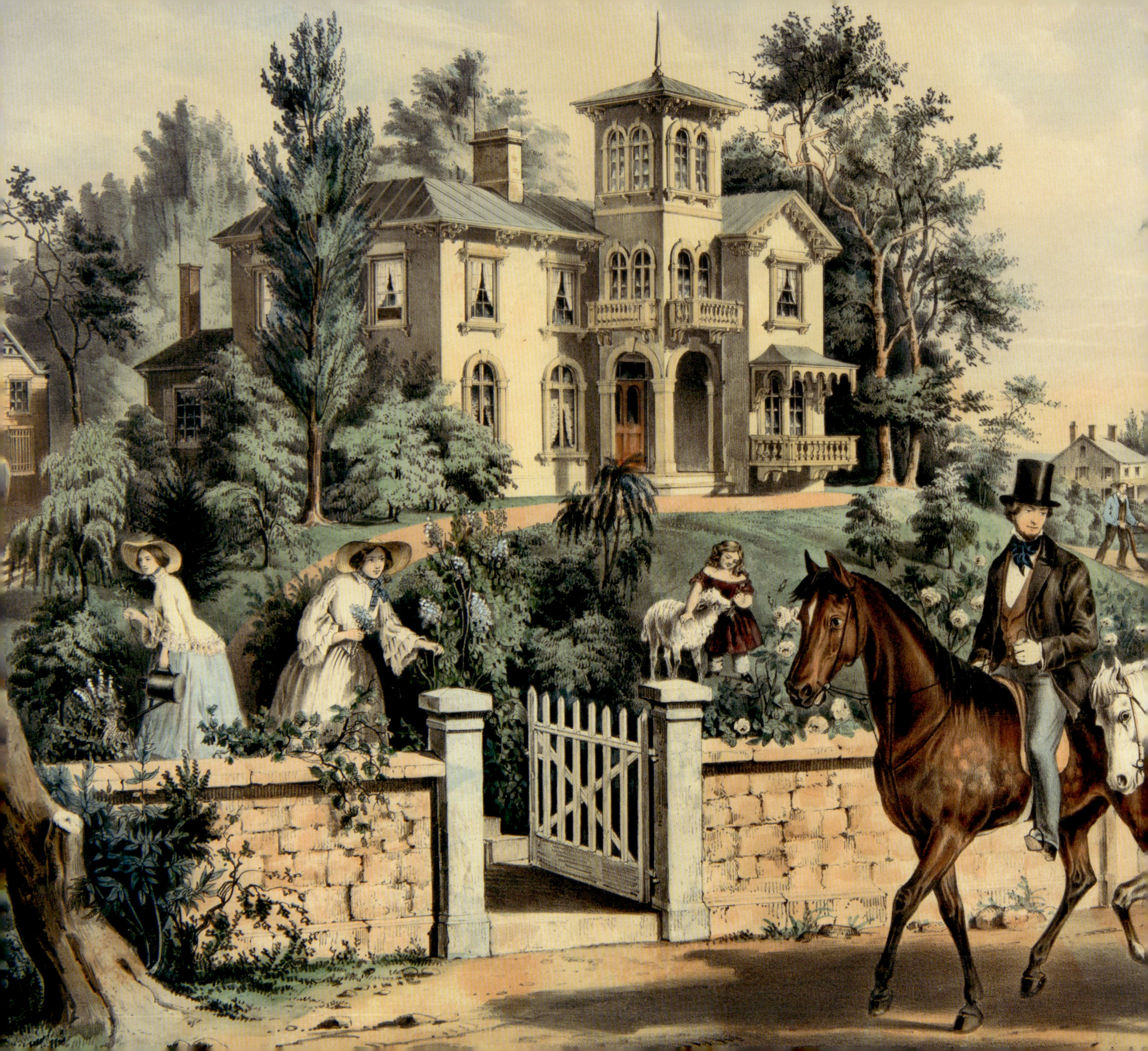

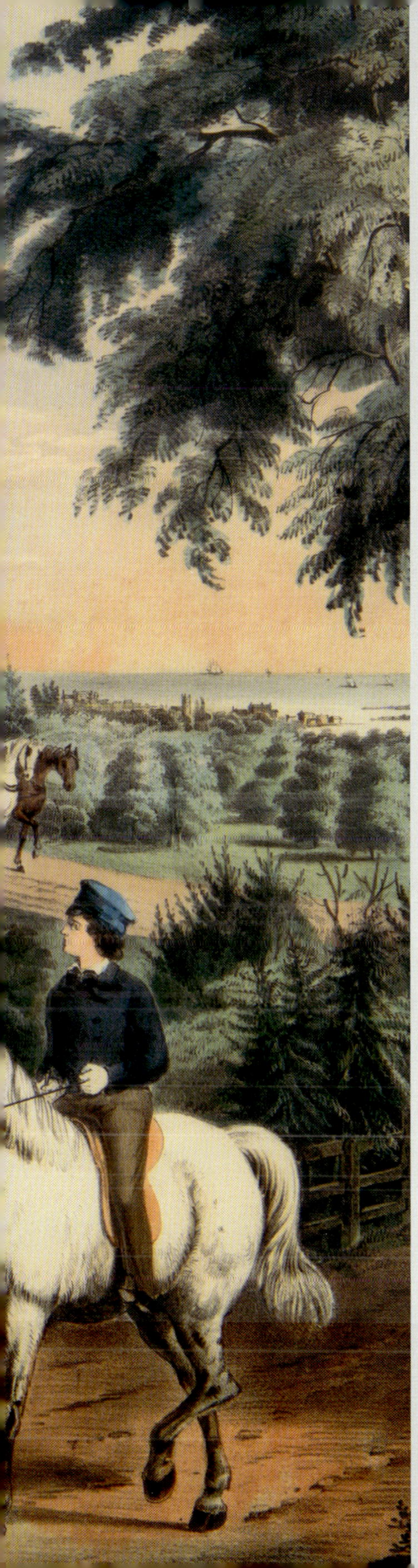

# DOMESTIC VISIONS

Just as rural Americans were dreaming of life in Currier & Ives's idealized vision of the city, urban Americans longed for the countryside they had left behind—or the one they imagined they had. Central to Victorian American culture, the home was a haven of peace, refinement, and morality, protecting the family from the world outside. The ideal home was also the domain of middle- and upper-class women, and prints played an important role in their home décor. Affordable works of art such as those offered by Currier & Ives reflected a woman's ability to create a nurturing environment for her family. As urbanization expanded in the second half of the nineteenth century, many American middle-class families moved to the city's fringes or dreamed of a second home in the country. Accordingly, Currier & Ives multiplied its offering of prints depicting prosperous farm life or ideal homesteads in suburban and rural landscapes. Focusing on leisure time enjoyed by the upper classes in the country, these images painted a rosy picture of the countryside, often using nostalgic symbols of Colonial America to remind viewers of simpler times marked by agricultural bounty and natural beauty.

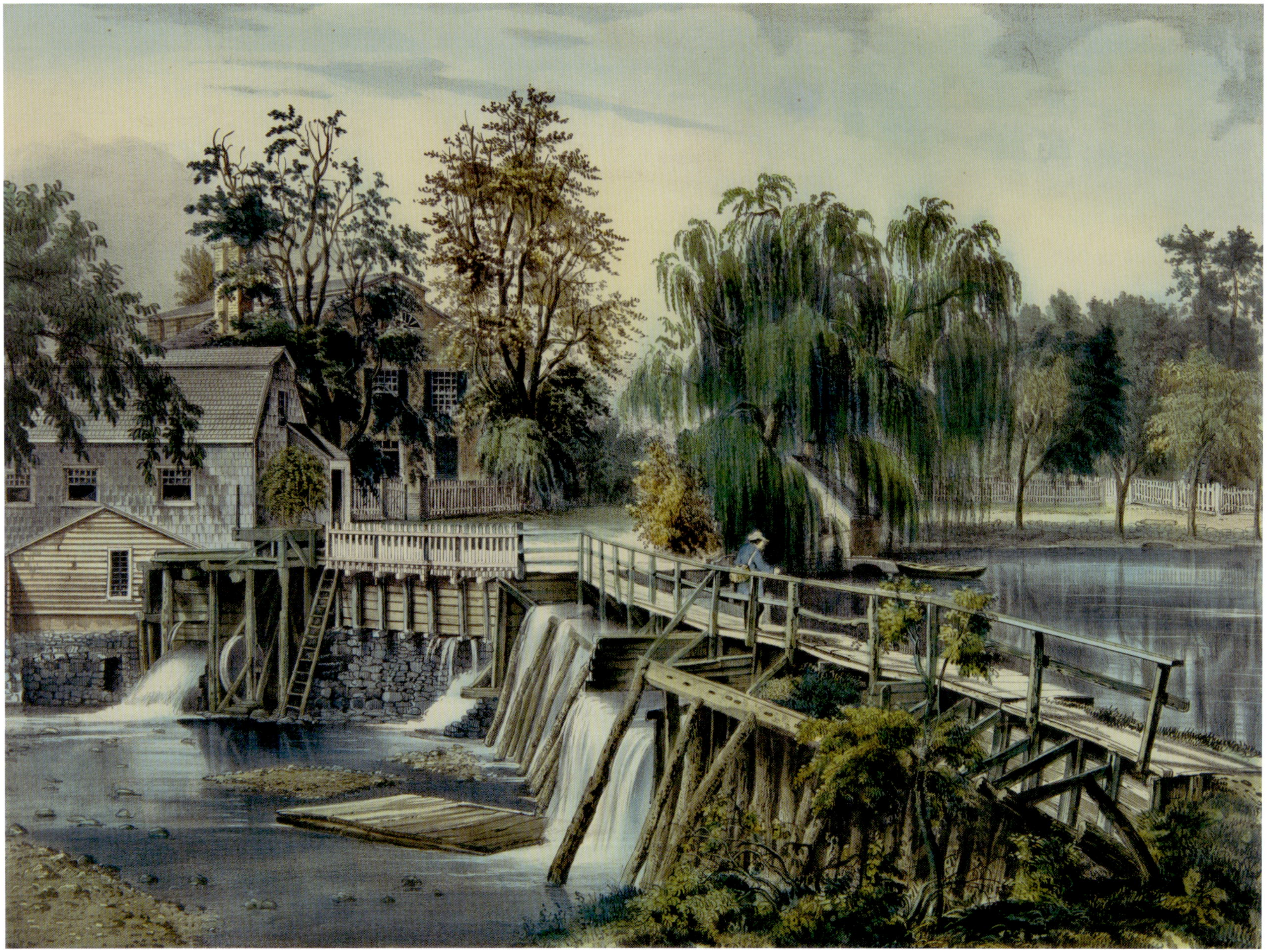

*The Mill-Dam at Sleepy Hollow*

ca. 1857–71

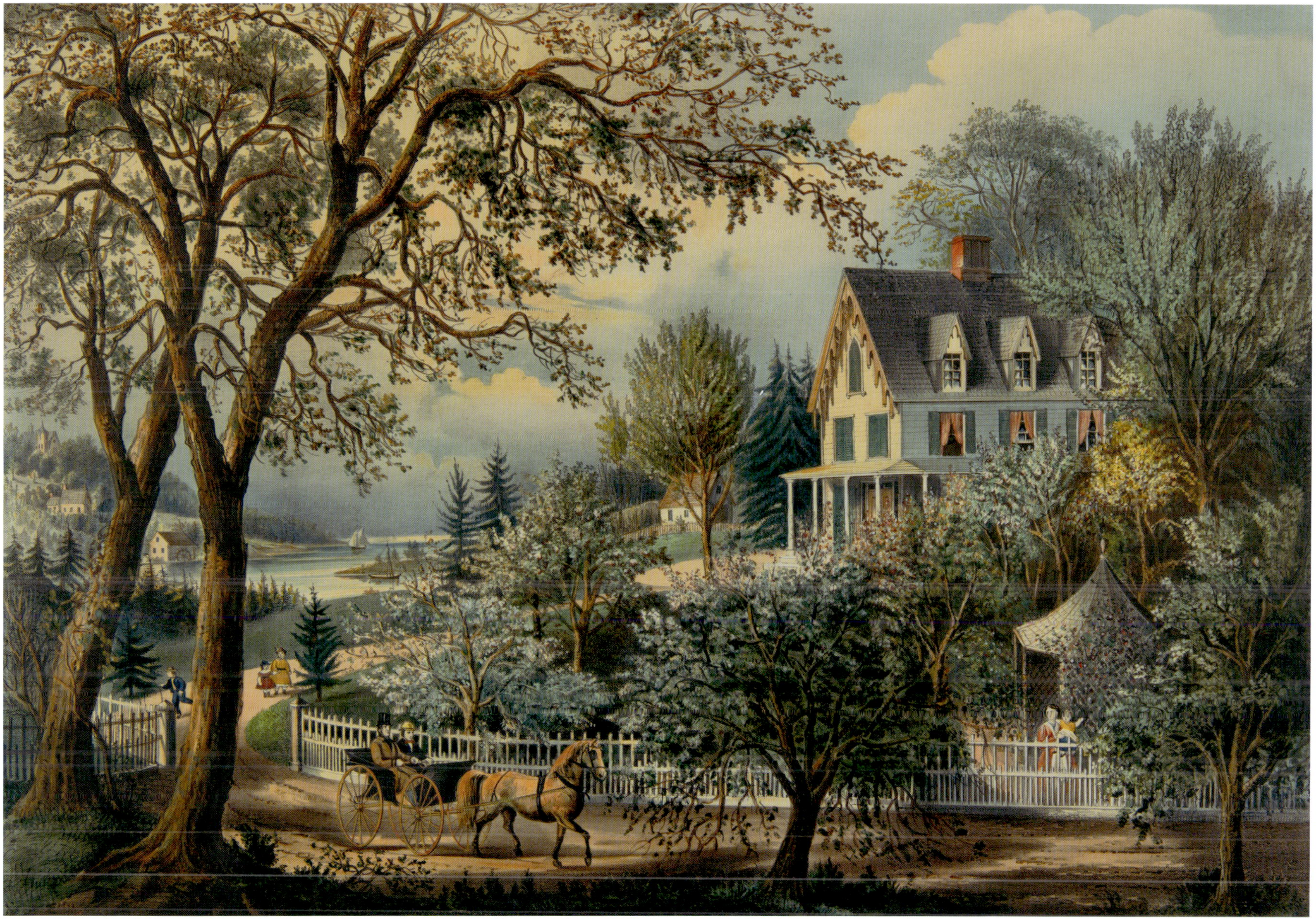

*The Season of Blossoms*

1865

Frances Palmer, AMERICAN (BORN ENGLAND), 1812–1876

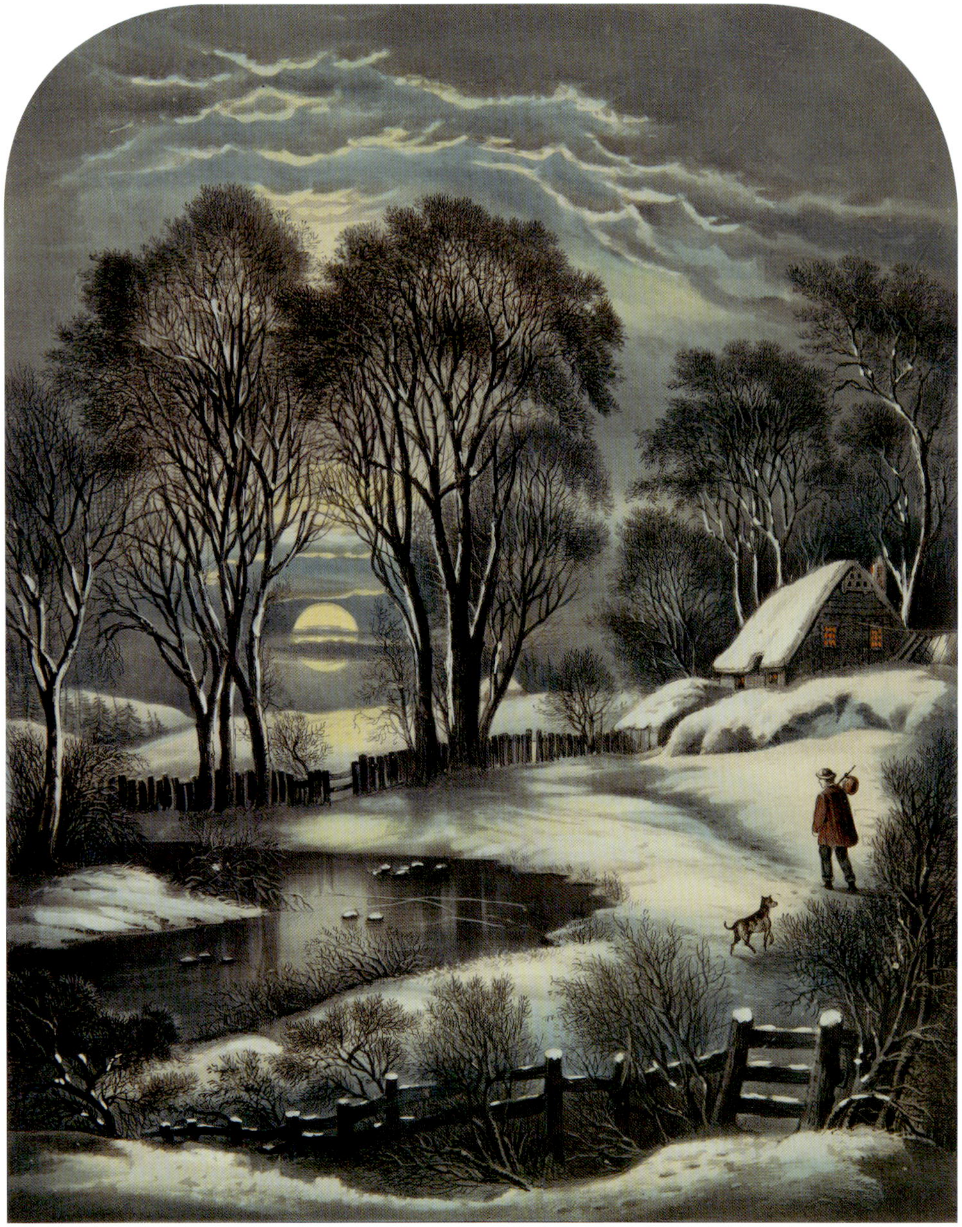

*Winter Moonlight*

1866

Frances Palmer, AMERICAN (BORN ENGLAND), 1812–1876

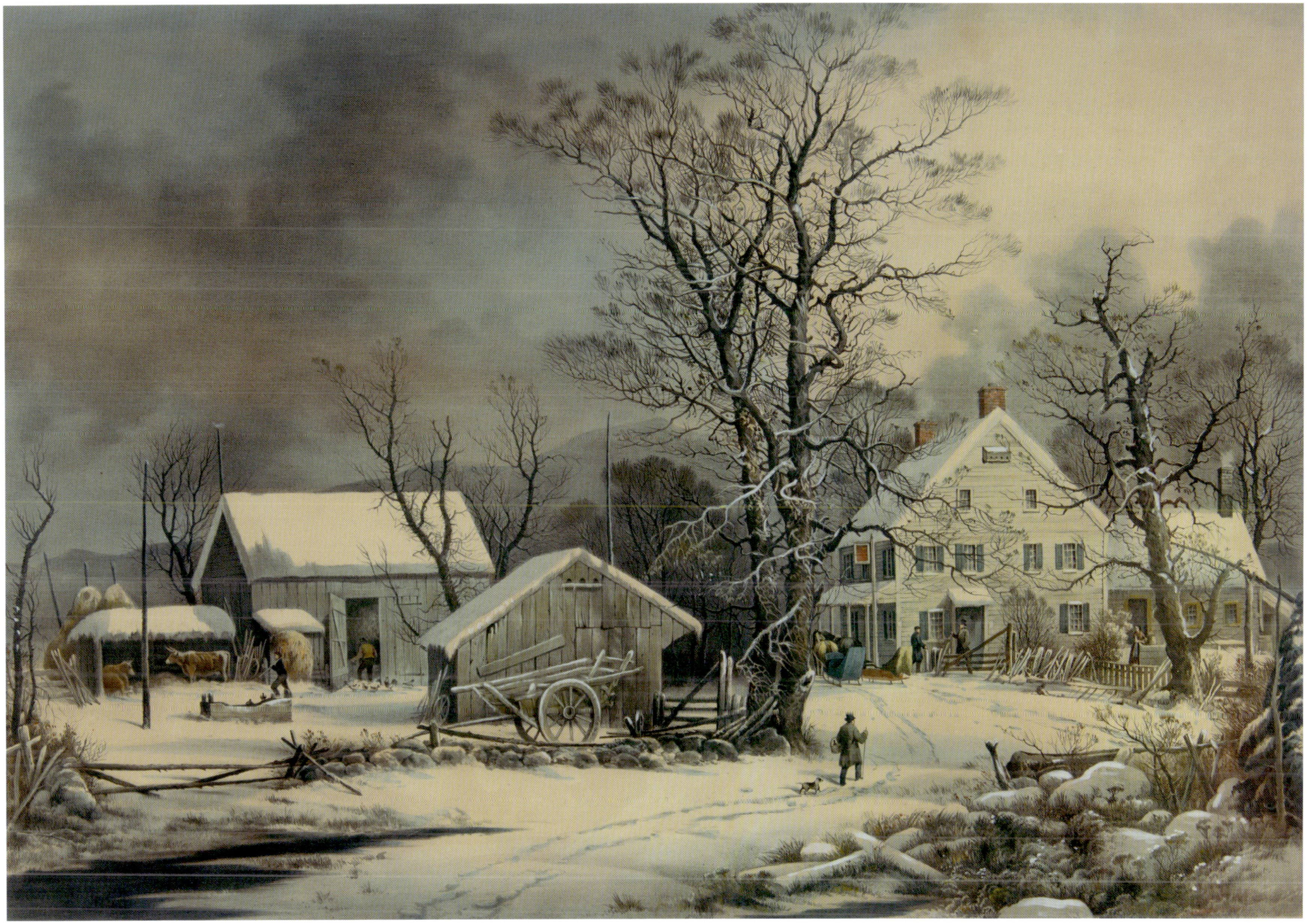

*Winter in the Country*

***A Cold Morning***

1864

George Henry Durrie, AMERICAN, 1820–1863

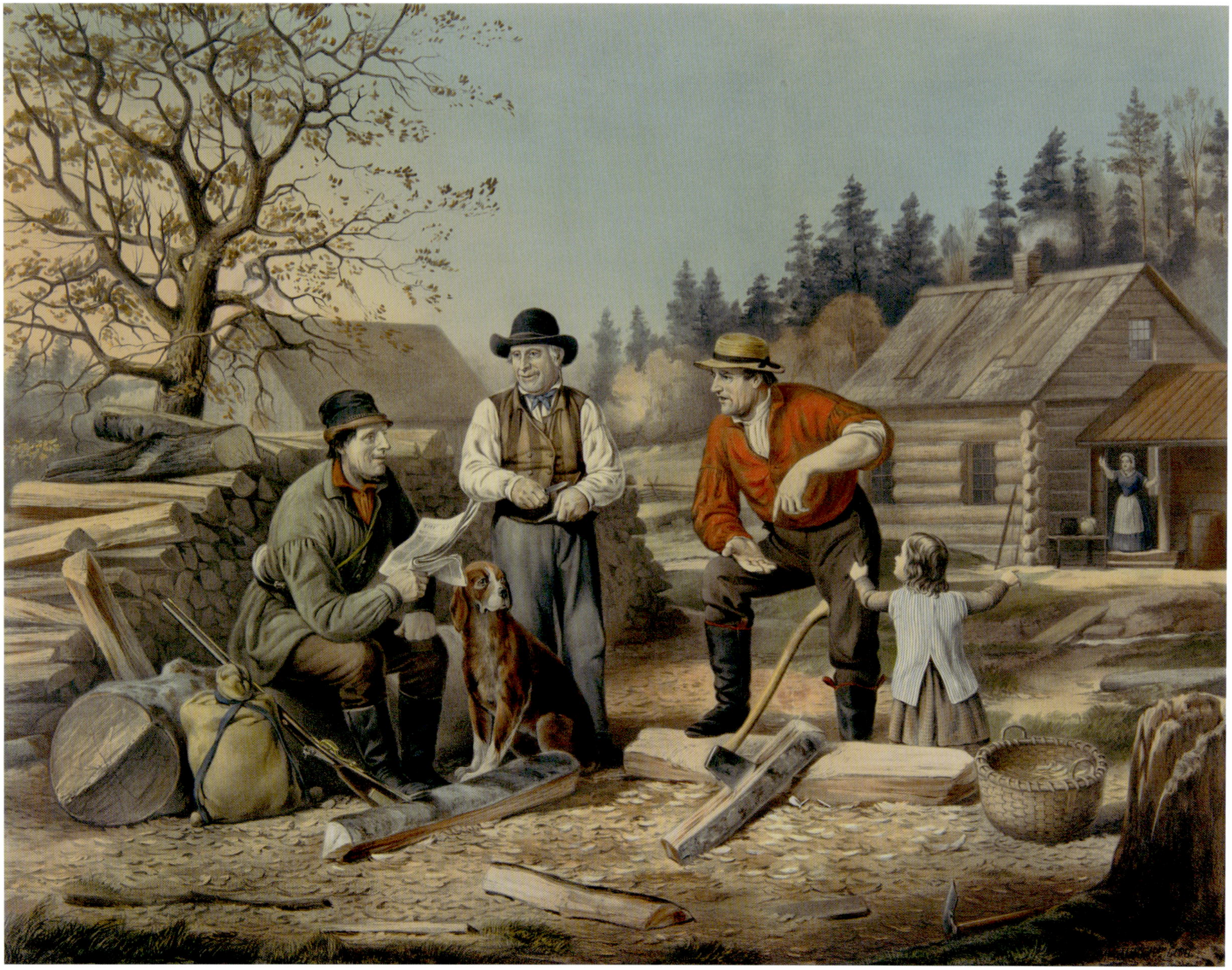

*Arguing the Point*

1855

Arthur Fitzwilliam Tait, AMERICAN (BORN ENGLAND), 1819–1905

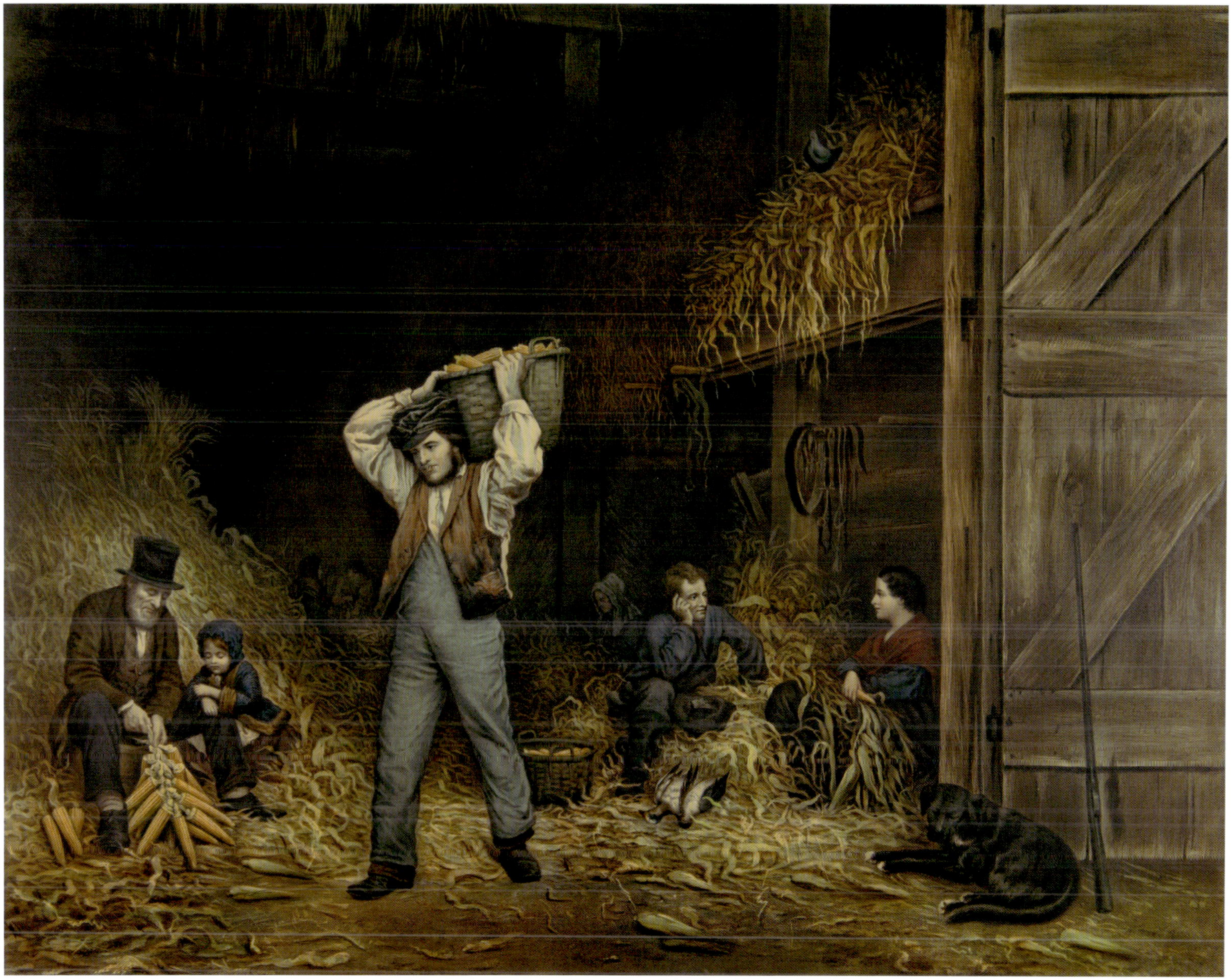

*Husking*

1861

Eastman Johnson, AMERICAN, 1824–1906

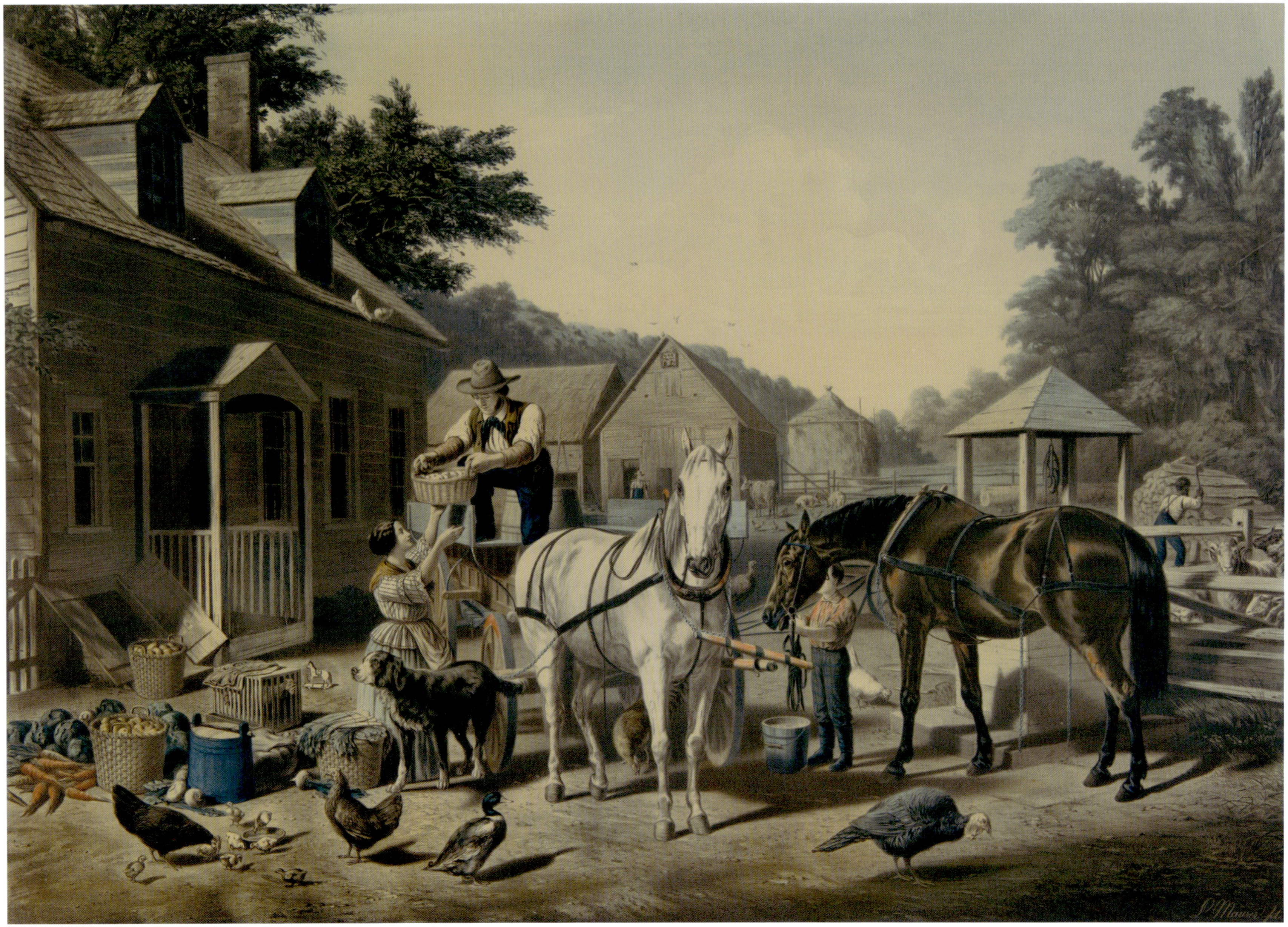

*Preparing for Market*

1856

Louis Maurer, AMERICAN (BORN GERMANY), 1832–1932

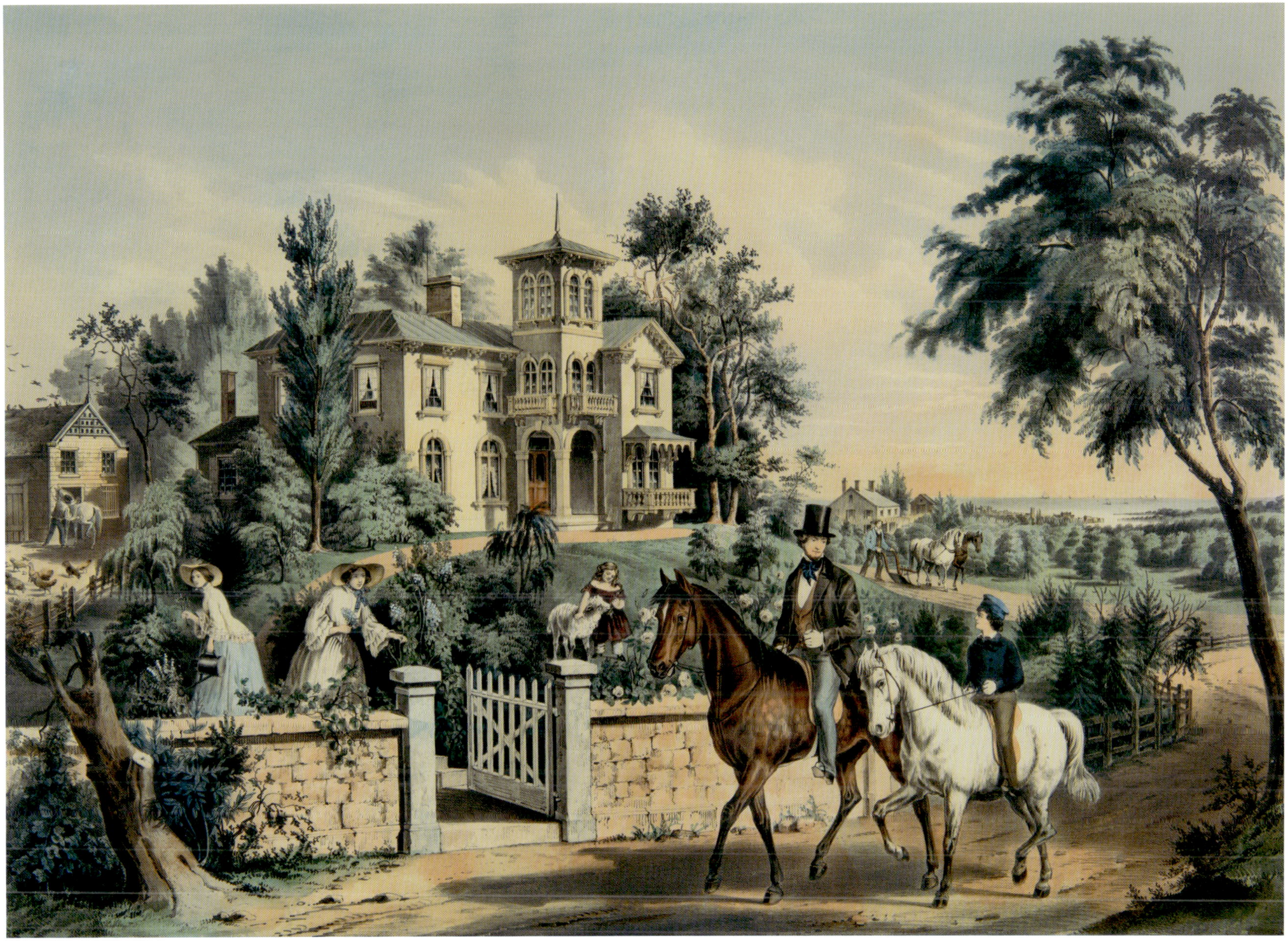

*American Country Life*

***May Morning***

1855

Frances Palmer, AMERICAN (BORN ENGLAND), 1812–1876

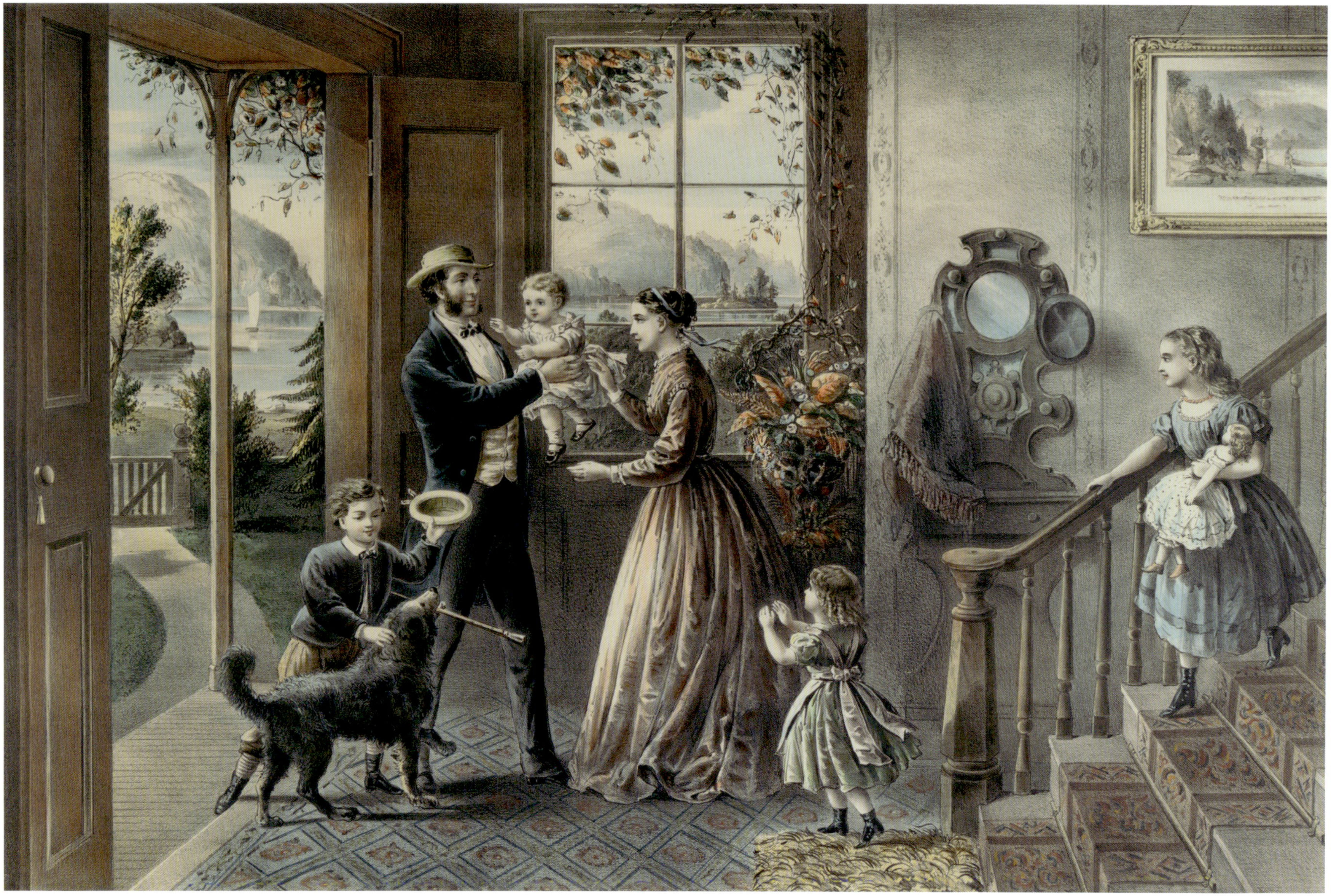

*The Four Seasons of Life: Middle Age*
*The Season of Strength*
1868
Charles Parsons, AMERICAN (BORN ENGLAND), 1821–1910

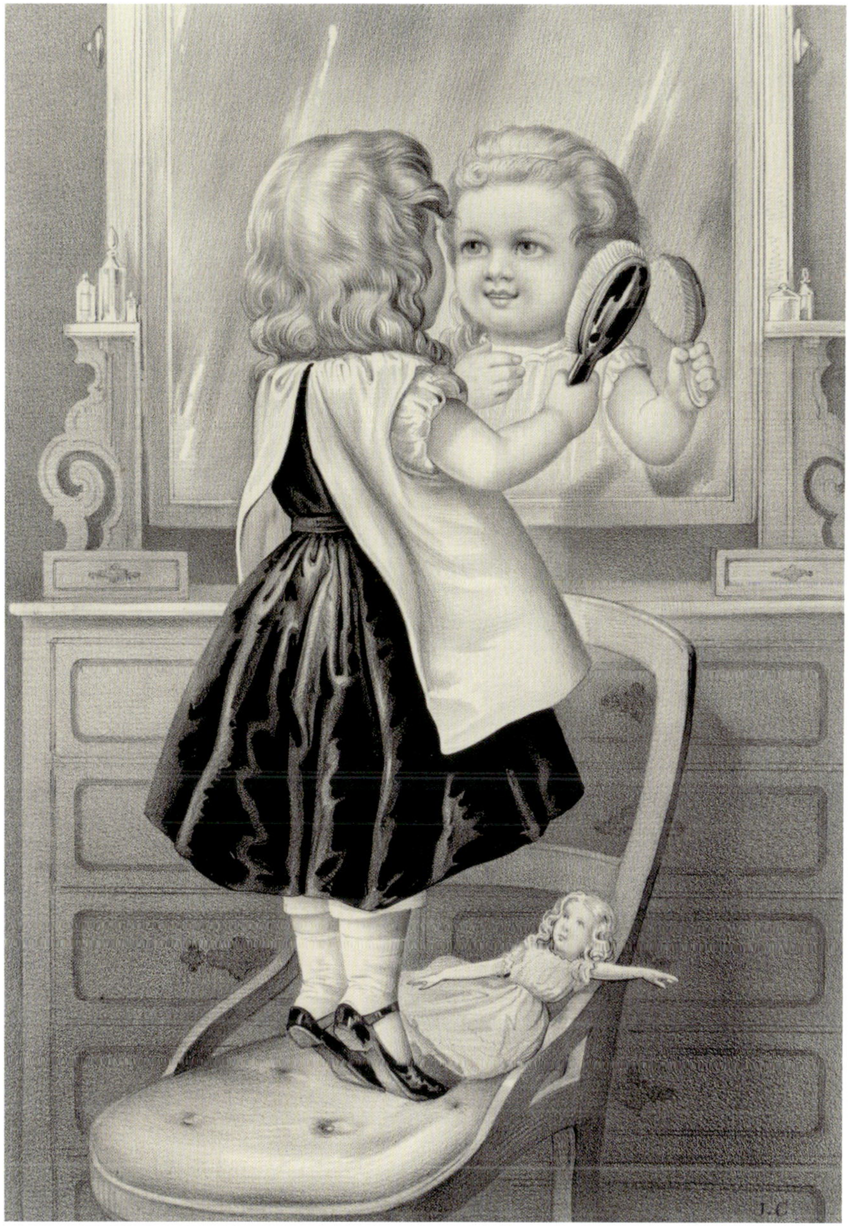

*The First Toilet*

1873

John Cameron, AMERICAN (BORN SCOTLAND), ca. 1828

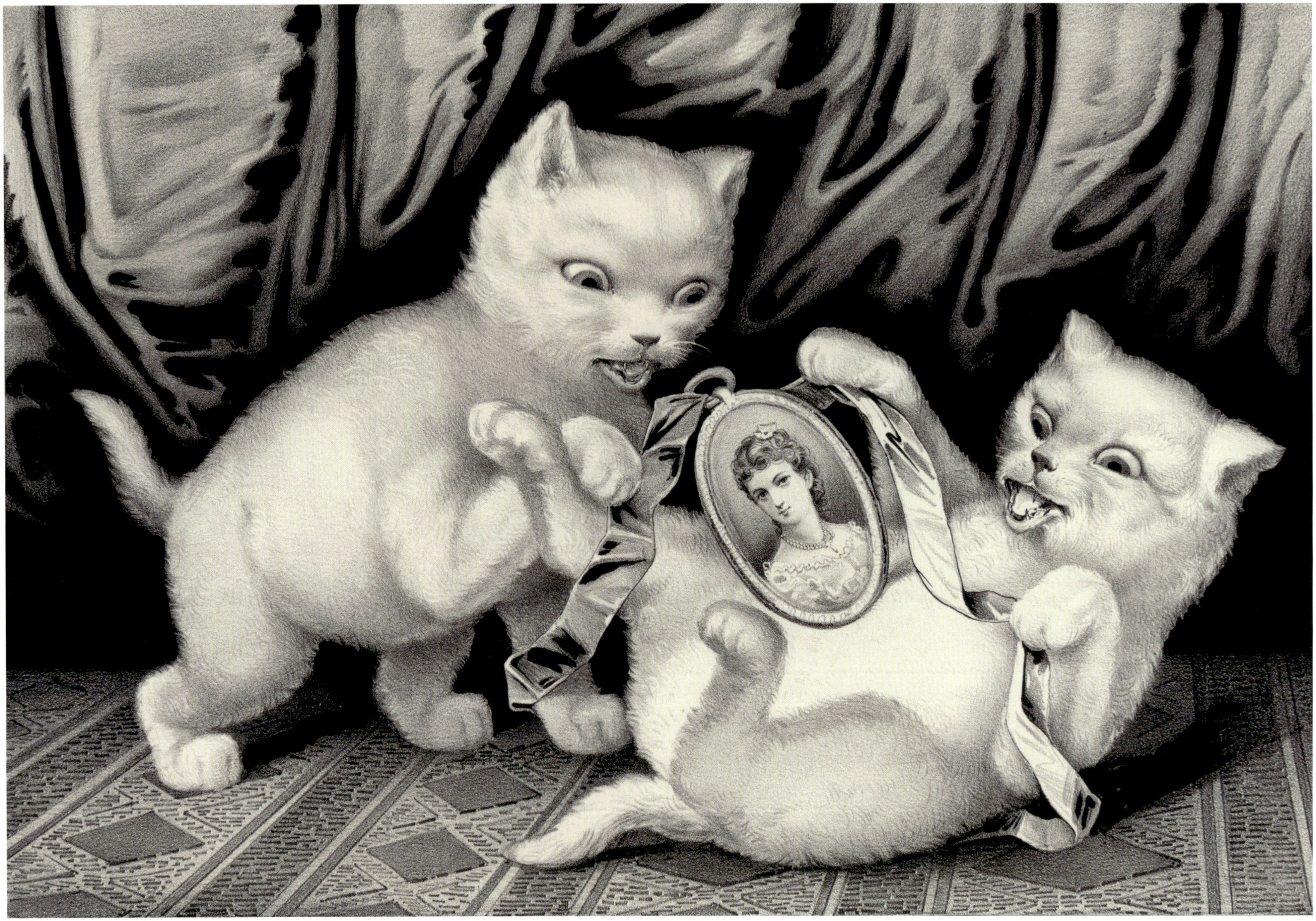

*My Little White Kitties*

1871

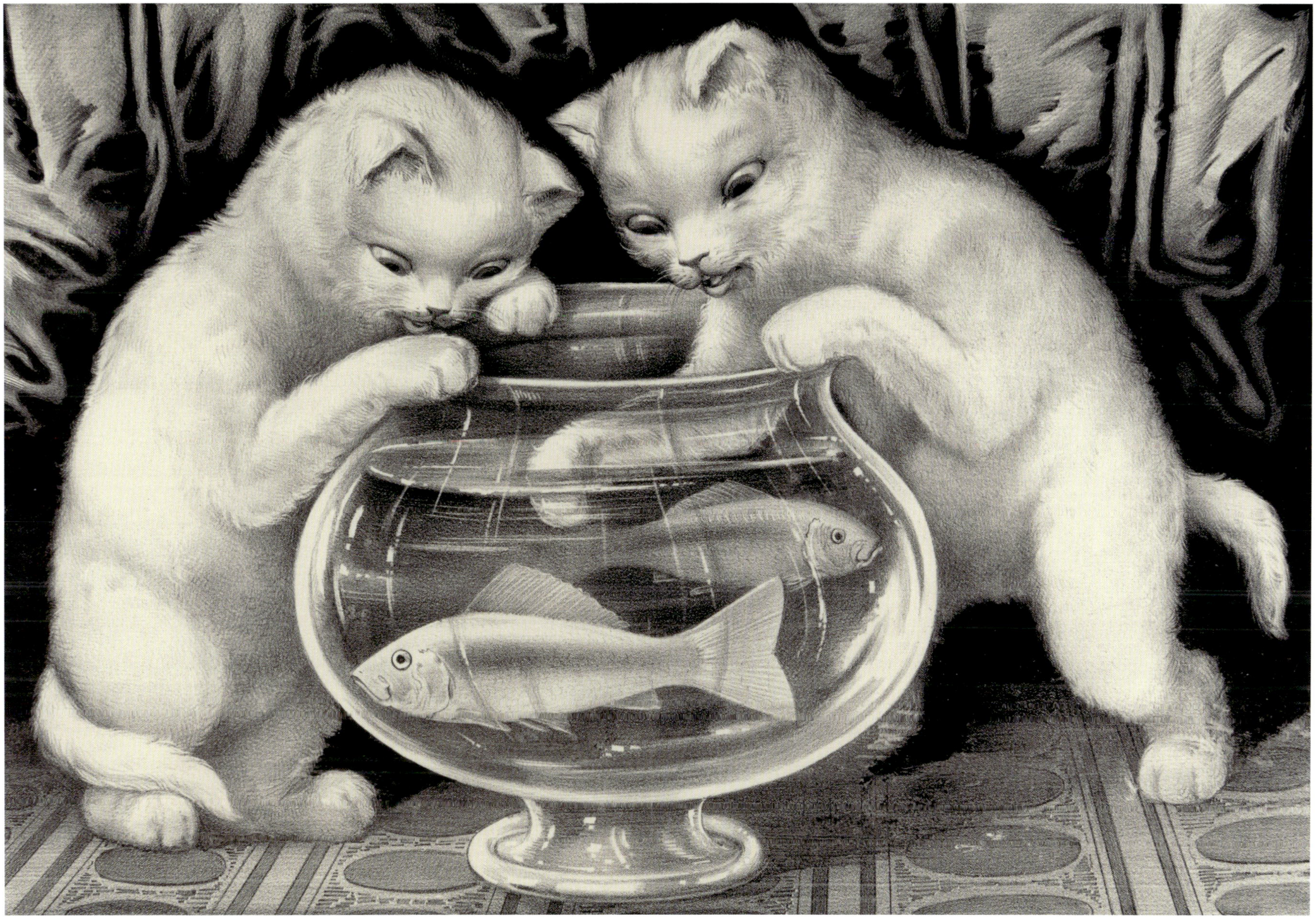

*Three Little White Kitties*
***Fishing***
1871

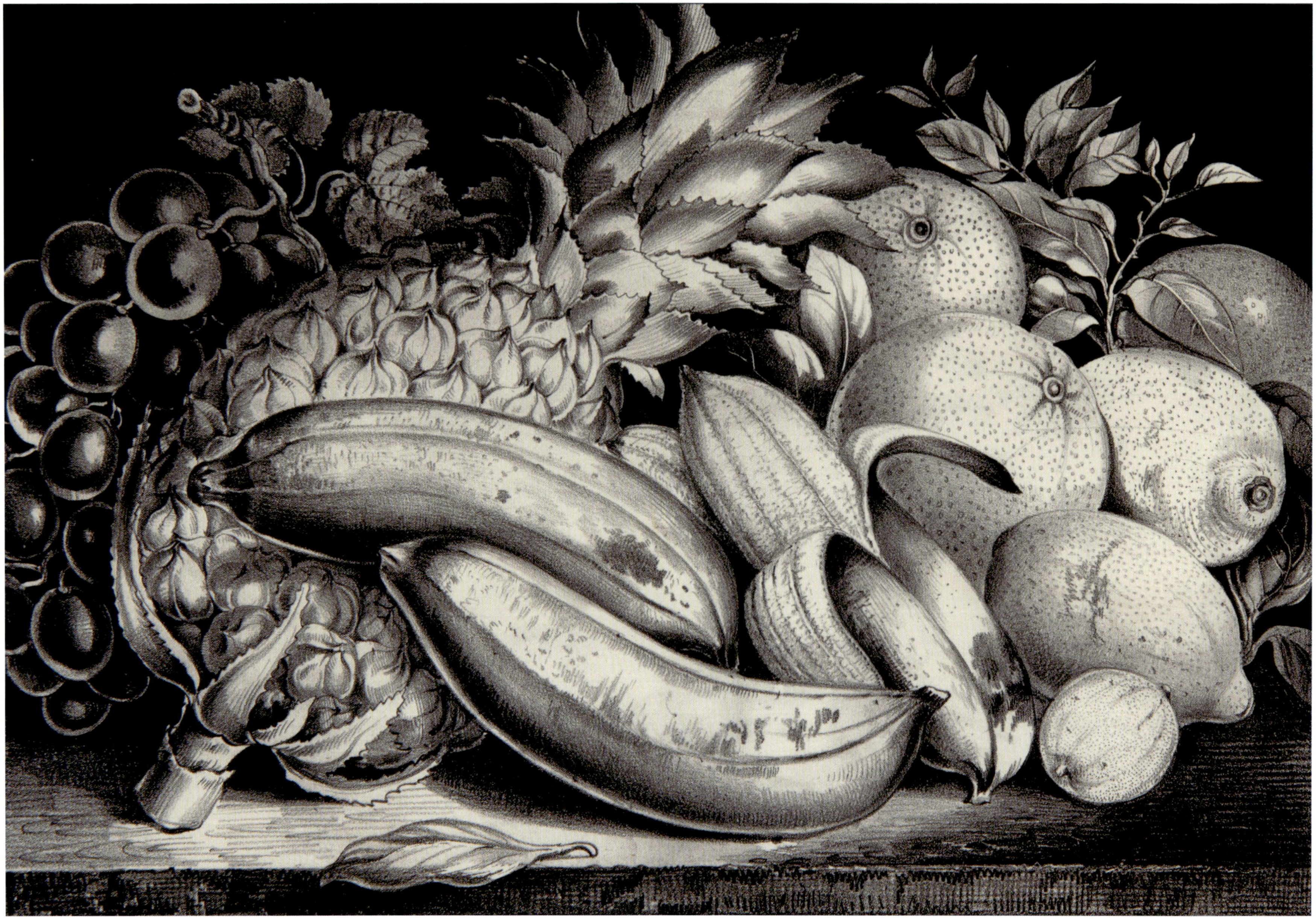

*Fruits of the Tropies* [sic]

1871

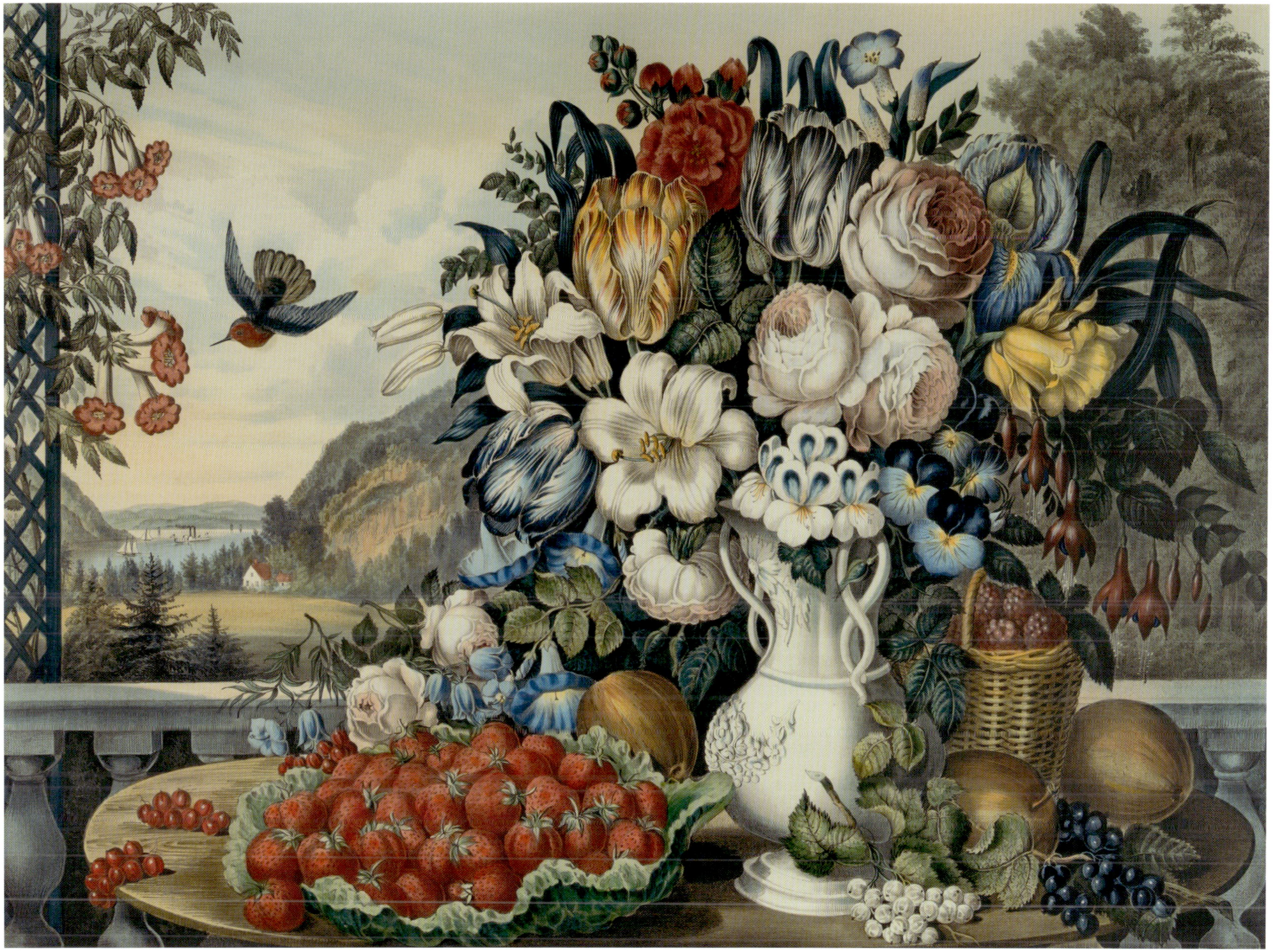

*Landscape, Fruit and Flowers*

1862

Frances Palmer, AMERICAN (BORN ENGLAND), 1812–1876

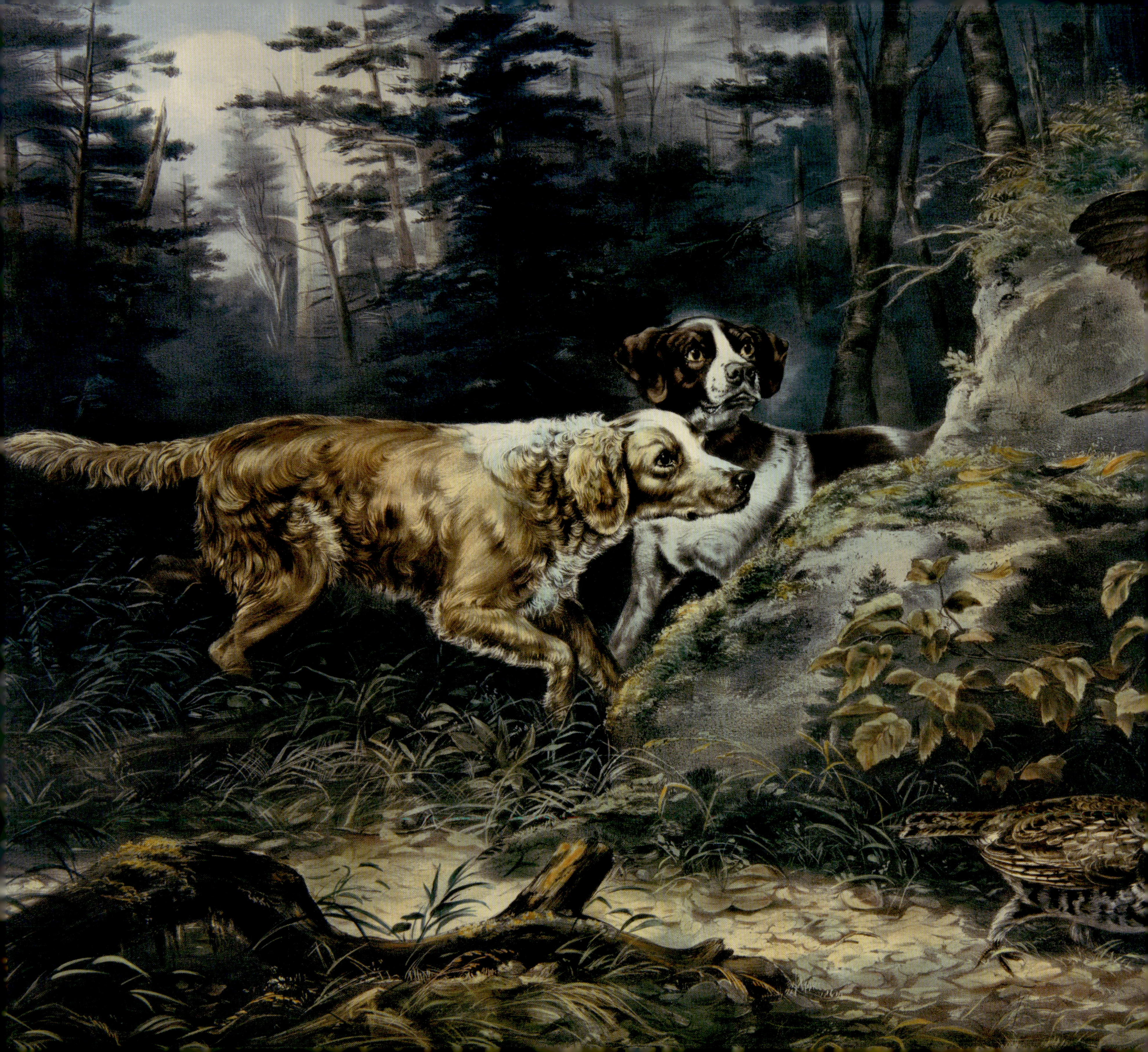

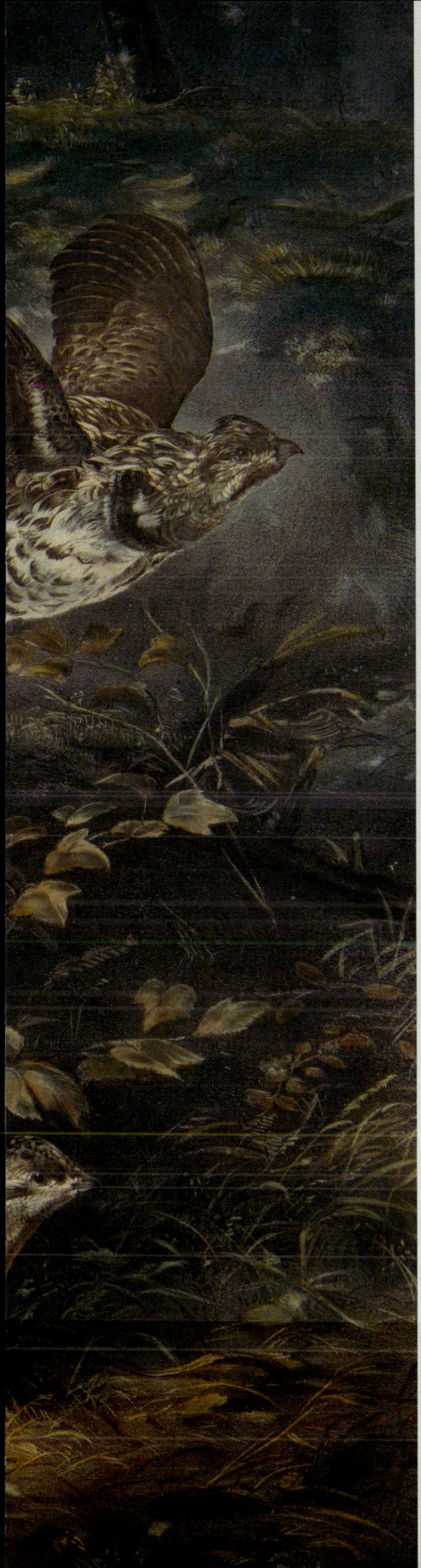

# SPORTING LIFE

As the nation became increasingly industrialized throughout the nineteenth century, Americans suddenly found themselves with leisure time to fill with sports and other activities. More regulated working schedules meant city dwellers were able to join in the sporting world as they had never done before. Middle- and upper-middle-class urban men participated in activities that offered close encounters with nature as a remedy against the ills and anxieties of urban life. Hunting and fishing were popular among rural and urban populations alike, yet Currier & Ives's images tended to represent hunters as fashionable and well-mannered metropolitan gentlemen. Arthur Tait, one of the firm's artists, was a well-known sportsman himself, renowned for his hunting scenes set in the Adirondacks. Horse racing became so popular that the firm produced more than seven hundred and fifty prints representing horses, racing, owners, and riders. Before the segregation of the sport, many Thoroughbred trainers and jockeys were African American—fifteen of the first twenty-eight Kentucky Derbies between 1875 and 1901 were won by Black jockeys. Images of these jockeys and trainers marked one of Currier & Ives's few depictions of African Americans that did not resort to debasing stereotypes and caricatures.

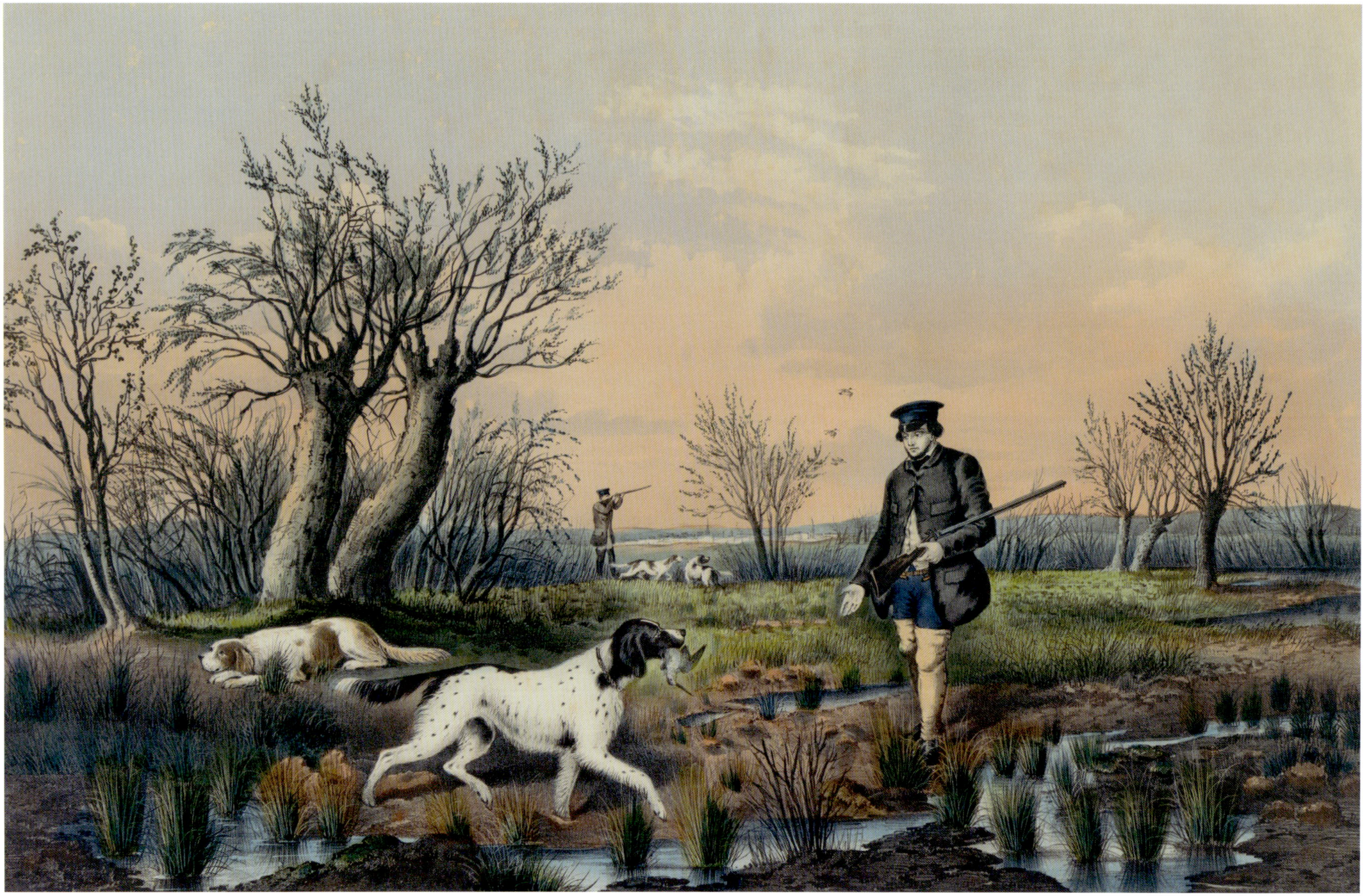

*Snipe Shooting*

1852

Frances Palmer, AMERICAN (BORN ENGLAND), 1812–1876

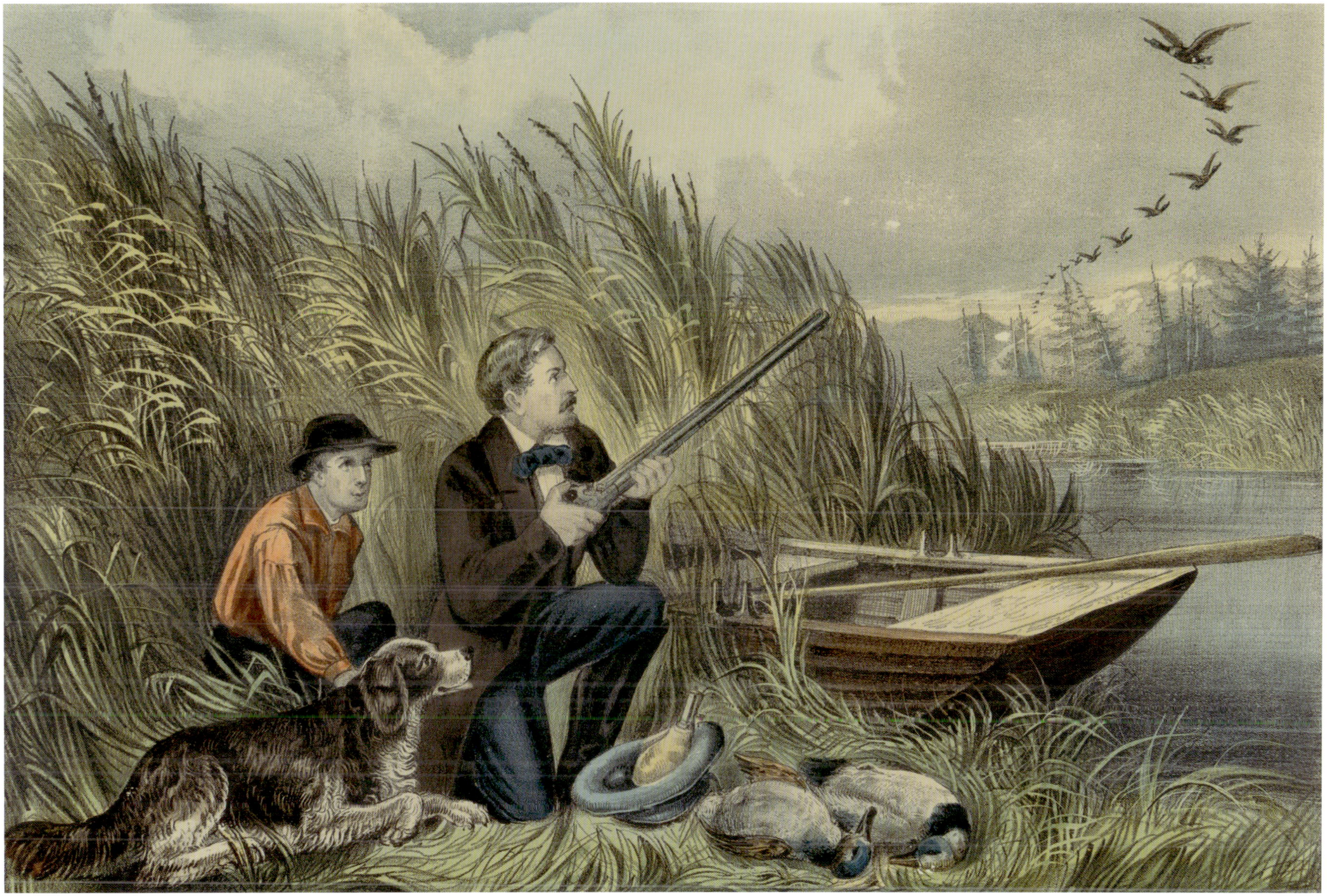

*Wild Duck Shooting*
*On the Wing*
1870

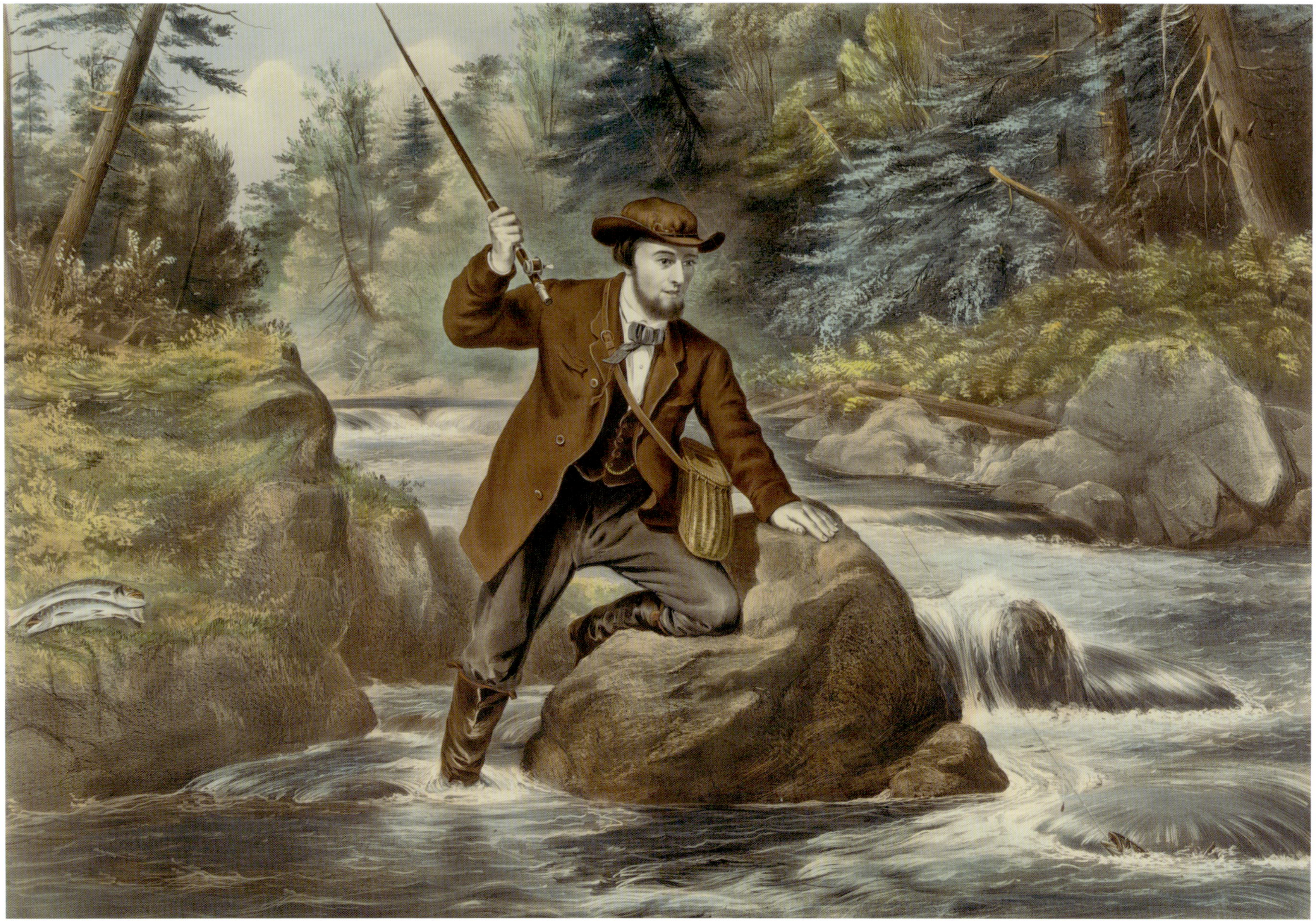

*Brook Trout Fishing*
***An Anxious Moment***
1862
Arthur Fitzwilliam Tait, AMERICAN (BORN ENGLAND), 1819–1905

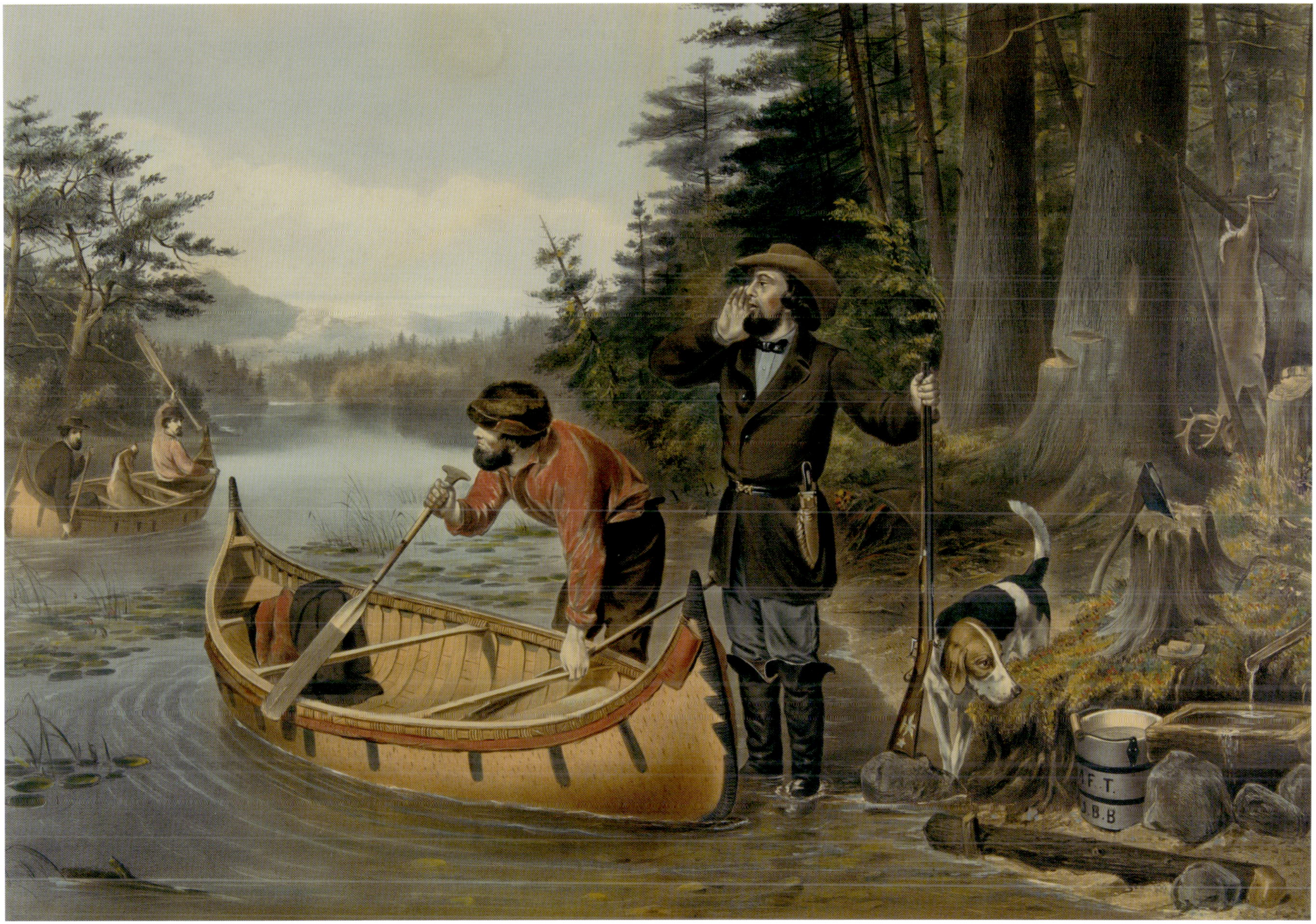

*American Hunting Scenes*

***An Early Start***

1863

Arthur Fitzwilliam Tait, AMERICAN (BORN ENGLAND), 1819–1905

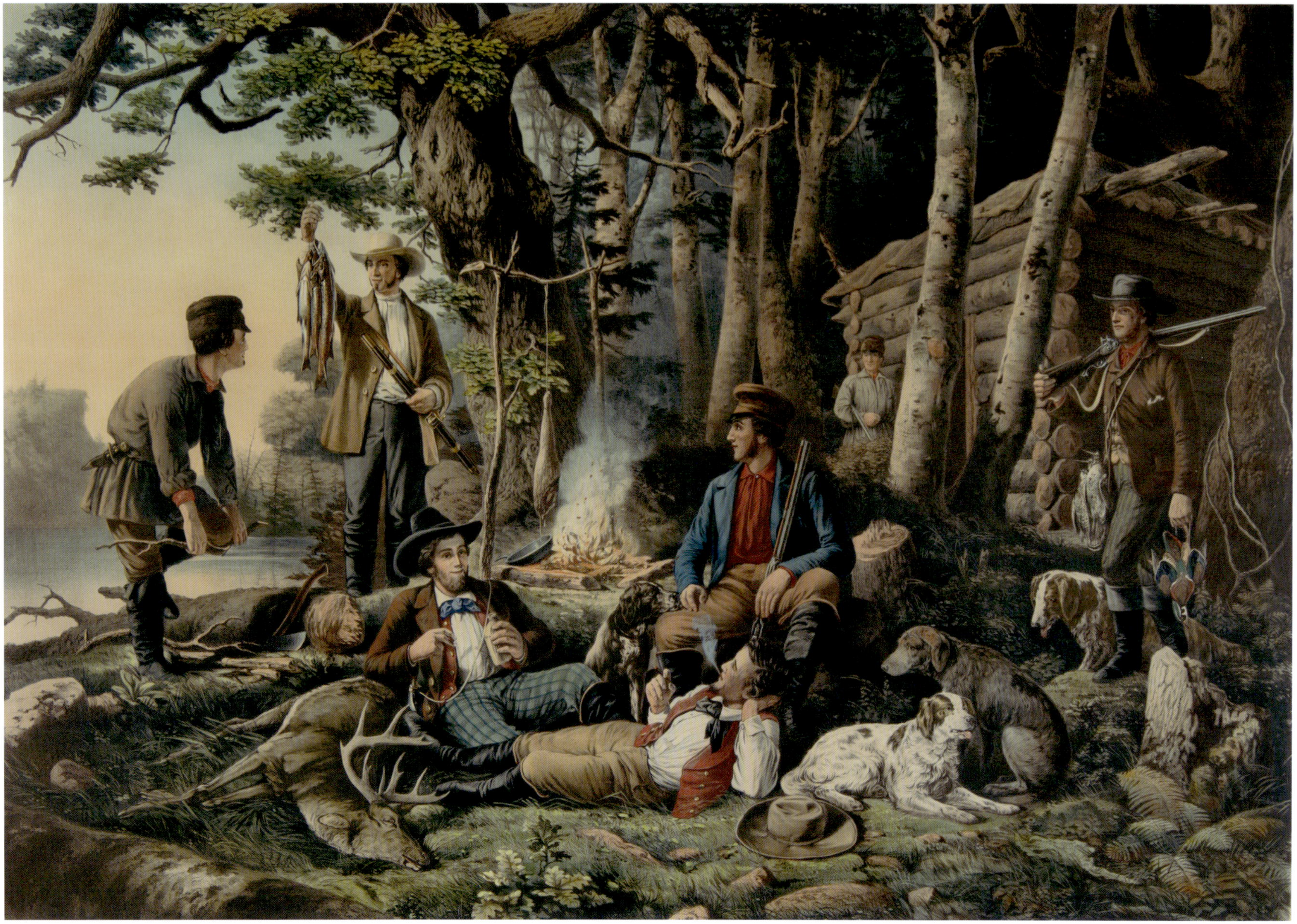

*Camping Out*

***Some of the Right Sort***

1856

Louis Maurer, AMERICAN (BORN GERMANY), 1832–1932

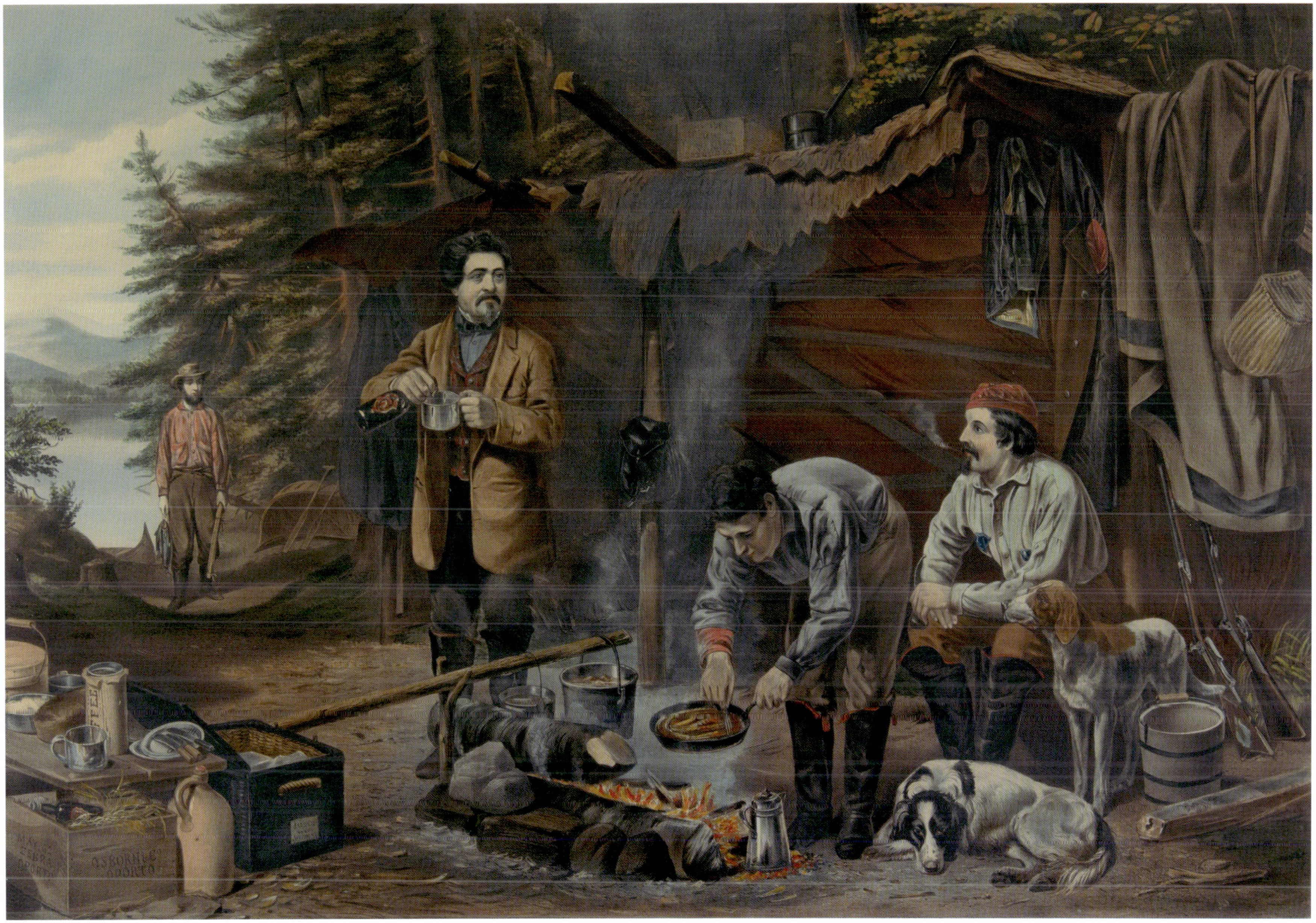

*Camping in the Woods*

***A Good Time Coming***

1863

Arthur Fitzwilliam Tait, AMERICAN (BORN ENGLAND), 1819–1905

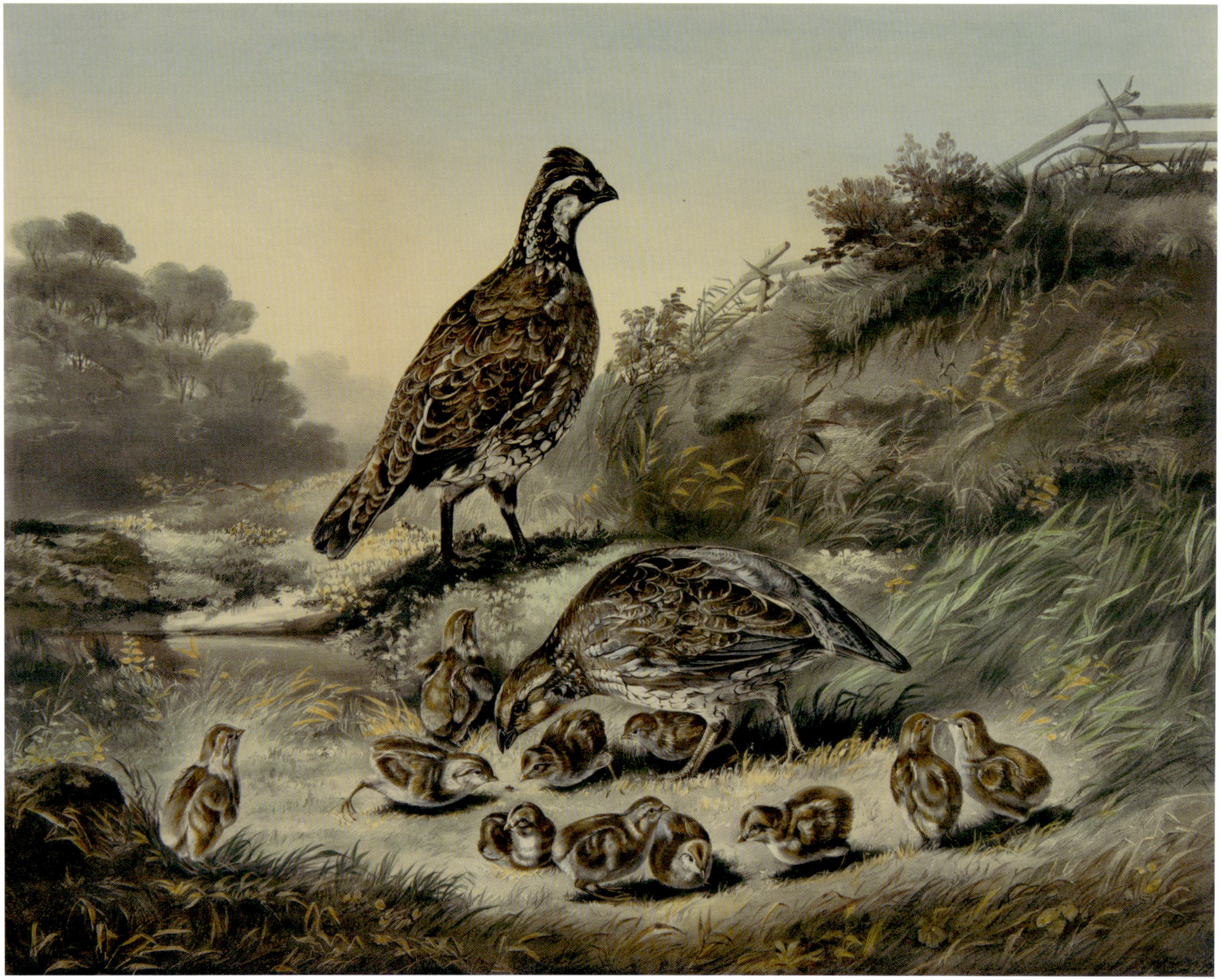

*The Cares of a Family*

1856

Arthur Fitzwilliam Tait, AMERICAN (BORN ENGLAND), 1819–1905

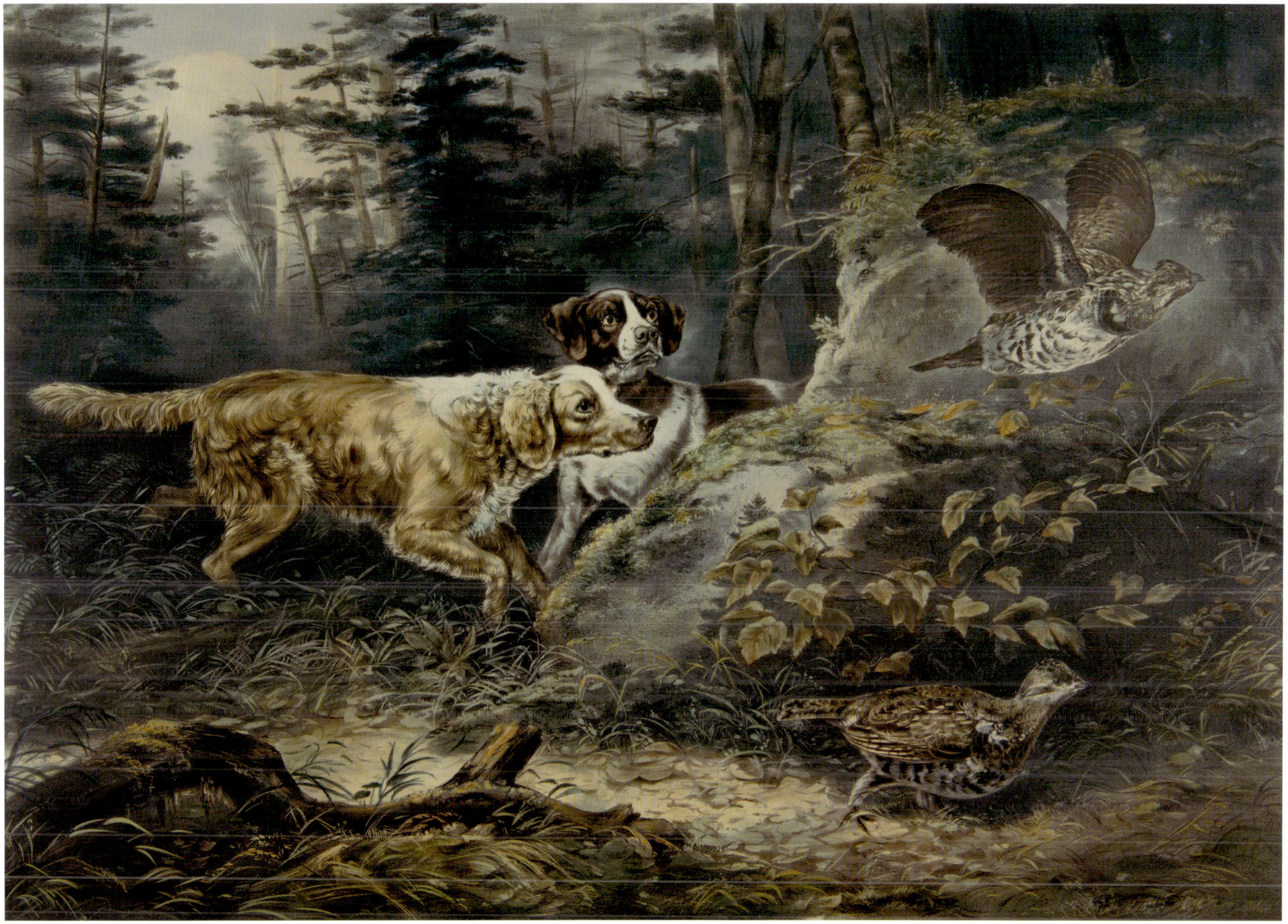

*American Field Sports*

1857

Arthur Fitzwilliam Tait, AMERICAN (BORN ENGLAND), 1819–1905

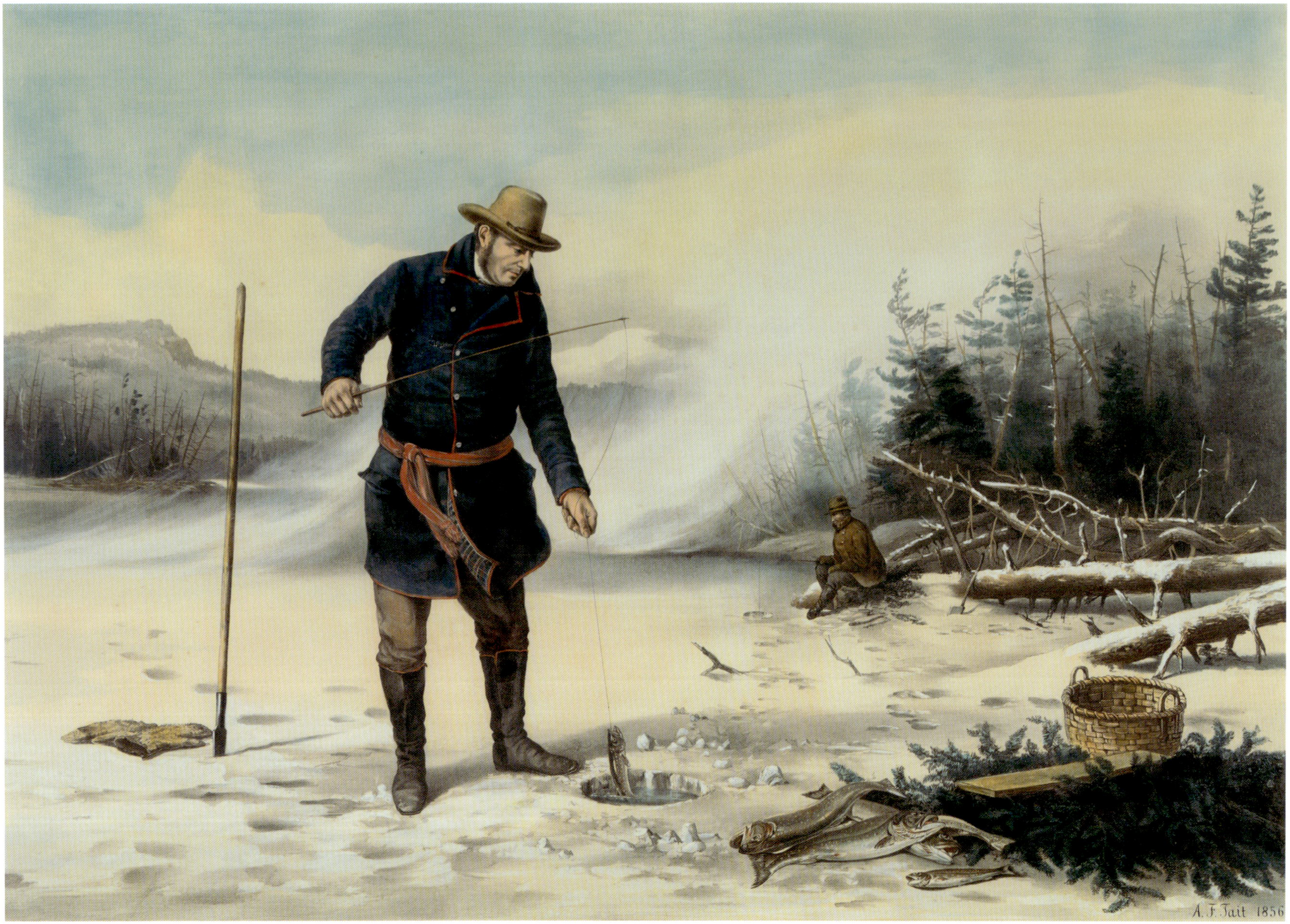


*American Winter Sports*
*Trout Fishing on Chateaugay Lake*

1856

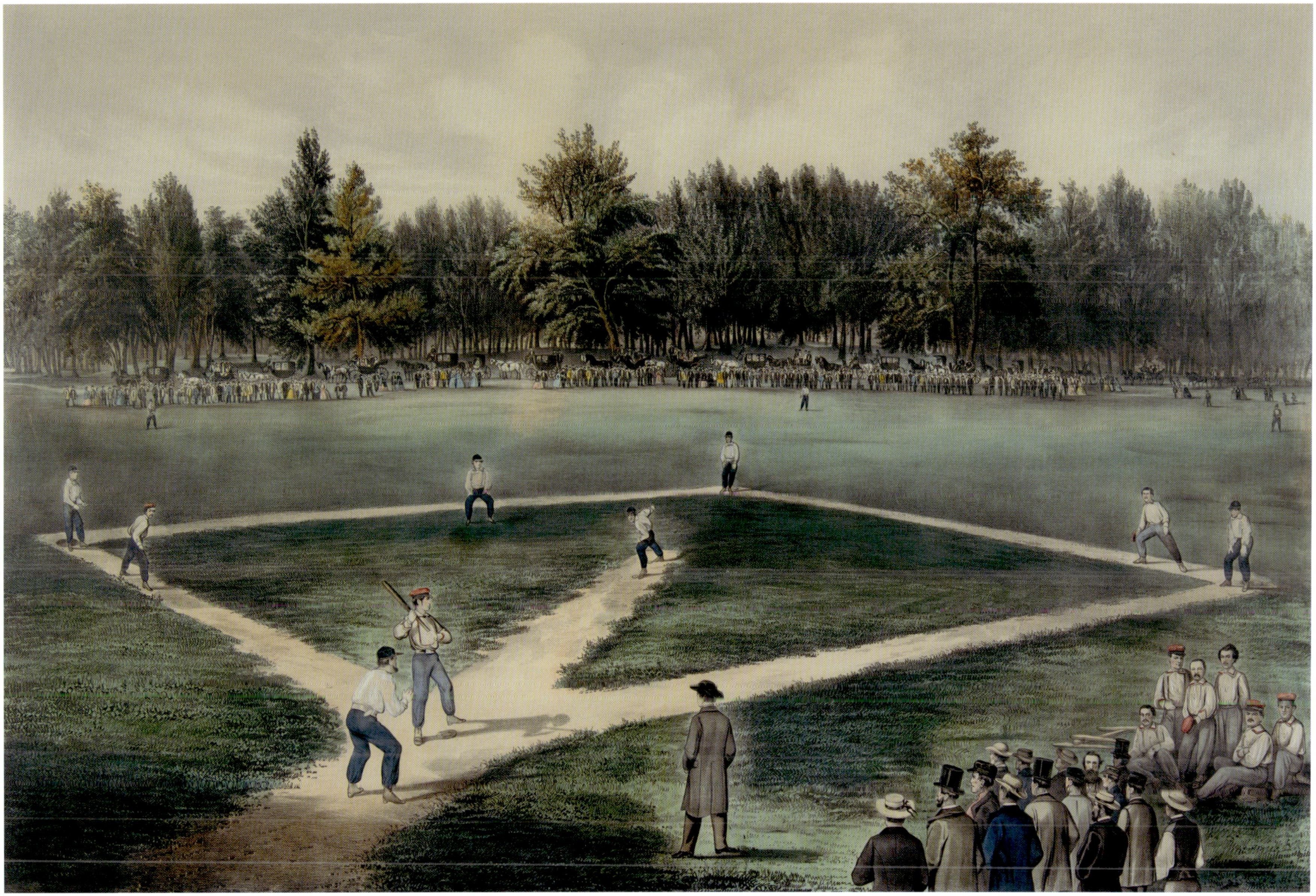

*The American National Game of Base Ball*
*Grand Match for the Championship at the Elysian Fields, Hoboken, N.J.*

1866

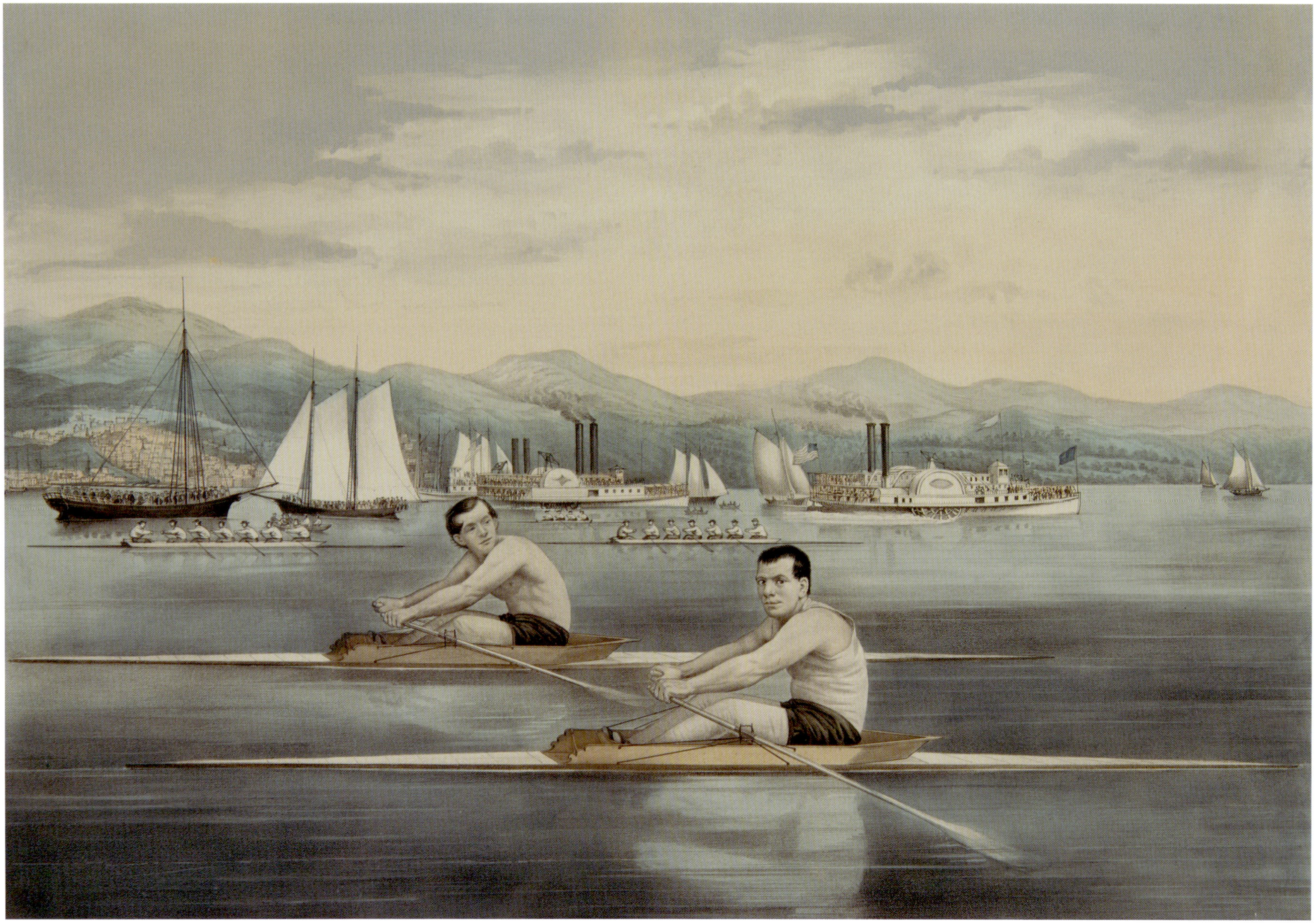

*James Hammill, and Walter Brown*
*In Their Great Five Mile Rowing Match for $4000 & the Championship of America*



1867

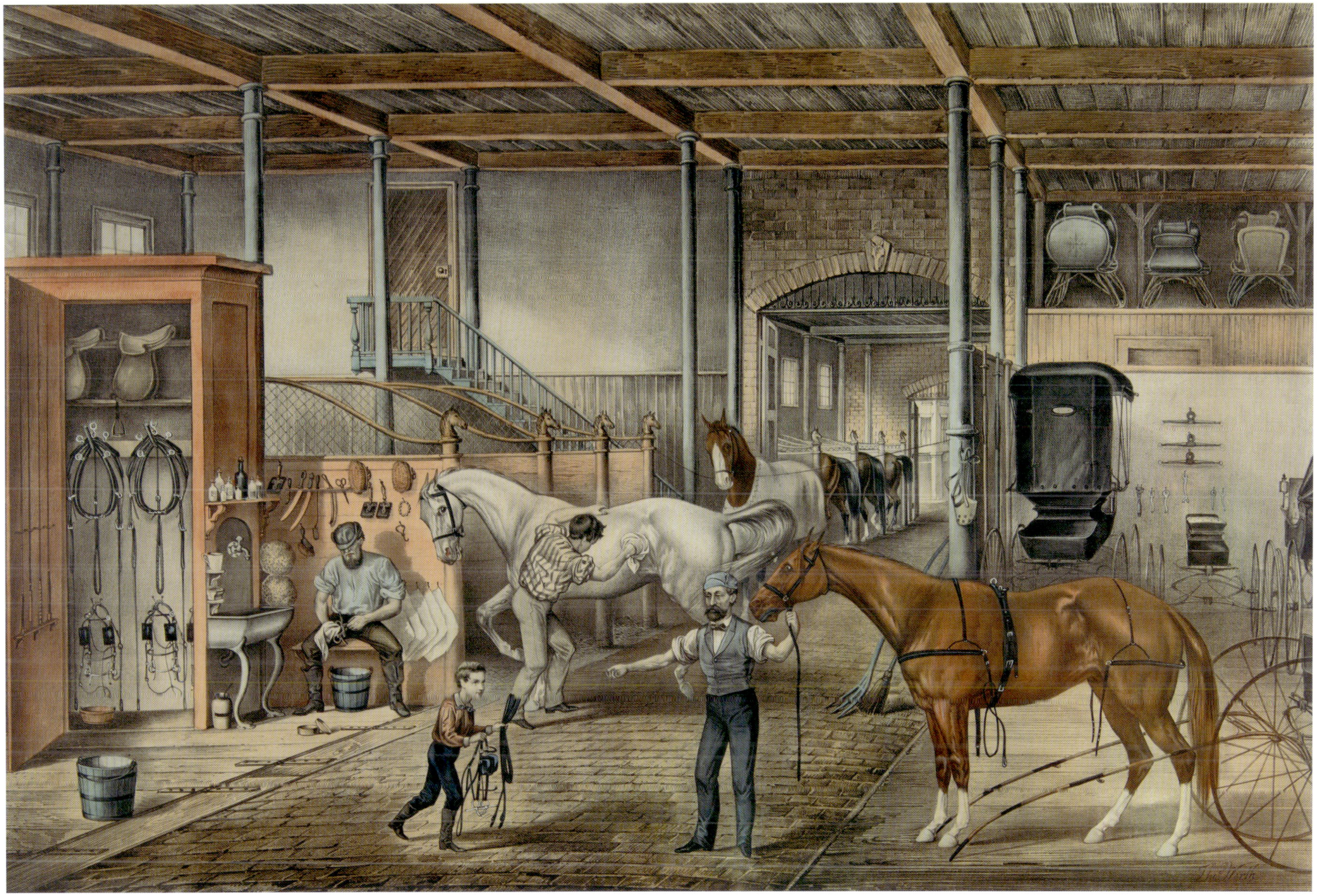

*Trotting Cracks at Home*

***A Model Stable***

1868

Thomas Worth, AMERICAN, 1834–1917

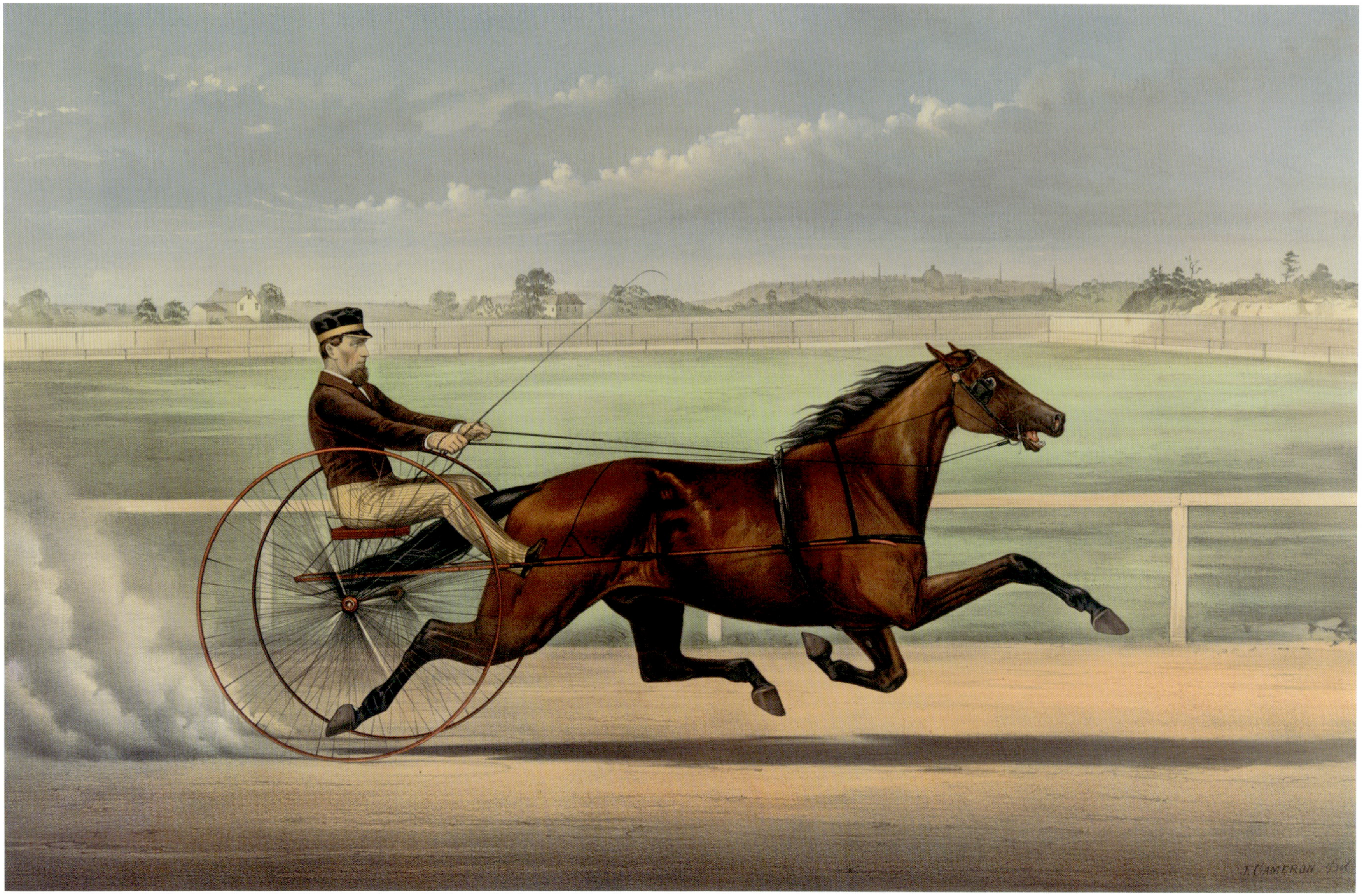


*Mr. Bonner's Horse Joe Elliott, Driven by J. Bowen*

1873

John Cameron, AMERICAN (BORN SCOTLAND), ca. 1828

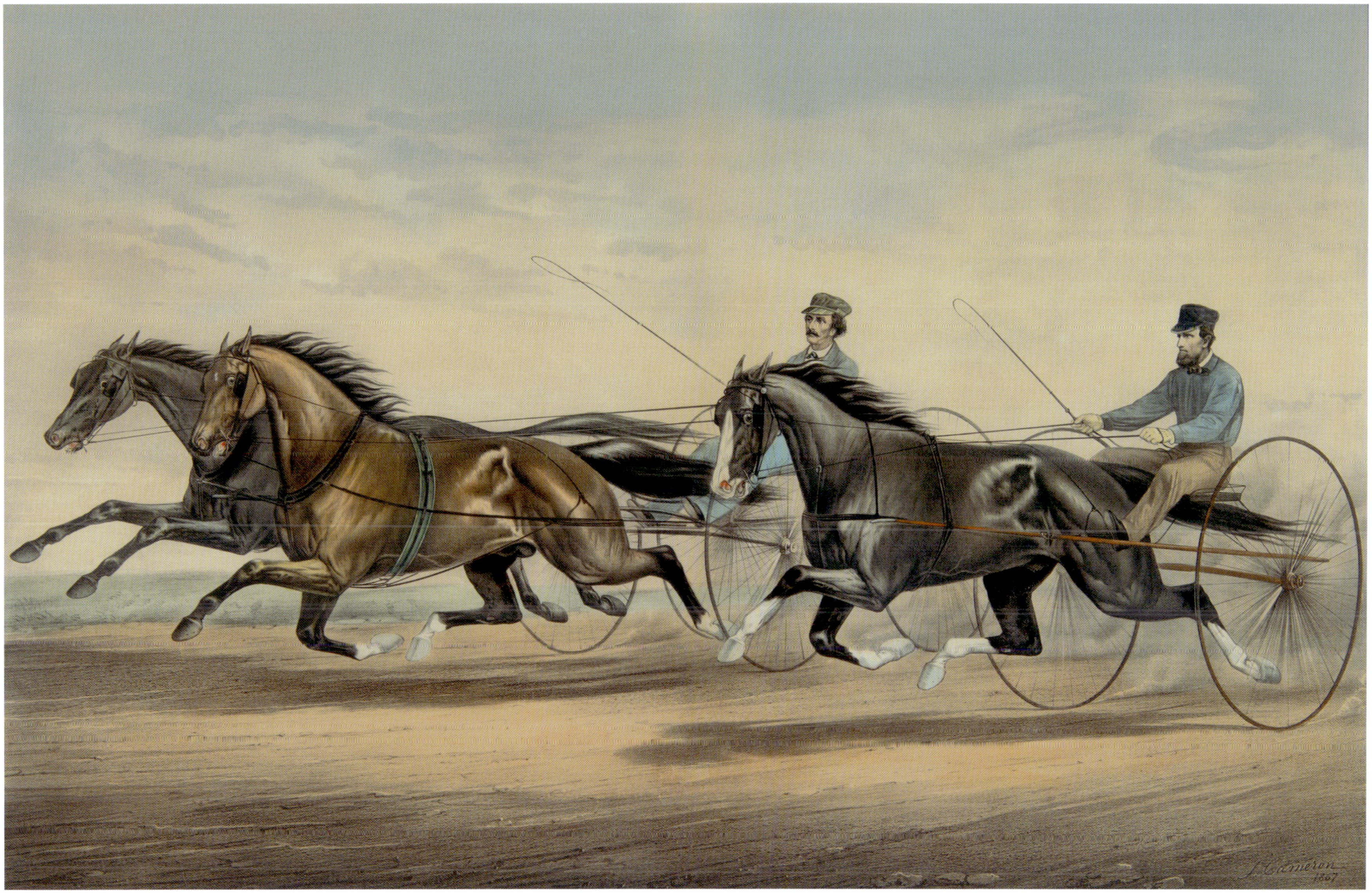


*Ethan Allen and Mate and Dexter*

***In Their Wonderful Race, over the Fashion Course, L.I. June 21st. 1867***

1867

John Cameron, AMERICAN (BORN SCOTLAND), ca. 1828

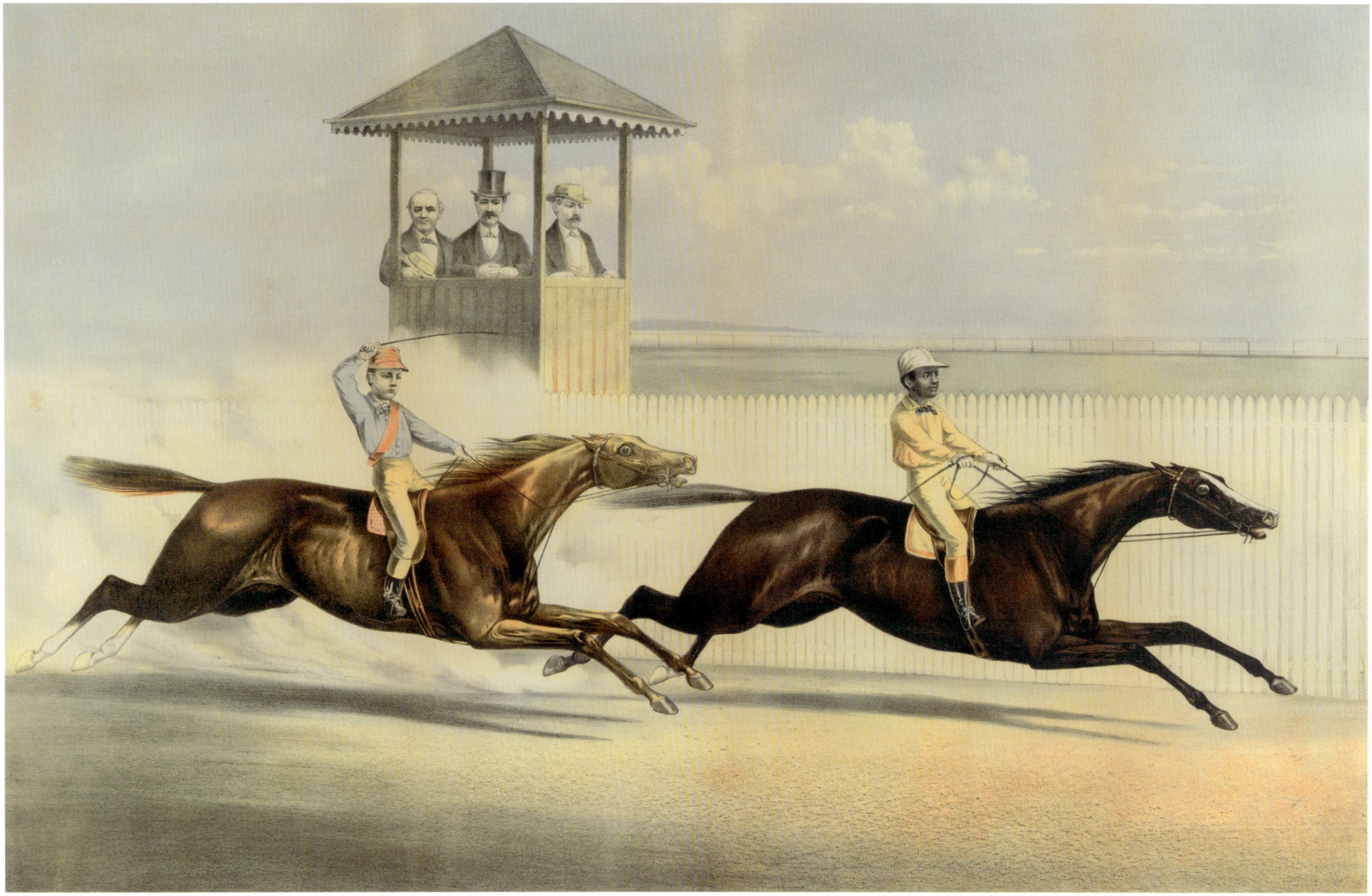

*Harry Bassett and Longfellow*
*In Their Great Races at Long Branch, N.J. July, 2nd and Saratoga, N.Y. July, 16th 1872*



1872

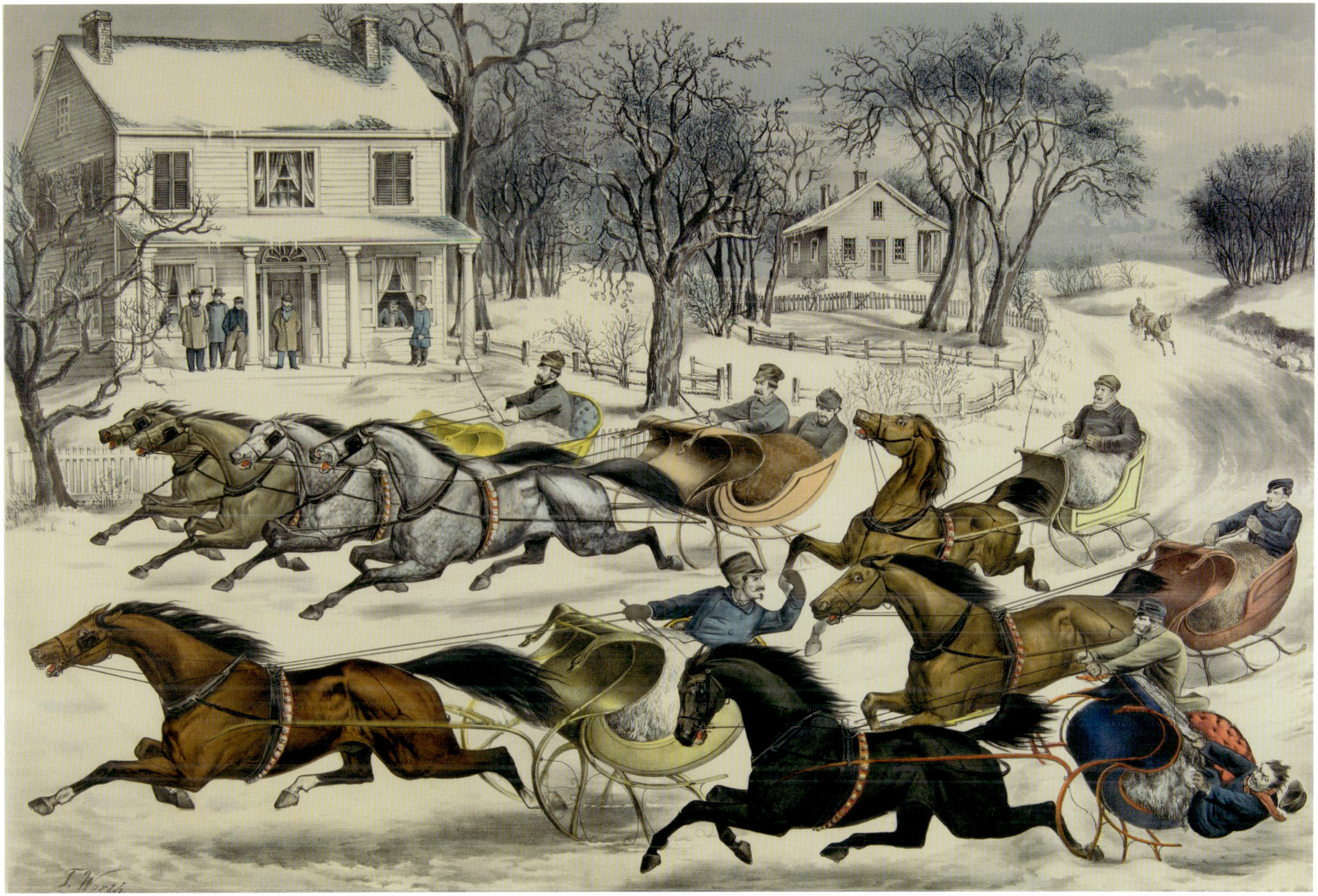

*A Brush for the Lead*
***New York Flyers on the Snow***
1867
Thomas Worth, AMERICAN, 1834–1917

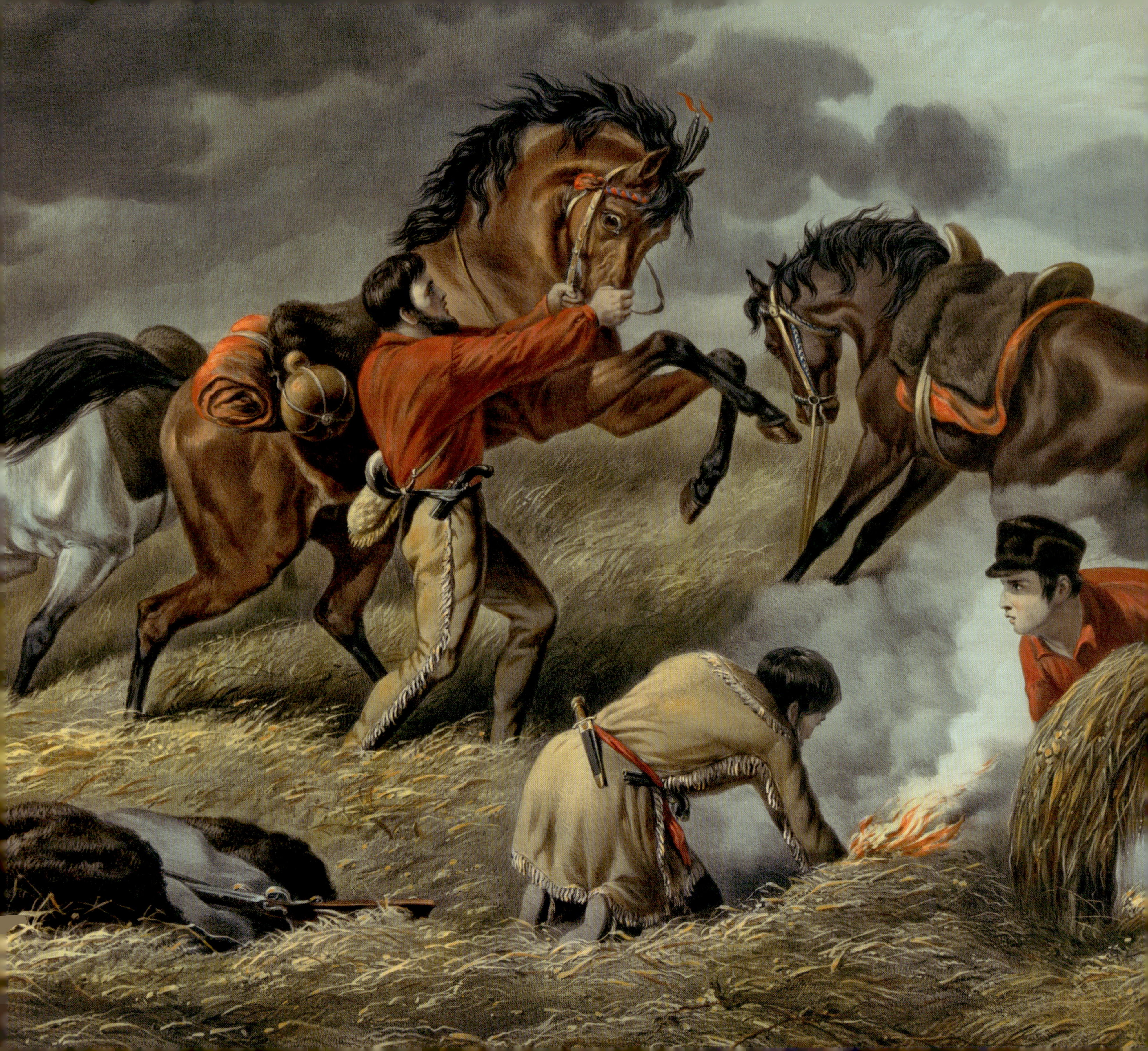

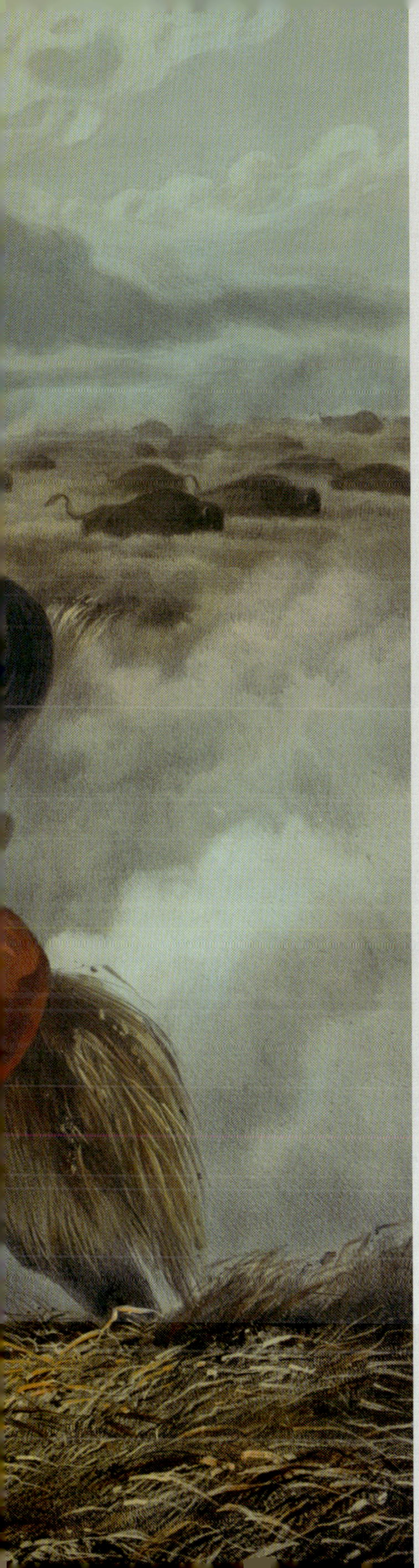

# THE FRONTIER

The myth of the western frontier increasingly appealed to nineteenth-century Americans facing rapid urbanization and social change. With women now working to help support their families, masculine ideals of independence and resourcefulness were challenged. The wild and rugged lifestyle embodied by frontiersmen was attractive to urban men, who looked to the fantasy of the west as they struggled with new gender roles. Currier & Ives produced numerous prints of frontier adventures, but like many renowned western painters of the era, their artists never left the east coast. Created in New York studios, Currier & Ives's images of the west provided a dramatic yet unrealistic account of life beyond the Missouri River. Enterprising individuals sought their fortunes in depictions of the California gold rush, embodying the dream of Manifest Destiny and the nation's wealth of fertile land. Frontiersmen navigated a seemingly unsettled wilderness or battled Native Americans, who were often stereotyped as violent and uncivilized. Depictions of Indigenous people also perpetuated the problematic idea of the "noble savage"—brave and shrewd, but ultimately inferior to white men. These action-filled prints also offered a counterimage of the Victorian husband, who was not only wild and rough, but a self-sufficient and resourceful independent actor in a dramatic landscape.

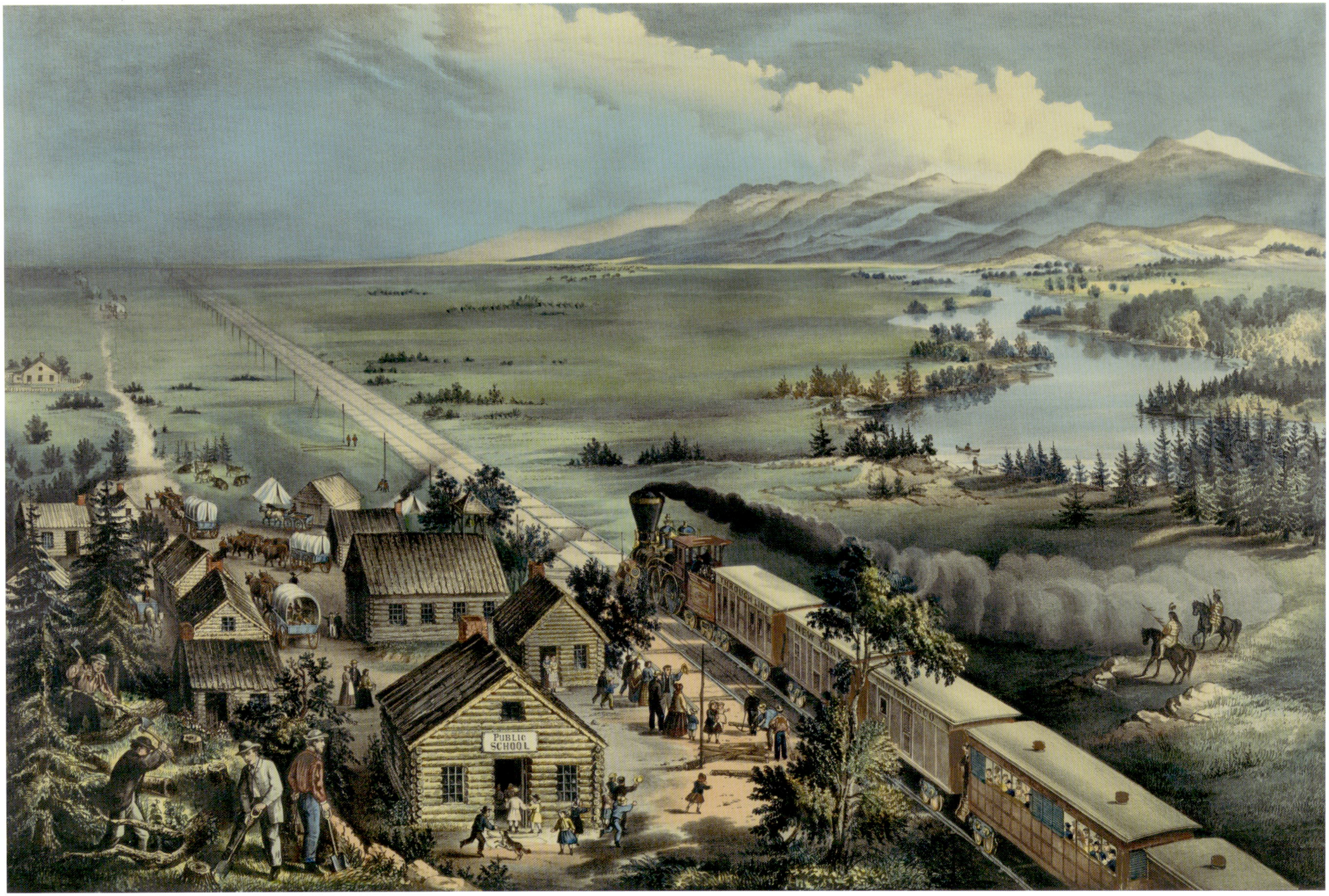


*Across the Continent*

*Westward the Course of Empire Takes Its Way*

1868

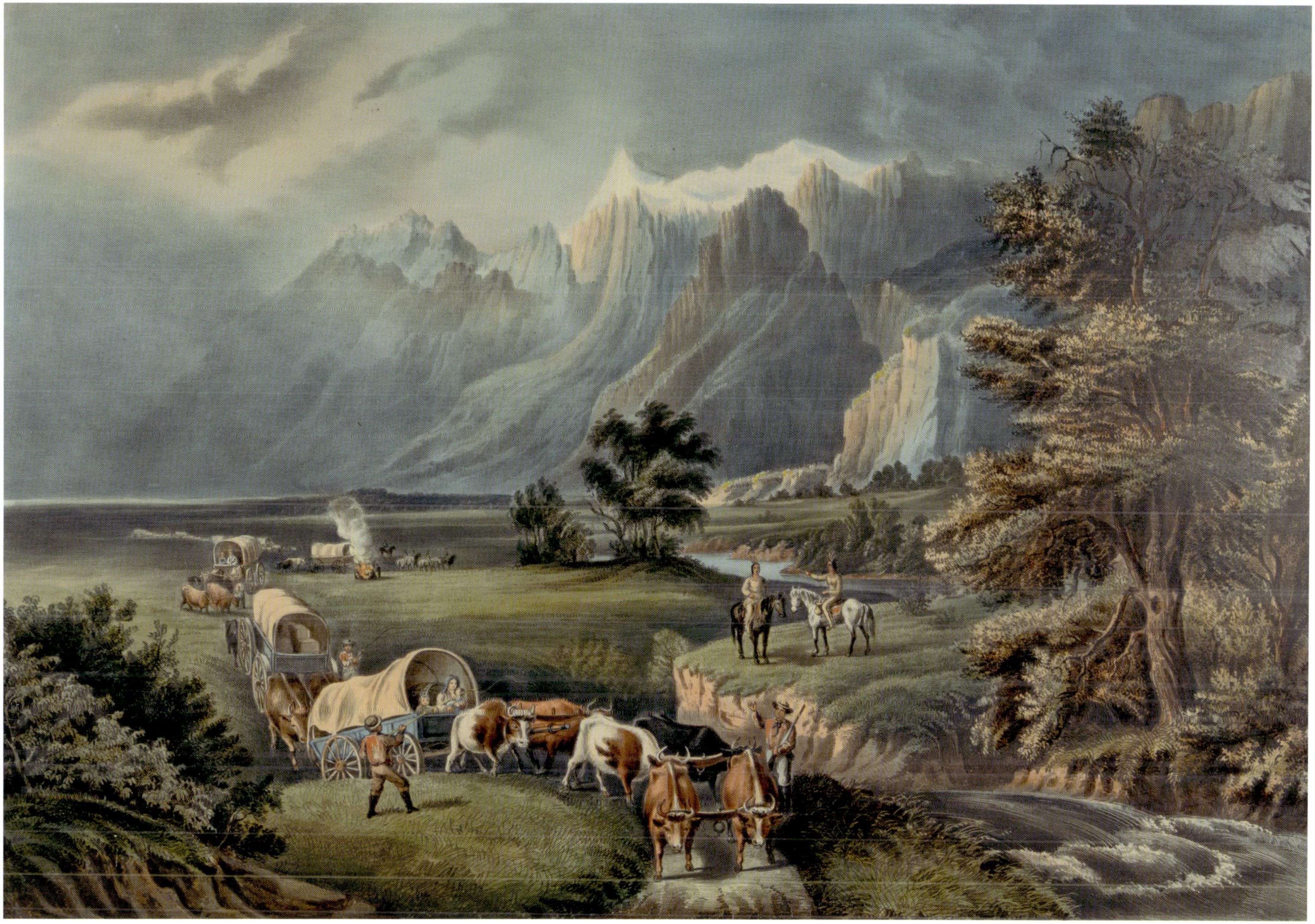

*The Rocky Mountains*

***Emigrants Crossing the Plains***

1866

Frances Palmer, AMERICAN (BORN ENGLAND), 1812–1876

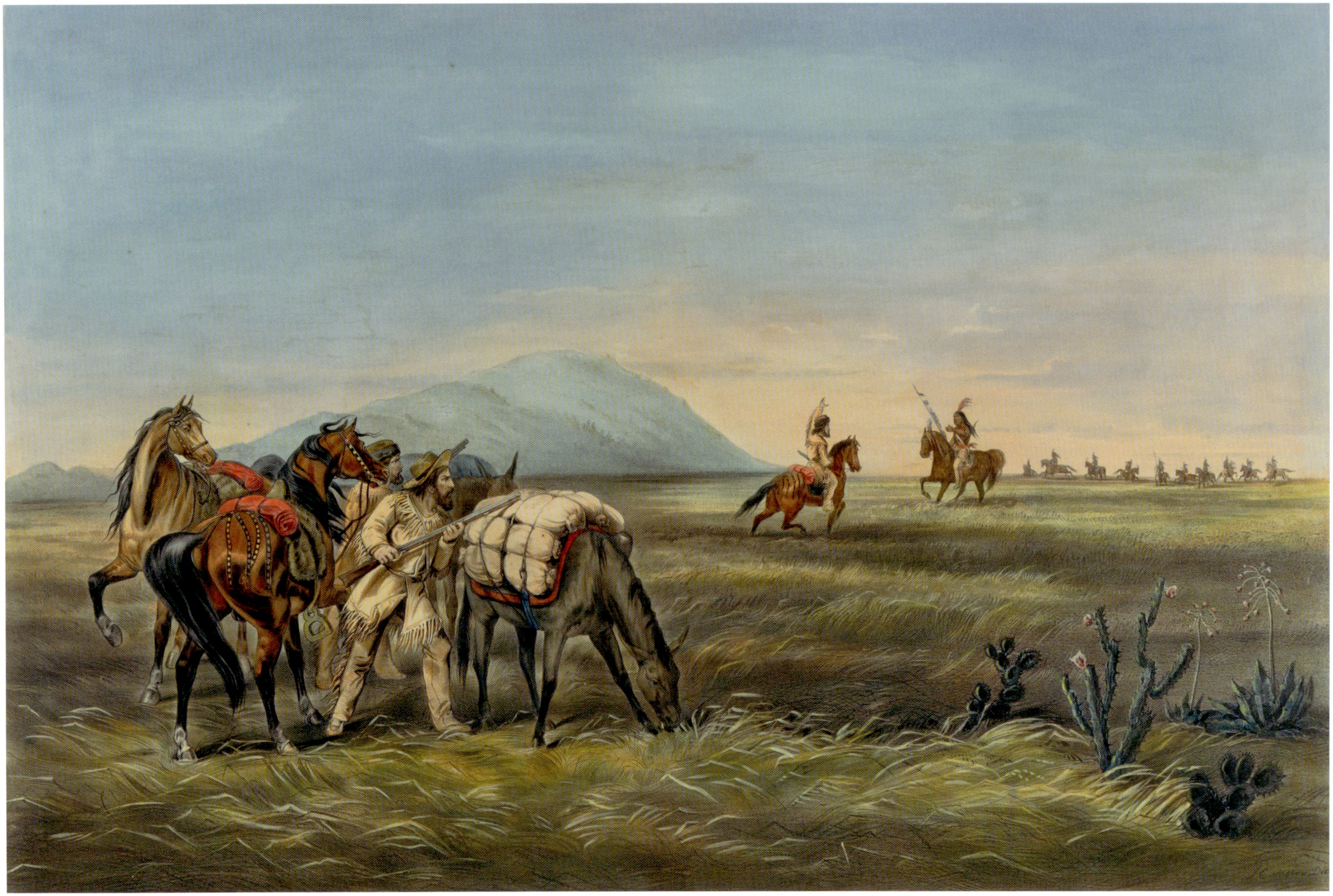

*A Parley*

***Prepared for an Emergency***

ca. 1866

John Cameron, AMERICAN (BORN SCOTLAND), ca. 1828

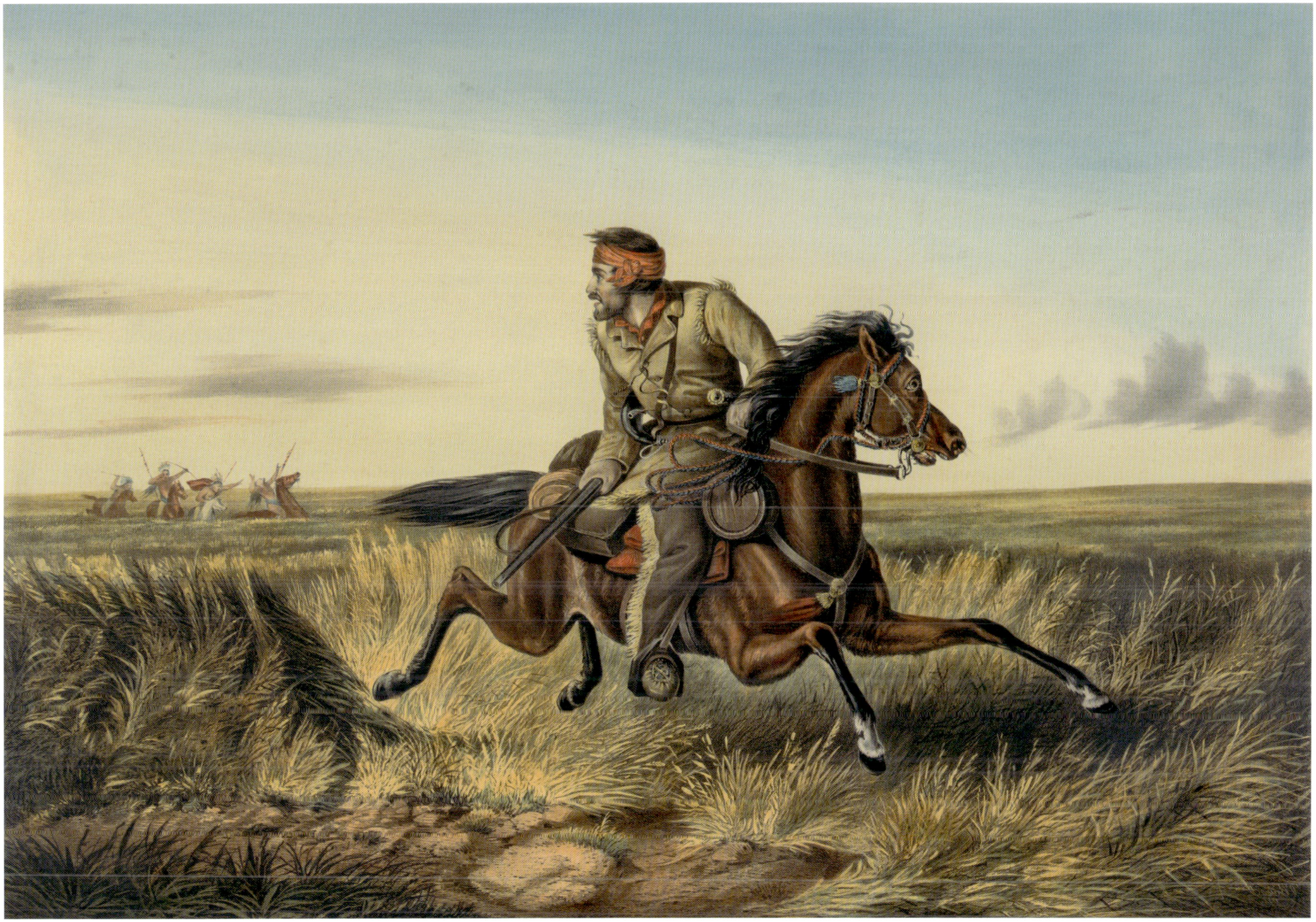

*The Prairie Hunter*
***One Rubbed Out***
1852
Arthur Fitzwilliam Tait, AMERICAN (BORN ENGLAND), 1819–1905

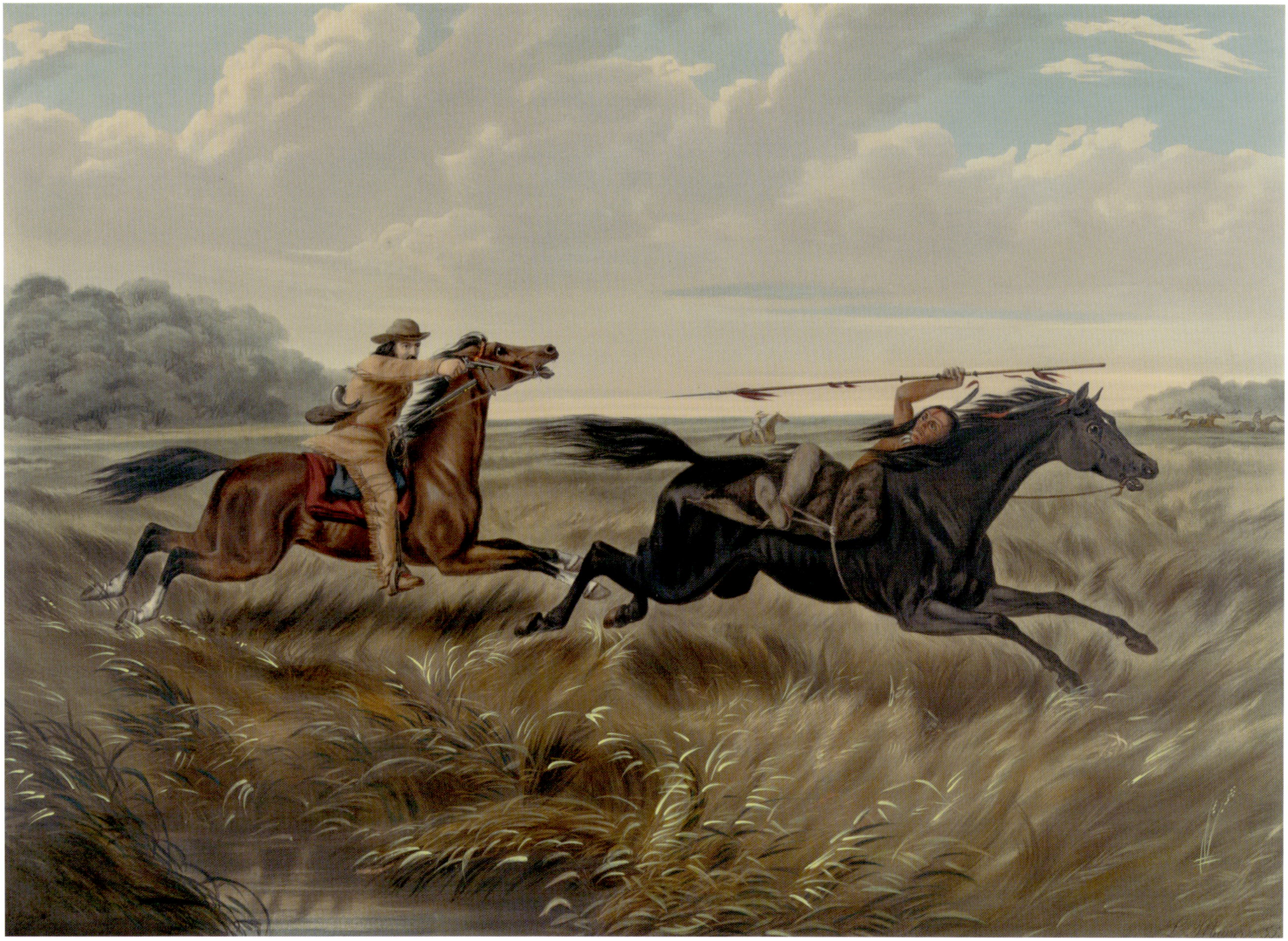

*The Pursuit*

1856

Arthur Fitzwilliam Tait, AMERICAN (BORN ENGLAND), 1819–1905

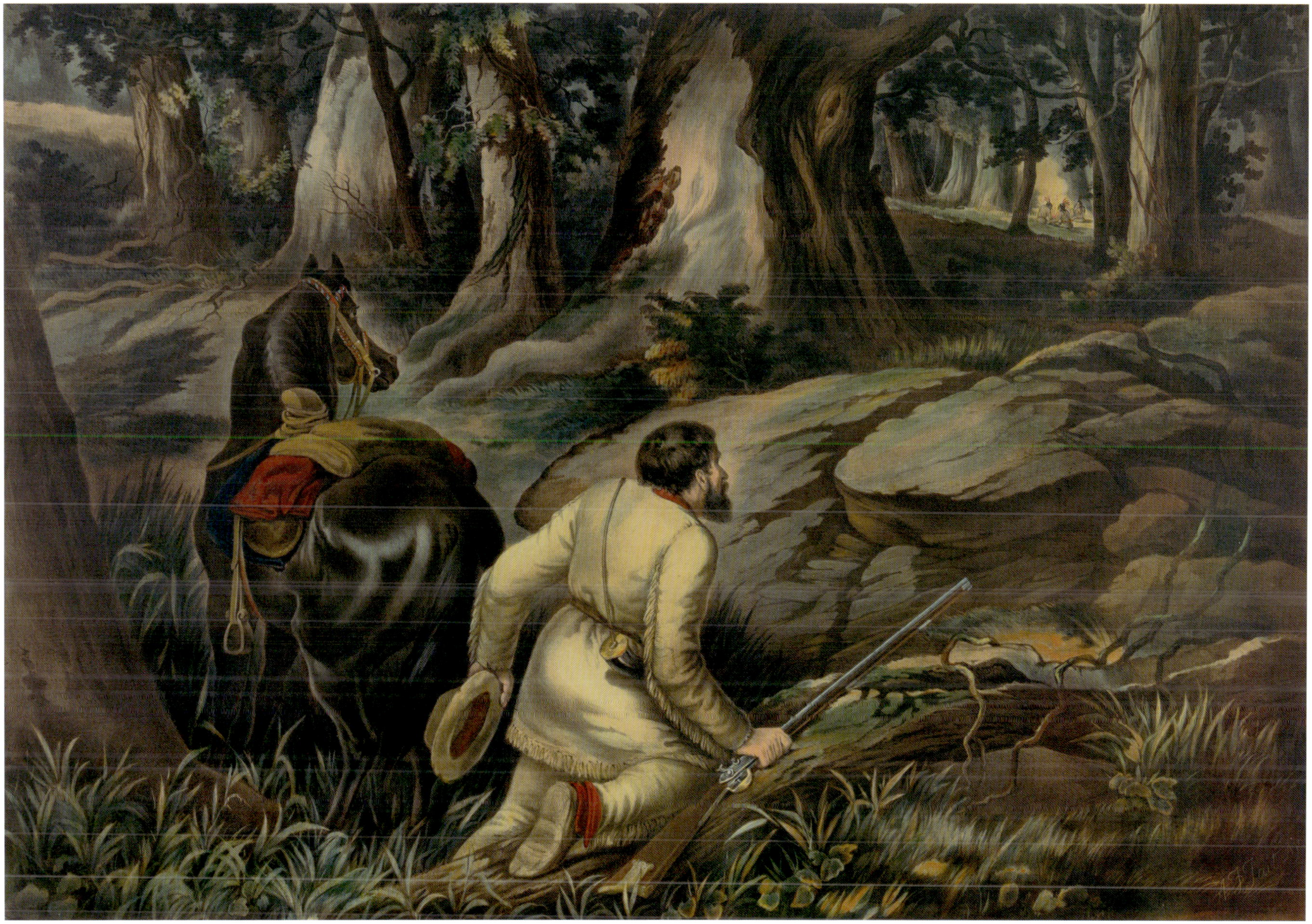

*American Frontier Life*

***On the War Path***

1863

Arthur Fitzwilliam Tait, AMERICAN (BORN ENGLAND), 1819–1905

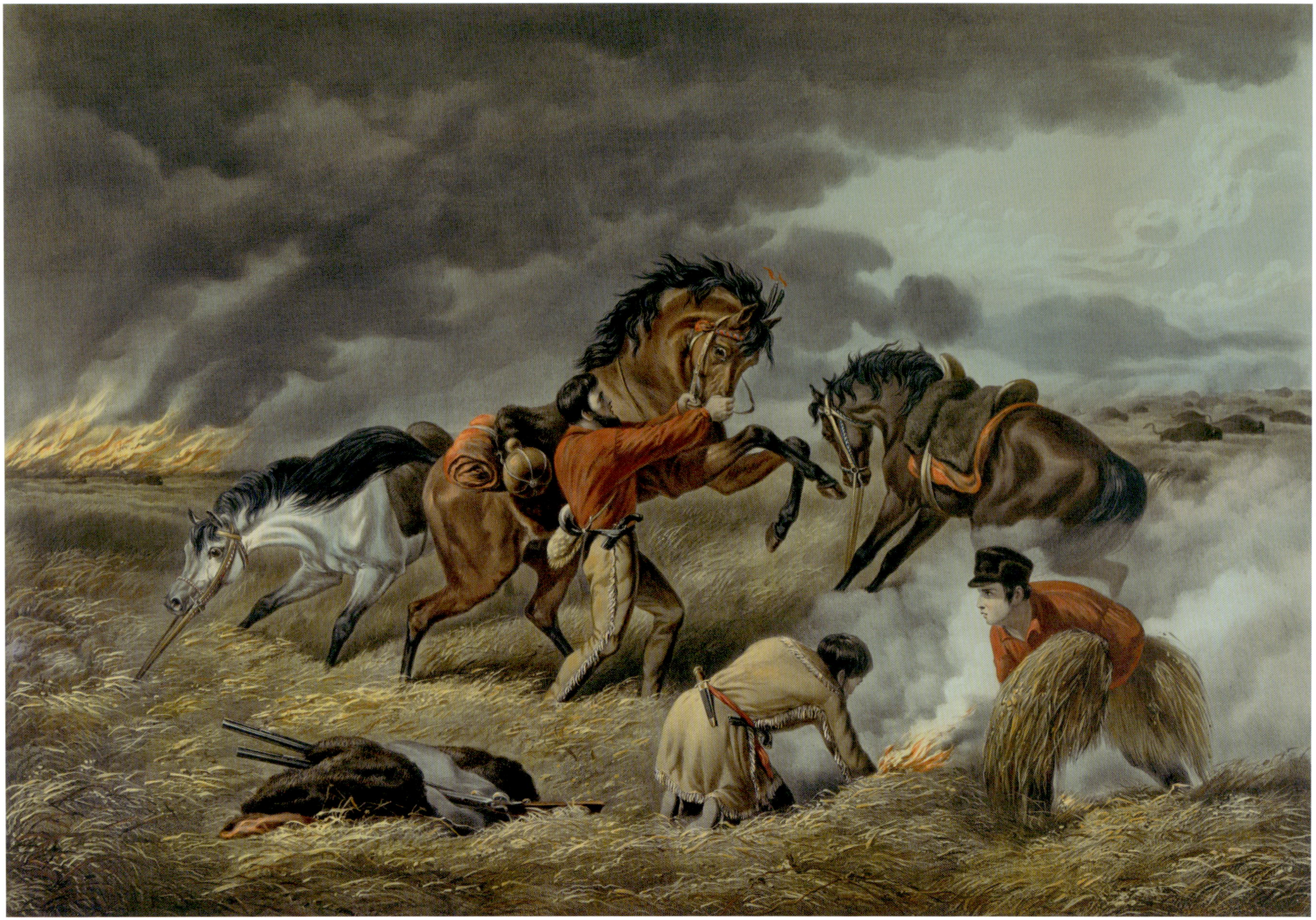

*Life on the Prairie*
*The Trappers Defence—Fire Fight Fire*
1862
Arthur Fitzwilliam Tait, AMERICAN (BORN ENGLAND), 1819–1905

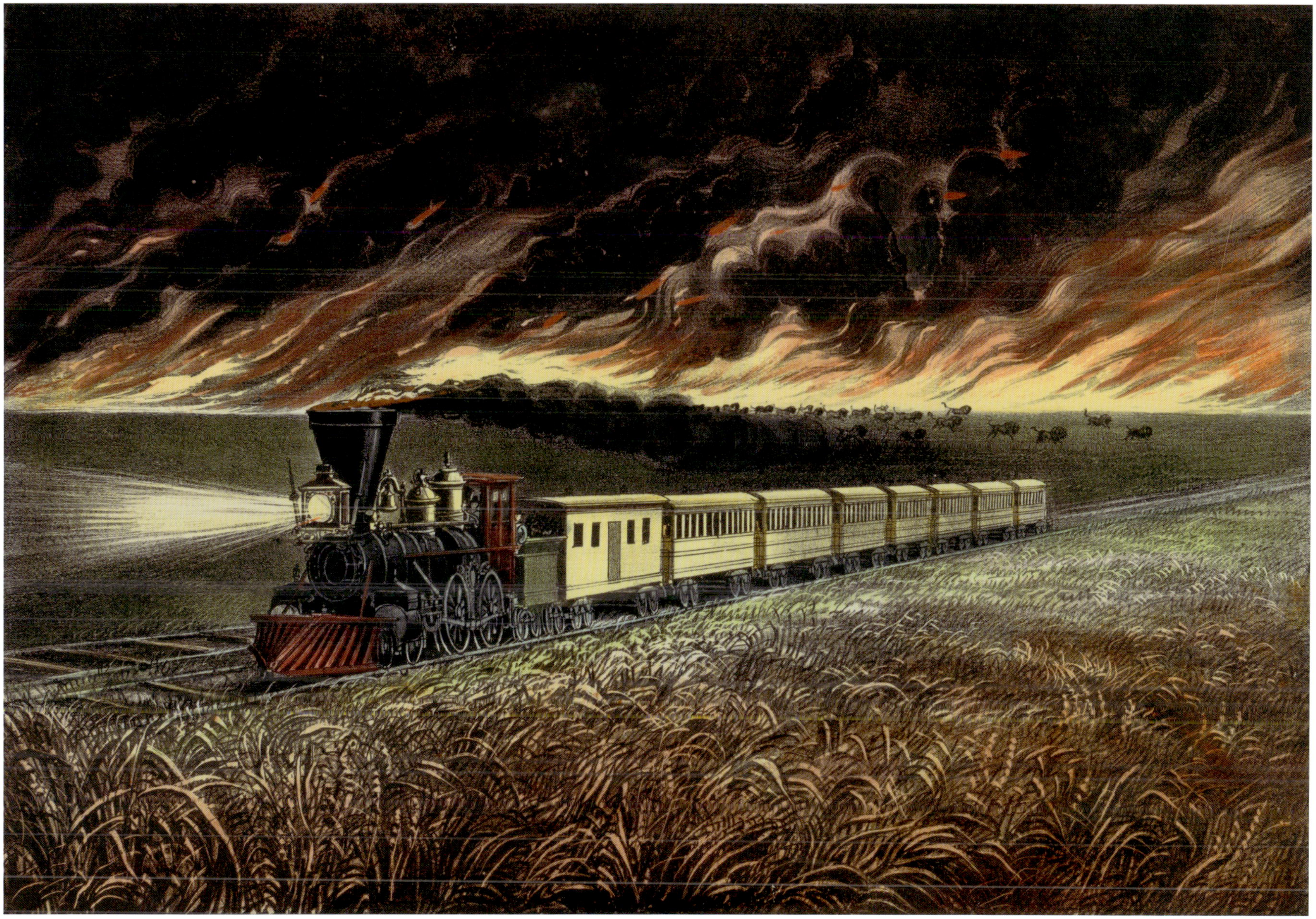

*Prairie Fires of the Great West*

1871

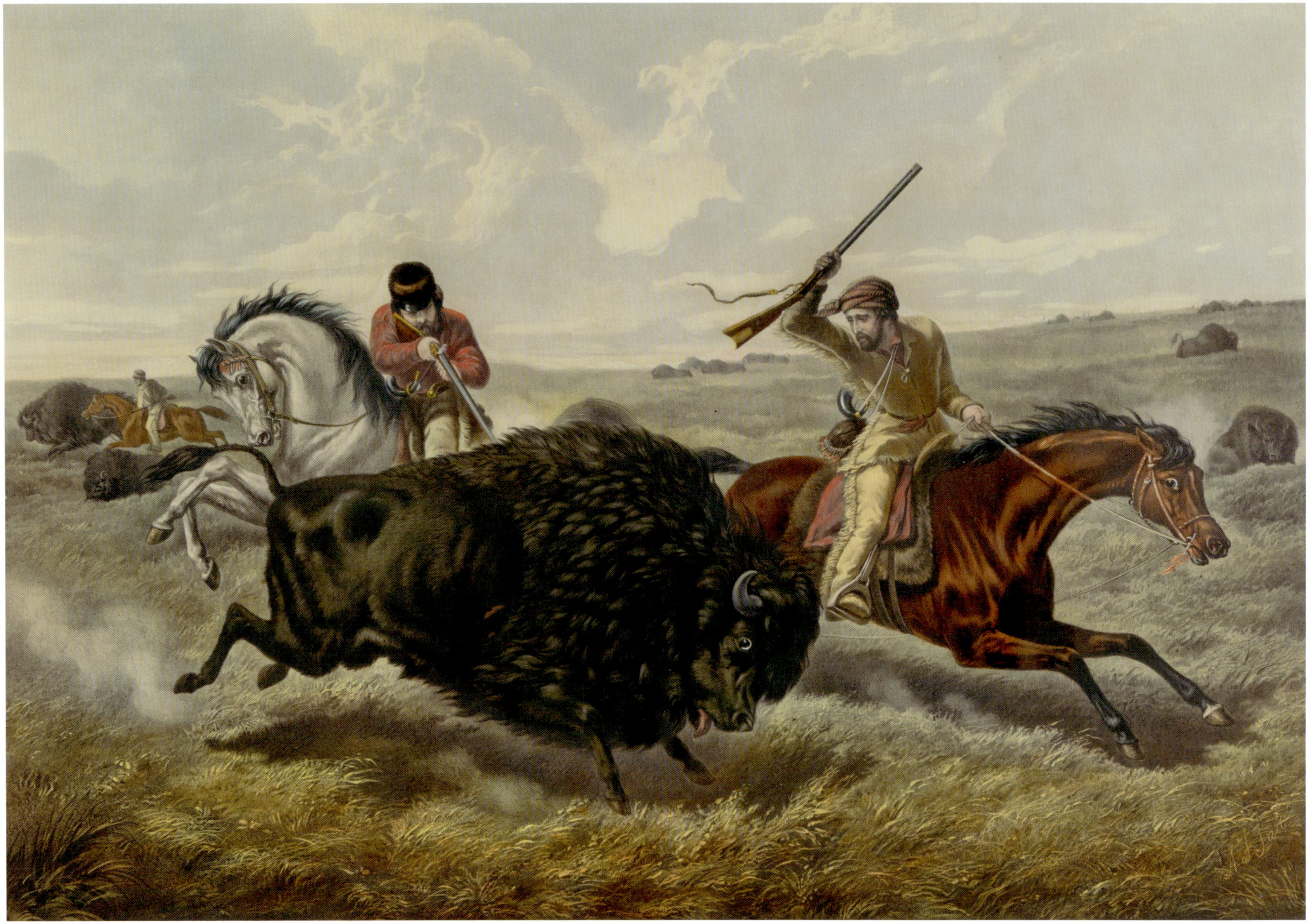

*Life on the Prairie*
***The Buffalo Hunt***
1862
Arthur Fitzwilliam Tait, AMERICAN (BORN ENGLAND), 1819–1905

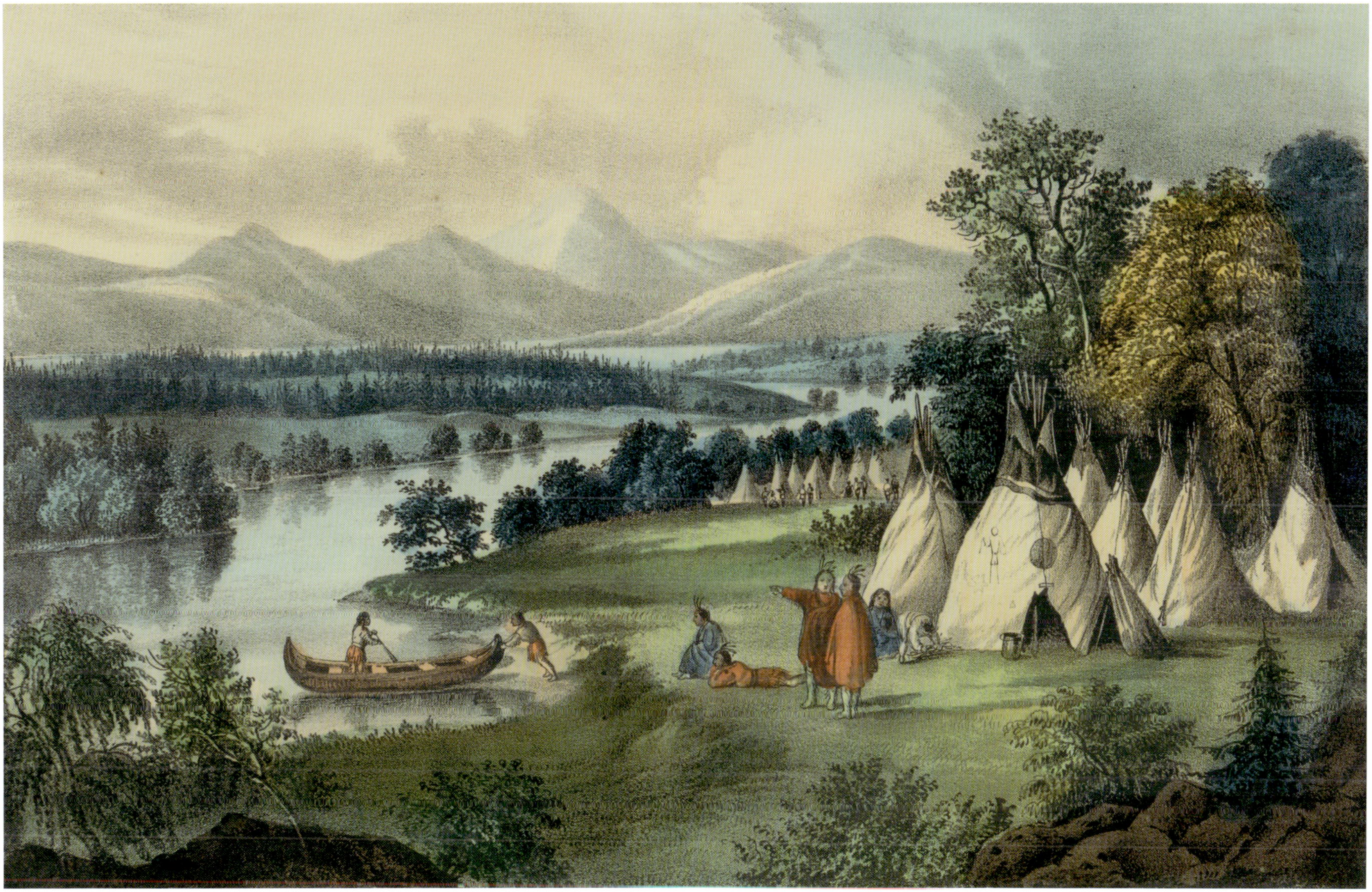

*Scenery of the Upper Mississippi*
***An Indian Village***
ca. 1874–78

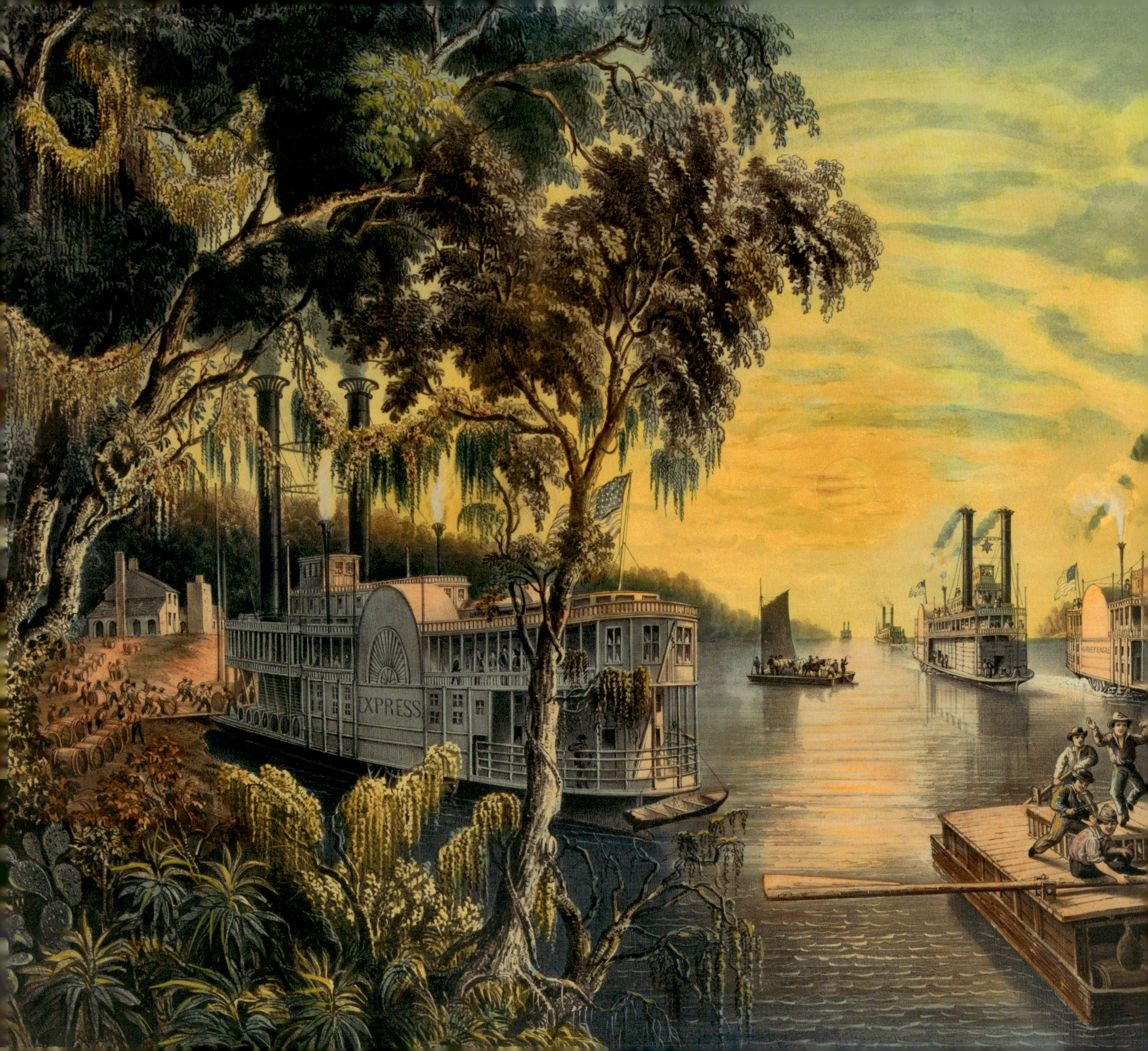
EXPRESS
GREYEAGLE

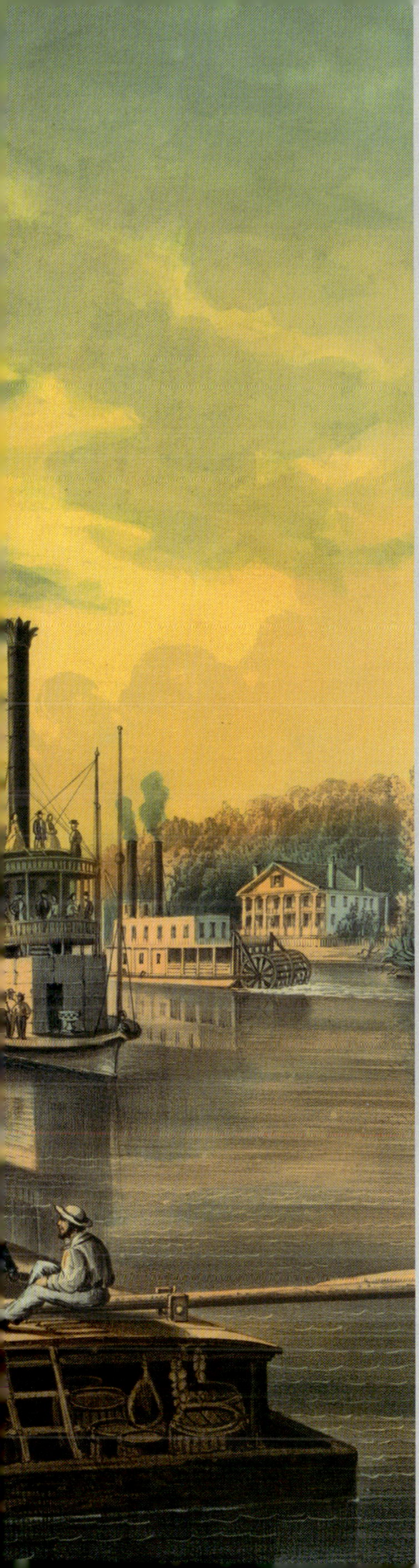

# THE SOUTH

Currier & Ives was an unreservedly Northern firm whose scenes of rural life heavily favored New England rather than the rural South. Before the 1870s, the company's depictions of the South were largely confined to the Civil War, including images of Confederate defeats on land and at sea. However, Currier & Ives stood as a moderate and less political alternative to the illustrated weekly newspapers' demonization of the Confederacy, and was more concerned with depicting a romantic ideal of war than its bloody reality. Despite its wartime pro-Union output, less than ten years after the war the firm began offering nostalgic visions of the antebellum South featuring thriving plantations and riverboats plying the Mississippi. These prints also catered to white customers' appetites for dehumanizing depictions of African Americans as enslaved, uneducated, and happily subservient, well after the Emancipation Proclamation of 1863. Currier & Ives followed cultural tastes as they shifted from placid depictions of enslaved people to a crude and mocking form of racist humor, which emerged in the late nineteenth century. These prints, where racial injustice was portrayed as humorous, helped to perpetuate stereotypes and caricatures about Black people that remain present in American consciousness. Although Currier & Ives had previously published at least one print condemning the evils of slavery, it sold poorly, and the firm instead chose to depict a view of life in the antebellum South that appealed to its customers' desires.

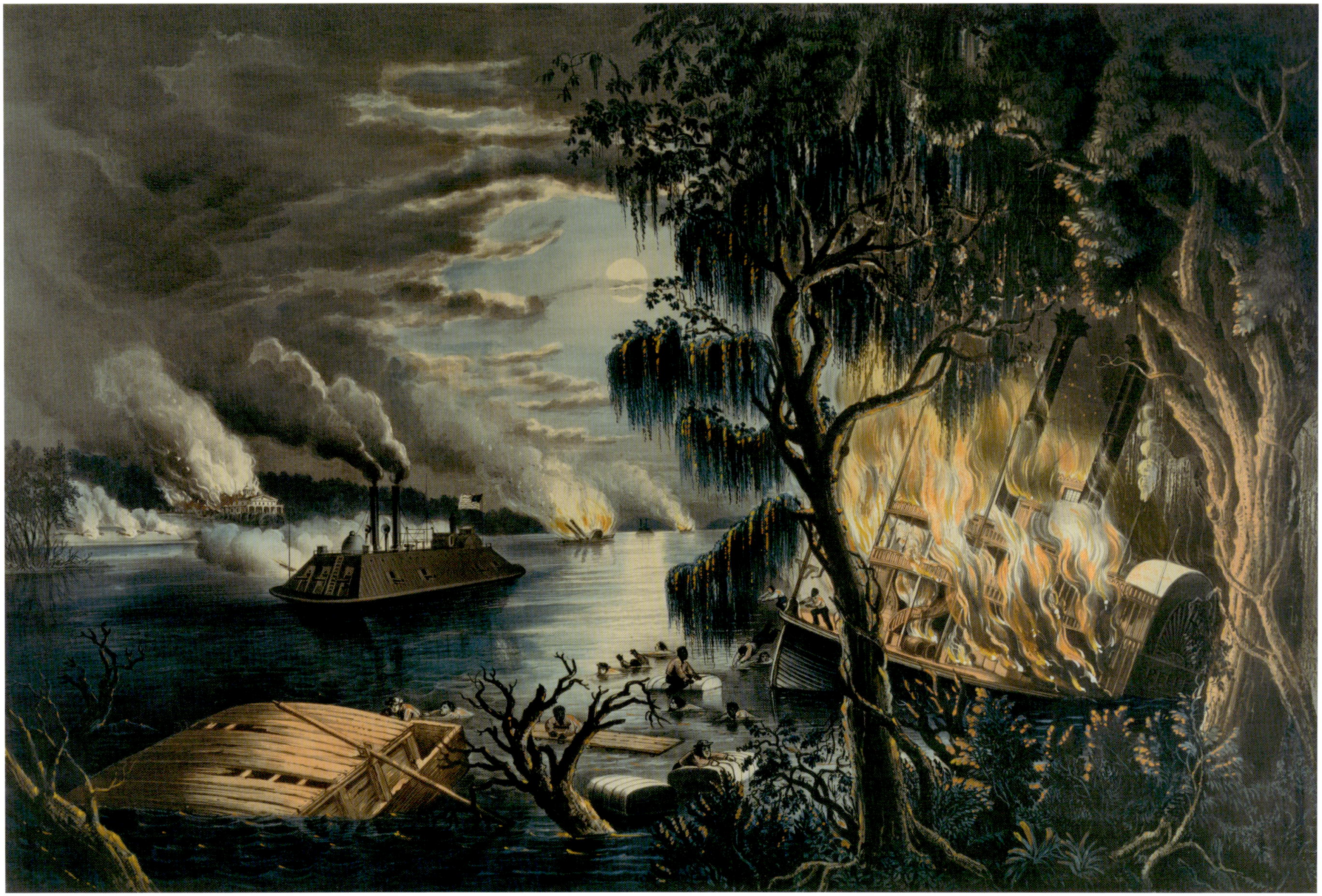

*The Mississippi in Time of War*

1865

Frances Palmer, AMERICAN (BORN ENGLAND), 1812–1876

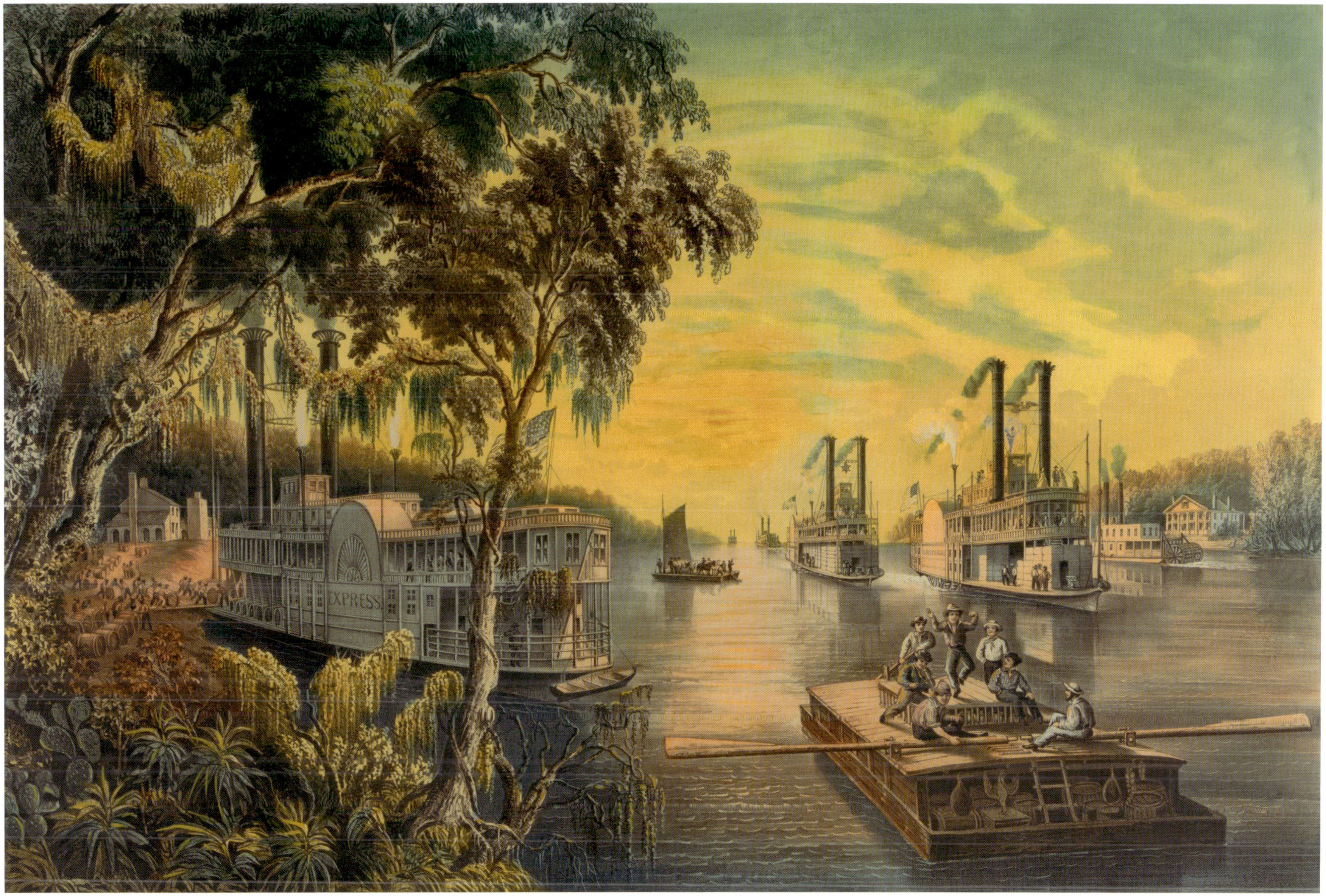


*The Mississippi in Time of Peace*

1865

Frances Palmer, AMERICAN (BORN ENGLAND), 1812–1876

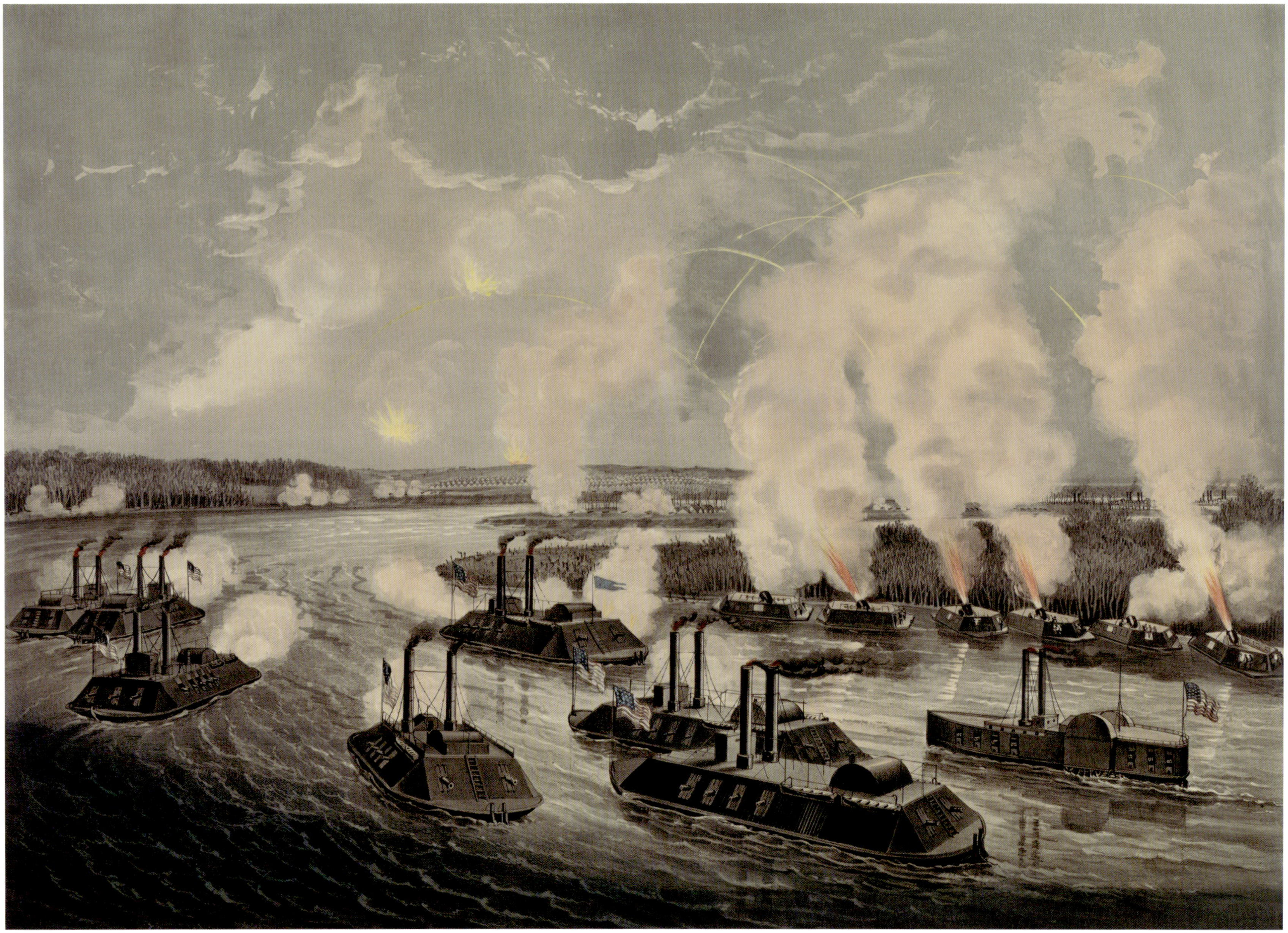

*Bombardment and Capture of Island Number Ten*

1862

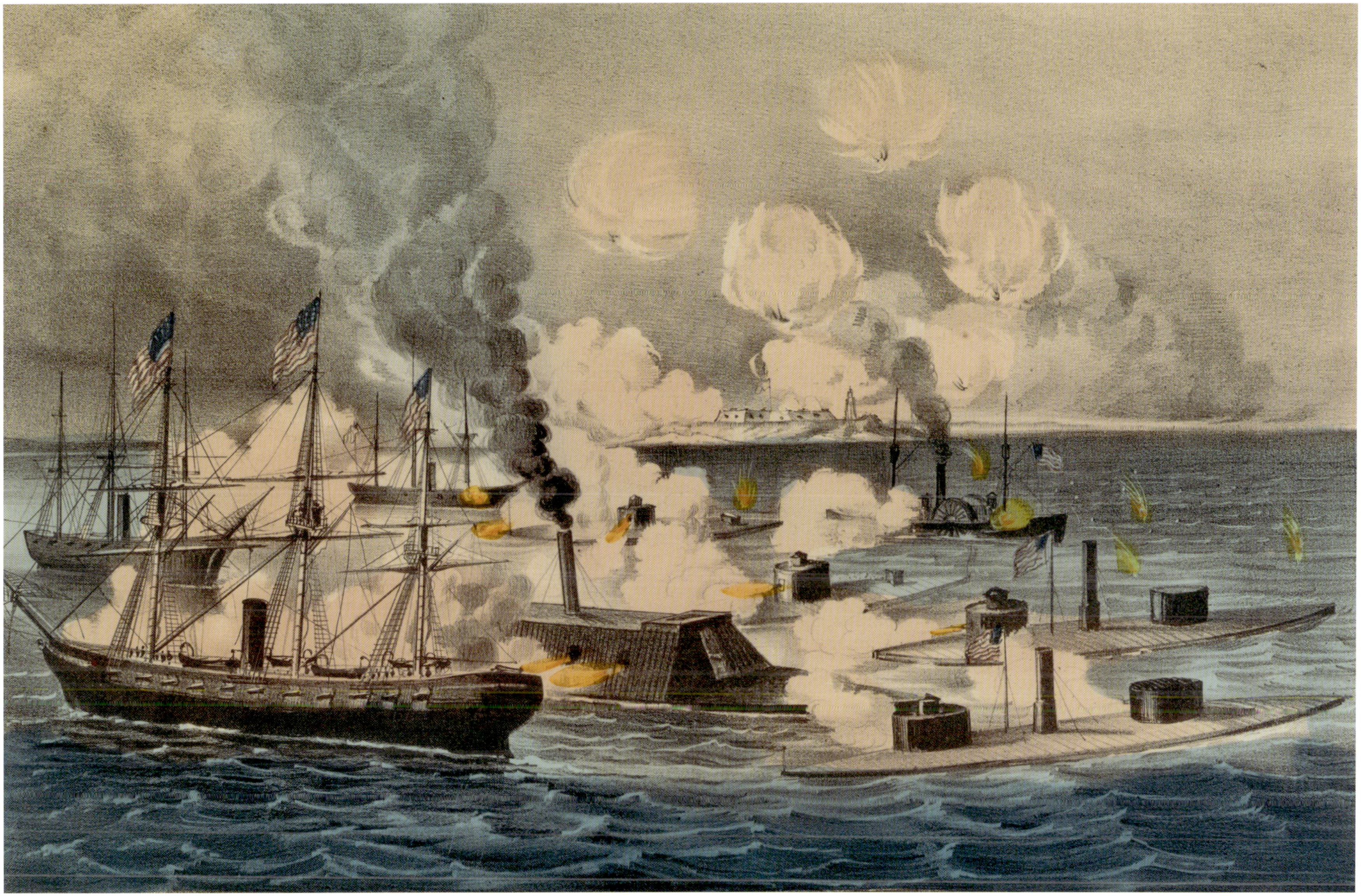

*The Great Naval Victory in Mobile Bay, Aug. 5th 1864*

ca. 1864

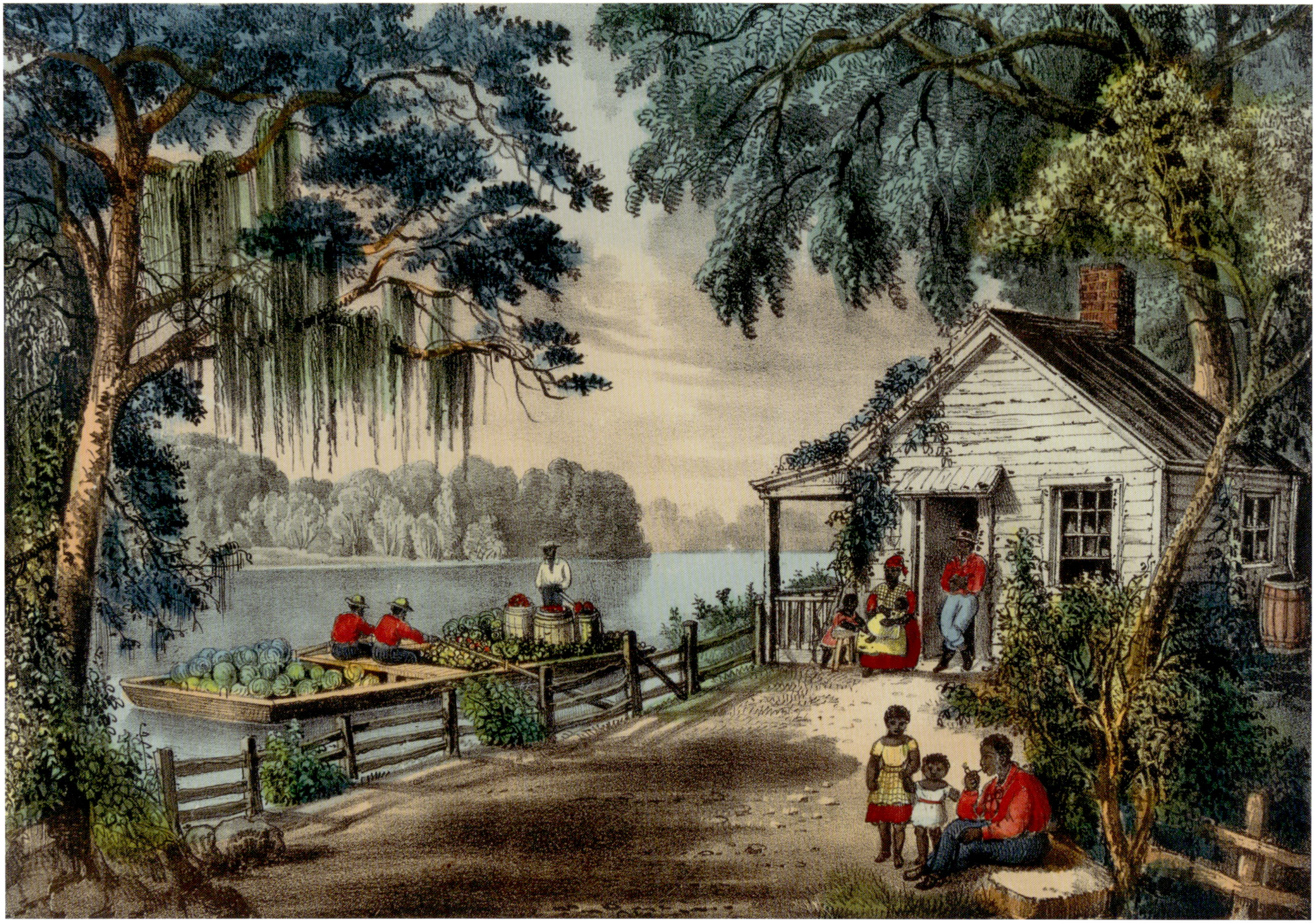

*Good Times on the Old Plantation*

ca. 1877–94

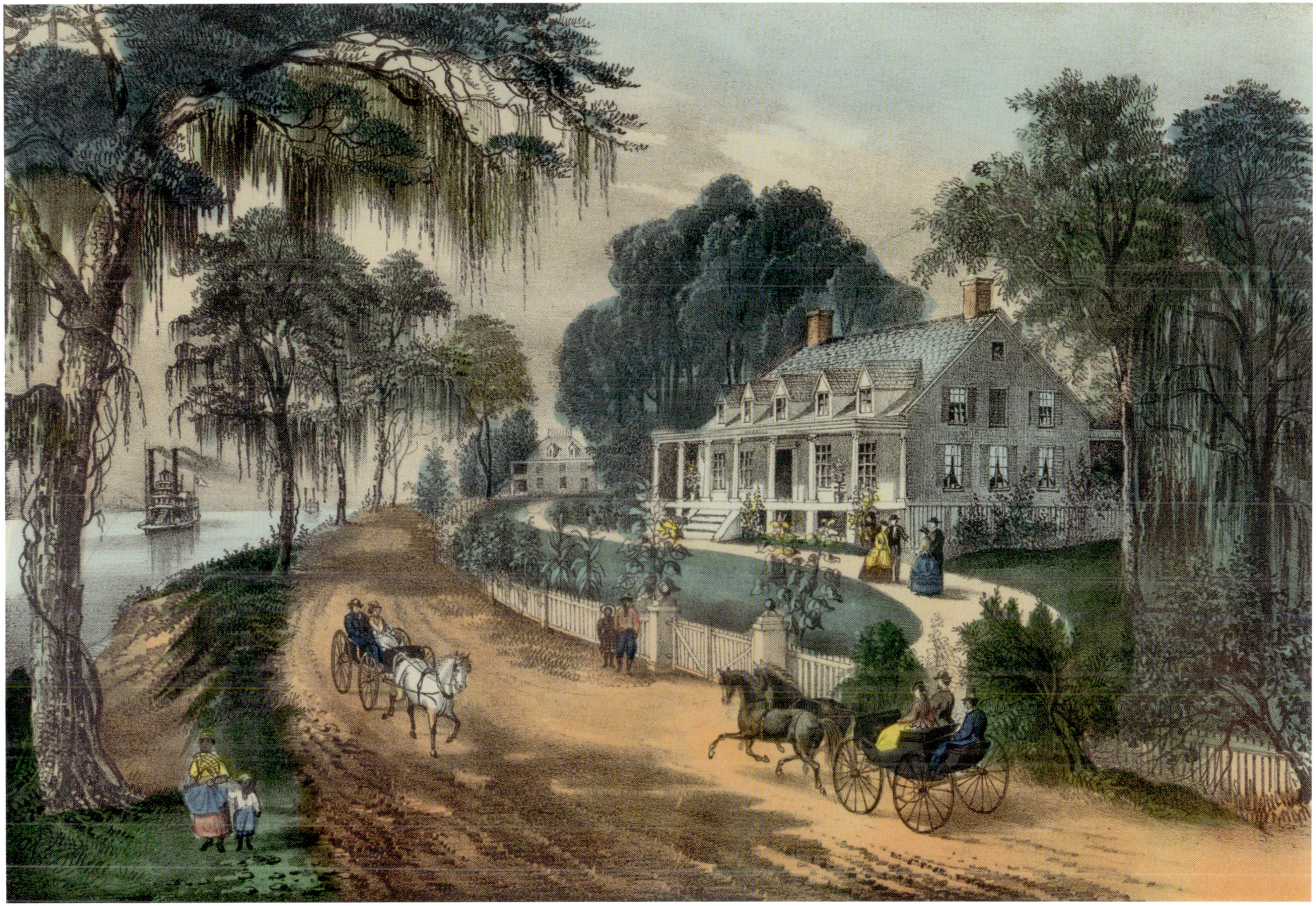

*A Home on the Mississippi*

1871

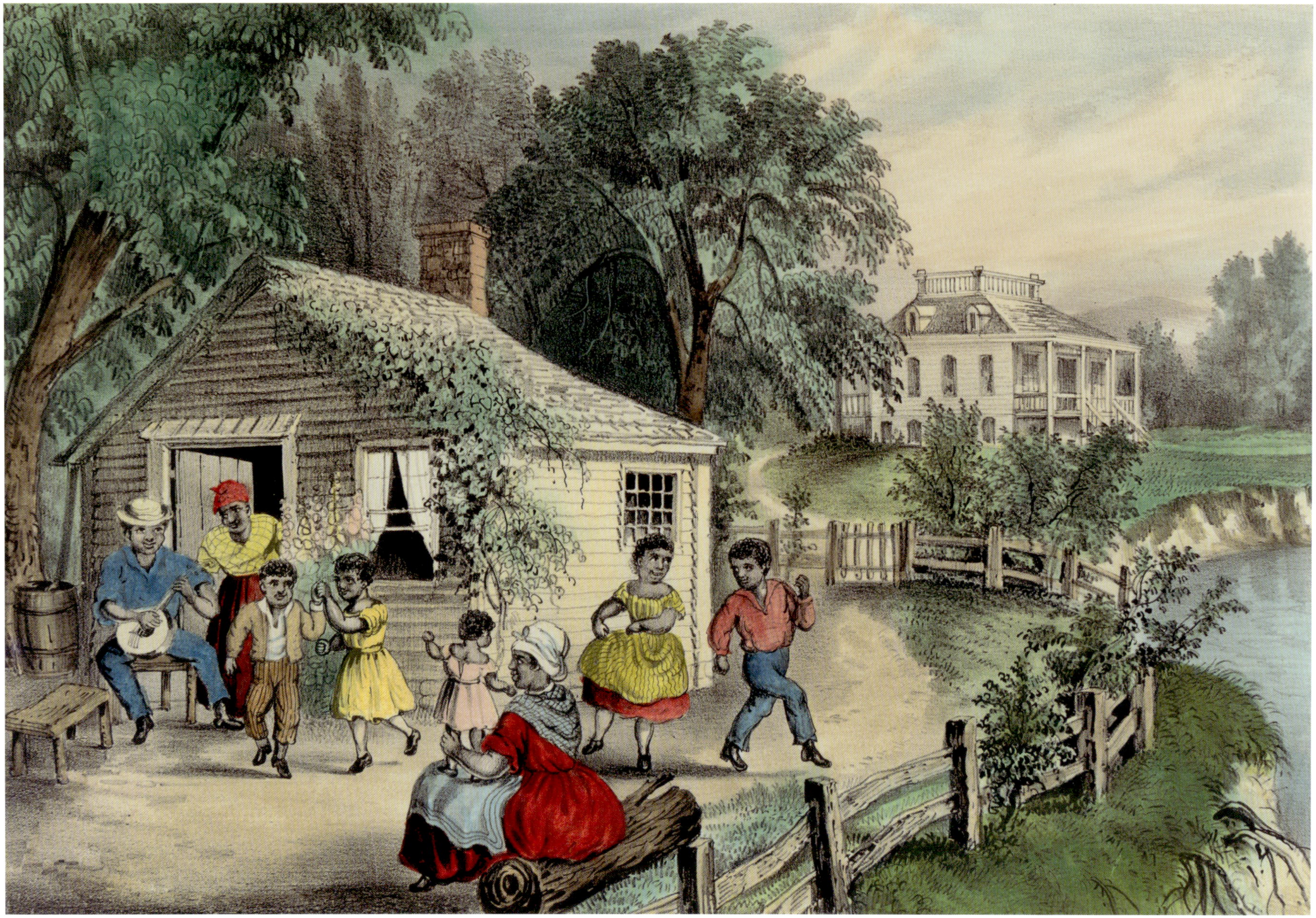

*The Old Plantation Home*

1872

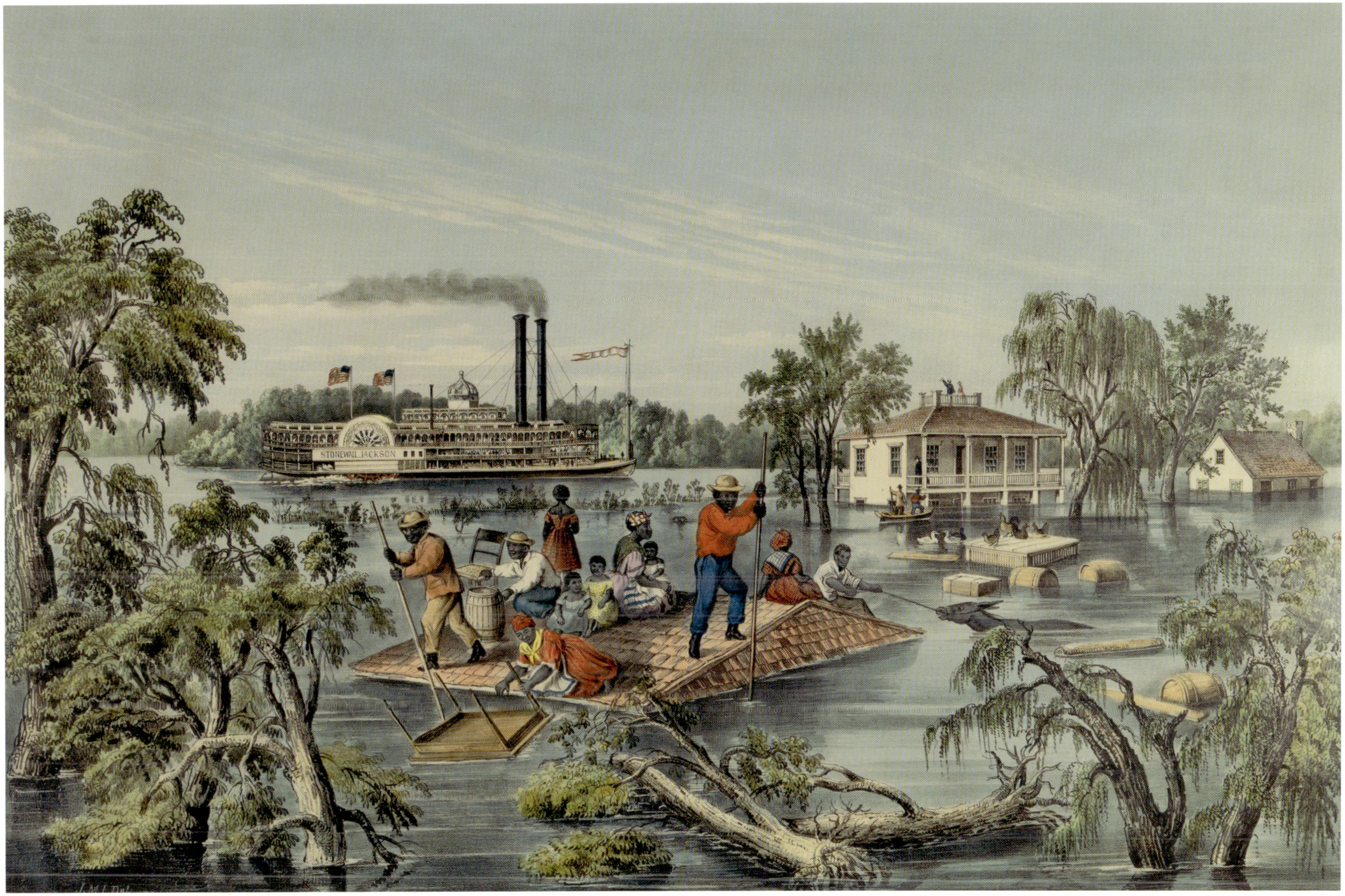


*High Water in the Mississippi*

1868

Frances Palmer, AMERICAN (BORN ENGLAND), 1812–1876

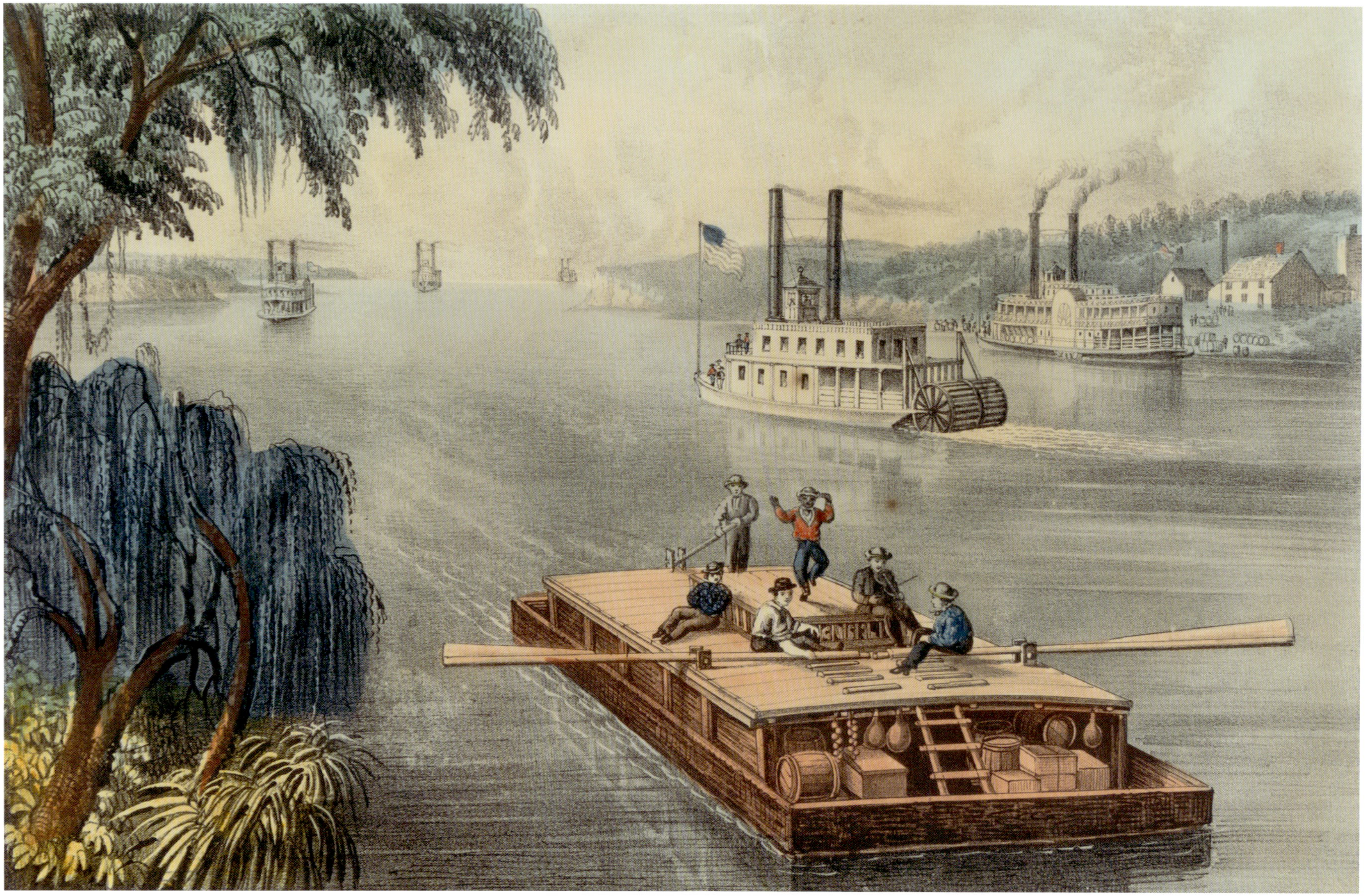

*Bound Down the River*

1870

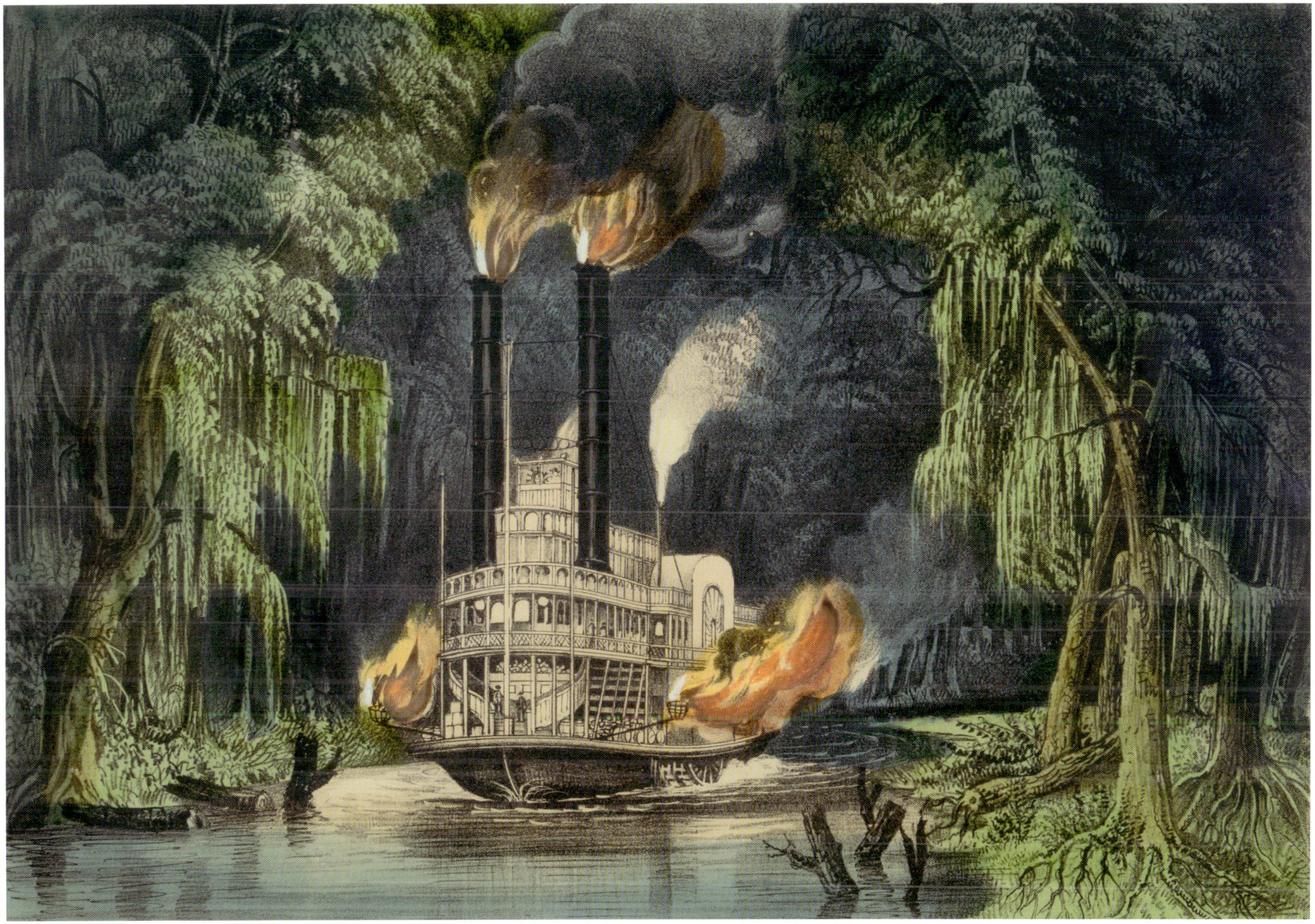

*Through the Bayou by Torchlight*

ca. 1877–94

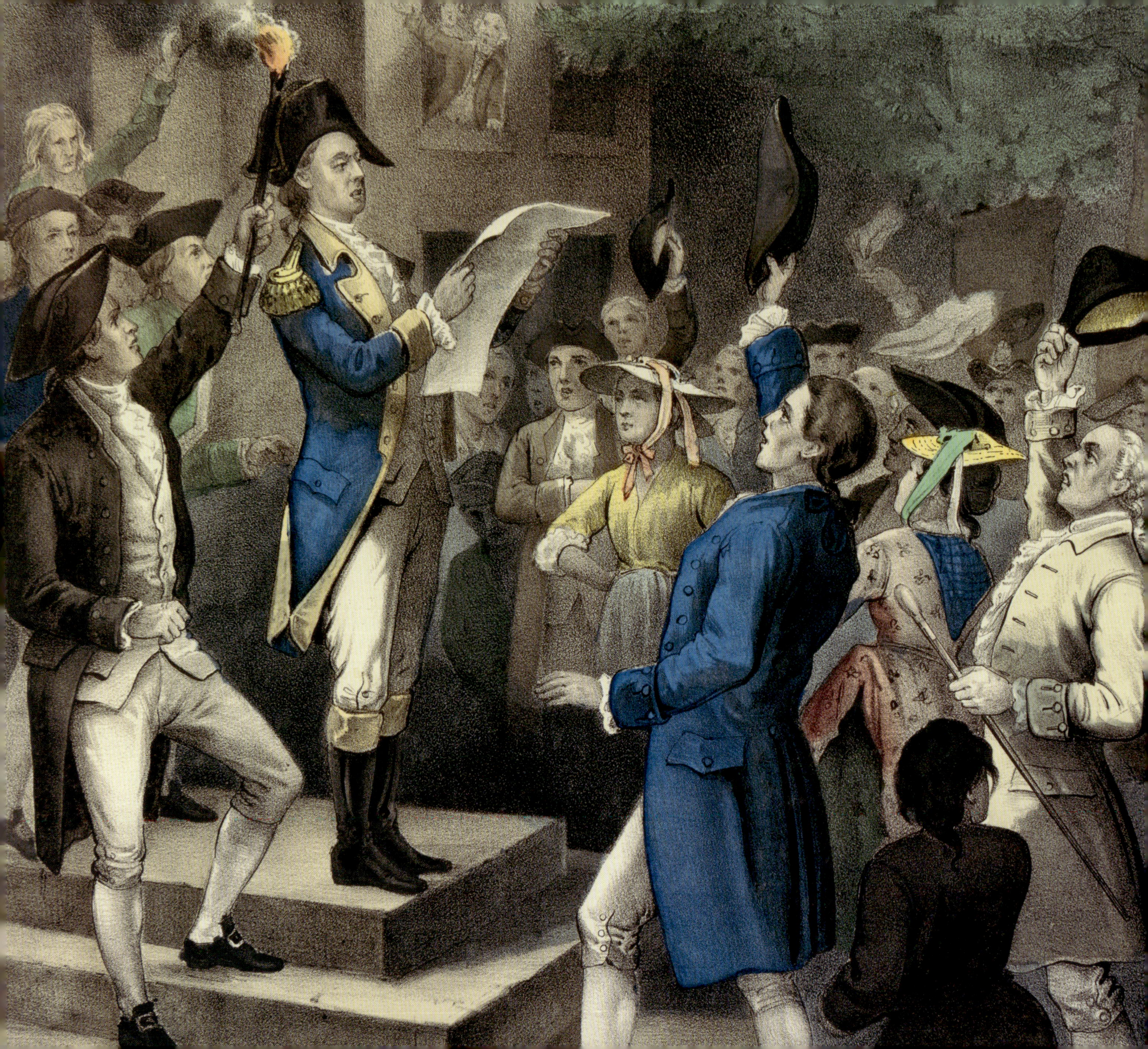

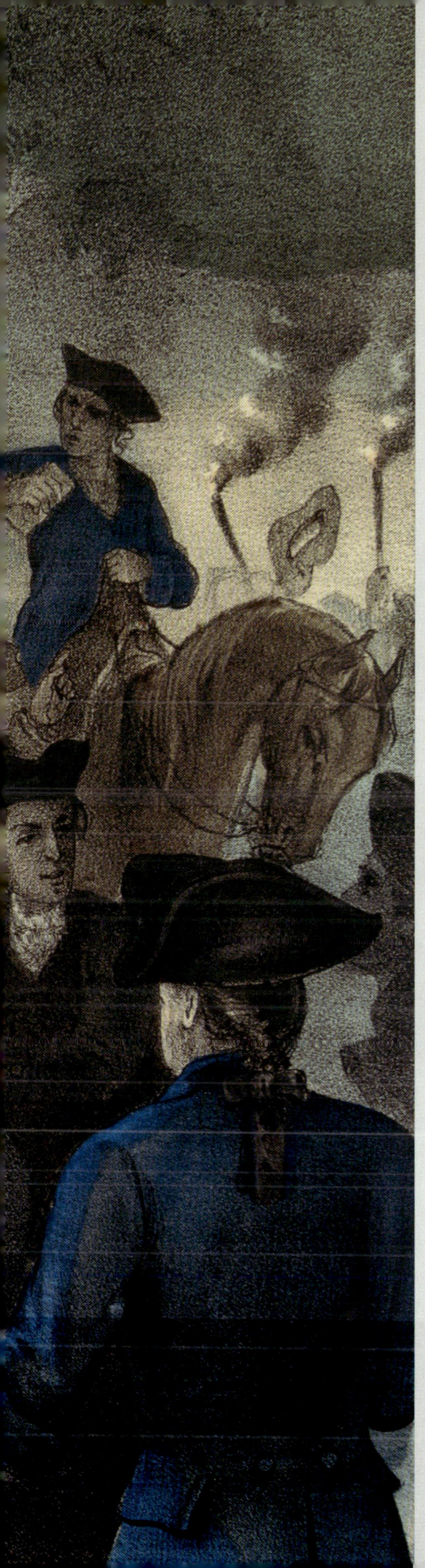

# AMERICA IN WAR AND PEACE

Although photography offered an immediate visual account of the Civil War, this new medium was limited to capturing static subjects, including landscapes, portraits, and the scene before or after a conflict. Currier & Ives and other lithography firms, whose artists could capture the action of a battle itself shortly after its occurrence, played a key role in picturing America's bloodiest war. While their illustrations documented the events of war as they were happening, the firm was undoubtedly pro-Union, and its images glorified the North. Yet it also pictured a more moderate and romantic view of war than did papers such as *Harper's Weekly*, which readily displayed atrocities perpetrated by the Confederacy in an effort to drum up support for the Union. Similar to its portrayal of the Civil War, Currier & Ives's depictions of the Revolutionary War celebrated American identity by romanticizing and immortalizing the war that founded the nation. In both conflicts, the firm lionized American presidents and heroes, such as George Washington and Abraham Lincoln. Lincoln, in particular, was a popular subject and appeared in many political cartoons while he was still a candidate. After his assassination, however, the former commander-in-chief was elevated to the status of national martyr and was embraced as the savior of the Union.

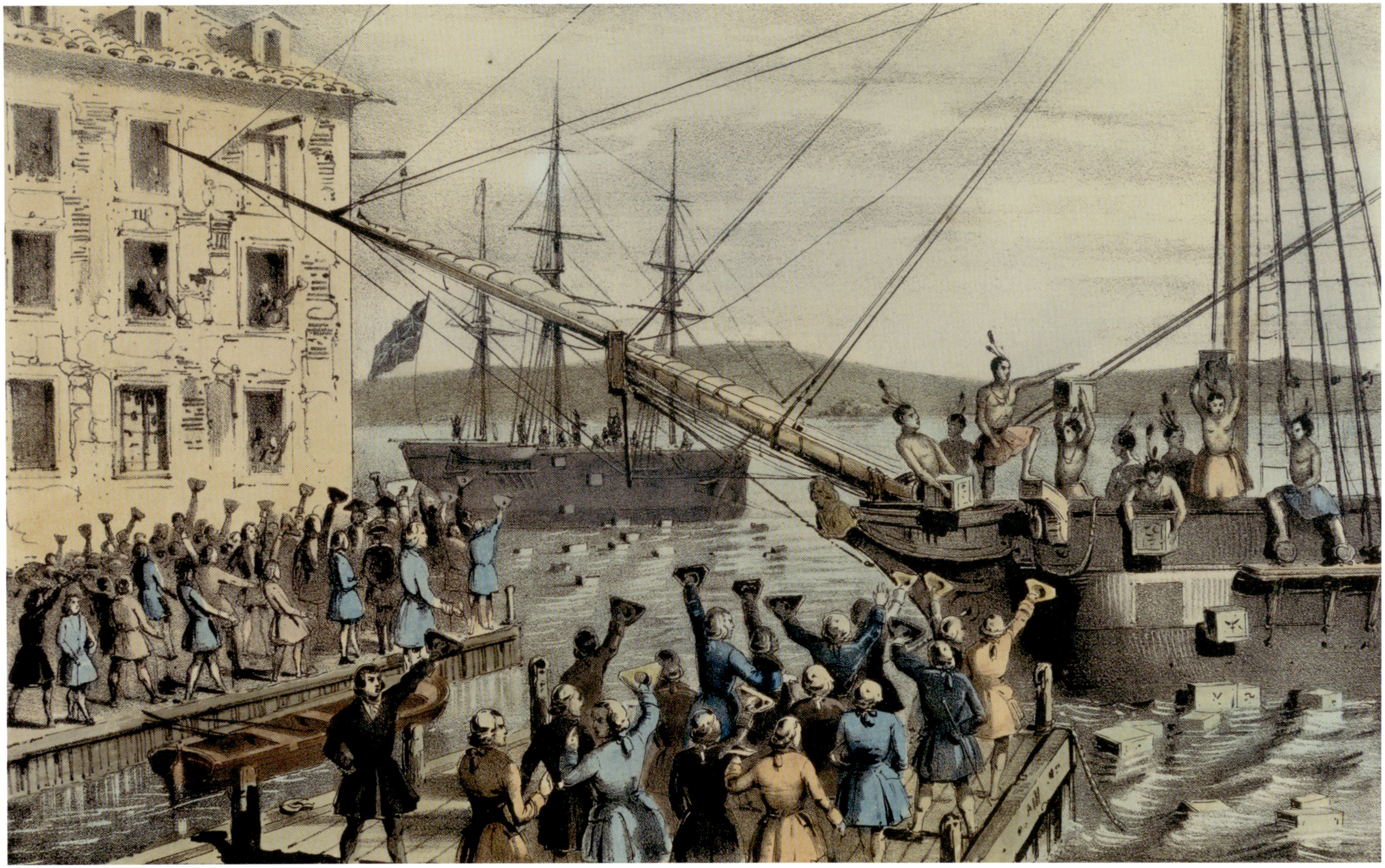

*The Destruction of Tea at Boston Harbor*

1846

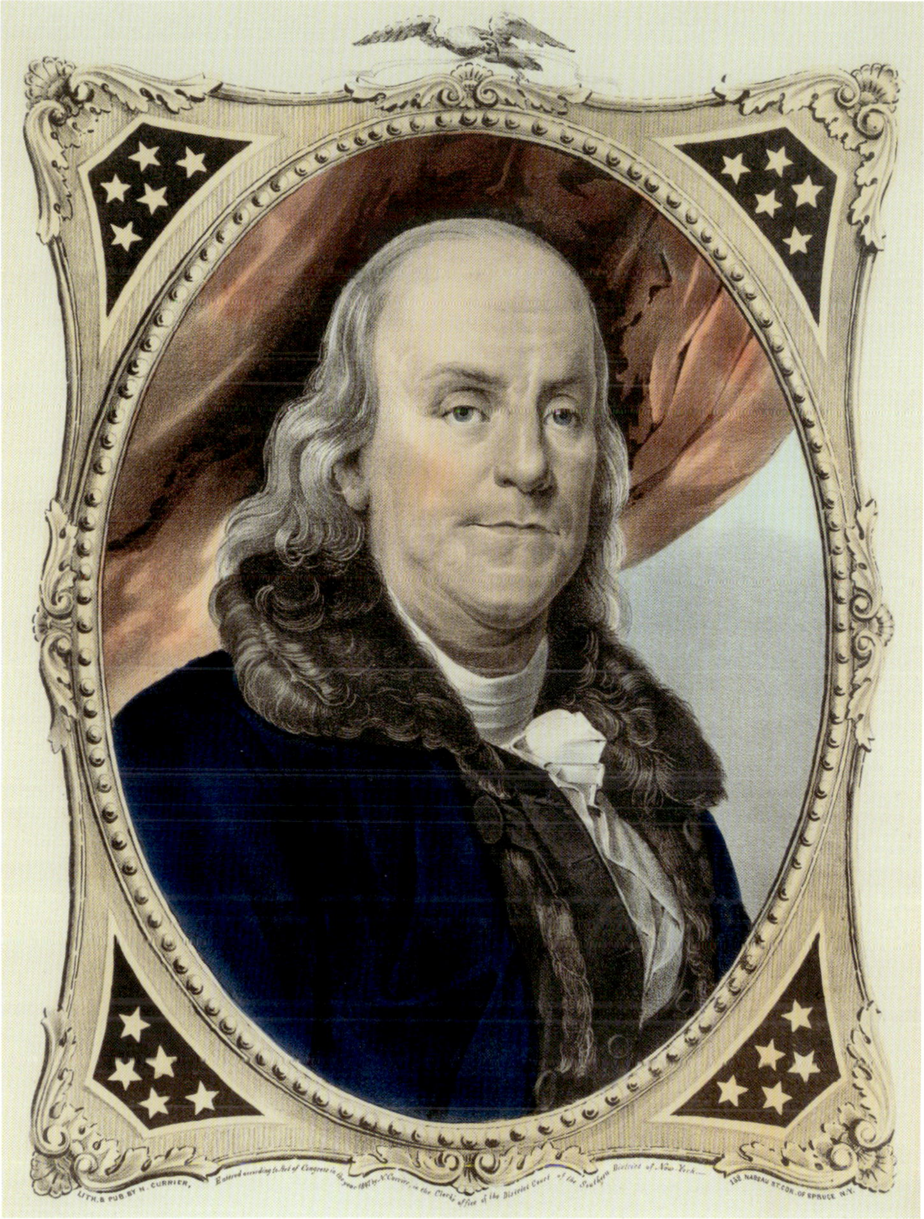


*Benjamin Franklin*
*The Statesman and Philosopher*
1847

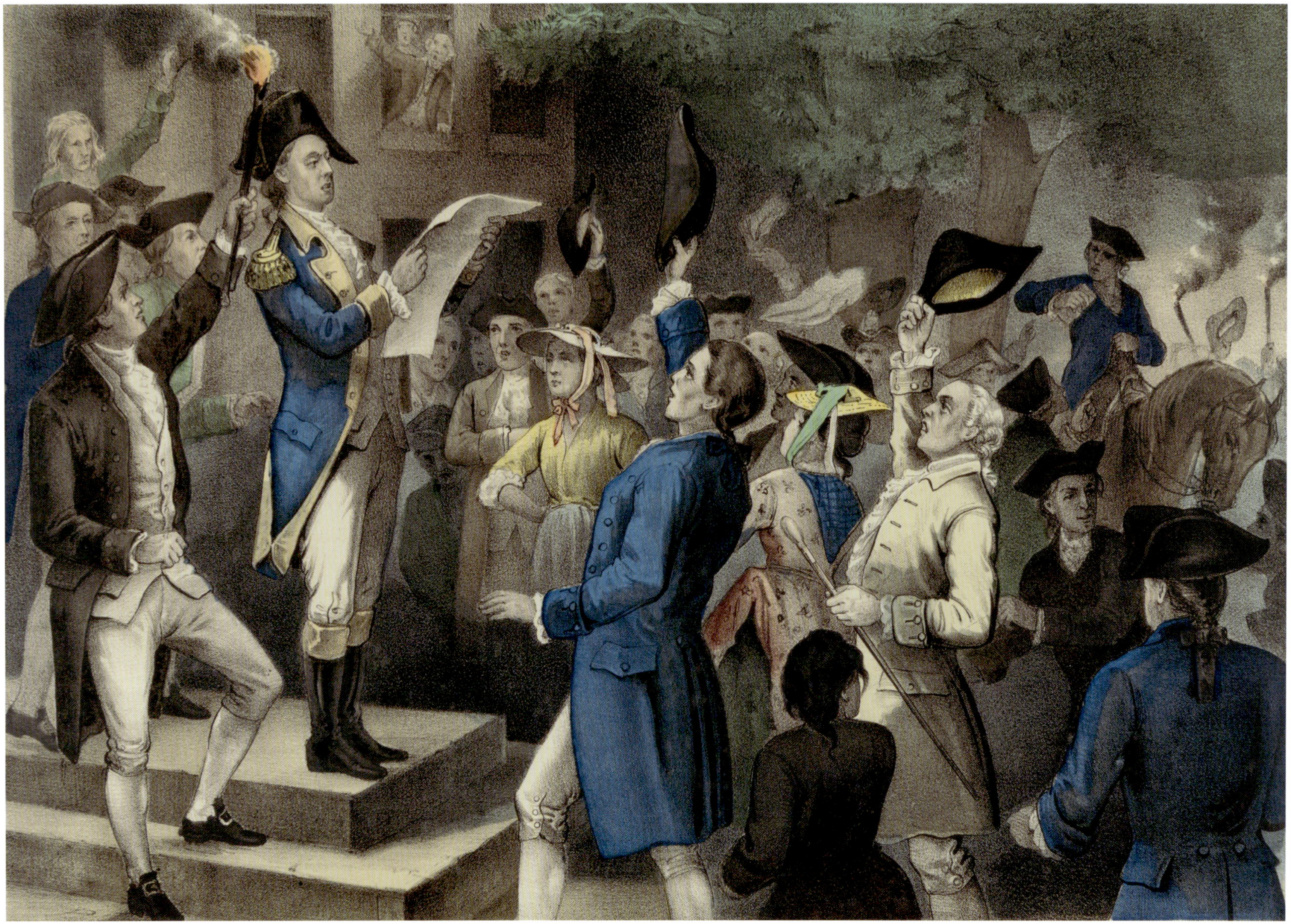

*Cornwallis is Taken!*

*Lieut. Col. Tighlman of Washington's Staff, Announcing the Surrender of Cornwallis, from the Steps of the State House, (Independence Hall,) at Midnight, October 23rd. 1781*

1876

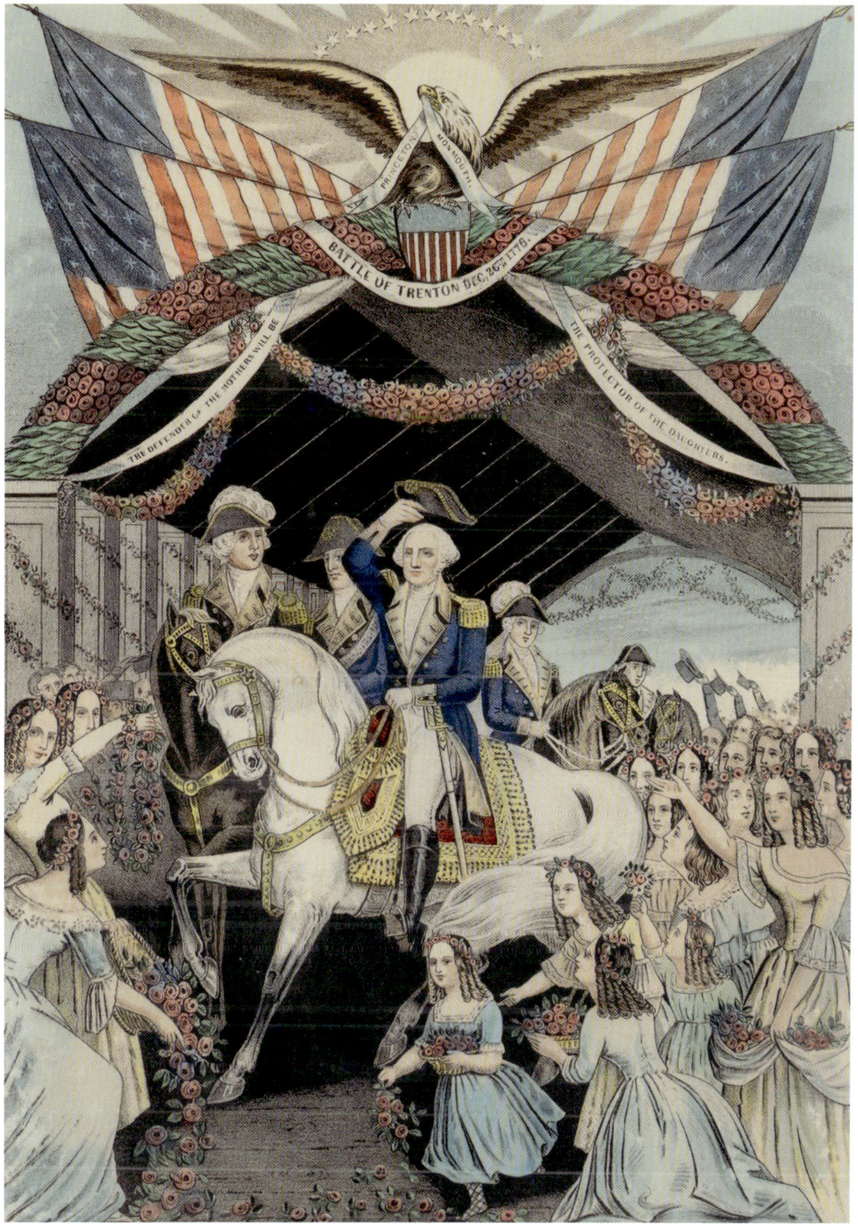


*Washington's Reception by the Ladies, On Passing the Bridge at Trenton, N.J. April 1789*

***On His Way to New York to be Inaugurated First President of the United States***

1845

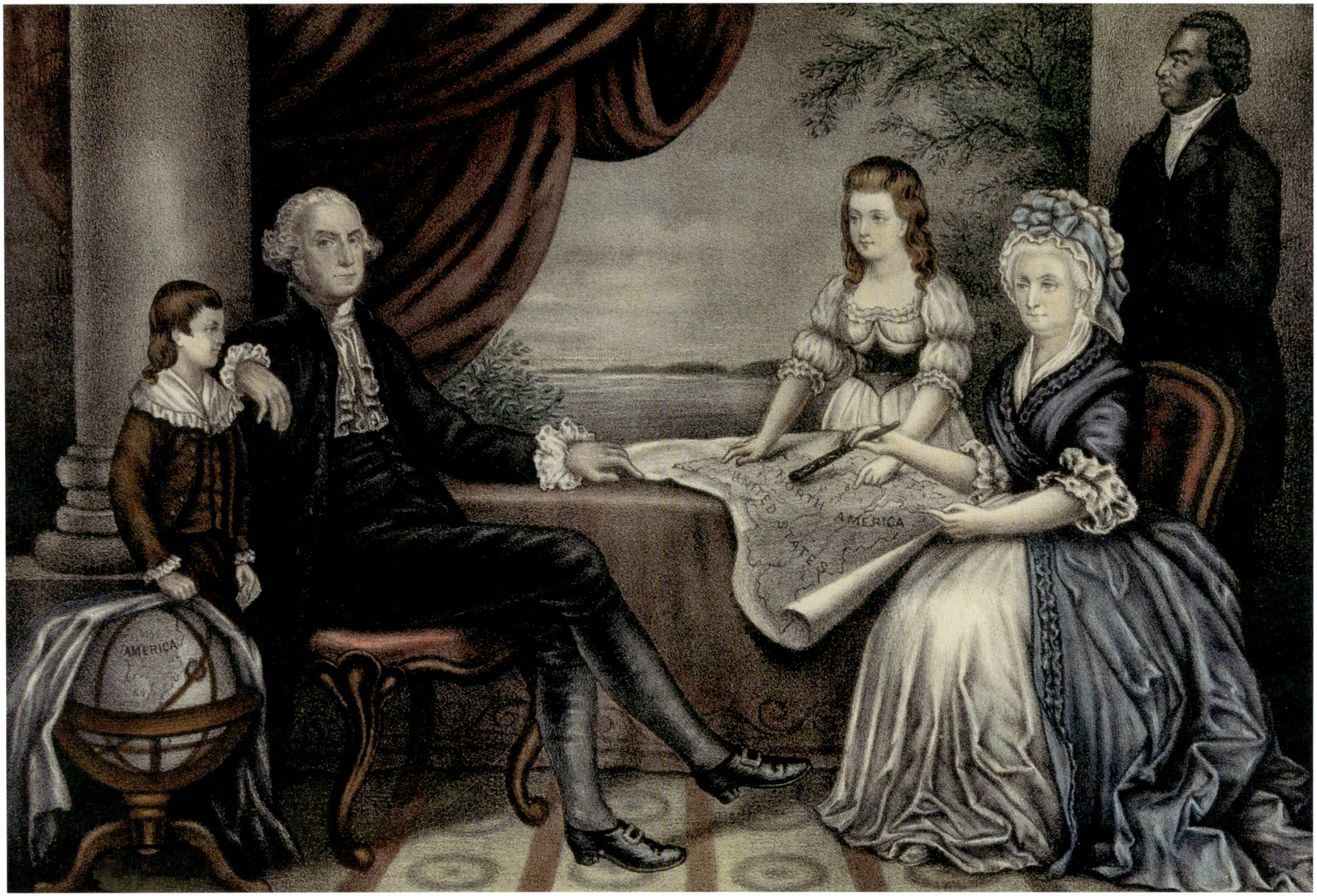


*The Washington Family*

n.d.

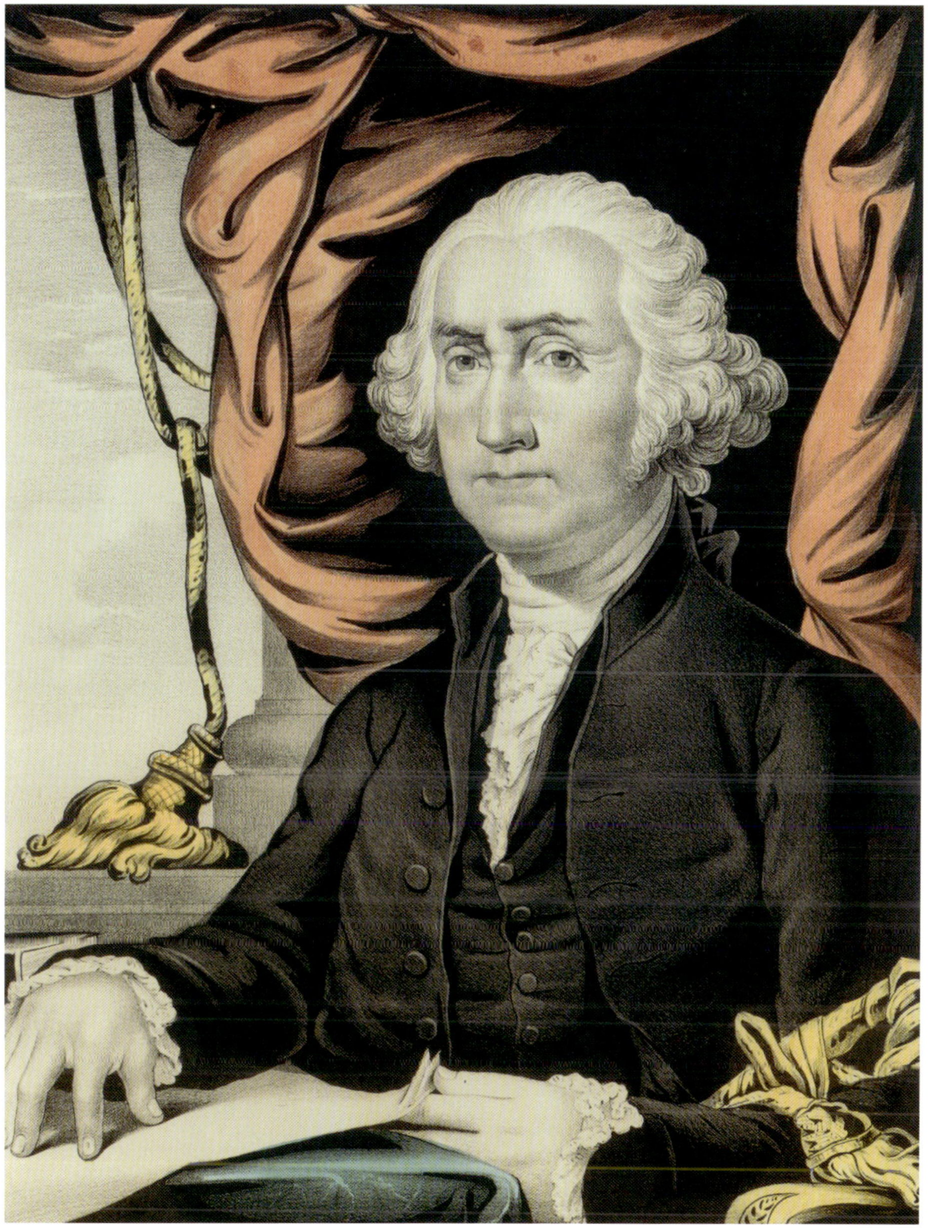

*George Washington*
*First President of the United States*
n.d.

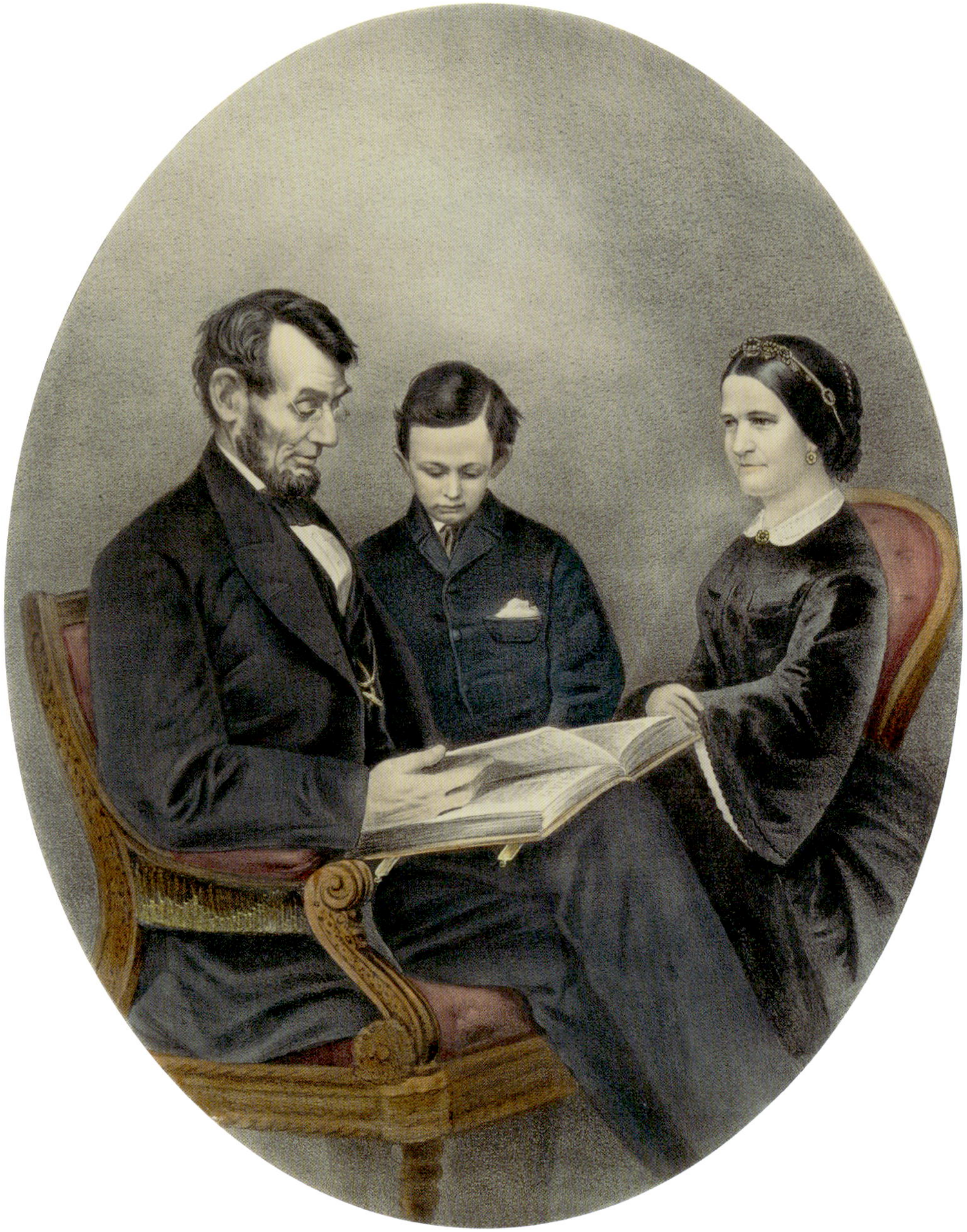

*President Lincoln at Home*
*Reading the Scriptures to His Wife and Son*
1865

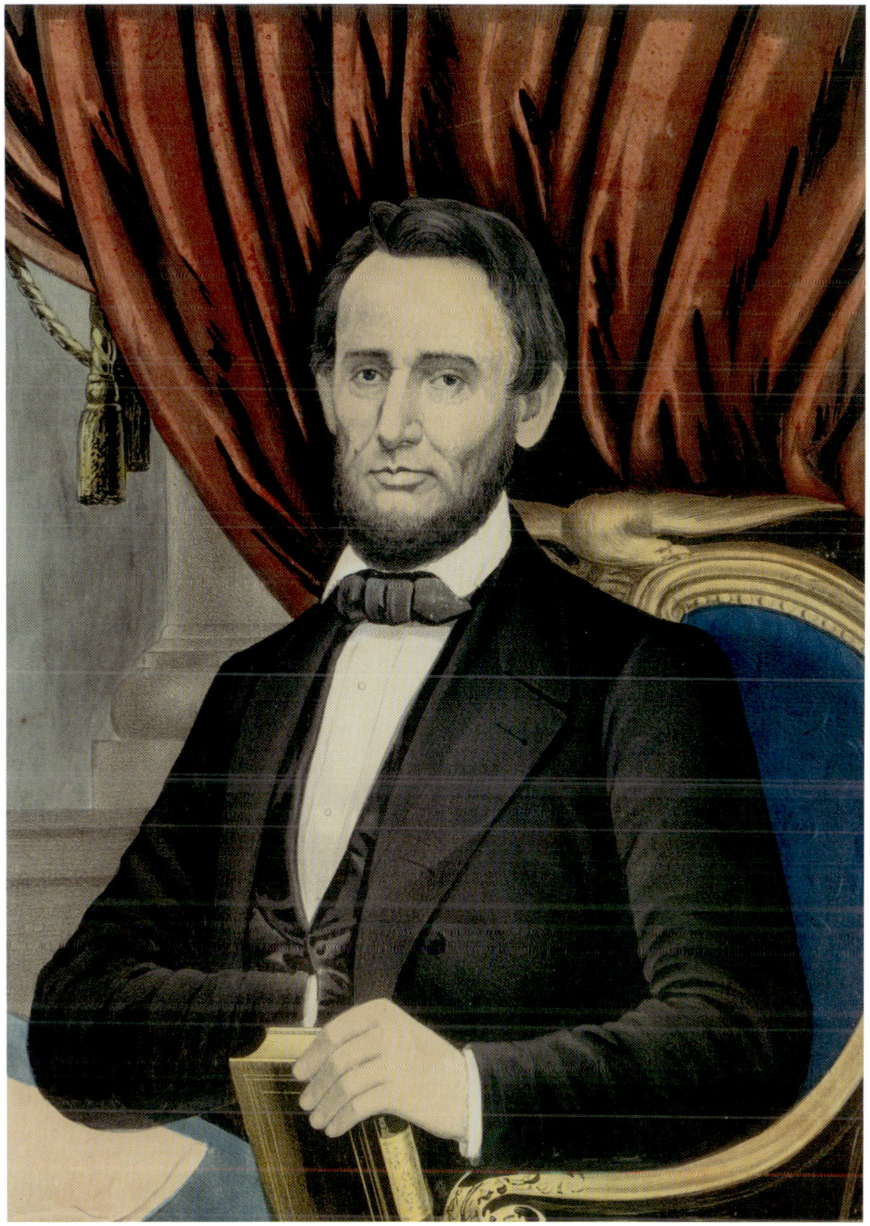

*Abraham Lincoln*
*Sixteenth President of the United States*
1861

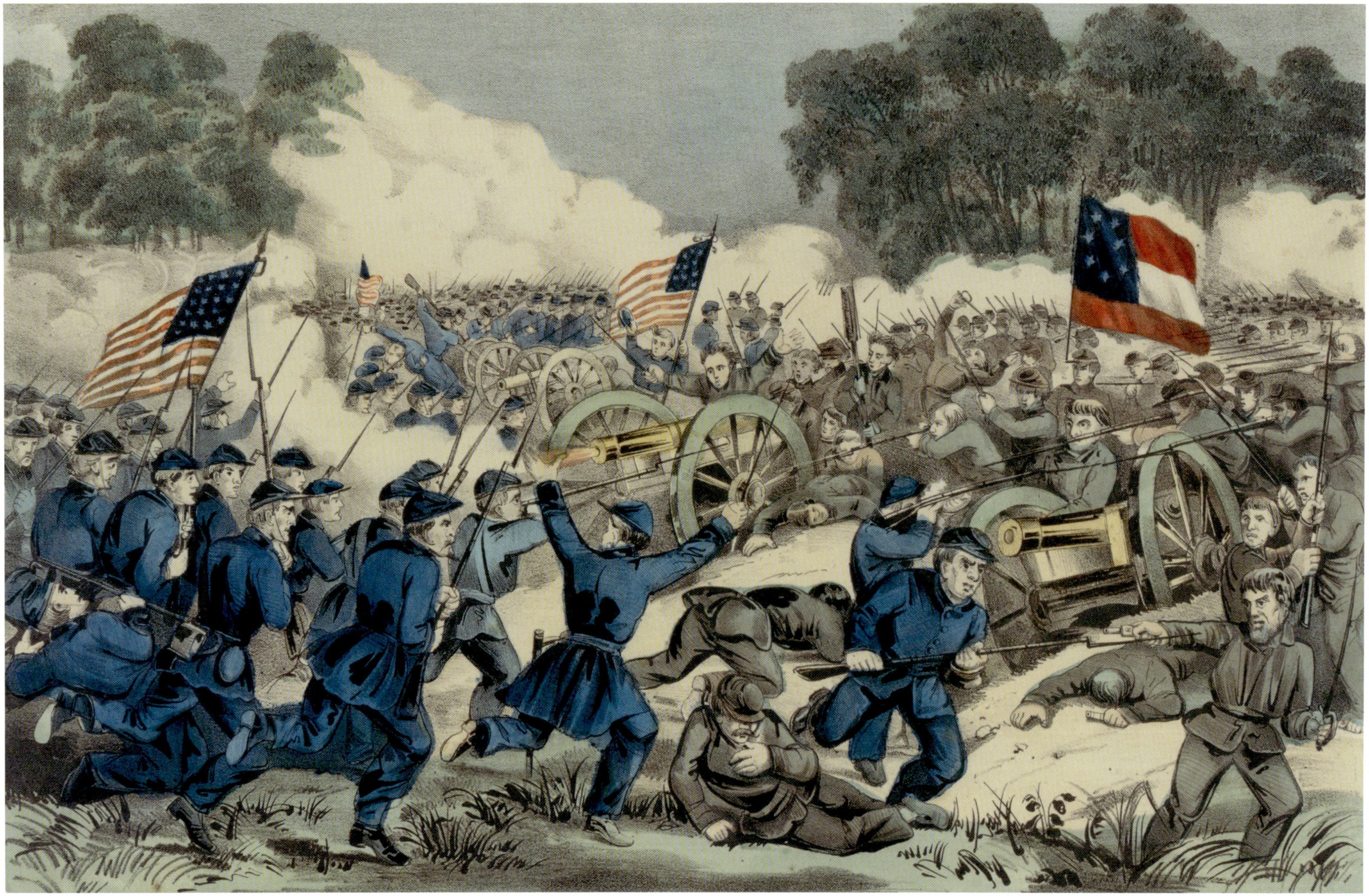

*The Battle of Gettysburg, Pa. July 3rd. 1863*

ca. 1863

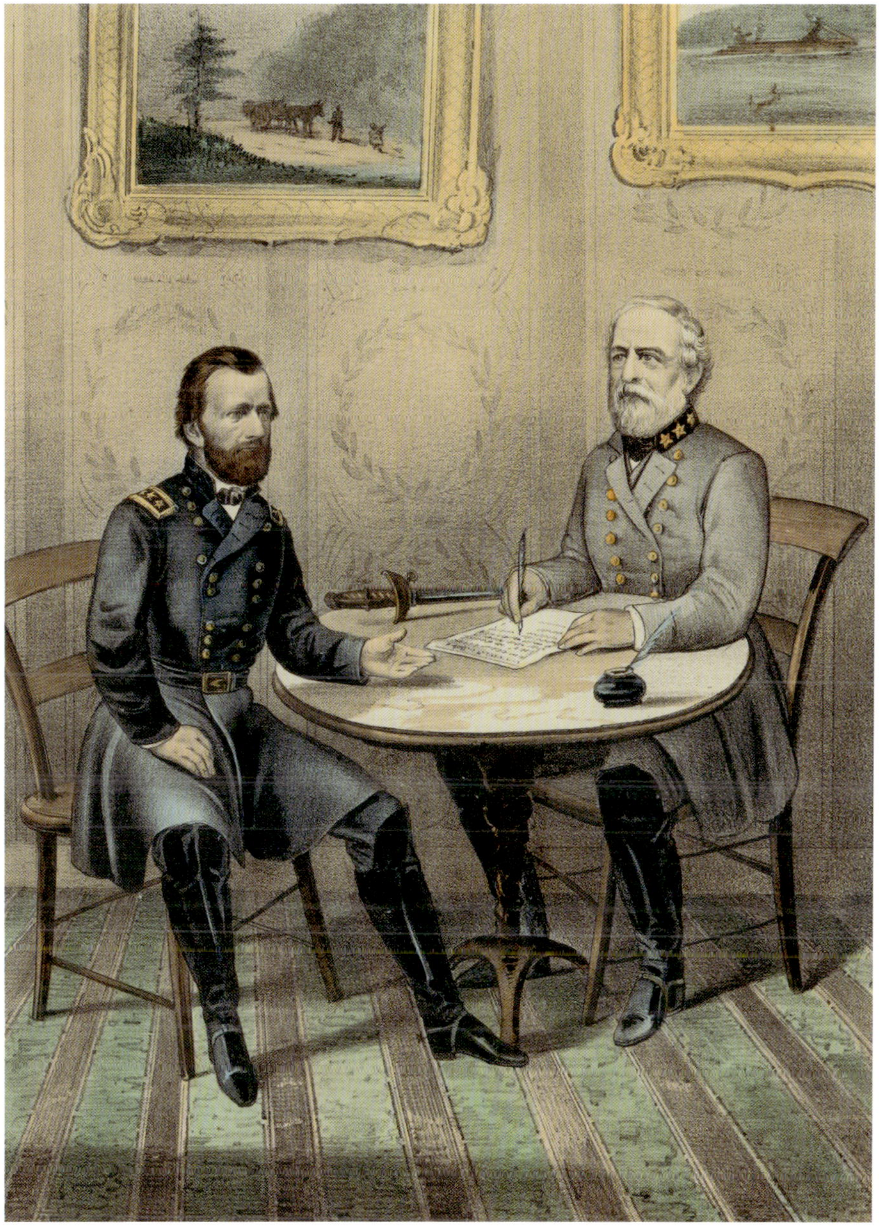

*Surrender of Genl. Lee, at Appomattox C.H. Va. April 9th. 1865*

1865

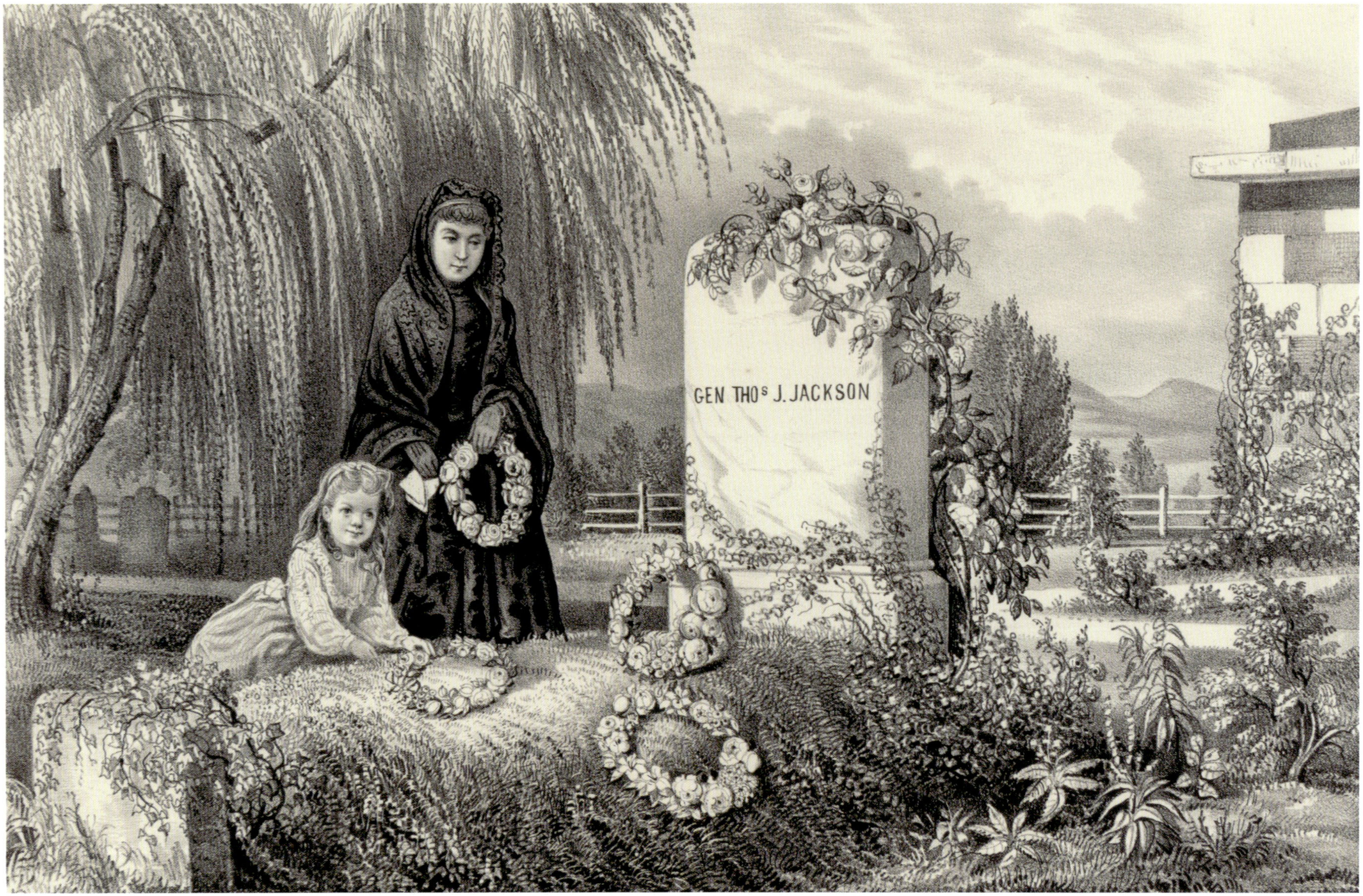


*The Grave of Stonewall Jackson*

*Lexington Virginia*

1870

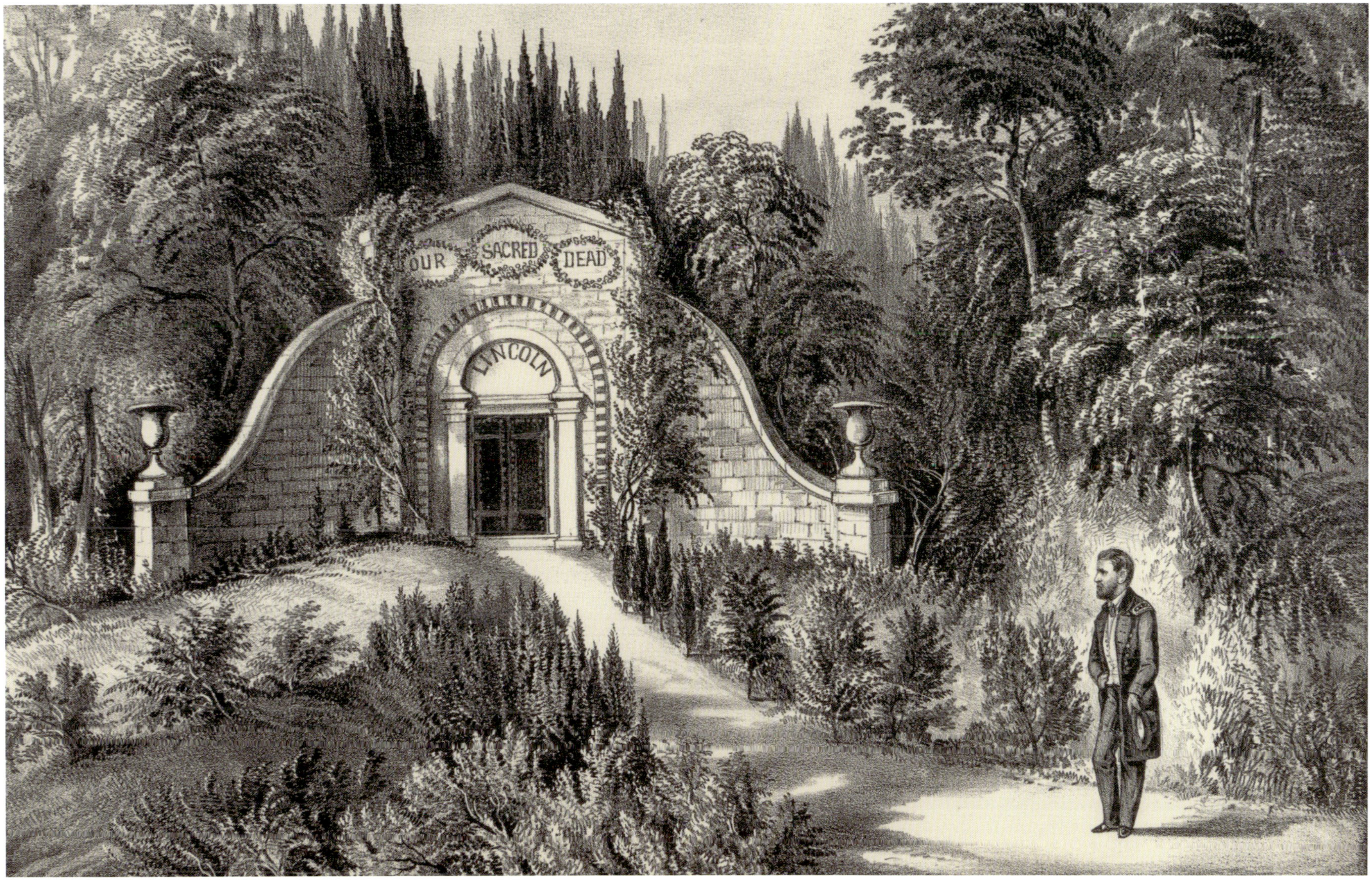


*General Grant at the Tomb of Abraham Lincoln*
***Oakridge Cemetery Springfield Illinois***
1868

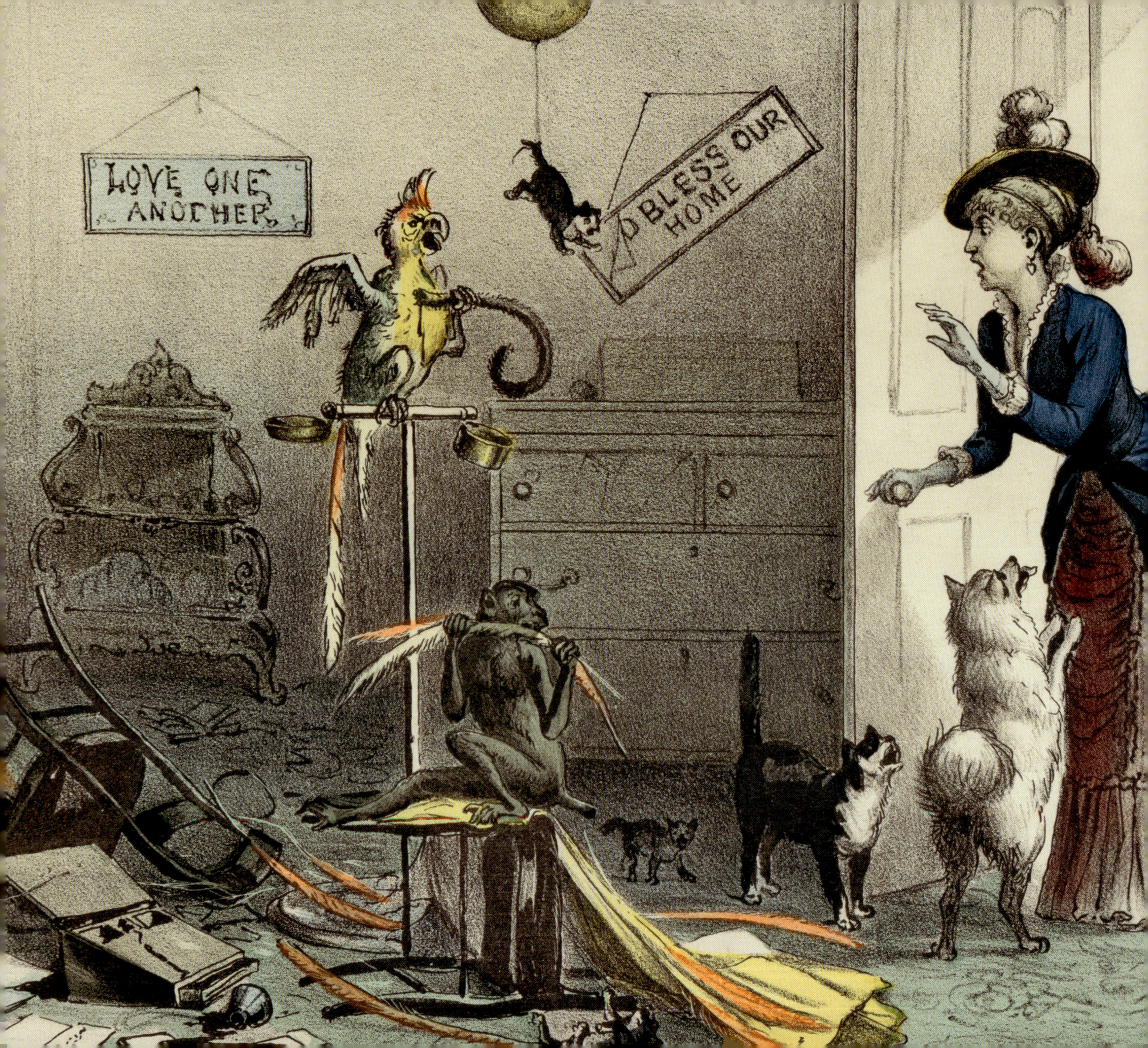
LOVE ONE ANOTHER
D BLESS OUR HOME

# HUMOR

Currier & Ives's humorous prints comprised a wide variety of "comics," including political cartoons, farcical sporting prints, and overtly racist sketches. Notably, however, their portrayal of Irish Americans was largely positive and at times even heroic, despite the virulent anti-Irish sentiment that was prevalent at the time. These lithographs, as well as the firm's numerous depictions of Catholic saints and leaders, point to an effort to cater to the large Irish-American population in New York. In their illustrations of white upper-class Americans at leisure, the company satirized home life as well as sports, such as horse racing, hunting, and fishing. Currier & Ives also produced numerous political cartoons, publishing more than five hundred over a period of nearly forty years. They were driven by profit over politics and did not endorse any particular candidate or party, instead choosing to follow national trends by focusing on the issues or politicians that captured the current moment. The firm aimed for the broadest possible market by avoiding partisanship, despite the rising polarization of American society and political turmoil at the time.

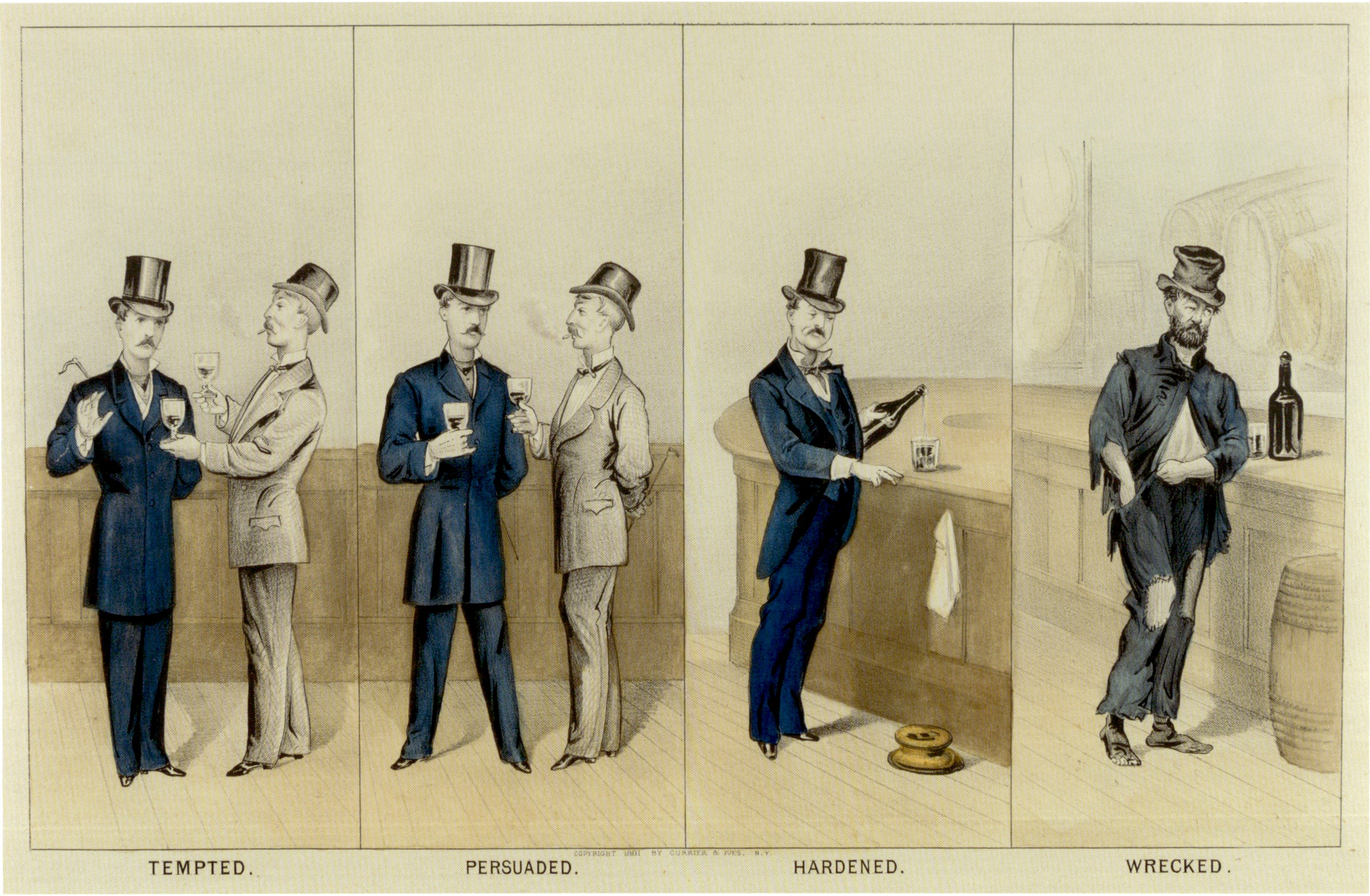


*The Progress of Intemperance*

1881

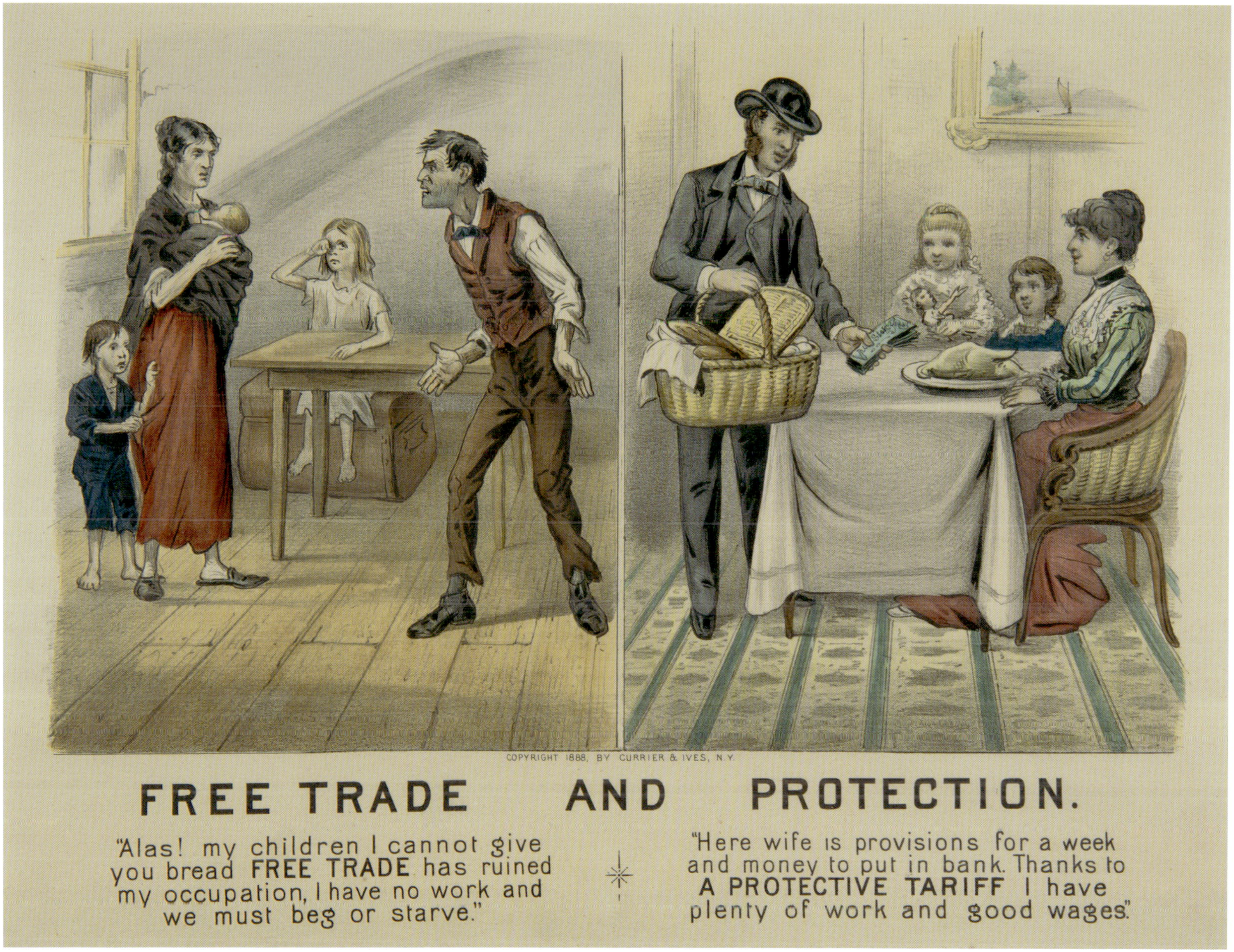


*Free Trade and Protection*

1888

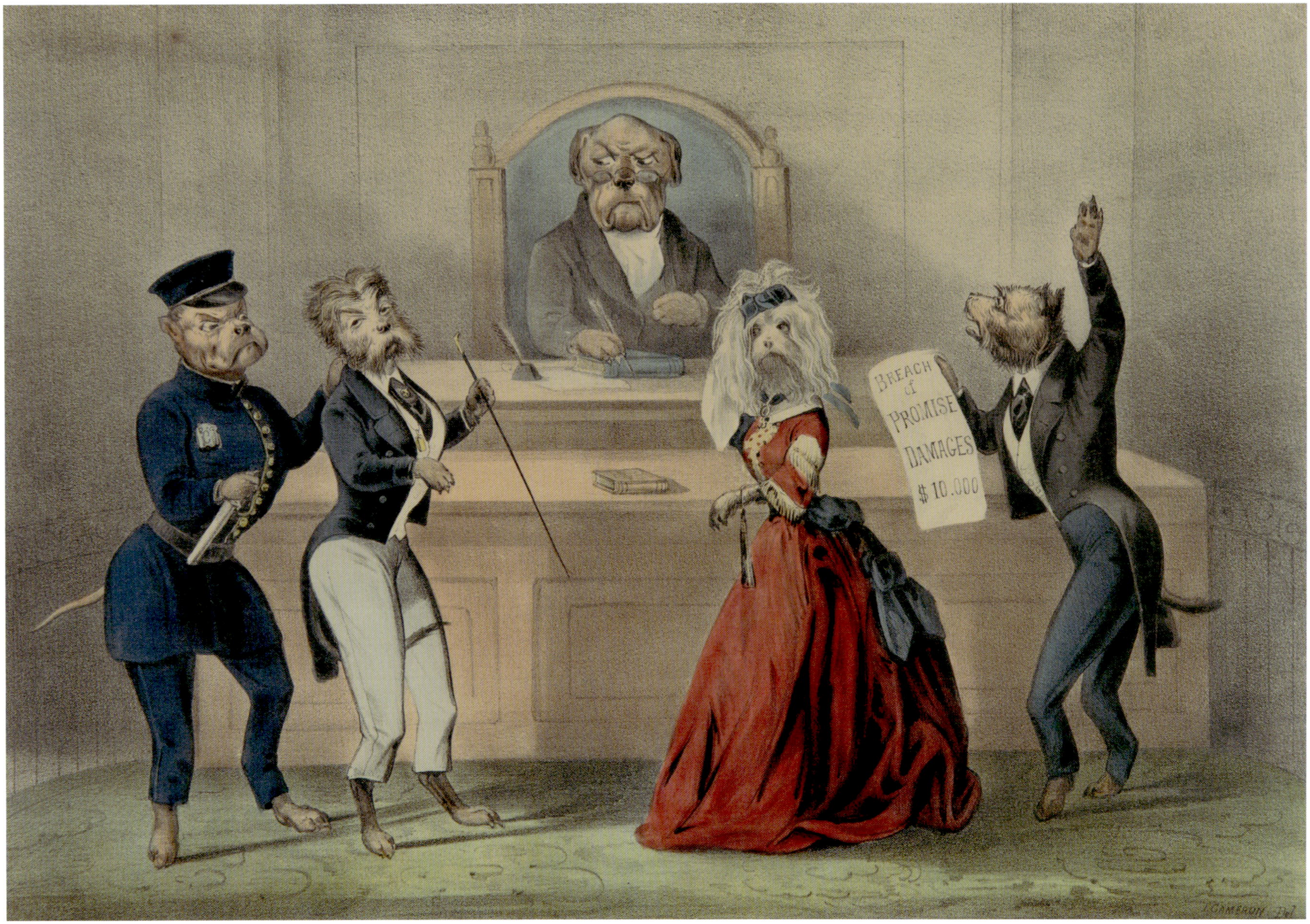


***The Gay Deceiver***

1871

John Cameron, AMERICAN (BORN SCOTLAND), ca. 1828

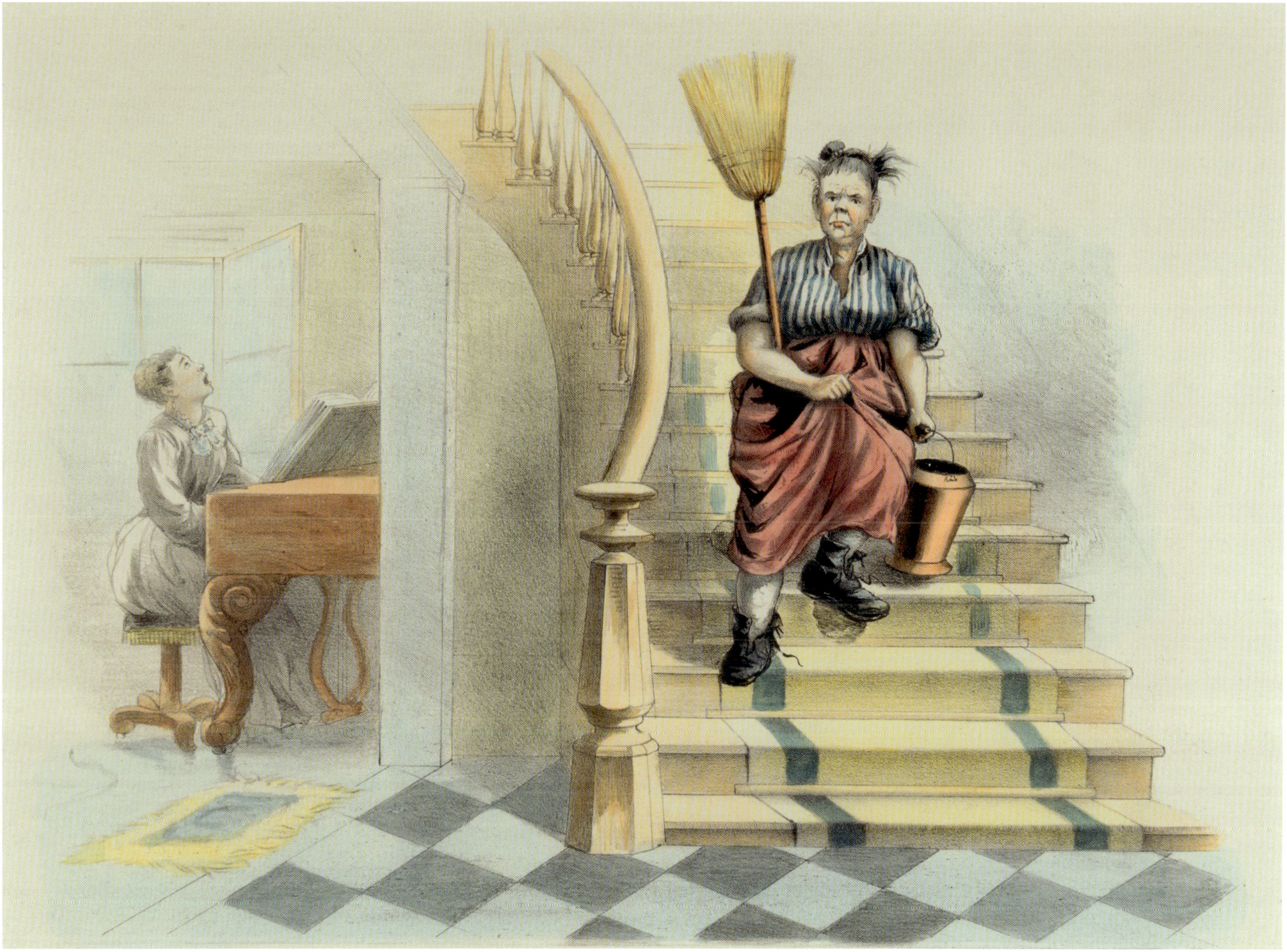

*Angel Footsteps*

***Hark! I Hear an Angel's Footsteps Coming Down the Shining Stairs***

1878

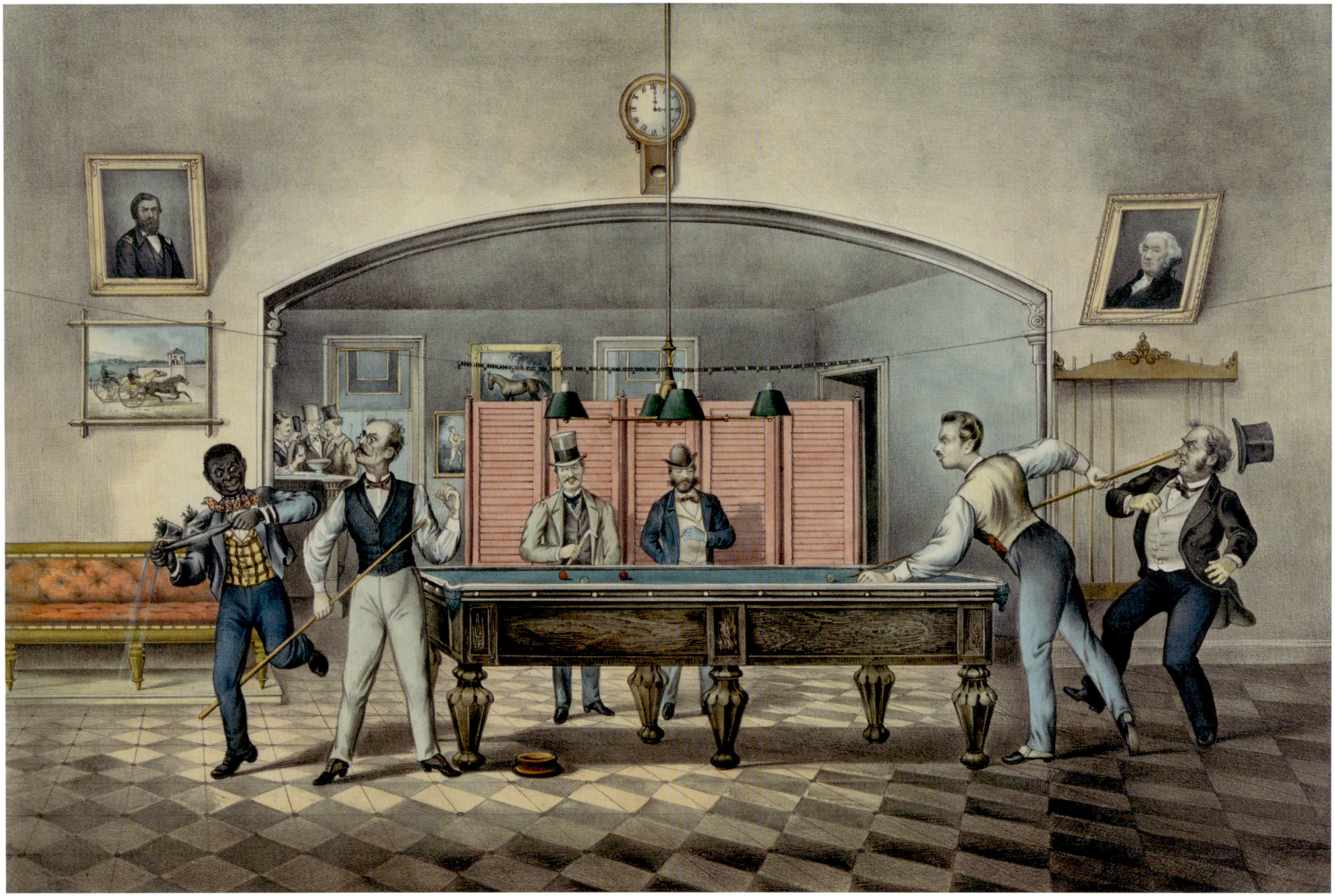

*The Beauties of Billiards*

*A Carom on the Dark Red*

1869

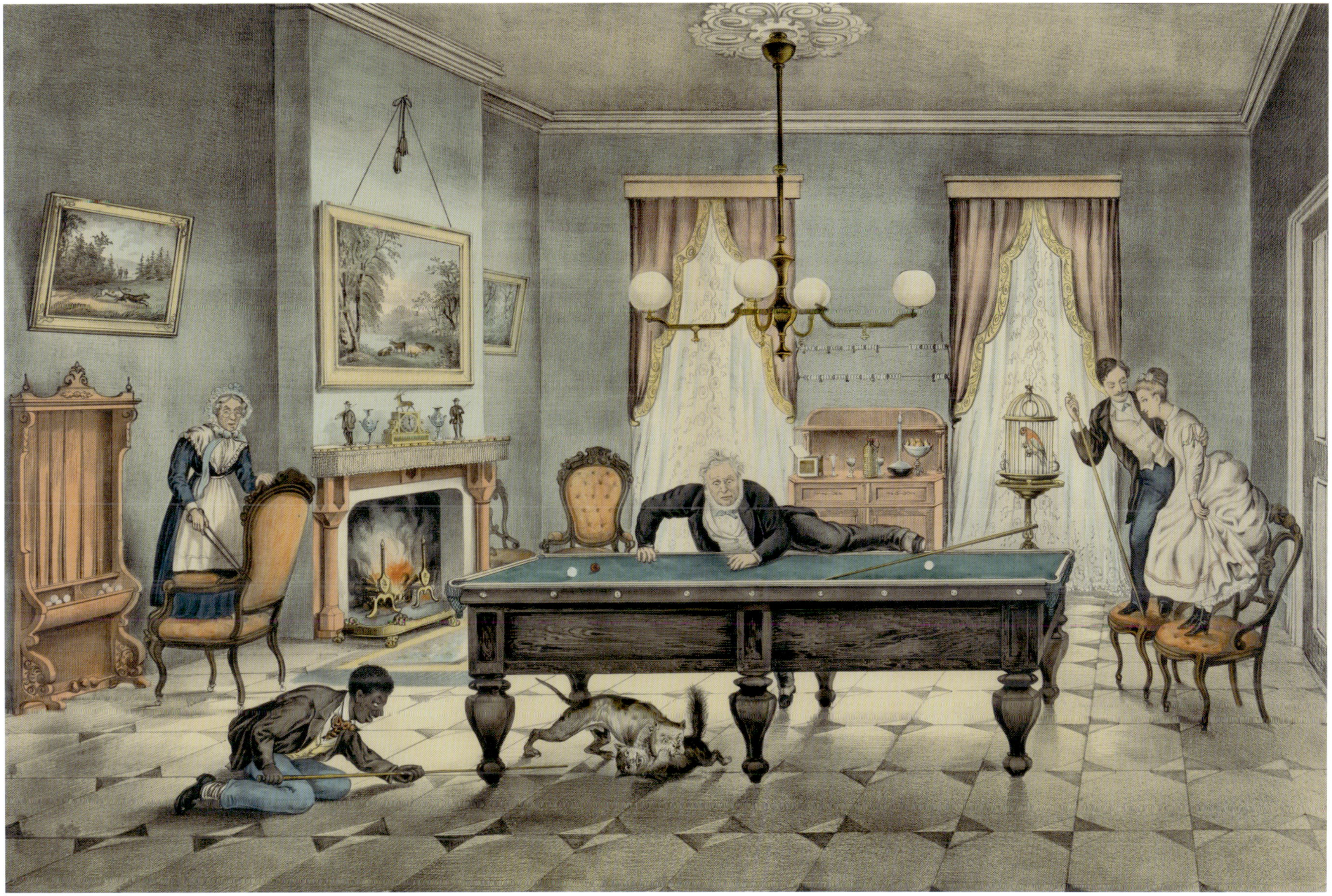

*The Chances of Billiards*
*A Scratch All Around*
1869

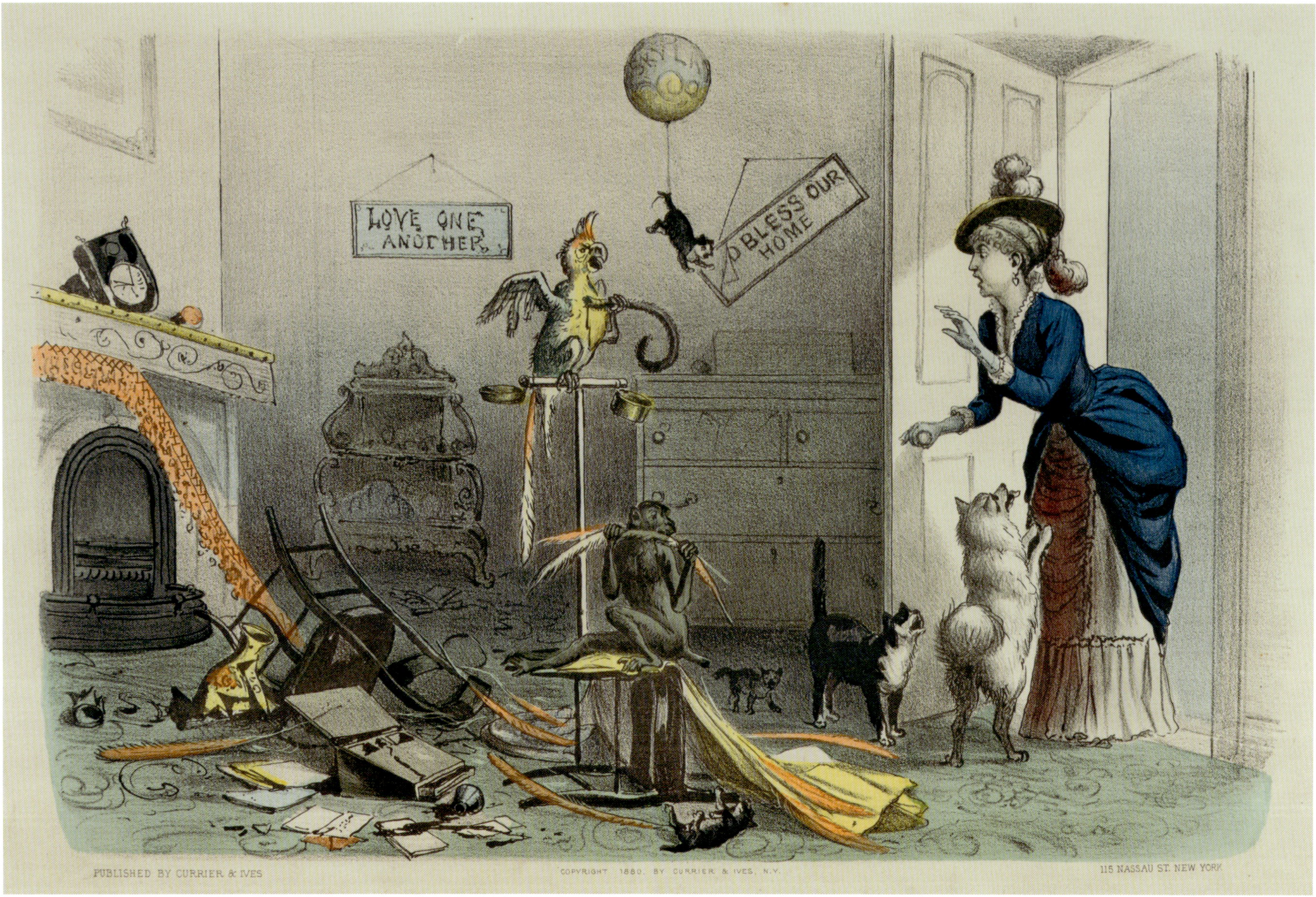


*We've Had a Healthy Time!*

1880

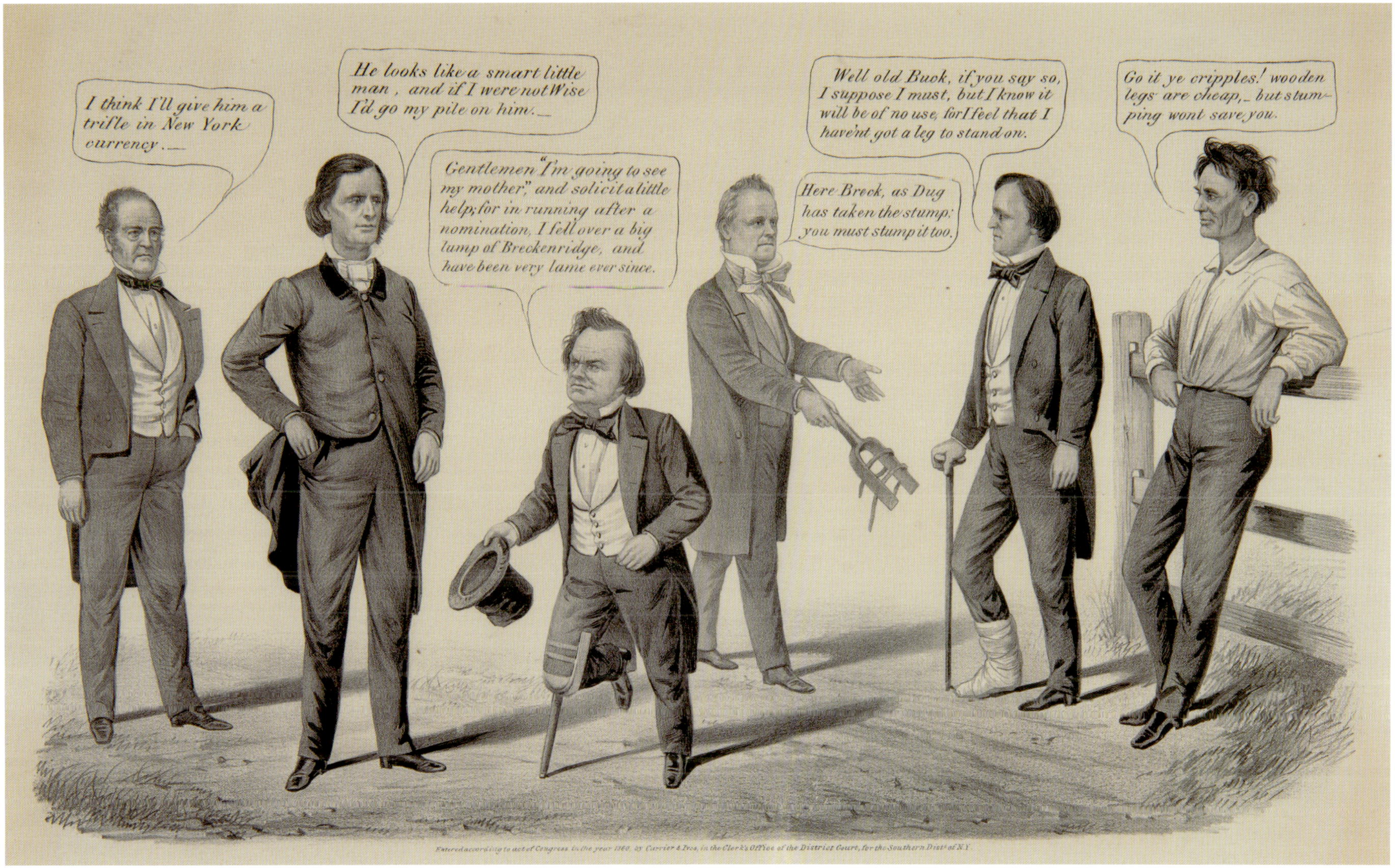



*Taking the Stump or Stephen in Search of his Mother*

1860

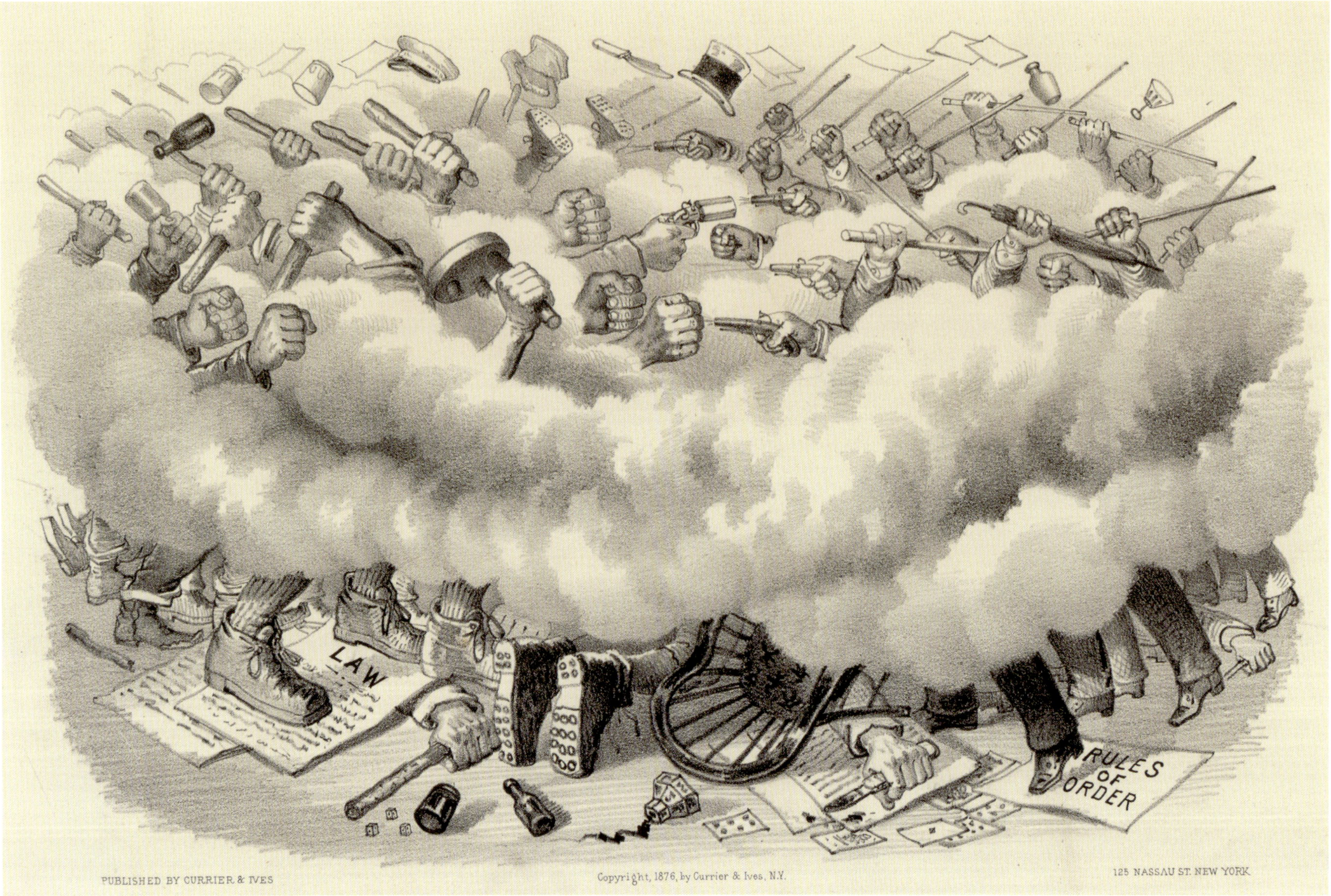


*Democratic Reformers in Search of a Head*

1876

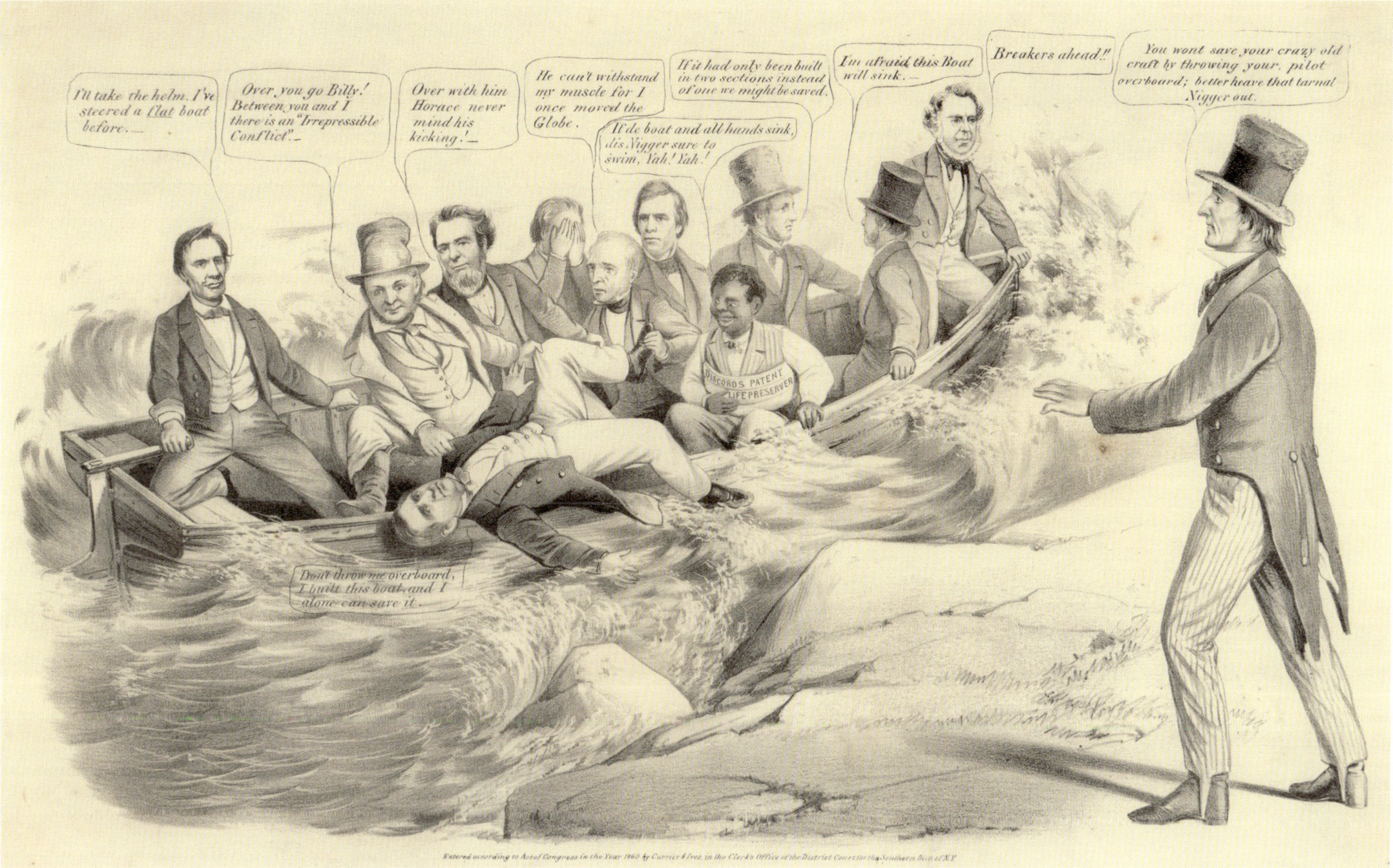


*The Irrepressible Conflict*

*Or the Republican Barge in Danger*

1860

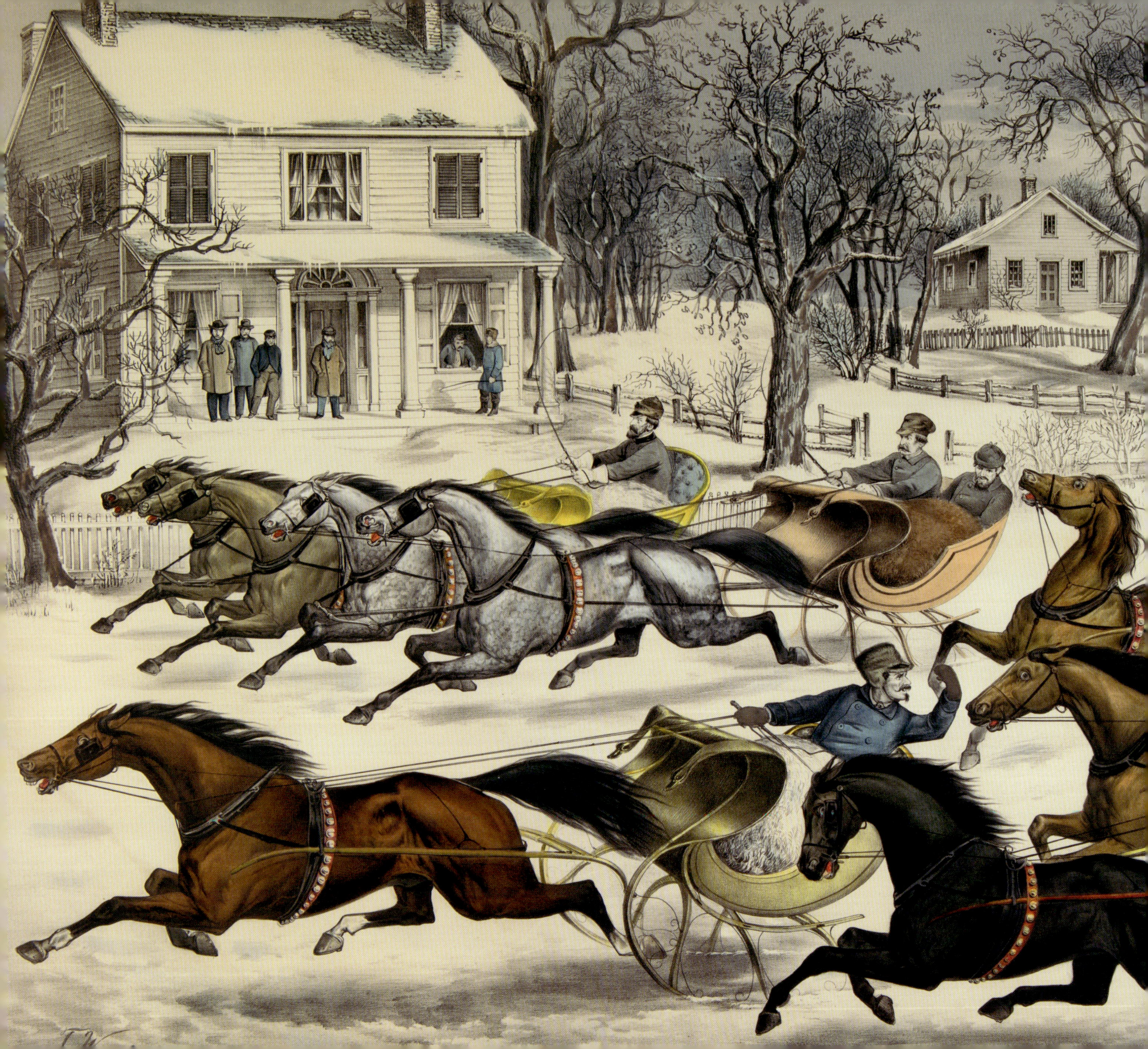

# CATALOGUE CHECKLIST

## *All Currier & Ives prints gift of Conagra Brands*

**SAILS, STEAM, AND SPEED**

James E. Butterworth, American
(born England), 1817–1894
*Clipper Ship "Flying Cloud,"* 1852
Lithograph
Image size: $15\frac{13}{16} \times 23\frac{1}{2}$ in.
Sheet size: $20\frac{3}{4} \times 27\frac{5}{8}$ in.
2016.20.406

Charles Parsons, American
(born England), 1821–1910
*Clipper Ship "Dreadnought" off Tuskar Light*, 1856
Lithograph
Image size: $16 \times 24\frac{5}{8}$ in.
Sheet size: $20 \times 28$ in.
2016.20.409

*Clipper Ship "Racer,"* 1854
Lithograph
Image size: $16 \times 23\frac{7}{8}$ in.
Sheet size: $20\frac{7}{8} \times 27\frac{5}{8}$ in.
2016.20.408

James E. Butterworth, American
(born England), 1817–1894
*The Wreck of the Steam Ship "San Francisco,"* 1854
Lithograph
Image size: $17 \times 25\frac{1}{2}$ in.
Sheet size: $21\frac{1}{4} \times 29$ in.
2016.20.448

*The Great Race on the Mississippi: From New Orleans to St. Louis 1210 Miles*, 1870
Lithograph
Image size: $18\frac{3}{4} \times 29\frac{1}{2}$ in.
Sheet size: $24\frac{5}{8} \times 34\frac{7}{8}$ in.
2016.20.454

Frances Palmer, American
(born England), 1812–1876
*Rounding a Bend on the Mississippi: The Parting Salute*, 1866
Lithograph
Image size: $18\frac{3}{8} \times 27\frac{7}{8}$ in.
Sheet size: $22\frac{3}{4} \times 31\frac{7}{8}$ in.
2016.20.450

Frances Palmer, American
(born England), 1812–1876
*Wooding Up on the Mississippi*, 1863
Lithograph
Image size: $17\frac{3}{4} \times 27\frac{5}{8}$ in.
Sheet size: $21\frac{1}{2} \times 31\frac{1}{2}$ in.
2016.20.398

*American Steamboats on the Hudson: Passing the Highlands*, 1874
Lithograph
Image size: $19\frac{1}{4} \times 33$ in.
Sheet size: $26\frac{3}{8} \times 39\frac{1}{2}$ in.
2016.20.458

William A. Walker, American,
1838–1921
*The Levee—New Orleans*, 1884
Lithograph
Image size: $20 \times 29\frac{7}{8}$ in.
Sheet size: $24\frac{7}{8} \times 33\frac{3}{4}$ in.
2016.20.422

*Western River Scenery*, 1866
Lithograph
Image size: $11\frac{3}{8} \times 16\frac{5}{8}$ in.
Sheet size: $15\frac{1}{2} \times 19\frac{3}{4}$ in.
2016.20.294

Frances Palmer, American
(born England), 1812–1876
*The Lightning Express Trains: Leaving the Junction,* 1863
Lithograph
Image size: $17\frac{3}{4} \times 27\frac{3}{4}$ in.
Sheet size: $24\frac{3}{8} \times 32\frac{5}{8}$ in.
2016.20.449

Frances Palmer, American
(born England), 1812–1876
*American Express Train*, 1864
Lithograph
Image size: $17\frac{1}{2} \times 27\frac{3}{4}$ in.
Sheet size: $22 \times 31\frac{3}{4}$ in.
2016.20.416

*The Route to California: Truckee River Sierra-Nevada*, 1871
Lithograph
Image size: $8\frac{3}{8} \times 12\frac{3}{8}$ in.
Sheet size: $11 \times 14\frac{3}{4}$ in.
2016.20.148

*American Railroad Scene: Snow Bound*, 1871
Lithograph
Image size: $8\frac{1}{2} \times 12\frac{7}{16}$ in.
Sheet size: $12\frac{3}{8} \times 16\frac{1}{16}$ in.
2016.20.80

*The Express Train*, 1870
Lithograph
Image size: $7\frac{7}{8} \times 12\frac{3}{8}$ in.
Sheet size: $13\frac{1}{4} \times 15\frac{7}{8}$ in.
2016.20.212

*Pensylvania* [sic] *Rail Road Scenery*, n.d.
Lithograph
Image size: $8\frac{3}{8} \times 12\frac{3}{8}$ in.
Sheet size: $11\frac{1}{2} \times 16\frac{1}{4}$ in.
2016.20.220

**URBAN EXPERIENCES**

*The Great East River Bridge: To Connect the Cities of New York & Brooklyn*, 1872
Lithograph
Image size: $8\frac{7}{16} \times 12\frac{3}{8}$ in.
Sheet size: $10\frac{15}{16} \times 14\frac{3}{4}$ in.
2016.20.108

*U.S. Post Office, New York*, n.d.
Lithograph
Image size: $9 \times 12\frac{7}{8}$ in.
Sheet size: $13\frac{7}{8} \times 17\frac{5}{8}$ in.
2016.20.114

*Broadway New York*, n.d.
Lithograph
Image size: $8 \times 12\frac{3}{4}$ in.
Sheet size: $11 \times 14\frac{3}{8}$ in.
2016.20.78

Charles Parsons, American
(born England), 1821–1910
*Central-Park, Winter: The Skating Pond*, 1862
Lithograph
Image size: $18 \times 26\frac{5}{8}$ in.
Sheet size: $24\frac{1}{8} \times 32$ in.
2016.20.397

*The Great St. Louis Bridge: Across the Mississippi River*, ca. 1874
Lithograph
Image size: $8 \times 13\frac{3}{4}$ in.
Sheet size: $13\frac{1}{8} \times 17\frac{5}{8}$ in.
2016.20.61

*City of New Orleans*, n.d.
Lithograph
Image size: $8 \times 12\frac{11}{16}$ in.
Sheet size: $12\frac{1}{4} \times 16\frac{13}{16}$ in.
2016.20.14

Louis Maurer, American
(born Germany), 1832–1932
*The American Fireman: Always Ready*, 1858
Lithograph
Image size: $16\frac{7}{8} \times 13\frac{1}{4}$ in.
Sheet size: $19\frac{5}{8} \times 16\frac{3}{4}$ in.
2016.20.335

Louis Maurer, American
(born Germany), 1832–1932
*The American Fireman: Rushing to the Conflict*, 1858
Lithograph
Image size: $17\frac{1}{8} \times 13\frac{1}{2}$ in.
Sheet size: $19\frac{5}{8} \times 15\frac{3}{4}$ in.
2016.20.334

*View of the Terrific Explosion at the Great Fire in New York: From Broad St. July 19th 1845*, 1845
Lithograph
Image size: $8\frac{1}{8} \times 12\frac{1}{4}$ in.
Sheet size: $12\frac{7}{8} \times 17\frac{1}{4}$ in.
2016.20.112

*Burning of the City Hall New York*, 1858
Lithograph
Image size: $7\frac{7}{8} \times 12\frac{1}{4}$ in.
Sheet size: $9\frac{3}{4} \times 13\frac{3}{4}$ in.
2016.20.196

*Ruins of the Merchant's Exchange N.Y.: After the Destructive Conflagration of Decbr. 16 & 17 1835*, 1835
Lithograph
Image size: $9\frac{3}{8} \times 12\frac{1}{4}$ in.
Sheet size: $12 \times 14\frac{5}{8}$ in.
2016.20.111

*The Great Fire at Chicago, Octr. 8th. 1871*, 1871
Lithograph
Image size: 17 × 25 in.
Sheet size: 21⅞ × 28⅞ in.
2016.20.473

**DOMESTIC VISIONS**

*The Mill-Dam at Sleepy Hollow*, ca. 1857–71
Lithograph
Image size: 14⅝ × 20⅛ in.
Sheet size: 20⅛ × 24¼ in.
2016.20.364

Frances Palmer, American (born England), 1812–1876
*The Season of Blossoms*, 1865
Lithograph
Image size: 15¾ × 23¼ in.
Sheet size: 22½ × 29½ in.
2016.20.404

Frances Palmer, American (born England), 1812–1876
*Winter Moonlight*, 1866
Lithograph
Image size: 17½ × 14¼ in.
Sheet size: 19¾ × 15¾ in.
2016.20.355

George Henry Durrie, American, 1820–1863
*Winter in the Country: A Cold Morning*, 1864
Lithograph
Image size: 18⅝ × 27⅛ in.
Sheet size: 23¼ × 31 in.
2016.20.417

Arthur Fitzwilliam Tait, American (born England), 1819–1905
*Arguing the Point*, 1855
Lithograph
Image size: 18¼ × 24 in.
Sheet size: 21¼ × 26¾ in.
2016.20.428

Eastman Johnson, American, 1824–1906
*Husking*, 1861
Lithograph
Image size: 21 × 27⅜ in.
Sheet size: 24 × 30 in.
2016.20.442

Louis Maurer, American (born Germany), 1832–1932
*Preparing for Market*, 1856
Lithograph
Image size: 18⅞ × 27⅛ in.
Sheet size: 22¾ × 31⅛ in.
2016.20.467

Frances Palmer, American (born England), 1812–1876
*American Country Life: May Morning*, 1855
Lithograph
Image size: 16⅞ × 23⅞ in.
Sheet size: 21⅛ × 26⅝ in.
2016.20.446

Charles Parsons, American (born England), 1821–1910
*The Four Seasons of Life: Middle Age, The Season of Strength*, 1868
Lithograph
Image size: 15¼ × 23½ in.
Sheet size: 22 × 28½ in.
2016.20.463

John Cameron, American (born Scotland), ca. 1828
*The First Toilet*, 1873
Lithograph
Image size: 11½ × 8¼ in.
Sheet size: 17¼ × 12¾ in.
2016.20.506

*My Little White Kitties*, 1871
Lithograph
Image size: 8⅛ × 12$^{1}/_{16}$ in.
Sheet size: 12⅜ × 15¾ in.
2016.20.252

*Three Little White Kitties: Fishing*, 1871
Lithograph
Image size: 8¼ × 12$^{3}/_{16}$ in.
Sheet size: 12⅜ × 15¾ in.
2016.20.272

*Fruits of the Tropies* [sic], 1871
Lithograph
Image size: 8⅜ × 12⅜ in.
Sheet size: 13 × 16¼ in.
2016.20.264

Frances Palmer, American (born England), 1812–1876
*Landscape, Fruit and Flowers*, 1862
Lithograph
Image size: 20 × 27½ in.
Sheet size: 24 × 32⅞ in.
2016.20.441

**SPORTING LIFE**

Frances Palmer, American (born England), 1812–1876
*Snipe Shooting*, 1852
Lithograph
Image size: 12¾ × 19⅞ in.
Sheet size: 17½ × 23½ in.
2016.20.338

*Wild Duck Shooting: On the Wing*, 1870
Lithograph
Image size: 8⅛ × 12½ in.
Sheet size: 10⅞ × 14⅜ in.
2016.20.217

Arthur Fitzwilliam Tait, American (born England), 1819–1905
*Brook Trout Fishing: An Anxious Moment,* 1862
Lithograph
Image size: 18½ × 27⅛ in.
Sheet size: 21⅝ × 29⅛ in.
2016.20.484

Arthur Fitzwilliam Tait, American (born England), 1819–1905
*American Hunting Scenes: An Early Start,* 1863
Lithograph
Image size: 18⅝ × 27½ in.
Sheet size: 22⅝ × 31¾ in.
2016.20.483

Louis Maurer, American (born Germany), 1832–1932
*Camping Out: Some of the Right Sort,* 1856
Lithograph,
Image size: 19 × 27½ in.
Sheet size: 23¾ × 32½ in.
2016.20.476

Arthur Fitzwilliam Tait, American (born England), 1819–1905
*Camping in the Woods: A Good Time Coming,* 1863
Lithograph
Image size: 18⅝ × 27½ in.
Sheet size: 23⅛ × 31¼ in.
2016.20.486

Arthur Fitzwilliam Tait, American (born England), 1819–1905
*The Cares of a Family*, 1856
Lithograph
Image size: 18½ × 23⅞ in.
Sheet size: 21¾ × 27 in.
2016.20.430

Arthur Fitzwilliam Tait, American (born England), 1819–1905
*American Field Sports*, 1857
Lithograph
Image size: 18⅜ × 26⅝ in.
Sheet size: 21⁹⁄₁₆ × 29¾ in.
2016.20.395

*American Winter Sports: Trout Fishing on Chateaugay Lake,* 1856
Lithograph
Image size: 17⅞ × 25¾ in.
Sheet size: 21⅜ × 28 in.
2016.20.413

*The American National Game of Base Ball: Grand Match for the Championship at the Elysian Fields, Hoboken, N.J.*, 1866
Lithograph
Image size: 19¾ × 29¾ in.
Sheet size: 23⅝ × 32½ in.
2016.20.487

*James Hammill, and Walter Brown In Their Great Five Mile Rowing Match for $4000 & the Championship of America*, 1867
Lithograph
Image size: 16⅝ × 24¾ in.
Sheet size: 19⅝ × 26½ in.
2016.20.372

Thomas Worth, American, 1834–1917
*Trotting Cracks at Home: A Model Stable*, 1868
Lithograph
Image size: 19 × 29 in.
Sheet size: 22¾ × 31⅞ in.
2016.20.382

John Cameron, American (born Scotland), ca. 1828
*Mr. Bonner's Horse Joe Elliott, Driven by J. Bowen*, 1873
Lithograph
Image size: 16¾ × 26½ in.
Sheet size: 25⅛ × 33⅛ in.
2016.20.377

John Cameron, American (born Scotland), ca. 1828
*Ethan Allen and Mate and Dexter In Their Wonderful Race, over the Fashion Course, L.I. June 21st. 1867*, 1867
Lithograph
Image size: 17 × 27⅛ in.
Sheet size: 22¾ × 31¾ in.
2016.20.378

*Harry Bassett and Longfellow In Their Great Races at Long Branch, N.J. July, 2nd and Saratoga, N.Y. July, 16th 1872*, 1872
Lithograph
Image size: 16⅞ × 26¾ in.
Sheet size: 23 × 31 in.
2016.20.466

Thomas Worth, American, 1834–1917
*A Brush for the Lead: New York Flyers on the Snow*, 1867
Lithograph
Image size: 19½ × 29⅜ in.
Sheet size: 25½ × 35⅛ in.
2016.20.488

**THE FRONTIER**

*Across the Continent: Westward the Course of Empire Takes Its Way*, 1868
Lithograph
Image size: 17⅝ × 27¼ in.
Sheet size: 21¾ × 29⅞ in.
2016.20.474

Frances Palmer, American (born England), 1812–1876
*The Rocky Mountains: Emigrants Crossing the Plains*, 1866
Lithograph
Image size: 17½ × 25¾ in.
Sheet size: 23½ × 32 in.
2016.20.433

John Cameron, American (born Scotland), ca. 1828
*A Parley: Prepared for an Emergency*, ca. 1866
Lithograph
Image size: 17⅛ × 26¼ in.
Sheet size: 21⅞ × 30 in.
2016.20.414

Arthur Fitzwilliam Tait, American (born England), 1819–1905
*The Prairie Hunter: One Rubbed Out*, 1852
Lithograph
Image size: 14¹⁄₁₆ × 20¹¹⁄₁₆ in.
Sheet size: 17⅝ × 23⅜ in.
2016.20.349

Arthur Fitzwilliam Tait, American (born England), 1819–1905
*The Pursuit*, 1856
Lithograph
Image size: 17⅞ × 25⁷⁄₁₆ in.
Sheet size: 22 × 29⅝ in.
2016.20.375

Arthur Fitzwilliam Tait, American (born England), 1819–1905
*American Frontier Life: On the War Path*, 1863
Lithograph
Image size: 18¼ × 26⅞ in.
Sheet size: 22⅜ × 29⅝ in.
2016.20.401

Arthur Fitzwilliam Tait, American (born England), 1819–1905
*Life on the Prairie: The Trappers Defence—Fire Fight Fire*, 1862
Lithograph
Image size: 18½ × 27⅛ in.
Sheet size: 21¾ × 29⅞ in.
2016.20.439

*Prairie Fires of the Great West*, 1871
Lithograph
Image size: 8⅜ × 12⅜ in.
Sheet size: 11 × 15 in.
2016.20.134

Arthur Fitzwilliam Tait, American (born England), 1819–1905
*Life on the Prairie: The Buffalo Hunt*, 1862
Lithograph
Image size: 18½ × 27¼ in.
Sheet size: 24⅞ × 35⅛in.
2016.20.418

*Scenery of the Upper Mississippi: An Indian Village*, ca. 1874–78
Lithograph
Image size: 7¹³⁄₁₆ × 12½ in.
Sheet size: 12 × 16⅛ in.
2016.20.165

**THE SOUTH**

Frances Palmer, American (born England), 1812–1876
*The Mississippi in Time of War*, 1865
Lithograph
Image size: 18¼ × 27¾ in.
Sheet size: 25 × 34 in.
2016.20.475

Frances Palmer, American (born England), 1812–1876
*The Mississippi in Time of Peace*, 1865
Lithograph
Image size: 18¼ × 27¾ in.
Sheet size: 24⅞× 34¼ in.
2016.20.440

*Bombardment and Capture of Island Number Ten*, 1862
Lithograph
Image size: 15⅞ × 22½ in.
Sheet size: 19 × 24⅜ in.
2016.20.444

*The Great Naval Victory in Mobile Bay, Aug. 5th 1864*, ca. 1864
Lithograph
Image size: 8⅛ × 12⅛ in.
Sheet size: 10 × 13¾ in.
2016.20.73

*Good Times on the Old Plantation*, ca. 1877–94
Lithograph
Image size: 8 1/2 × 12 7/16 in.
Sheet size: 10 9/16 × 14 7/16 in.
2016.20.127

*A Home on the Mississippi*, 1871
Lithograph
Image size: 8 3/8 × 12 3/8 in.
Sheet size: 11 7/8 × 15 7/8 in.
2016.20.126

*The Old Plantation Home*, 1872
Lithograph
Image size: 8 7/8 × 12 3/8 in.
Sheet size: 13 1/4 × 17 1/4 in.
2016.20.131

Frances Palmer, American (born England), 1812–1876
*High Water in the Mississippi*, 1868
Lithograph
Image size: 18 × 28 in.
Sheet size: 23 3/4 × 32 1/4 in.
2016.20.420

*Bound Down the River*, 1870
Lithograph
Image size: 7 7/8 × 12 3/8 in.
Sheet size: 10 11/16 × 14 5/8 in.
2016.20.215

*Through the Bayou by Torchlight*, ca. 1877–94
Lithograph
Image size: 9 1/2 × 12 1/2 in.
Sheet size: 12 3/16 × 15 3/4 in.
2016.20.11

**AMERICA IN WAR AND PEACE**

*The Destruction of Tea at Boston Harbor*, 1846
Lithograph
Image size: 7 3/4 × 12 7/16 in.
Sheet size: 9 7/8 × 14 1/8 in.
2016.20.84

*Benjamin Franklin: The Statesman and Philosopher*, 1847
Lithograph
Image size: 11 3/4 × 9 in.
Sheet size: 13 7/8 × 9 3/4 in.
2016.20.38

*Cornwallis is Taken!: Lieut. Col. Tighlman of Washington's Staff, Announcing the Surrender of Cornwallis, from the Steps of the State House, (Independence Hall,) at Midnight, October 23rd. 1781*, 1876
Lithograph
Image size: 8 3/4 × 12 5/8 in.
Sheet size: 12 1/2 × 16 1/8 in.
2016.20.83

*Washington's Reception by the Ladies, On Passing the Bridge at Trenton, N.J. April 1789: On His Way to New York to be Inaugurated First President of the United States*, 1845
Lithograph
Image size: 12 × 8 3/4 in.
Sheet size: 14 7/8 × 10 in.
2016.20.81

*The Washington Family*, n.d.
Lithograph
Image size: 8 1/16 × 12 1/4 in.
Sheet size: 10 7/8 × 13 3/4 in.
2016.20.125

*George Washington: First President of the United States*, n.d.
Lithograph
Image size: 12 7/16 × 9 in.
Sheet size: 13 7/8 × 10 in.
2016.20.55

*President Lincoln at Home: Reading the Scriptures to His Wife and Son*, 1865
Lithograph
Image size: 12 1/8 × 9 7/8 in.
Sheet size: 14 3/4 × 11 7/8 in.
2016.20.69

*Abraham Lincoln: Sixteenth President of the United States*, 1861
Lithograph
Image size: 11 3/8 × 8 1/2 in.
Sheet size: 13 7/8 × 9 7/8 in.
2016.20.270

*The Battle of Gettysburg, Pa. July 3rd. 1863*, ca. 1863
Lithograph
Image size: 8 × 12 1/2 in.
Sheet size: 13 × 17 3/8 in.
2016.20.31

*Surrender of Genl. Lee, at Appomattox C.H. Va. April 9th. 1865*, 1865
Lithograph
Image size: 11 7/8 × 8 7/8 in.
Sheet size: 14 1/8 × 11 7/8 in.
2016.20.24

*The Grave of Stonewall Jackson: Lexington Virginia*, 1870
Lithograph
Image size: 7 7/8 × 12 3/8 in.
Sheet size: 10 13/16 × 16 1/2 in.
2016.20.209

*General Grant at the Tomb of Abraham Lincoln: Oakridge Cemetery Springfield Illinois*, 1868
Lithograph
Image size: 7⅞ × 12½ in.
Sheet size: 13 × 17⅜ in.
2016.20.238

**HUMOR**

*The Progress of Intemperance*, 1881
Lithograph
Image size: 8¼ × 13⅝ in.
Sheet size: 12⅞ × 17 in.
2016.20.268

*Free Trade and Protection*, 1888
Lithograph
Image size: 8⅞ × 14¼ in.
Sheet size: 13 × 16¾ in.
2016.20.304

John Cameron, American (born Scotland), ca. 1828
*The Gay Deceiver*, 1871
Lithograph
Image size: 10 × 14⅝ in.
Sheet size: 11⅞ × 15⅝ in.
2016.20.303

*Angel Footsteps: Hark! I Hear an Angel's Footsteps Coming Down the Shining Stairs*, 1878
Lithograph
Image size: 8⅞ × 12 in.
Sheet size: 13 × 17¼ in.
2016.20.318

*The Beauties of Billiards: A Carom on the Dark Red*, 1869
Lithograph
Image size: 16 × 24¾ in.
Sheet size: 22⅝ × 29⅞ in.
2016.20.368

*The Chances of Billiards: A Scratch All Around*, 1869
Lithograph
Image size: 16¼ × 24¾ in.
Sheet size: 22¾ × 30 in.
2016.20.447

*We've Had a Healthy Time!*, 1880
Lithograph
Image size: 9 × 13¾ in.
Sheet size: 12⅜ × 16½ in.
2016.20.247

*Taking the Stump or Stephen in Search of his Mother*, 1860
Lithograph
Image size: 9¼ × 16 in.
Sheet size: 13⅛ × 17¾ in.
2016.20.308

*Democratic Reformers in Search of a Head*, 1876
Lithograph
Image size: 9 × 14½ in.
Sheet size: 12⅜ × 15 in.
2016.20.91

*The Irrepressible Conflict: Or the Republican Barge in Danger*, 1860
Lithograph
Image size: 9¾ × 16¼ in.
Sheet size: 12⅞ × 17½ in.
2016.20.307

This book is published in conjunction with the exhibition *Revisiting America: The Prints of Currier & Ives*, presented at Joslyn Art Museum.

Funding for this publication was provided by

HENRY LUCE FOUNDATION



ISBN: 978-1-64657-010-2
Library of Congress Control Number: 2020938351

Published by Joslyn Art Museum
www.joslyn.org

Distributed by ARTBOOK | D.A.P.
75 Broad Street, Suite 630
New York, NY 10004
www.artbook.com

Produced by Lucia | Marquand, Seattle
www.luciamarquand.com

Edited by Melissa Duffes
Designed by Meghann Ney and Ryan Polich
Typeset in Sagona by Maggie Lee
Proofread by Ivy Long
Color management by iocolor, Seattle
Catalogue photography by Joshua Ferdinand
Printed and bound in Singapore by Pristone

## Contributors

**Emma Westbrook** was the 2018–2019 Weitz Fellow at Joslyn Art Museum, where she is currently a curatorial assistant. She received her BA from Carleton College in 2018 with dual majors in Studio Art and Art History. She is a practicing artist.

**Marie-Stéphanie Delamaire** is the Associate Curator of Fine Arts at Winterthur Museum, Garden, and Library, and an affiliated Assistant Professor in the Winterthur Program in American Visual Culture at the University of Delaware. Her research involves American art from the Colonial Era to World War I, and she has published essays on Antebellum genre painting and sculpture, Currier & Ives, and nineteenth-century American cartoons. In 2016, she curated *Lasting Impressions: The Artists of Currier & Ives* for the Winterthur Museum.

**Michael Clapper** is an Associate Professor of Art History at Franklin & Marshall College. His scholarship primarily focuses on understanding the broad appeal of mass-reproduced, popular art in the United States from the mid-nineteenth century to the present, including chromolithographs, Rogers Groups, and Thomas Kinkade prints. His current projects are on the art of Maxfield Parrish and Norman Rockwell.

**Baird Jarman** is an Associate Professor of Art History at Carleton College. His research focuses on nineteenth-century American popular illustrations, especially Gilded Age satire and Civil War reportage. He is currently completing a book about political caricature during the Reconstruction era.